Series on
Foreign Language Acquisition
Research and Instruction

Barbara F. Freed
General Editor

Foreign Language Acquisition Research and the Classroom

Barbara F. Freed, Editor
Carnegie Mellon University

D. C. Heath and Company
Lexington, Massachusetts   Toronto

Acquisitions Editor: Denise St. Jean
Production Editor: Janice Molloy
Designer: Judith Miller
Production Coordinator: Chuck Dutton

Published simultaneously in Canada.

Printed in the United States of America.

International Standard Book Number: 0–669–24263–2

Library of Congress Catalog Card Number: 90–81520

10 9 8 7 6 5 4 3 2

To the memory of my father

Acknowledgments

The papers in this volume are based on presentations made at a conference of the same name held in October 1989 at the University of Pennsylvania. A conference of this scope does not happen by itself. It is the culmination of months of work by numerous individuals and of logistic and financial support from several institutions, all of whom contributed in specific and valuable ways. While there are too many people to name specifically, the contributions of some must be singled out. To begin with, the conference and the resulting volume would not have occurred without the existence and support of the Consortium for Language Teaching and Learning and its dynamic and intellectually energetic director, Peter Patrikis. The generous contributions of the School of Arts and Sciences at the University of Pennsylvania also helped to make the conference possible.

Three individuals above all others, each in unique and invaluable ways, must be recognized. Madeline Rawley Crouse with unique talent and unusual personal sacrifice attended to every minute detail of organizing the conference. Her devotion will always be remembered. Shearer Norris Weigert participated in the initial planning stages of the conference and then returned to provide meticulous attention to all editorial aspects of completing this volume. Her good humor, unfailing eye, and indefatigable energy are greatly appreciated. Erin Downey contributed countless hours to carrying out innumerable requests from the most menial to the most responsible. Her cheery willingness to complete a task and then ask for more work will never be forgotten. In addition, appreciation is extended to the members of the Conference Planning Committee who offered advice and recommendations and to students and staff of the Department of Romance Languages for all their behind-the-scenes help. Denise St. Jean is also thanked for her ready accessibility and efforts to find an immediate answer to every imaginable question. Finally, as in all such endeavors, there is a family in the background. To my mother, my sister, Alice Freed, and my husband, Sheldon Tabb, go my deepest thanks for their continual encouragement, confidence, and unfailing indulgence.

Barbara F. Freed

Contents

Foreword

Peter C. Patrikis

The Consortium for Language Teaching and Learning

In October 1989, the Consortium for Language Teaching and Learning conducted a conference on Foreign Language Acquisition Research and the Classroom at the University of Pennsylvania. The Consortium is an assembly of eleven distinguished private research universities: Brown University, the University of Chicago, Columbia University, Cornell University, Dartmouth College, Harvard University, the Massachusetts Institute of Technology, the University of Pennsylvania, Princeton University, Stanford University, and Yale University. It was created to enhance the quality of language teaching, to consolidate and build upon the strengths of the programs of its member institutions, and to provide support for new efforts in foreign language education. This conference, which attracted 150 participants from some one hundred institutions and organizations, was the occasion for the papers in this volume. The different parts of the title of this event are familiar. It has now become customary in many quarters to differentiate foreign language acquisition (FLA) research from second language acquisition (SLA) research. The differences between those two domains is the direct or indirect subject of many of the essays in this volume.

In the recent past there have been opportunities to examine these differences between FLA and SLA, and there have been occasions to discuss the nature of foreign language acquisition research theory. For this conference and for this volume we have attempted to shift the focus to prospects and promises for classroom-based acquisition. For some people, the shift of focus toward the classroom represents a recognition of the reality of language teaching today: three to five hours a week in class, some unspecified number of hours in a language laboratory, homework, perhaps some time at a computer, perhaps some time watching a film or television broadcast. . . . That reality can be stated differently: much language learning in this country is cognitive rather than experiential. But the classroom is no single conceptual monolith, and not all of our students proceed from the first to the second to the third year of language instruction. Travel, study abroad programs, internships in foreign companies, and other opportunities are radically altering the abilities of students, the nature of the classroom, and the responsibilities of the language teacher.

This conference was the third in a series of national conferences intended to address major issues in foreign language education. The first conference in 1987 examined the complex issues of the governance of foreign language teaching and learning: the status, credentials, and professional development of foreign language teachers in research universities.[1] Few people need to be told that the profession is changing and that there are increasing demands placed on foreign language teachers. Some of the factors contributing to those increasing demands are renewed demands for accountability, the trends in assessment, the opportunities provided by advanced technology, the pragmatization of language learning, rapidly rising enrollments in many of the less commonly taught languages, among others. Indeed, the expansion of the field of foreign language acquisition research is itself another contributing factor.

In 1988 a second conference examined language learning and liberal education.[2] What is the place of language learning in undergraduate education? The perennial tensions in American education between general education and pragmatic training have resurfaced in the discussions of foreign language education. It is unlikely that we shall ever achieve consensus about the goals of foreign language instruction, and there is probably little reason for us to do so. Our goals, however, must be explicit, and they will necessarily inform the nature of the classroom and the kind of foreign language acquisition research that can be done.

This third conference shifts the perspective from academic organization and the undergraduate curriculum to the domain of research. Paradoxically, this domain of acquisition research is at the same time rich and poor. It is rich, because so much has been accomplished and because so much remains to be done. It is poor, because much of the research remains unknown or unused by classroom teachers and because too few classroom teachers are aware of the research possibilities open to them in their classes and programs. This conference established a new meeting ground—tentative, exploratory, and promising—and it offered classroom teachers and researchers alike a new opportunity to rethink their work. It is the hope of those who commissioned these papers that they will serve to provoke discussion, to provide a stimulus for foreign language teachers to look more deeply and more frequently into foreign language acquisition research, and to encourage foreign language acquisition specialists to think more creatively about the needs of the foreign language classroom.

ENDNOTES

1. Peter C. Patrikis, ed. 1988. *The Governance of Foreign Language Teaching and Learning: Proceedings of a Symposium, Princeton, New Jersey, 9–11 October 1987.* New Haven, Conn.: The Consortium for Language Teaching and Learning.

2. Peter C. Patrikis, ed. 1988. *Language Learning and Liberal Education: Proceedings of a Symposium, the University of Chicago, 15–17 April 1988.* New Haven, Conn.: The Consortium for Language Teaching and Learning.

*Foreign Language
Acquisition Research
and the Classroom*

Section I

Introduction

Chapter 1

Current Realities and Future Prospects in Foreign Language Acquisition Research[1]

Barbara F. Freed

Carnegie Mellon University

This book, and the conference on which it is based, has been motivated by the need to provide a unified collection of papers that examine major issues in foreign language acquisition research, primarily in the setting of our schools and colleges, The book, therefore, will serve to assess the general state of current foreign language acquisition research and its relationship to the classroom, with the goal of fostering a confrontation of theoretical and practical concerns.

An appropriate beginning might be recognition of the fact that as recently as five years ago a conference such as this would not have been organized. To be sure, other scholarly meetings have either implicitly or explicitly focused on the relationship between second language acquisition and foreign language learning.[2] For the most part, however, these previous meetings have attracted students and scholars in the field of second language acquisition. In this instance, the audience consisted of those whose primary training and area of specialization has tended to be in some aspect of foreign language study.

Given that there has been extensive focus on second language acquisition research in the past fifteen years, contrasted with the paucity of attention to foreign language acquisition research, one might reasonably ask why foreign language research has been neglected.

This neglect of foreign language acquisition research can be attributed to several factors.

1. The first is that the teaching of foreign languages has traditionally been embedded in departments of foreign languages and literatures. This is not necessarily an unreasonable location within the academy for the teaching of foreign languages to take place. But it has meant that the teaching of language has always been associated with a "higher goal," that of teaching literature,

literary analysis, and criticism. Despite our insistence on teaching for communicative competence, that goal introduced by Savignon's work in the early 1970s, we are acutely aware that literature still lurks in the background. Language teaching has long been a service function of our departments, while those involved in teaching languages and conducting research on language learning or language teaching have usually remained at the lower end of the academic hierarchy.[3]

2. The second fact that has contributed to the dearth of theoretically motivated, psycholinguistically oriented research in classroom-based foreign language acquisition is the absence of well-trained foreign language researchers. As Ferguson and Huebner have pointed out (1989, 2), most American second language acquisition specialists are descendants of the TESOL profession, belonging to an English-oriented group, who, for the most part, do not have foreign language specializations. There are few foreign language specialists who have received the requisite training to conduct the caliber of research that is required.

3. The third factor, which is in part responsible for the neglect of foreign language acquisition research, is that such research has been divorced from the very field with which it should be associated. The two areas, second language acquisition and foreign language learning, have been separated intellectually in the minds of scholars, and physically in the departments in which they reside. Foreign language acquisition, as Kramsch has noted, is a field in search of definition (1987, viii).

This situation, one that distinguishes between foreign and second language acquisition, has bred a false dichotomy, one that has led to a fragmentation that distorts, retards, and ultimately replicates.

In what follows, these themes will be developed by examining what is traditionally meant by studies in *second* language acquisition as opposed to *foreign* language acquisition, and then by providing some perspective on many of the major issues facing the profession today.

The study of foreign languages, of course, is not new. It dates at least to the second century B.C. with the teaching by the Greeks of their language to foreigners. This early interest in the teaching and learning of various "foreign" languages has continued over the centuries in myriad formats, with countless methods that seem to be invented and reinvented with every new decade, in classrooms throughout the world. The term *foreign language* has usually been used to refer to the teaching or learning of a non-native language *outside* of the country or speech community where it is commonly spoken (Stern 1983, 16).

Second language, as contrasted with the term *foreign language*, is applied to non-native language learning or language use, which takes place *within* one of the speech communities where that language is traditionally used. Thus, the term *foreign language learning* does not refer to the massive amount of language learning and teaching that takes place worldwide in what are known as natural or untutored learning situations, which arise by virtue of languages in contact in various bilingual and multilingual situations. Nor does *foreign language learning* refer to formal classroom learning that also takes place in indigenous environments throughout the world. Thus, the teaching, learning, or use of English in the United States, the field known as ESL, and the teaching, learning, or use of French in Canada are considered second language activities, whereas the teaching and learning of English in France or French in the United States are considered foreign language activities.

This distinction between second and foreign language learning arose after the Second World War in international organizations to satisfy certain nationalist sensitivities in discussions of language use and learning (Stern 1983, 16). The French in Morocco, for example, did not consider French a "foreign" language. This distinction has served to mislead some, satisfy others, and confuse even more. What has emerged, however, from these two seemingly related but subtly distinct learning environments, are two complementary but, until recently, almost unrelated traditions of research. Each has developed its own focus, its own research agenda, its own professional organizations and, to a large extent, its own publications. Historically, and to our misfortune, there has been relatively little overlap between the two.

Foreign language learning research has tended to be associated with the general field of education, on the assumption that classroom-based learning, be it mathematics, sociology, or foreign language, belongs to the field of educational inquiry.[4] We have thus faced the consequences of separating an area of study from its own self-correcting discipline. With a few notable exceptions, this has meant that most of the large-scale research has focused on comparisons of various methods of teaching, on issues related to curriculum, materials, testing, and, more recently, to technological advances in the teaching of foreign languages. By contrast, research on the acquisition of *second* languages has been closely associated with the general field of linguistics, frequently with a psycholinguistic, sociolinguistic, or cognitive orientation. Second language acquisition (SLA) research has addressed fundamental questions in the acquisition of nonprimary languages, investigating such areas as processes and strategies in second language acquisition, the development of interlanguages, the effects of instruction, transitional stages, and sequences in the acquisition of a second language, as well as the role of primary languages and of transfer. Researchers have also tested hypotheses regarding causal factors in SLA and have worked to develop theories and models of the acquisition process. This research has tended to be more learner-centered and process-oriented, unlike research in foreign language learning, which tended to focus on manipulations of methods, teaching techniques, and materials. As a result, we have the surprising legacy of two individual and historically quite separate traditions of research, both related to a very similar, if not identical, area of inquiry: the acquisition or learning of nonprimary languages.

This twofold situation has bred several distinct and unfortunate consequences. The first, and most obvious, is that there has been little theoretically based and psycholinguistically oriented research in classroom-based foreign language acquisition, and little research that tells us anything about the learner and the language learning process. Second, and intimately related to point one, is the fact that certain general assumptions about second language acquisition have been formed and used as the basis for more research, which rather than being cross-linguistic has focused primarily on the acquisition of English as a second language. Finally, and again related to previous points, is the fact that those few foreign language learning specialists who are interested in theoretically motivated research have had no field to call their own. They have not been easily integrated into the ranks of English-dominated SLA research; yet there is no field of inquiry with which they can comfortably identify.

Within the very recent past, some of those whose interests and professional lives are devoted to the teaching and learning of foreign languages have been attracted by the vigorous research tradition of those in second language acquisition. Some of these foreign language researchers and teachers have daringly claimed that they, too, are engaged in second language acquisition research. Some have even asked, "Is there any real difference between the acquisition of a 'second' and a 'foreign' language? Despite real differences in contexts of learning and perhaps of motivation and need, isn't the process, after all, the same?"

Indeed, some well-known scholars have disclaimed a difference between second and foreign language acquisition. For instance, while acknowledging a potential difference in the way language acquisition proceeds, Ellis has written that

> *Second* language acquisition is not intended to contrast with *foreign* language acquisition. SLA is used as a general term that embraces both untutored (or "naturalistic") acquisition and tutored (or "classroom") acquisition (1986, 5).

Similarly, Littlewood, in his book *Foreign and Second Language Learning,* decided that the term *second language acquisition* would be used as a cover term for both "foreign" and "second" language acquisition (1984, 2). Others, such as Anderson, 1990, Gass (1990) and Kramsch (1990), have tried to identify the similarities and differences in second and foreign language acquisition, but in the end they too have suggested that foreign language learning should be understood as similar to and within the overall domain of second language acquisition. That is, the study of the acquisition of nonprimary languages, second or foreign, is essentially one and the same field.

One might consider the following questions as illustrative of the confusion that results when an artificial distinction is imposed on the boundaries between foreign and second language acquisition. Which term, second or foreign language, should be used to describe the situation of an American student who studies French as a *foreign language* in an American classroom context, but who then goes abroad to study French in France for six months? Is that student then studying French as a *second language?* And upon return to the United States, will this student once again be studying French as a *foreign language?*

These queries notwithstanding, it would be a misleading oversight to imply that all scholars are in agreement on this issue. There are some who have carefully attempted to define the similarities and differences between second and foreign language acquisition and who have developed a different perspective. (See for example VanPatten, 1988; VanPatten and Lee, 1988 and 1990; VanPatten, Dvorak, and Lee, 1987.) Their efforts have been to delineate a more limited role for the label *second language acquisition,* one that does not totally cover or embrace foreign language learning, but with which it partially overlaps. Such a distinction emphasizes important variables that have been referred to above: function of the language for the learner, goals and attitudes of the learner, and, perhaps most significant, the context in which learning takes place.

This position, illustrated in Figure 1 with a schema adapted from VanPatten (1988, 105), focuses on the intersection of natural or untutored second language learning, classroom-based second language learning, and classroom-based foreign language learning.

The inherent problem with this interpretation of the relationship between second and foreign language acquisition is that, while it places SLA at the center of the visualized sphere, the overlap of the three areas creates the impression, at least visually, that SLA is actually the smallest part of the domain when, in fact, SLA is the field of inquiry itself. Functions of the language for the learner and

Figure 1

A New Relationship for SLA and FLL (adapted from VanPatten, 1988).

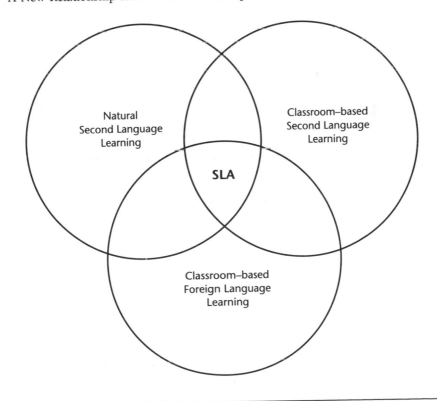

contextual differences in learning situations are indeed crucial variables, but they may or may not account for differences in the *process* of acquisition. It would appear that such a visualization places undue emphasis on these variables. It may ultimately be proven that yet other variables (learner age, for example) are the crucial variables in the process of acquisition.

A more comprehensive and global view of the relationship between FLA and SLA might be portrayed as in Figure 2. Such a visualization characterizes SLA as *the* domain that accounts for the acquisition of all nonprimary languages. This schematization does not conceptualize the field as one bounded by what may prove to be artificial distinctions between second and foreign language acquisition, nor does it exclude the potential impact of other identifiable variables. It may be that these differences are, after all, as Ferguson and Huebner (1989, 4) have recently affirmed, differences in degree if not in kind.

Whichever the case, we have come to understand that research into the acquisition of a nonprimary language, be it termed foreign or second, whatever

— Figure 2 ———————————————————————

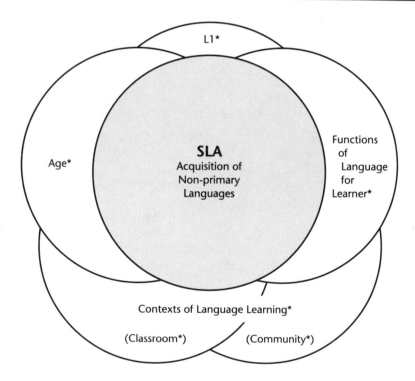

*Illustrative of some of the variables that may affect the process of second language acquisition

the circumstances of learning, must comprise a multitude of orientations: psychological, linguistic, educational, as well as sociological and anthropological. All of these, in turn, must focus on the learner and the learning environment. In our desire to be more "scientific" and to bridge the gap between second and foreign language acquisition research, we must also be scrupulously careful not to reject or discredit a priori the possible contributions of educational research. In disclaiming any potential value of pedagogical insights from the classroom, we not only perpetuate the traditional stigma associated with educational inquiry, but we also reject the notion that teaching can inform research and not merely the other way around.

A step in this direction has been made in recent attempts to describe classroom-based SLA (see Chaudron, 1988 for a summary). This research has provided us with instruments for observing classroom language learners' activities and outcomes in light of SLA theory, and has isolated variables that appear to influence the learning process: for example, participation patterns, task type, and wait time.

There is little doubt that we have ready populations for such research. While we constantly decry the fact that foreign language learning is not a greater national priority and repeatedly cite statistics that underscore how few students study foreign language, the truth is that we have a huge cohort for study. If the usual negative figures are turned upside-down and given a new slant, there is cause for cautious optimism. If, for example, we note that more than half of all American high schools offer foreign languages (Ferguson and Huebner, 1989, 1) and that almost 60% of our institutions of higher learning require foreign language study (Brod, 1989, 17), meaning that approximately four and one-half million secondary school students study foreign language (Dandonoli, 1987, 457), and over one million undergraduates also pursue language study (Brod, 1988, 39), 50% of them continuing beyond the first year (Steel, 1989, 15), then we have a massive captive audience, possibly the largest in the world—an audience that lends itself to inquiries centered on the acquisition of foreign languages in the classroom environment.

Given this perspective, we might turn here to consider some of the issues that confront the profession: debates, questions, and goals. For instance, there is little disagreement with the claim that, except in cases of the severest deprivation or retardation, language acquisition is a normal, natural, automatic, and species-specific process. Yet, this incontrovertible fact about first language acquisition is confounded in the case of second language acquisition. There is the common belief, bolstered by considerable research, that young children immersed in a second language speech environment achieve perfect mastery of a second language and become nativelike, if not native, speakers of this second language. Beyond this, there is little evidence that acquisition of nativelike competence in a second language is at all probable or perhaps even possible.

Inquiries of various types have demonstrated that the acquisition of nativelike competence in a second language is constrained in almost all language learning settings: untutored language learning situations and bilingual immersion programs, as well as second and foreign language classrooms (Swain, 1985; Swain and Lapkin 1982, 1989; Coppieters, 1987; Harley, 1984). Thus, learner age is a factor in any study of ultimate proficiency in a second language. Recent studies on adult second language learning, particularly evidence reported by Swain and her colleagues on Canadian immersion programs (Swain and Lapkin, 1989), seem to suggest that in some respects "older is better," or at least that adults have cognitive and literacy skills, which tend to enhance their learning of a second language. At the same time, there is other impressive evidence from a major study by Johnson and Newport (1989) that reaffirms the long-held view of the overall advantage young children have in matters of language learning. It may be that older is better only at first, as with many types of learning, and that ultimately younger has the advantage.

These conflicting findings are of importance both to those interested in psycholinguistic questions of language learning and to those who are concerned with the organization of second language learning environments and the potential achievement of various cohorts of learners.

Beyond questions of the role of learner age in the acquisition of second languages are research questions that seek to identify causal factors in second language acquisition and the impact of instruction on second language learners. Accumulating evidence has led us to reevaluate both the influence of first languages and the role of language transfer, as well as the value of contrastive analysis in research on these areas. That is not to say that first language influence has been eliminated from research questions, but rather that it has been rethought. We have come to recognize the differentiated role of a first language in second language acquisition and have been influenced by Chomskyan notions of universal grammar and parameter-setting in the acquisition of second languages (Pica, 1989; Zobl, 1980; Tarone, 1980; Ferguson and Huebner, 1989; Flynn, 1988; White, 1990).

In addition to newly emerging views on universal tendencies in language acquisition, there are renewed efforts to define the role of the environment in second language learning. Unfortunately, it is difficult to pinpoint with any specificity the various effects of a natural language learning environment and those of the formal classroom situation. Ultimately, there will be much to learn from comparisons of cross-linguistic evidence gathered from major European studies of language learning in natural speech environments (Perdue, 1984) with large-scale studies of language learning in classroom contexts.

Recent efforts to control for differences in these two contexts have been of two types. One has compared the acquisition of *specific syntactic features* by learners in formal and informal learning contexts (for example, VanPatten's study of clitics, forthcoming, and Eubank's 1987 and 1990 studies of negation). The second has focused on foreign language learners in study-abroad environments. Despite widespread belief to the contrary, preliminary evidence indicates that there may not be enormous advantages, or at least advantages that we have thus far been able to measure and identify, between classroom-based language learning and "picking it up abroad" (Day, 1985; Freed, 1989, 1990; DeKeyser, 1986; Spada 1985, 1986). While there is some conflicting evidence, it appears that the *crucial variables* are not the classroom versus the natural environment per se, but rather such things as the type of instruction, form versus content, the level of instruction, and significant individual differences, as each of these interact with out-of-class contact in the target environment (DeKeyser, 1986; Freed, 1989, 1990, Spada 1985, 1986). Indeed, we are now more aware of the significance of the role of individual differences in learners, as well as learner strategies, in all forms of second language acquisition. As foreign language acquisition research progresses, we can also look forward to learning more about the differential effects of the classroom and the natural speech environment.

Discussions on the impact of the environment on language acquisition lead naturally to investigations of the role of formal instruction on eventual proficiency. The general conclusions seem to be that formal instruction has little or no effect on the sequence of second language acquisition, but that it does affect both the rate and ultimate success of second language learning (Ellis, 1986, 245; Long, 1988, 135). Within the context of any discussion of formal instruction are the ubiquitous questions as to the relative roles of grammar and accuracy in instruction, as contrasted with the role of communication. The sometimes virulent controversy regarding grammar versus communication, though still unresolved, has abated somewhat as we have come to understand that in order to help learners acquire communicative language proficiency, it is the integration of form and content that ultimately matters (Bratt-Paulston, 1987). Moreover, particularly with respect to selection and sequence of grammatical rules and assessment of learner readiness (Pica, 1989, 14) new evidence is emerging, which may lead us to revise existing interpretations regarding the role of instruction (Pienemann, 1984, 1985; Doughty 1988; Gass, 1982).

A debate of similar, if not greater, passion continues regarding the respective roles of *comprehensible input* (Krashen, 1985) and *comprehensible output* (Swain, 1985). Despite Krashen's unyielding insistence on the role of comprehensible input as the crucial variable in the SLA process, investigators such as Long (1985) and Pica *et al.* (1987) have pointed to the role of negotiated interaction in facilitating comprehension and thereby aiding the acquisition process. This controversy promises to provide us with new insights, as investigation as to the respective roles of these major factors continues. It is possible that we will find that input, interaction, and output each assume a major role at different stages in the acquisition sequence.

There is still more to learn about the role of error correction in language learning. Despite the intractable tendencies of classroom teachers to correct learner errors overtly , until quite recently there has been an assumption based on prior research evidence that learner errors are a crucial part of the learning process and that they are resistant to teacher correction. Now, however, more recent theory and research (Bley-Vroman, 1986; Schachter, 1984; White, 1987) seem to indicate that there may be a role for explicit and/or implicit error correction.

There remain yet other issues, which have not been alluded to here. Included among them are research on the topics of language teaching methodology, second and foreign language initiatives outside the United States, discourse and communication strategies in the acquisition of cultural competence, the interdependence of literacy skills and language learning, and research design itself.

This volume will elaborate on these and other issues as it takes stock of the cutting edge of foreign language acquisition research and its ultimate relationship to the classroom setting. It might further serve to provoke new dialogues between foreign language educators and second language acquisition researchers, thereby encouraging future generations of foreign language specialists to conduct empirical and theoretically motivated research. Such research will provide the profession with much-needed cross-linguistic evidence to bolster our understanding of the second language acquisition process as it unravels in the classroom setting. In such a fashion, our recognition of the contributions to be made to second language acquisition theory by classroom-based foreign language acquisition research will be acknowledged. By examining what is already known about second language acquisition with what can be observed and analyzed in classroom environments, we will further elucidate the processes and sequences of language development and identify the variables that may make a crucial difference in the acquisition of any nonprimary language. It is ultimately this reciprocity of language acquisition theory and research integrated with classroom practice that will best serve the profession.

This section began with the thought that five years ago this conference and the resulting volume would not have been organized. It ends with the suggestion that five years from now these issues will be taken for granted.

OVERVIEW OF THE VOLUME

This volume is divided into ten major sections. With the exception of the introduction and the conclusion, each section contains two or more chapters that summarize basic research in one fundamental area. Included in that chapter, or presented in a succeeding chapter, is a discussion of implications for the classroom of research on various aspects of foreign language acquisition.

These chapters approach foreign language acquisition research from numerous perspectives. Despite the integrity of each individual section, there is much valuable and intended overlap. Therefore, throughout the volume, certain themes appear and reappear, each time with an interesting variation and slightly different orientation. These recurrent themes represent current preoccupations of the profession and are indicative of underlying currents that confront those committed to research on the teaching and learning of foreign languages in the United States today.

SECTION II: THE ROLE OF INSTRUCTION IN
FOREIGN LANGUAGE ACQUISITION

Reference has been made to research on the role of instruction in the learning of foreign languages. Several issues might be considered within this general category. These include the formal teaching of specific structural features, the respective roles of grammar and communication, the role of error correction, and the role of environmental factors of the classroom.

This section focuses on one aspect of instruction and/or curricular organization that has preoccupied, some would say polarized, many in the profession, namely the role of grammar and accuracy vis à vis the role of communication in classroom-based foreign language acquisition. In reading the papers in this section it immediately becomes obvious not only that there is a dearth of well-defined research to support one or the other position, but that confusion is also considerable with respect to the meaning of focus on form versus focus on message or function. Interestingly enough, despite the longstanding debate over these issues, each of the authors in this section acknowledges the need for both. In fact, two of the authors go so far as to question the form versus function debate. Nor does anyone reject the need for communication *and* linguistic accuracy. It seems, from these positions and from papers that appear later in the volume, that the profession is slowly reaching a new level of understanding regarding these issues.

The opening chapter by Savignon provides a broad perspective on the communicatively oriented classroom. Savignon suggests that research findings must be interpreted within a broader context, one that includes program goals and resources, pre- and in-service teacher education, realities of the classroom, and even national priorities for foreign language learning. While Savignon identifies several programs that successfully demonstrate the value of focus on communication, she goes on to point out what may be a pervasive confusion between the focus on form versus function. This theme is further developed by Garrett later in this section.

Higgs, like Savignon, discusses research on the role of grammar and accuracy in relationship to program goals and learner needs and expectations. Within the context of reviewing the relevant research, Higgs defends the value of teaching for linguistic accuracy, but simultaneously recognizes the need to help students develop communicative strategies.

The next two chapters by VanPatten and Garrett address implications for the classroom of research on grammar and/or communication in classroom-based foreign language acquisition. Each, however, approaches the question of pedagogical implications in very different ways.

VanPatten reflects Savignon in his references to expression, interpretation, and negotiation of meaning. He begins by reviewing certain theoretical research on the roles of grammar and communication in instruction. He then goes on to sketch out three general stages of language acquisition: early, mid, and advanced. This is followed by suggestions on how communication and communicative skills can be developed in the classroom. His emphasis is on defining a global foreign language curriculum that builds on natural processes of language acquisition. In sketching out this curriculum, which is organized topically rather than grammatically, VanPatten provides concrete examples of a communication-centered syllabus that reflects natural learning processes. Within the context of this discussion, VanPatten discusses the role of grammar in a communication-based curriculum, providing once again a series of usable and specific examples.

Garrett, unlike VanPatten, questions the very possibility of extracting meaningful pedagogical principles from extant research on the role of grammar versus the role of communication in classroom-based foreign language acquisition. Garrett begins by questioning the form versus meaning debate and enumerates several problems in attempting to extrapolate either "theoretical significance or pedagogical guidelines" from this research. She goes on to claim that "those who argue for *some* focus on form and those who argue against it, do not in fact disagree very much as to the communicative importance of formal accuracy." She elegantly and convincingly identifies weaknesses in the traditional debate, which pits form versus meaning by examining the role that form plays in meaning as well as the role meaning assumes in form. ". . . We have allowed the assumption to develop that meaning can be separated from form and can be conveyed independent of it; indeed, in a great deal of the pedagogical literature, meaning is defined *in opposition* to grammatical form."

She suggests that the terms *competence, communicative competence, meaning,* and *grammar* have been blurred and politicized, a situation that has resulted in a confusion that keeps the profession locked in "unresolvable pedagogical issues." Such a situation precludes serious interpretation and implementation of any research findings in the "focus on form . . . focus on meaning" debate.

Garrett ends by taking the position that for the moment "a focus on SLA must be kept independent of pedagogical manipulation." Until we are able to "generate testable hypotheses about individual classroom language learners' processing and acquisition," research attempts to evaluate usefulness of focus on form or focus on meaning will remain relatively unproductive.

SECTION III: LEARNING ENVIRONMENTS IN FOREIGN LANGUAGE ACQUISITION

The learning environment has been identified as one of the variables that affects the acquisition of a second language. In a foreign language learning situation, the most common and most obvious learning situation is the more-or-less traditional language classroom. The limited research on foreign language acquisition that has been completed to date has focused on methodological manipulation or classroom interaction (see Chaudron, 1988). There are, however, other learning environments in which increasing numbers of students participate. These include immersion programs, study-abroad experiences, and, with the advance of technology, we see an emerging technological environment. Each of these learning contexts presents new variables that potentially interact with whatever internal mechanisms the learner brings to the language learning task. These three chapters treat each of these learning environments.

The section begins with Swain's paper on learning French in a Canadian immersion situation. There have been numerous reports on various aspects of immersion learning (Swain and Lapkin, 1982, 1989; Genesee, 1987; Lambert, this volume). This chapter reports on the French language and content-area (academic) skills of "later" immersion students (those who begin at ages twelve to fourteen) and "sheltered" students (those who begin with the university-level programs). Swain summarizes the findings of both groups of students' learning of French as well as their learning of an academic subject: thus the "two for one" reference in her title. In her discussion Swain continues her well-known hypothesis regarding students' needs for comprehensible output as a possible explanation of immersion students' relatively weak productive skills. Of particular interest to American foreign language educators is the finding that students who have had more than one year of "core" instruction in French (that is, basic language instruction) succeed essentially as well in their academic subjects as do native speakers who are pursuing the same course. This finding has important implications for Americans who are considering the implementation of content-area foreign language programs.

DeKeyser continues the examination of alternative learning environments in his study of foreign language acquisition in a study-abroad environment. What is noteworthy about this article is that it is one of the first to focus in depth on American foreign language students in a target language environment. Most previous studies have addressed either international students learning ESL in the United States or immigrant and foreign workers learning a second language in a native speaking environment. In his study DeKeyser compares the Spanish skills of two groups of students: a study-abroad group and an at-home group. Despite popular expectations to the contrary, his conclusions are that the differences between the two groups were far less significant than were individual differences among students in the study-abroad group. Given his own findings and the supposed advantages of "picking it up" abroad, DeKeyser asks why it is that study abroad can make a big difference in proficiency despite the fact that his findings did not reveal a radical change in communicative processes. He answers the question by hypothesizing three possible reasons. Of these, one putative explanation is the interaction of focus on form and focus on meaning, which occurs when living abroad is combined with a (high) intermediate course. This hypothesis is supported by newly emerging evidence from other studies (Spada 1985, 1986; Freed 1989, 1990). With respect to implications for the classroom, DeKeyser notes in his conclusion the need to address students' level of achievement before the study-abroad experience. This suggestion is of major importance to the growing group of researchers who are interested in analyzing the linguistic effects of a study abroad experience on American foreign language students.

The final chapter in this section is by Noblitt and Bland. Their chapter describes the results of a pilot study of first and second semester students in French who used Système D (a software system that serves as a writing assistant for French) for creative writing assignments. In the course of their discussion, Noblitt and Bland emphasize the potential of computer-aided language learning (CALL) for "creating an interactive learning environment" and "a new environment for language study." They underscore the potential that the technological environment has for providing insights into learner strategies and processes as the computer tracks learner behavior in the course of instructional activities. On the basis of their pilot study, they summarize three benefits of tracking the learner in a CALL environment: "enhancements of the data base," "insights into error analysis," and "formulation of pedagogical and theoretical questions about the language learning process."

SECTION IV: FOREIGN LANGUAGE ACQUISITION RESEARCH OUTSIDE THE UNITED STATES

The last twenty years have witnessed considerable European activity in the general area of second language acquisition (SLA) research, activity which has been encouraged in large part by the great influx of migrant workers into Western Europe. Unlike most foreign language learning research in the United States, which has been predominantly situated in the classroom, most of the European SLA research has focused on the acquisition of a second language in everyday communication in a natural context. To this extent European SLA research has tended to have a more functional orientation than much of the corresponding American research.

This section includes three chapters, which address various aspects of what might be called the European tradition. Within the context of these three chapters, distinctions from and comparisons with recent American perspectives and initiatives in SLA research are made, with some attempt by the authors to extract implications for the American foreign language classroom. Each of the authors has chosen to highlight one or another of the major European projects and to discuss its orientation as well as some preliminary findings. Interpreted as a group, these chapters suggest that while there may be no such thing as a totally integrated and unified European approach, and while European and American research reflects some common concerns and has proceeded in some similar directions, there are, in fact, some important basic differences to be identified.

In the first chapter von Stutterheim provides an overview of European SLA research within the last fifteen years and includes a brief introduction to the work of several of the major projects (the Kiel Group, the Heidelberger Projekt *Pidgindeutsch,* the Zisa project, the GRAL Group, and the work of the European Science Foundation coordinated by the Max-Planck-Institute). Rather than concentrating on the general findings of each of these groups, she has chosen to present a detailed analysis of one group of interrelated concept-oriented studies, which focus on the acquisition of temporality. Subsequent to this discussion she provides a brief description of several other current research domains, including transfer, communication and interaction, and sociopsychological factors in SLA. In searching for implications for the classroom based on the direction of this work, she is led to conclude that, as yet, such "scientific models for language teaching . . . cannot be derived from studies on 'natural' L2 acquisition."

Huebner begins the second chapter by setting out those areas of European SLA research that he finds particularly useful and that contrast the most with American SLA research. In particular he refers to the European view of SLA, which is within the historical and social context in which it occurs, and which is "one aspect of a larger 'epiphenomenon' of language contact, acquisition, change, and loss." He juxtaposes this situation with what he suggests has been the American tendency to divorce SLA "from 'parent disciplines' of linguistics and psychology . . . supported by an infrastructure of educational programs. . . ." He supports this personal perspective with examples from several major European projects. Huebner concludes this discussion with remarks that he terms both "obvious and speculative" regarding applications of these findings for foreign language teaching. Suggesting that such applications can only be made with extreme caution, he points to possible support for a focus both on form and communicative interaction in the foreign language classroom.

In the final chapter in this section, Valdman offers yet another perspective on comparisons between foreign language learning in the United States and abroad. His first objective is to clarify some of the important distinctions that exist in these two settings: the marginal role of foreign language instruction in the United States, the dominance of ESL in the United States, and the very special role of English instruction within Europe. Valdman then proceeds to offer three taxonomies of SLA research, which he subsequently uses to clarify and interpret the differences in these research traditions. Utilizing numerous examples from the work of European scholars not covered by von Stutterheim and Huebner, he compares some of this work with that of several American foreign language scholars, ultimately concluding that American foreign language research tends to be "product oriented and experimental," whereas European research is more likely to focus on the "process of learning." He attributes this to the highly specific context of foreign language instruction in the United States, which accounts at least in part for our focus on structural features in language, as opposed to those that reveal underlying psycholinguistic processes.

SECTION V: THE ACQUISITION OF CULTURAL COMPETENCE

Recognition of the importance of cultural competence has grown enormously within the recent past. Originally considered an aspect of a broadly defined communicative competence, there have been increasing efforts to develop a broad notion of cultural competence, one based on ethnography, anthropological linguistics, and cross-cultural pragmatics.

When read together, the two chapters that comprise this section give some insight into what might be meant by cultural competence, particularly from the vantage point of the language learner. Understandably, these chapters do not pretend to provide an index or guide to the acquisition of cultural competence, but they do offer insights into the directions, topics, and issues that must be confronted in searching to provide students with a consciousness of themselves and others, their world and other worlds, in the development of cross-cultural awareness.

In the first chapter, Kramsch addresses the issue through an exploration of language as discourse. In a well-developed argument, she explicates the limitations of traditional views of "language in discourse" and identifies previously unidentified limitations in the profession's current formulations of communicative language teaching. These include some inherent problems with the currently articulated "focus on the learner," "negotiation of meaning," and authentic contexts. Kramsch identifies the restricted sense that "procedures of exclusion" have imposed on each of these areas, resulting in a situation in which "discourse has been decontextualized and is now taught according to structuralist principles of learning."

In elaborating a broad interpretation of language as discourse, she suggests a tri-part, cross-cultural approach to the teaching of language: "the container," "the collage," and "the montage" metaphors of language teaching. The examples Kramsch provides illustrate the direction one might take in further developing a pedagogy that extends beyond an exclusive focus on linguistic forms to include, in Kramsch's terms, "the pragmatic and cultural aspects of language in use and to link them to a broader definition of discourse. . . ."

The chapter by Byrnes continues the theme begun by Kramsch, namely, that for "learners to be communicatively competent in another language, they must not only be cross-linguistically but also cross-culturally competent." In this respect, Byrnes further elaborates on certain limitations of the notion of communicative language teaching as it is currently conceived and as it can be taught within the American education system.

Unlike much previous work in this area, which has concentrated on interactive oral ability, Byrnes has chosen to focus on written texts and their potential for helping learners access the cultural foundations of the text and the speech community. It is her contention that written texts better illustrate crucial issues in the development of cross-cultural communicative competence. Within the course of her discussion, Byrnes identifies five constraints on teaching for cultural competence and offers numerous suggestions for dealing with these constraints. Among these suggestions is an important one, which provides for a gradual progression from emphasis on C1 to C2, one which would bring additional rigor and intellectual content to language courses frequently criticized for their anti-intellectual focus on skills to the exclusion of content. Byrnes offers not so much implications, but rather thought-provoking suggestions on how one might proceed in developing and in helping students acquire cultural competence. Her emphasis throughout is that the process of developing cultural competence is more important than the product (frequently, the accumulation of isolated or fragmented cultural facts).

SECTION VI: THE ACQUISITION OF LITERACY SKILLS

Both chapters included in this section reflect and encourage increased attention to the acquisition of literacy skills. Beyond this, however, these chapters continue themes that have been developed elsewhere in this volume with respect to our emerging understanding of the integration of numerous phenomena in the acquisition of communicative language competence and in the broad roles played by cognition and cultural studies in the acquisition of any aspect of language use. As Swaffar so aptly states, we are becoming aware of the extent to which "language learning is more than learning language."

Bernhardt begins the first chapter by exploring the reading-writing relationship. She quotes a new area of inquiry, which suggests that these two processes must be viewed as complementary rather than as separate linguistic phenomena. With this background, she retrospectively reviews nine strands of research in reading and writing (word recognition, background knowledge, text structure, oral-aural factors, syntactic factors, cross-lingual processing strategies, metacognitive factors, testing, and instruction). Concluding that there is considerable ambiguity in the existing research, she goes on to explicate several reasons for some of the conflicting findings and then outlines prospects for future reading-writing research.

The second chapter, by Swaffar, relates to issues also discussed by Rivers, Byrnes, and Kramsch. In developing the theme that language learning is more than learning language, Swaffar focuses on two major extralinguistic factors, metacognitive processes and prior knowledge, that must be considered in developing materials or instructional strategies for the teaching of reading.

Within a context that accords significant importance to cognitive processing, Swaffar argues for a revised learning sequence by matching speaking and listening, which deal with "immediacy tasks" and reading and writing, which deal with "recursive tasks," a coupling that contradicts the more traditional association of the productive (speaking/writing) and reactive (listening/reading) skills. In a detailed examination of several current textbooks that purport to focus on authentic and communicative language use, Swaffar reveals inconsistencies between stated goals and the resulting materials. She extracts from current research several basic implications for revising the instructional sequence and expanding the curriculum at the beginning levels, to help students use their cognitive strengths to develop linguistic competence.

SECTION VII: PERSPECTIVES ON LANGUAGE TEACHING METHODOLOGY

This section provides new perspectives on language teaching methodology. Rather than describing and evaluating the pendulum swings from one methodological approach to another, information readily available in most methods textbooks, the authors of these two chapters have chosen to consider methodology in a more abstract and more theoretical sense. The first chapter, by Rivers, presents an overview of current theories of learning and cognition that would in principle validate any language teaching methodology. The second chapter, by Jarvis, provides perspectives on methodological research, which in turn would corroborate that research, a sorely lacking quality in much previous research on language teaching methodology.

Rivers begins this section with an ambitious and unique approach to the question of methodology. Rather than seeking to identify specific implications for classroom practices from research on various methods of language teaching, she forces the reader to consider current concepts in linguistics and cognitive psychology, which might validate any methodology selected for foreign language instruction. Rivers introduces her discussion by asking what she believes is the fundamental question in second language teaching: how do we internalize a language system so that we can enter into meaningful communication with speakers or writers of that language? She then attempts to answer that question by considering what that internalization might be and how it takes place. Beyond this, she considers mental representation and relationships to linguistic activity, cognitive psychology, theoretical models of Universal Grammar, and innate cognitive structures. She discusses memory processes, as developed in neo-connectionist parallel processing systems and the Adaptive Control of Thought (ACT*) model of cognition, as they might relate to the acquisition of a foreign language.

Rivers uses these theories to demonstrate how current approaches to memory support the emphasis on contextual learning of languages. She further points out how each of these theories encourages the design of certain types of courses useful to a dynamic view of language learning. She concludes by integrating the knowledge of these theories to suggest how they might interact in the language classroom to help students develop the ability "to convey what they really want to convey in pragmatically, culturally, syntactically, and semantically appropriate ways."

Jarvis's chapter, in addition to providing a review of methodological research of the past thirty years, identifies numerous limitations of that research. In addressing the shortcomings of this research, Jarvis identifies many of the features of that research that have given educational inquiry in language teaching a bad name. Jarvis maintains a belief, nonetheless, in the "potential of inquiry into classroom behavior" and enumerates desirable directions for future research on teaching methodology. Included among prospects for the future in this area are increased options for collaborative research, for the improved preparation of language researchers, for more descriptive studies, and, like Rivers, for a greater emphasis on research on learning.

SECTION VIII: RESEARCH DESIGN IN FOREIGN LANGUAGE ACQUISITION RESEARCH

The four chapters in this section reinforce each other in their description of the characteristics, limitations, and potential of various approaches to research design in foreign language acquisition research. They reflect each other as well in their frequent reference to the need for theoretical underpinning in planning and conducting such research. As might be anticipated, there is valuable overlap and amplification of discussion in these chapters with issues raised elsewhere in this volume. Particular reference can be made to the examination of methodological research first discussed by Jarvis, to the analysis of bilingual immersion programs reported on by Swain, to the need for better-trained foreign language researchers mentioned by Jarvis and Bernhardt, and perhaps most significant, to the idea that language learning and language learning research must make reference to and include far more than linguistic analysis, a frequent theme throughout the volume.

Long's chapter presents an overview of three major phases in foreign language learning research within the last thirty years. Long first identifies these three categories: product-oriented methods comparisons of the 1960s and 1970s, process-oriented microstudies of the 1970s and 1980s (and others that continue today), and process-process and process-product experiments, which began to appear in the late 1980s. He then illustrates each research approach, citing major research studies in each and offering valuable critical analysis along the way.

Lambert begins his chapter by admitting a preference for "tight designs and quantitative checkouts" in language learning research because he finds "all other alternatives . . . too subjective and personally biased." Recognizing his commitment to putting hypotheses to "a serious quantitative experimental test," he discusses the advantages and disadvantages he sees in a quantitative approach. The chapter is organized around three macro concerns in quantitative research design: size of language-related research, product versus process research, and deeper forms of process. Throughout the chapter Lambert reports on major bilingual studies in the United States and Canada (an added benefit of the chapter), identifying major flaws in some studies while specifying strengths in others. Lambert includes in his discussion a detailed examination of four studies, which utilize a "hypothetical-deductive research model," and which exemplify the need for researchers to attend to relevant theoretical ideas, both of which Lambert underscores as crucial to progress in second and foreign language research.

The third chapter, by Erickson, focuses on what he calls "interpretive" research, a designation that avoids the false dichotomy that he believes exists in the terms *quantitative* and *qualitative*. Interpretive research encompasses a variety of related research approaches that utilize description and analysis of routine events and the meanings of these events to the participants in them. Included in this category are approaches variously called ethnography, case study, documentation, sociolinguistic microanalysis, and qualitative analysis. Such research is usually accomplished by means of participant-observation and interviews. Erickson emphasizes that it is not uncommon to quantify some of the data collected in qualitative research; hence one sees the confusion potentially caused by opposing quantitative and qualitative approaches. Erickson situates his discussion of interpretive methods within the context of two theoretical notions: the nature of social interaction as a learning environment and the nature of communicative competence. By providing numerous examples of the varying nature of social interaction and the meanings of these interactions, Erickson provides a perspective on how interpretive research is valuable to those interested in language acquisition research. He details several advantages and disadvantages of interpretive, survey, and experimental research, including problems of "the lurking variable," ecological validity, and generalization, among others.

The final chapter in this section, that by Packard, considers implications for classroom-based research of various research designs. Packard argues that, despite common beliefs to the contrary, quantitative and qualitative (interpretive) research can, in fact, be complementary and used to bolster each other. He defends this position by demonstrating that many alleged limitations of each approach may be equally true of the other. Moreover, he illustrates how potential problems in either approach might reasonably be resolved. Packard concludes his discussion by urging that more classroom-based foreign language research be conducted, no matter how modest the size or scope, in the belief that all research ultimately contributes to our understanding of the field.

SECTION IX: CURRENT FOREIGN LANGUAGE LEARNING PROJECTS AND THEIR IMPLICATIONS FOR FOREIGN LANGUAGE ACQUISITION RESEARCH

This section presents three thematically related but quite distinct chapters. The first two chapters describe ongoing foreign language projects that capitalize on the use of new technologies. The first chapter deals with an experiment in CALL, which uses the computer to teach writing in French. The second chapter describes the use of video in a program for teaching spoken Japanese. The third chapter analyzes both of these projects in terms of their applicability to foreign language acquisition research.

Barson's chapter describes a bold initiative in the use of the electronic classroom to create a collaborative cross-country (Massachussets-California) electronic-mail project. Barson first describes the conceptual framework for this model, which utilizes what he calls the computer's "instrumental" and "agentive" potential. He continues by describing the various e-mail projects in which he and his students have participated, providing along the way reflections on various pedagogical implications for students and teachers alike.

In a similar manner, Jorden describes the development of her video project for the teaching of spoken Japanese. Jorden clarifies her choice of video as being the new technology that best permits the instruction of the spoken language with a culturally authentic orientation. Jorden discusses the range of sociolinguistic cues and stylistic choices that characterize every utterance in Japanese, and the degree to which the use of video helps sensitize learners to this phenomenon. In this respect, we find repeated once again an emphasis on the fact that the linguistic code is only one aspect of the total language learning experience.

The third chapter in this section represents a bridge between the classroom and research. Pica introduces her chapter by specifying the common interests shared by teachers and researchers despite the different objectives that their work often obliges. She acknowledges the sometimes divisive situation created by researchers' seeming reluctance to specify pedagogical implications from their research findings, and enumerates several constraints on the applicability of research findings to the language classroom. The central focus of Pica's chapter resides in her analysis of researchable themes in Barson's and Jorden's language learning projects. As part of this analysis, Pica interprets some of the well-known and controversial issues in language learning research (the roles of comprehensible input, student interaction, interlanguage, grammar, error correction, and fossilization). Pica concludes by urging more classroom description, more focused research (and the design of experimental classrooms), so that foreign language learning projects may assume a more significant role in the broader context of language learning research.

SECTION X: CONCLUSION

We conclude this volume with a final chapter by Charles Ferguson. Ferguson offers a personal perspective on the themes that emerge in this volume. He draws attention to the fact that these themes and the resulting discussion confirm our growing understanding of "the complexity of human language and the complexity of the classroom." Ferguson emphasizes that despite our varied vantage points and the varied circumstances in which second language learning takes place, we must not lose sight of a "unified conceptual framework" in focusing on the field that ultimately concerns us all: "the acquisition of nonmother tongues."

ENDNOTES

1. Appreciation is extended to Alice Freed, Lila Gleitman, Jerry Packard, and Teresa Pica for insightful comments and useful suggestions on the conference keynote address on which this revised and expanded chapter is based. Similar appreciation is offered to David Goldberg for his prompt efforts to supply figures on national foreign language enrollments.

2. Notable among these meetings are those organized by Bill VanPatten and James Lee at the University of Illinois. The first of these meetings was held in the spring of 1987. A selection of papers from that conference, which focused on the relationship between SLA and FLL from a researcher's point of view, appears in VanPatten and Lee, 1990.

3. Recent efforts are under way to change this perception by creating new courses and programs that emphasize content as well as skills in the acquisition of foreign languages. Francois Hugot, supported by a grant from FIPSE, is developing a model for Foreign Language Studies as an Academic Discipline. Numerous institutions, inspired in part by the Canadian model (see Wesche, 1985 for discussion), are also creating new courses that combine language with content-area instruction. Among major new initiatives are those under way at the Monterey Institute for International Studies under the direction of Jon Strolle. Supported by a grant from the PEW Foundation, MIS

has implemented a three-year program on Issues in the Integration of Subject Matter and Foreign Language Instruction.

4. References to the impact of American educational inquiry on the focus of foreign language teaching, learning, and research have been developed elsewhere. See Jarvis, Huebner, and Valdman (all in this volume) as well as VanPatten, Dvorak, and Lee, 1987.

REFERENCES

Anderson, Roger. 1990. "Models, Processes, Principles and Strategies: Second Language Acquisition Inside and Outside the Classroom." *Second Language Acquisition–Foreign Language Learning*. Eds. Bill VanPatten and James F. Lee. Clevedon, UK: Multilingual Matters. 45–68.

Bley-Vroman, Robert. 1986. "Hypothesis Testing Second Language Acquisition Theory." *Language Learning* 36.3: 353–76.

Bratt-Paulston, Christina. 1987. "Educational Language Policies in Utopia: A Reaction Paper to the Development of the Bilingual Proficiency Project." Paper presented at the 1987 annual meeting of AAAL, Chicago, Ill.

Brod, Richard. 1988. "Foreign Language Enrollments in U.S. Institutions of Higher Education—Fall 1986." *ADFL Bulletin* 19: 39–44.

Brod, Richard, and Monique Lapointe. 1989. "The MLA Survey of Foreign Language Entrance and Degree Requirements, 1987–1988." *ADFL Bulletin* 20: 17–41.

Chaudron, Craig. 1988. *Second Language Classrooms: Research on Teaching and Learning*. Cambridge, England: Cambridge UP.

Coppieters, R. 1987. "Competence Differences Between Native and Near-Native Speakers." *Language* 63.3: 544–73.

Dandonoli, Patricia. 1987. "Report on Foreign Language Enrollment in Public Secondary Schools, Fall 1985." *Foreign Language Annals* 20: 457–70.

Day, Richard. 1985. "The Use of the Target Language in Context and Second Language Proficiency." *Input in Second Language Acquisition*. Eds. Susan Gass and Carolyn Madden. Rowley, Mass.: Newbury House. 257–271.

DeKeyser, Robert. 1986. "From Learning to Acquisition in a U.S. Classroom and During a Semester Abroad." Unpublished Ph.D. Diss., Stanford University.

Doughty, Catherine. 1988. "The Effects of Instruction on the Acquisition of Relative Clauses in English as a Second Language." Unpublished Ph.D. Diss., University of Pennsylvania.

Ellis, Rod. 1986. *Understanding Second Language Acquisition*. Oxford: Oxford UP.

Eubank, Lynn. 1987. "The Acquisition of German Negation by Formal Language Learners." *Foreign Language Learning: A Research Perspective*. Eds. Bill Van-

Patten, Trisha Dvorak, and James F. Lee. Rowley, Mass.: Newbury House. 33–51.

———. 1990. "Linguistic Theory and the Acquisition of German Negation." *Second Language Acquisition–Foreign Language Learning.* Eds. Bill VanPatten and James F. Lee. Clevedon, UK: Multilingual Matters. 73–94.

Ferguson, Charles, and Thom Huebner. 1989. "Foreign Language Instruction and Second Language Acquisition Research in the United States." *NFLC Occasional Papers.* 1–9.

Flynn, Suzanne. 1988. "Second Language Acquisition and Grammatical Theory." *Linguistics: The Cambridge Survey Vol. 2, Linguistic Theory: Extensions and Implications.* Ed. Frederick Newmeyer. Cambridge, England: Cambridge UP. 53–73.

Freed, Barbara. 1989. "Informal Language Contact and Its Effect on Foreign Language Proficiency." Paper presented at the RP-ALLA 1989 Conference, Ohio State University, November, 1989.

———. "Language Learning in a Study Abroad Context: The Effects of Interactive and Non-interactive Out-of-Class Contact on Grammatical Achievement and Oral Proficiency." To be published in the proceedings of the Georgetown University Round Table on Languages and Linguistics 1990. *Linguistics, Language Teaching, and Language Acquisition: The Interdependence of Theory, Practice, and Research.* Washington, D.C.: Georgetown University Press.

Gass, Susan. 1982. "From Theory to Practice." *On TESOL '81.* Eds. M. Hines and William Rutherford. Washington, D.C.

———. 1990. "Second and Foreign Language Learning: Same, Different or None of the Above?" *Second Language Acquisition–Foreign Language Learning.* Eds. Bill VanPatten and James F. Lee. Clevedon, UK: Multilingual Matters. 34–44.

Genesee, Fred. 1987. *Learning Through Two Languages: Studies of Immersion and Bilingual Education.* New York: Newbury House.

Harley, Birgit. 1984. "Age as a Factor in the Acquisition of French as a Second Language in an Immersion Setting." *Second Language: A Cross-Linguistic Perspective.* Ed. Roger Anderson. Rowley, Mass.: Newbury House.

Johnson, Jacqueline S., and Elissa L. Newport. 1989. "Critical Period Effects in Second Language Learning: The Influence of Maturational State on the Acquisition of English as a Second Language." *Cognitive Psychology* 21: 60–99.

Kramsch, Claire. 1987. Foreword. *Foreign Language Learning: A Research Perspective.* Eds. Bill VanPatten, Trisha R. Dvorak, and James F. Lee. Rowley, Mass.: Newbury House.

———. 1990. "What Is Foreign Language Learning Research?" *Second Language Acquisition–Foreign Language Learning.* Eds. Bill VanPatten and James F. Lee. Clevedon, UK: Multilingual Matters. 27–33.

Krashen, Stephen. 1985. *The Input Hypothesis.* London: Longman.

Littlewood, William. 1984. *Foreign and Second Language Learning.* Cambridge, England: Cambridge UP.

Long, Michael. 1985. "Input and Second Language Acquisition Theory." *Input in Second Language Acquisition.* Eds. Susan Gass and Carolyn Madden. Rowley, Mass.: Newbury House. 377–93.

———. 1988. "Instructed Interlanguage Development." *Issues in Second Language Acquisition: Multiple Perspectives.* Ed. Leslie M. Beebe. New York: Newbury House/Harper and Row. 115–41.

Perdue, Clive, ed. 1984. *Second Language Acquisition by Adult Immigrants: A Field Manual.* Rowley, Mass.: Newbury House.

Pica, Teresa. 1989. "Research on Second and Foreign Language Learning: How Can It Respond to Classroom Concerns?" Manuscript. University of Pennsylvania.

Pica, Teresa, Richard Young, and Catherine Doughty. 1987. "The Impact of Interaction on Comprehension." *TESOL Quarterly* 2.4: 737–58.

Pienemann, Manfred. 1984. "Psychological Constraints on the Teachability of Languages." *Studies in Second Language Acquisition* 6.2: 186–214.

———. 1985. "Learnability and Syllabus Construction." *Modeling and Assessing Second Language Acquisition.* Eds. K. Hyltenstam and Manfred Pienemann. London: Multilingual Matters. 23–75.

Savignon, Sandra. 1972. *Communicative Competence: An Experiment in Foreign Language Teaching.* Philadelphia: Center for Curriculum Development.

Schachter, Jacqueline. 1984. "A Universal Input Condition." *Universals and Second Language Acquisition.* Ed. William Rutherford. Amsterdam: John Benjamins.

Spada, Nina. 1985. "Effects of Informal Contact on Classroom Learners' Proficiency: A Review of Five Studies." *TESL Canada Journal* 2: 51–62.

———. 1986. "The Interaction Between Types of Contact and Types of Instruction: Some Effects on the Second Language Proficiency of Adult Learners." *SSLA* 181–99.

Steele, Ross. 1989. "Teaching Language and Culture: Old Problems, New Approaches." Paper presented at the 1989 Georgetown University Roundtable on Languages and Linguistics, Washington, D.C.

Stern, H. H. 1983. *Fundamentals of Language Teaching.* Oxford: Oxford UP.

Swain, Merrill. 1985. "Communicative Competence: Some Roles of Comprehensible Input and Comprehensible Output in Its Development." *Input in Second Language Acquisition.* Eds. Susan Gass and Carolyn Madden. Rowley, Mass.: Newbury House. 235–53.

Swain Merrill, and Sharon Lapkin. 1982. *Evaluating Bilingual Education: A Canadian Study.* Clevedon, Avon: Multilingual Matters.

———. 1989. "Canadian Immersion and Adult Second Language Teaching: What's the Connection?" *Modern Language Journal* 75: 150–59.

Tarone, Elaine. 1980. "Some Influences on the Syllable Structure of Interlanguage Phonology." *International Review of Applied Linguistics* 8.2: 139–52.

VanPatten, Bill. 1988. "Theory and Research in Second Language Acquisition and Foreign Language Learning: On Producers and Consumers." *IDEAL* 3: 99–109.

———. Forthcoming. "Classroom and Naturalistic Learning: Two Case Studies." *Studies in Hispanic Phonology Sociolinguistics and Applied Linguistics.* Eds. T. Morgan, James F. Lee, and Bill VanPatten.

VanPatten, Bill, Trisha Dvorak, and James F. Lee. 1987. *Foreign Language Learning: A Research Perspective.* Rowley, Mass.: Newbury House.

VanPatten, Bill, and James F. Lee. 1988. "Exploring the Relationship Between Second Language Acquisition and Foreign Language Learning." *IDEAL* 3: 69–74.

———. 1990. "Content, Processes and Products in Second Language Acquisition and Foreign Language Learning." *Second Language Acquisition–Foreign Language Learning.* Eds. Bill VanPatten and James F. Lee. Clevedon, UK: Multilingual Matters. 240–245.

Wesche, Marjorie. 1985. "Immersion and the Universities." *Canadian Modern Language Review* 41: 931–35.

White, Lydia. 1987. "Implications of Learnability Theories for Second Language Learning and Teaching." Paper presented at the 1987 AILA Congress, Sydney, Australia.

———. 1990. "Second Language Acquisition and Universal Grammar." *Studies in Second Language Acquisition* 12:2: 121–133.

Zohl, Helmut. 1980. "The Formal and Developmental Selectivity of L2 Influence on L2 Acquisition." *Language Learning* 30.1: 43–57.

Section **II**

The Role of Instruction in Classroom-Based Foreign Language Acquisition

Research on the Role of Communication in Classroom-Based Foreign Language Acquisition: On the Interpretation, Expression, and Negotiation of Meaning

Sandra J. Savignon

University of Illinois at Urbana-Champaign

What is language? How is it acquired? These are simple questions with straightforward answers. Language is a social system of communication. Individuals develop their language skills through use, through involvement in communicative events.

Is the same true of second language skills? Simply stated, yes. Bilingualism and multilingualism occur naturally around the world. Bilinguals and multilinguals develop language skills to meet their social and professional needs in a variety of contexts. They often code mix and code switch, as appropriate, and their language experiences are not without an influence on one another. Is their style or manner of expression richer or poorer for this influence? In other words, is bilingualism a liability or an asset? The judgment depends on one's view of language and language change, as well as of individual autonomy and self-realization. The influence is nonetheless inarguable and inevitable, just as are the routine acquisition and use of one, two, three, or more languages as required to meet communicative needs.

Such is the world of multilanguage acquisition and use. Classroom language learning, on the other hand, appears far from routine. How learners learn and what teachers can do to help them learn remain the focus of continued discussion. Are the issues really so complex as they seem?

Classroom L2 learning, or acquisition, if one prefers, can be understood only within the broad sociopolitical context of which it is a part. Any discussion of research findings in classroom learning/acquisition properly belongs in a context that includes both the goals of a program and its resources. Program goals may include some measure of communicative competence in terms of the currently formulated framework, that is, grammatical competence, discourse competence, sociolinguistic competence, and strategic competence. Numerous reasons might be provided for establishing this particular goal. The experience of communicating in other than one's mother tongue and the sense of communicative confidence that presumably results might be seen to contribute in turn to a more general appreciation of linguistic—that is, *cultural*—difference, promoting tolerance and understanding both at home and across national borders. A more tangible outcome, no doubt, would be the maintenance and expansion of L2 contacts through continued study, reading, travel, personal relations, and other means, with a resulting increase in L2 competence for personal and/or professional enrichment. With either outcome, the broader social benefits are clear.

Another, more traditional goal of school L2 study is a cognitive awareness of language structure as part of a general education. In the case of formative language programs where linguistic description is the focus, development of some measure of communicative ability is but an incidental outcome. In the recent history of both public and private education, the study of Greek and Latin and, subsequently, *modern* languages has been valued, above all, for the analytical skills this study entails. Maintenance of language requirements has been seen as an assertion of value, of rigor in academic programs.

Program resources typically reflect program goals. They include the time available for L2 study—hours per day, hours per week, number of years in a sequence. They include teacher preparation and professionalism. These resources depend, in turn, on parental, community, and state support. Programs with a goal of communicative competence have needs strikingly different from those of more traditional, formative programs. An appreciation of these differences has led some to propose that not only are formative language programs that give explicit attention to grammatical structure the norm in U.S. schools and representative of our limited national commitment to foreign language study (zero to two years of study for the majority of secondary school graduates) but also continues to make them the most reasonable option (Valdman, 1989). Disagreeing, no doubt, are those who say, "Yes, but there is hope for change." The success of elementary-level immersion programs in cities like Milwaukee (Curtain and Pesola, 1987), curriculum reform and L2 study for all secondary school students in the state of New York (New York State Department of Education), recent efforts to establish functional criteria for meeting language requirements at major universities, such as the University of Pennsylvania (Freed, 1984) and the University of Minnesota (Lange, 1988), lend support to their challenge of the status quo.

Support for formative programs, on the other hand, comes from teachers who have been trained in linguistic analysis and feel most comfortable with a focus on form, as well as from administrators who find program resources inadequate to ensure a commitment to the development of communicative skills. And while eloquent cases have been made for untying the tongues of monolingual Americans, for example, Simon (1980), the preeminence of English as an international language of trade and technology leaves many taxpayers unconvinced.

A research agenda presupposes an agreement on program goals. In any discussion of research findings on the role of communication in language learning, the need to clarify goals and resources merits elaboration. This is all the more true in those situations where there is an apparent lack of consensus among teachers and program developers. With goals unclear, confusion persists, and articulation remains problematic. Research data are cited in support of one or another pedagogical practice—for example, to teach or not explicitly to teach a particular grammatical rule, when what really may be in question is not the practice as much as the goals of the program.

WHAT THE RESEARCH SAYS

The following discussion of research on the role of communication in classroom L2 programs assumes a goal of communicative competence, a measure of functional L2 ability that includes not only the grammatical but the pragmatic competence required for the interpretation, expression, and negotiation of meaning. Such interpretation, expression, and negotiation presupposes texts and a well-defined context of situation. Language structures and vocabulary are viewed as tools for doing, not as facts for knowing (Savignon, 1983).

Where communication is a goal, learner involvement in communication seems a reasonable demand to make of classroom activities. Communicative language teaching emphasizes the need for active learner participation in communicative events. The success of immersion programs in developing functional skills stands out as a well-documented example of learners leaning to communicate by communicating (Stern, 1984; Lapkin and Swain, 1984; Genesee, 1985; Swain, this volume). U.S. immersion programs in Spanish, French, and German have looked for guidance to the well-established and widely supported Canadian immersion programs in French (Anderson and Rhodes, 1984). On the other hand, U.S. immersion programs in English for an increasing number of non-native speaker residents have attracted attention abroad. The French daily *Le Figaro* (May 3, 1989) has cited the success of New York City public school ESL and bilingual programs for thousands of school-age children who often live in neighborhoods where the only language they hear is their native Spanish, Chinese, or Haitian creole.

The content-based curriculum of immersion programs has provided a useful model for establishing as the course focus a topic—geography, history, art, no matter, as long as it reflects learner needs and interests—in place of language per se, thus providing a more natural environment for the development of L2 skills. Teacher qualifications include knowledge of subject matter, L2 fluency appropriate for the context, and the ability to incorporate language arts activities that relate to learner experience in communication (Savignon, 1983; Swain and Lapkin, 1988). Content-based L2 instruction has been described at length by Mohan (1986). Within a university setting, upper division literature and civilization courses taught in the L2 provide a similar classroom immersion environment.

Within more traditional, language-focused classrooms, a concern for developing communicative competence has led to a number of initiatives in terms of materials, scope and sequence, classroom decentralization. Berns (forthcoming) provides a comprehensive analysis of communicative language teaching materials and their underlying functional linguistic theory. Savignon and Berns (1984, 1987) provide examples of the integration of communicative teaching and evaluation practices in programs selected for their international scope and diversity. Communicative curriculum design has been treated at length by Breen and Candlin (1980), van Ek (1975), Savignon (1983), Yaldin (1987), and others.

Insights into the communicative nature of the acquisition of particular sets of language skills abound in recent professional literature. Reading skills, for example, neglected in the audiolingual emphasis of U.S. foreign language programs during the past quarter of a century, are currently described as involving both top-down and bottom-up approaches to text interpretation. Schema theory characterizes the negotiation that takes place as the reader seeks to interpret the writer's intent in light of her own experiences and expectations. All texts assume certain kinds of knowledge of a reader. Readers, in turn, seek to relate what seems to be new information to something that is already known. Skimming for specific information, getting the gist of a report, following a narration, and savoring a style of expression are among the many purposes of reading that should be considered when providing activities for learners. Interest is sustained and interpretation facilitated when learners have prior knowledge of the topic and text type (Carrell, 1983; Dubin, Eskey, and Grabe, 1986).

Teaching of composition has benefited similarly from new focus and fresh insights. Written expression of meaning is seen now as something quite different from translation, transformation exercises, or the recombination of memorized phrases. As in the case of reading, texts, not sentences incorporating particular morphosyntactic features, are the route to self-expression. The criterion for text identification, whether a poem, an advertisement, or a grocery list, is not form or length but coherence. (Widdowson, 1987; Savignon, 1983; Connor and Kaplan, 1987). Having learners keep journals with short periodic entries for the teacher is but one example of a communicative approach to writing that has been used successfully and recommended by teachers for use with beginners. This type of activity provides a context, gives learners the initiative, and, when teachers respond with comments and requests for clarification, leads to a fruitful negotiation of meaning between writer and reader. Such activities are not meant to replace language arts activities that focus on spelling, word choice, and morphosyntactic features, but rather are meant to provide a communicatively rich context for attention to such formal matters. Focus on form is related to communicative needs and experience.

Contemporary perspectives on the acquisition of reading and writing skills in particular are important to understanding the role of communication in the development of communicative competence in general, precisely because they have been obscured in discussions of U.S. foreign language teaching by the excessive attention that has been focused on speaking. Bilingual, ESL, and EFL programs, on the other hand, understandably have been concerned with the development of academic reading and writing skills, and a wide array of attractive communicative materials has resulted.

As for conversation, in Wardhaugh's terms, "the most generalized form of talk," the need for early learner involvement in the negotiation of meaning is no longer seriously disputed. Such was not the case at the time of the Savignon (1972) study of adult classroom acquisition of French, which distinguished between sentence-level grammatical competence and a broader communicative competence that subsequently would be described in terms of grammatical competence, discourse competence, sociolinguistic competence, and strategic competence (Canale and Swain, 1980; Canale, 1981). By encouraging students to ask for information, to seek clarification, to use circumlocution, to resort to whatever linguistic and nonlinguistic resources they could muster to negotiate meaning, to stick to the communicative task at hand, teachers were invariably leading learners to take risks, to speak in other than memorized patterns. In the prevailing behaviorist view of the times, this meant that bad "habits" would result and that structural accuracy would suffer. In fact, when test results were compared at the end of the eighteen-week, five-hour-per-week program, learners who had practiced communication in lieu of laboratory pattern drills for one hour a week performed with no less accuracy on discrete-point tests of structure. On the other hand, their communicative competence as measured in terms of fluency, comprehensibility, effort, and amount of communication in a series of four unrehearsed tasks significantly surpassed that of learners who had had no such practice. Learner reactions to the test formats lent further support to the view that even beginners respond well to activities that let them focus on meaning as opposed to formal features. The overriding criterion for the communicative activities provided in both the practice and test settings was that learners have the opportunity to say things they really wanted to say, even if the expression of their thoughts did not fit the confines of the sample phrases or structures in their textbook.

Today, discussions focus not so much on whether learners should be given the opportunity to communicate, but on whether explicit attention to rules of usage is of help in the acquisition of functional, that is, communicative, skills. In a given classroom context, how much time should be given to drawing attention to the L2 code, that is, language arts, and how much to providing opportunities for communication? Second language acquisition studies, in general, suggest that teaching the code is less significant than was previously thought. Route of acquisition is largely unaffected by teaching. Attempts to force learners to use a particular structure before they are ready may appear successful in short term, highly monitored exercises of the type "Describe what you did yesterday. Use five reflexive verbs," but they have no subsequent influence on learner language (Lightbown, 1983; Pienemann, 1984; Ellis, 1985). The formal focus of such exercises, moreover, should not be confused with a focus on the expression of meaning.

Confusion of form and function persists in research design as well as in teaching materials and discussions of classroom practice. Considerable attention is thus required to interpret outcomes. Where communicative competence is a goal, the construct validity of test instruments remains an overriding concern. Reliability, while essential to validity, by no means establishes validity (Savignon, 1985; Bachman and Savignon, 1987; Bachman, 1990).

To illustrate, among a number of recent studies that purport to investigate the value of explicit teaching of grammar is one by Scott (1989). (For additional discussion of this study, see also Valdman, this volume.) Two classes of fourth semester college French students participated in the study, which involved ten minutes of instruction a day for six consecutive class periods (over a total of two weeks) for each of two selected grammatical structures: relative pronouns *qui, que, dont, ce qui, ce que, ce dont*, and subjunctive tense formation and usage. Explicit review of French relative pronouns was provided in one class: a different relative pronoun was presented each day with a grammatical rule followed by teacher modeling of five example sentences. The other class heard a six-episode story in French, which had the same relative pronouns embedded "naturally" in the text. Each episode had an average of twenty-five relative pronouns. After reading the episode, the teacher asked questions with regard to the content of the story and then quickly reread the text. The class was not told to focus on any particular grammatical structure. A similar procedure was then followed for the subjunctive, with the groups and presentations reversed.

Mean gain scores on both written and oral pretests and posttests for each group were compared. There were no significant between-group differences on the oral test. Both written and total test score differences showed significance, however, and the researcher concluded that "students who had been taught the target structures explicitly performed better overall than those who were exposed to an implicit presentation of the same grammar content" (Scott, 1989, 18). Her findings presumably lend support to the position detailed in the introduction to her paper, namely that "overtly teaching the rules and grammatical structures [is important] in order to organize, efficiently and accurately, linguistic elements for communicative purposes" (Scott, 1989, 14).

A detailed critique of this particular study is beyond the scope of this paper. A few observations are nonetheless in order, since they pertain generally to classroom research on the role of communication in the development of communicative competence. No theorist to my knowledge has made the assertion that doses of concentrated "exposure" to a particular structure constitute "implicit teaching" and are likely to promote grammatical competence. Rather, a careful distinction has been made between input and *intake*, which involves learners in the negotiation of meaning. (Krashen, 1985; Long, 1981). Nor does the embedding of twenty-five relative pronouns or fifteen subjunctive verbs in a short passage result in a "natural" text. Such distortion deprives learners of the opportunity to interpret authentic discourse, to exploit its natural redundancy in the negotiation of meaning. When texts are created by teachers as pretexts for grammar display, there is little incentive for learners to focus on meaning. (It is noteworthy in the example text provided in the research report, moreover, that the first sentence contains two errors in verb form. In the first error, the subjunctive form is inappropriate; in the second, the subjunctive is required: *Je ne crois pas que les six*

mois que nous ayons *passés à New York m'* ont *convaincue que j'étais américaine.*
Even teachers sometimes have trouble applying the rules they provide!) The
sample pretest and posttest items confirm the formal, monitored nature of these
measures. Lists of unrelated sentences are provided, and learners are told to fill in
the correct pronoun or verb form. In the language lab learners are told to "answer
using the subjunctive." This is hardly the kind of request they would be likely to
hear in a communicative setting. The researcher recognizes the problem and
notes in her discussion that "since the students under the implicit teaching
condition were never given the opportunity to organize their information under
grammatical headings such as 'relative pronoun' or 'subjunctive' they may have
been at a disadvantage" (Scott, 1989, 19). One can only wonder, then, why she
relied on this form of assessment. A final observation relates to the length of time
between presentation and assessment. Since all learners had had a previous introduction to pronoun and subjunctive use in French, the six ten-minute presentations amounted to a review. What better way to review for the kind of test that
would immediately follow than to have summary rules presented, with examples?
Nothing in the data suggests, however, that the pronoun and subjunctive forms
presented will be used appropriately by learners when they express their own
meaning, either orally or in writing, two, twenty, or fifty weeks hence. In other
words, there is no evaluation of learner grammatical competence as a component
of communicative competence.

A more promising avenue of inquiry for teachers interested in promoting
classroom L2 acquisition is an analysis of classroom talk and an identification of
the opportunities for developing not only grammatical, but discourse, sociolinguistic, and strategic competence. Not until we are able to describe the nature of
classroom L2 use under different conditions will we be ready to relate this use to
learning outcomes and make recommendations for classroom practice (Kramsch,
1985; Tardif and Weber, 1987; Van Lier, 1988; Chaudron, 1988; Allwright,
1988).

An early study of foreign language teacher talk was conducted by Guthrie
(1984), who found persistent form/focus confusion even when teachers felt they
were providing an optimal classroom acquisition environment by speaking only
in the L2. Transcriptions of teacher/learner dialogue reveal the unnaturalness,
that is, incoherence, of much of the discourse.

More recently, a study by Kinginger (1990) has examined the nature of
learner/leaner talk associated with a variety of task types involving small group or
pair work. Thirty-two conversations representing four distinct task types were
observed in two different college-level French programs. The conversations were
examined with respect to turn-taking and topic management, with generalizations regarding the degree of learner participation and initiative, and to negotiation and repair strategies. Her data show that when learners are constrained by
formal considerations or provided with a structure-embedded text as a basis for
conversation, their talk has many of the same characteristics as form-focused
teacher talk. The following transcript from her study illustrates the noncommuni-
cative nature of an exchange between three beginning adult learners of French,

one of whom was given a "conversation card" with a list of questions in English (A) to be asked of a partner (B). The third learner (C) had a card with the French versions of the same questions and was assigned the role of linguistic monitor.

A um. um. qu'est-ce que tu, no. . . . um. qu'est-ce que tu, no. quel penses tu? à quel?
[*um. um. what, no . . . um. what, no. which do you think? to which?*]

C à.
[*to.*]

A à quoi!
[*to what!*]

C oui. à quoi.
[*yes. to what.*]

A à quoi penses-tu? euah! la vie . . .
[*to what do you think? that euah! life . . .*]

C le verbe est ressembler.
[*the verb is ressembler.*]

A que, so à quoi penses-tu
[*that, so to what do you think*]

C à quoi re-
[*to what re-*]

A oh.

C ressemblerait
[*would resemble*]

A à quoi ressemblerait? (laughs) . . . à quoi ressemblerait . . . la vie?
[*to what would resemble? . . . to what would resemble . . . life?*]

C vie.

A dans. sur. en. (laughs) de?
[*in. on. in. of?*]

C de
[*of*]

A de cette pays,
[*of this country,*]

C de tous les jours.
[*of every day.*]

A oh. aaah. (laughs)

C de tous les jours. la vie de tous les jours.
[*of every day. everyday life.*]

A so: à quoi ressemblerait? la vie? wait! de tous les jours dans . . . de cette pays.
[*so: to what would resemble? life? wait! of every day in . . . of this country.*]

C dans.
[*in.*]

A aagh! dans cette—ce pays.
[*in this(f.)—this (m.) country.*]

C oui.
[*yes*]

A hoo. boy. . . . comprends?
[*understand?*]

B no!
(laughter)

Analyses of the interactions resulting from other task types showed them to differ with respect to both quality and quantity of language use. They include examples of ways in which communicative experience can be provided in classroom settings.

Negotiation of meaning is similarly the focus of a study by Pica *et al.* (1989) in which native speaker (NS)—non-native speaker (NNS) pairs collaborated on three different communicative tasks. Participants in this instance were intermediate-level adult Japanese learners of English and native speakers of English with no teaching background. The NS signal type was found to have a significant impact on the type of NNS response. NNS modification of expression occurred most often when NSs signaled an explicit need for clarification rather than providing a model utterance for confirmation. Among the other interesting findings of this study was the influence of gender on the nature of the negotiation. Male NNSs were much more likely to modify their expression, to participate in negotiation with the female NSs participating in the study than were their female counterparts. This observation led the researchers to note that "NNS production of comprehensible output was not simply an outcome of a single factor such as task type, but a host of inter- and intrapersonal variables as well" (Pica *et al.*, 1989, 84), and to recommend that both gender and ethnicity of participants be taken into account in the design of further research on learner expression and negotiation. Analysis of interaction of this kind represents a rich source of data, not only for understanding the nature of NS-NNS negotiation, as the researchers conclude, but for understanding the potential of NNS-NNS negotiation in foreign language classroom settings. The Kinginger study (1990) represents a step in this direction.

Descriptions of the nature of this negotiation under different conditions are preliminary to establishing any but the most general relations with learning outcomes. In the meantime, however, the preeminence of formative language instruction in U.S. programs leaves considerable room for providing learners with communicative experiences, not only in conversation, but in reading and writing as well, *if* in fact communicative competence is a goal *and* the needed resources are available. Long experience with teaching and emphasizing structural accuracy has shown that communicative ability does not result. Discouraged by lack of accomplishment, such as a lack of communicative confidence and/or disappointing results on a placement exam, entering college or university students may abandon the language they have "studied" for two or more years in high school to begin the study of yet another language, often with no better results. The results of an oft-cited study by Carroll of the oral communicative ability of foreign language majors, back in 1967 when structural accuracy and error avoidance dominated methodological discussion, show a similarly disappointing level of accomplishment.

From the perspective of communicative competence, secondary school programs suffer from a lack not only of appropriate materials but, more important, a cadre of teachers ready to implement and supplement them, and sufficient time in which to do so. When compared with other major nations, U.S. commitment to language study has been and remains minimal. True, the precipitous decline in enrollments in the 1960s has been arrested, and graduation requirements in second language study have been gradually reinstated. In 1983, 47% of comprehensive U.S. colleges/universities had such a requirement, and by 1988 the percentage had increased to 58%. Entrance requirements show a similar increase but remain low. Twenty-six percent (26%) of these same colleges/universities reported entrance requirements in 1988, up from 14% in 1983 (Brod and Lapointe, 1989). Similarly, the total number of students studying languages at both the secondary and college levels has increased, but not dramatically. Most of the increase has been in Spanish, and more than 90% of the enrollments are in first and second year courses. Recommendations for research on classroom learning and the interpretation of findings should not neglect the nature of this context.

Teacher preparation and expectations are another part of the overall picture. Surprisingly little systematic inquiry has been conducted into foreign language teachers' perceptions and practices. A study by Kleinsasser (1989) is an important exception. Based on a sociological model of inquiry developed by Rosenholtz (1989), his observations and conversations with secondary school foreign language teachers have led him to identify two different technical cultures, one uncertain and routine, the other certain and nonroutine. To summarize from his findings, "all language teachers perceive that they possess a technical culture. One group's technical culture uses routine tasks and relies on routine instruction that supports teachers' uncertainty about instructional practice. The second group's technical culture uses nonroutine tasks and relies on nonroutine instruction that supports teachers' certainty about instructional practice" (156). Heavy reliance on the textbook and nonexistent or infrequent opportunities for spontaneous, communicative L2 interaction were classroom characteristics of those teachers with an uncertain and routine culture.

Undergraduate teachers in training are often quick to note the discrepancies between what they learn in methods courses about the importance of opportunities to interpret, express, and negotiate meaning and what they sometimes observe in foreign language classrooms. The following comments excerpted from the observation reports of foreign language teacher education majors at a large midwestern university provide a note of realism in the discussion of research findings:

> The chairs in both classes were arranged in straight parallel rows set up so that they faced the teacher.
> It was obvious that the focus of the course was on the form of the language

rather than on the function. Class time was spent on doing exercises out of the textbook as well as filling in the blanks on worksheets.

As in the first year class, all grammar explanations occurred in the L1. Whether it was review or a new lesson, English prevailed. In a third year class, I had hoped to see more extensive use of Spanish.

Of the four components of communicative competence, grammatical competence was definitely the most prominent. Every day there was some sort of grammar activity. The activities varied often enough, but grammar was always at the root. On the Monday following Spring Break, I was surprised to find out that the main activity for the hour was for the students to mingle around the room and talk about their vacations. At last some sociolinguistic practice! But my feeling of surprise soon wore off when the teacher spent half of the hour reviewing the preterite *tú* form of every verb one might want to use when discussing one's vacation.

The fourth year class was similar to the first year class in the amount of French that was used. All student and teacher talk was in English.

Discourse and strategic competencies were sadly neglected. There was little opportunity for the students to develop the ability to understand the overall meaning of a given text, either written or oral. No readings in Spanish were used, and the teacher spoke in English most of the time.

The second year class started with Herr Schultz using a little German small talk about student likes and dislikes. There was not a good response. Then they had a vocabulary quiz. Although the teacher's manual had excellent examples of circumlocution for the entire vocabulary list, Herr Schultz gave the L1 equivalent.

After 16 hours of observation in two French classes, intermediate-level and advanced conversation, I painfully realized that the road to a communicative approach to language teaching will be long and bumpy, not so much because of the teacher's lack of effort, but because of an ingrained fear that the new approach "won't work with high school kids that must pass tests that are structurally based." The teacher feels that the communicative approach will work only in a university setting where students are presumably more motivated, serious, and committed to language learning.

If these few observations are to any extent representative of the larger national scene, then communication in no way can be said to have claimed the day, displacing structural analysis as the center of attention. To the contrary, the amount of language practice in typical classrooms would appear to be quite small. Again, recommendations for methods and materials must take into account the realities of classroom instruction.

In Asia and Europe at present there is much talk about lowering linguistic barriers to education and economic development. In Japan, private language schools flourish alongside the more academic state school programs. In France, the Ministry of Education has announced that second language study for all learners will begin at age nine and continue for nine years, with a third language introduced at age thirteen. At the April 1989 Etats Généraux des Langues in Paris, an international symposium on language learning and teaching, was sounded the theme of mandatory plurilingualism in a united Europe. "Barriers will disappear when Europeans have understood that the use of a single national language encloses them in a world too narrow to contain their whole life" (Garibaldi-Jallet, 1989). The preparation of teachers to meet the needs of a plurilingual society was also considered:

> Teachers who are meant to educate learners towards "international learning" must be "international learners" themselves. . . . [They] should aim to adopt the role and function of social and intercultural interpreter, not ambassador. . . . Teachers should develop further appropriate communication skills in language which are suited for negotiation both in the classroom and in intercultural communication situations outside. They should have and develop further text skills, i.e., the ability to deal with all forms of authentic data (Edelhoff, 1989).

At issue in the United States at present is not the research evidence supporting the need for involving learners in communicative transactions, in the interpretation, expression, and negotiation of meaning so that they may develop text skills. Language teachers can teach, and learners will learn in an environment that values functional L2 skills and provides a range of integrated form and strategy focused language arts along with experience in communication both inside and outside the classroom. Debates within the American foreign language profession on morphosyntactic "accuracy," explicit presentation of grammar rules, "natural" approaches to teaching, and the like often serve to obscure the real issue, that of the goals and resources of school programs. Given present resources and commitment, should the goals of useful second language communicative skill development be abandoned as utopian? Should more traditional, general educational goals of linguistic awareness be reaffirmed in their stead? Herein lies the real debate.

REFERENCES

Allwright, Richard. 1988. *Observation in the Language Classroom*. London: Longman.

Anderson, Helena, and Nancy Rhodes. 1984. "Immersion and Other Innovations in U.S. Elementary Schools." *Initiatives in Communicative Language Teaching*. Eds. S. Savignon and M. Berns. Reading, Mass.: Addison-Wesley. 167–81.

Bachman, Lyle. Forthcoming. *Fundamentals of Language Testing*. Oxford: Oxford UP.

Bachman, Lyle, and Sandra J. Savignon. 1987. "The Evaluation of Communicative Language Proficiency: A Critique of the ACTFL Oral Interview." *Modern Language Journal* 70: 380–90.

Berns, Margie S. Forthcoming. *Contexts of Competence: English Language Teaching in Non-Native Contexts*. New York: Plenum.

Breen, Michael, and Christopher Candlin. 1980. "The Essentials of a Communicative Curriculum in Language Teaching." *Applied Linguistics* 1: 89–112.

Brod, Richard, and Monique Lapointe. 1989. "The MLA Survey of Foreign Language Entrance and Degree Requirements, 1987–1988." *ADFL Bulletin* 20: 17–41.

Canale, Michael. 1981. Introduction. *Ontario Assessment Instrument Pool for French as a Second Language.* Toronto: Ontario Ministry of Education.

Canale, Michael, and Merrill Swain. 1980. "Theoretical Bases of Communicative Approaches to Second Language Teaching and Testing. *Applied Linguistics* 1: 1–47.

Carrell, Patricia. 1983. "Three Components of Background Knowledge in Reading Comprehension." *Language Learning* 33: 183–207.

Carroll, John B. 1967. *The Foreign-Language Attainment of Language Majors in the Senior Year: A Survey Conducted in U.S. Colleges and Universities.* Cambridge, Mass.: Graduate School of Education, Harvard University.

Chaudron, Craig. 1988. *Second Language Classrooms.* Cambridge, England: Cambridge UP.

Connor, Ulla, and Robert Kaplan, eds. 1987. *Writing Across Languages: Analysis of L2 Text.* Reading, Mass.: Addison-Wesley.

Curtain, Helena, and Carole Ann Pesola. 1987. *Languages and Children—Making the Match.* Reading, Mass.: Addison-Wesley.

Dubin, Fraida, David Eskey, and William Grabe, eds. 1986. *Teaching Second Language Reading for Academic Purposes.* Reading, Mass.: Addison-Wesley.

Edelhoff, Christophe. 1989. "Institutions and Training: Past, Present and Future." Paper presented at the Etats-Généraux des Langues, Paris, 26–29 April, 1989.

Ellis, Rod. 1985. *Understanding Second Language Acquisition.* Oxford: Oxford UP.

Freed, Barbara. 1984. "Proficiency in Context: The Pennsylvania Experience." *Initiatives in Communicative Language Teaching.* Eds. S. Savignon and M. Berns. Reading, Mass.: Addison-Wesley. 211–40.

Garibaldi-Jallet, Annita. 1989. "1992: The Consequences of the Single European Act." Paper presented at the Etats-Généraux des Langues, Paris, 26–29 April, 1989.

Genesee, Fred. 1985. "Second Language Learning Through Immersion." *Review of Educational Research* 55: 541–61.

Guthrie, Elizabeth. 1984. "Intake, Communication, and Second Language Teaching." *Initiatives in Communicative Language Teaching.* Eds. S. Savignon and M. Berns. Reading, Mass.: Addison-Wesley. 35–54.

Kinginger, Celeste. 1990. "Task Variation and Classroom Learner Discourse." Diss., U. of Illinois.

Kleinsasser, Robert. 1989. "Foreign Language Teaching: A Tale of Two Technical Cultures." Diss., U. of Illinois.

Kramsch, Claire. 1985. "Classroom Interaction and Discourse Options." *Studies in Second Language Acquisition* 7: 169–83.

Krashen, Stephen. 1985. *The Input Hypothesis.* New York: Longman.

Lange, Dale. 1988. "Assessing Foreign Language Proficiency in Higher Education in the United States." Paper presented at the American Association of Applied Linguistics Annual Meeting, New Orleans, December 28, 1988.

Lapkin, Sharon, and Merrill Swain. 1984. "Research Update." *Language and Society.* Ottawa: Ministry of Supply and Services. 48–54.

Lightbown, Patricia. 1983. "Exploring Relationships Between Developmental and Instructional Sequences in L2 Acquisition." *Classroom-Oriented Research in Second Language Acquisition.* Eds. H. Seliger and M. Long. Rowley, Mass.: Newbury House. 217–245.

Long, Michael. 1981. "Input, Interaction and Second Language Acquisition." *Annals of the New York Academy of Sciences* 379: 259–78.

Mohan, Bernie. 1986. *Language and Content.* Reading, Mass.: Addison-Wesley.

New York State Department of Education. 1985. *Foreign Language Curriculum Guide.* Albany, N.Y.

Pica, Teresa, Lloyd Holliday, Nora Lewis, and Lynelle Morgenthaler. 1989. "Comprehensible Output as an Outcome of Linguistic Demands on the Learner." *Studies in Second Language Acquisition* 11: 63–90.

Pienemann, Manfred. 1984. "Psychological Constraints on the Teachability of Languages." *Studies in Second Language Acquisition* 6: 186–214.

Raimes, Ann. 1987. *Exploring Through Writing.* New York: St. Martin's Press.

Rosenholtz, Susan J. 1989. *Teachers' Workplace.* New York: Longman.

Savignon, Sandra J. 1972. *Communicative Competence: An Experiment in Foreign Language Teaching.* Philadelphia: Center for Curriculum Development.

———. 1983. *Communicative Competence: Theory and Classroom Practice.* Reading, Mass.: Addison-Wesley.

———. 1985. "Evaluation of Communicative Competence: The ACTFL Provisional Proficiency Guidelines." *Modern Language Journal* 69: 129–134.

Savignon, Sandra J., and Margie S. Berns, eds. 1984. *Initiatives in Communicative Teaching.* Reading, Mass.: Addison-Wesley.

———, eds. 1987. *Initiatives in Communicative Language Teaching II.* Reading, Mass.: Addison-Wesley.

Scott, Virginia, M. 1989. "An Empirical Study of Explicit and Implicit Teaching Strategies in French." *Modern Language Journal* 73: 14–22.

Simon, Paul. 1980. *The Tongue-Tied American: Confronting the Foreign-Language Crisis.* New York: Continuum.

Stern, H. H. 1984. "The Immersion Phenomenon." *Language and Society*. Ottawa: Ministry of Supply and Services. 4–7.

Swain, Merrill, and Sharon Lapkin. 1988. "Canadian Immersion and Adult Second Language Teaching: What's the Connection?" Keynote paper presented at the first OSU/MLJ Conference on Research Perspectives in Adult Language Learning and Acquisition, Ohio State University, October 21, 1988.

Tardif, Claudette, and Sandra Weber. 1987. "French Immersion Research: A Call for New Perspectives." *Canadian Modern Language Review* 44: 67–77.

Valdman, Albert. 1989. "The Role of Grammar Analysis in Formative Language Instruction." Paper given at the SLATE Fifth Anniversary Seminar Series, University of Illinois at Urbana-Champaign, April 13, 1989.

Van Ek, J., ed. 1975. *Systems Development in Adult Language Learning: The Threshold Level in a European Unit Credit System for Modern Language Learning by Adults*. Strasbourg: Council of Europe.

Van Lier, Leo. 1988. *The Classroom and the Language Learner*. New York: Longman.

Wardhaugh, Ronald. 1985. *How Conversation Works*. Oxford: Basil Blackwell.

Widdowson, Henry, G. 1987. *Teaching Language as Communication*. Oxford: Oxford UP.

Yaldin, Janice. 1987. *Principles of Course Design for Language Teaching*. Cambridge, England: Cambridge UP.

Research on the Role of Grammar and Accuracy in Classroom-Based Foreign Language Acquisition

Theodore V. Higgs
San Diego State University

This paper seeks an answer to two distinct questions: "To what extent is linguistic accuracy an important factor in oral communication?" and "To what extent is it a credible and achievable goal of instruction in the context of university-level foreign language classroom instruction?" Although the answer to the second question represents perhaps one of the major points of contention in our profession, the answer to the first question is, I trust, quite noncontroversial, even in such a potentially contentious gathering as the present symposium. Stated simply, the more accurately a message is transmitted, the greater the possibility is for successful communication.

The reasons for this assertion are many and obvious. At the lower end of an arbitrary ability scale, for example, if a message fails even to attain the threshold of intelligibility, no communication is possible. Even on the plus side of the intelligibility threshold, however, there are severe limitations on both the quality and the quantity of successful communication that can take place. Full, interactive communication is hampered on the speaker's side by the inability to negotiate with precision the desired content, that is, his or her own meaning, and on the listener's side by the disproportionate loading of conversational responsibility and the uncertainty that what has been received is in fact what has been transmitted.

The uncertainty is caused not only by a lack of full specification of the message, but also by the listener's being forced to attend to sundry linguistic units, such as pronunciation features, words, and higher-order constructions, as individual objects demanding of his attention rather than as elements of an undifferentiated Gestalt. In Polanyi's (1962, 57) observations on the "transparency of language," such units "become slightly opaque and prevent my thought from passing through them unhindered to the things they signify."

At the higher end of the ability scale, when the speaker's usage of the target language is less intrusive, both cognitive and affective variables are very well served by the greater linguistic accuracy. If the grammar of the communicator, using *grammar* here in its broadest construction, is essentially isomorphic with respect to the grammar of the listener, the communicative signal is virtually unaffected by channel noise, and information can be transmitted not only successfully, but in exquisite detail if necessary. Affectively, speakers are motivated to express themselves fully, and listeners not only are confident that they have received the message, but also participate willingly and fully in the conversational exchange, secure in the knowledge that the communicative burden is being shared equally.

The perception that successfully negotiating one's own meanings accurately in another's language is both desirable and important is not limited to foreign language teachers and second language acquisition specialists. Historically, phonetic accuracy has perhaps never been graded so harshly as in ancient Israel during the period of the Book of Judges. The compiler of this Old Testament book tells us that forty-two thousand members of the tribe of Ephraim were slain by the Gileadites when the former were unable to pronounce the word *shibboleth* to the latters' satisfaction (Judg. 12:5–6).

In a more contemporary and less life-threatening sense, it is instructive to consider the patterns of multilingualism among various indigenous tribes inhabiting the northwest Amazon area comprised by the Vaupés River and its tributaries. In this region, roughly the size of New England, are found many different tribes, each of which speaks its own language. According to Sorensen (1967), "Almost every individual is polylingual—he knows three, four, or more languages well."

This multilingual machine is fueled by a tradition of mandatory exogamy in which one never marries inside of one's own tribe and language group. "A prospective bridegroom, if he does not know it already, learns his prospective wife's language from his prospective mother-in-law" (1967, 672).

> There is a preference, though not an obligation, for a man to marry into his mother's tribe, so there is an added cultural incentive for a man to know his mother's language. If he has little opportunity to learn it—if she, for instance, is the only one of her tribe in the longhouse, and her tribe lives at a distance—his mother, nevertheless, will teach him lists of words in her language and how to say various things in it. . . .
>
> The Indians do not practice speaking a language that they do not know well yet. Instead, they passively learn lists of words, forms, and phrases in it and familiarize themselves with the sound of its pronunciation. . . . They may make an occasional preliminary attempt to speak a new language in an appropriate situation, but if it does not come easily, they will not try to force it. One of the preconditions of language-learning in the area is a passive familiarity with lists of words (including inflected and derived forms) in languages likely to be learned. . . . Informants estimate that it takes them from at least one to two years to learn a new language fluently, regardless of language family. Most of them also estimate that it takes longer to learn Spanish than to learn Tukano [a lingua franca of the region] or another Eastern Tukanoan language.

An Indian [from this area], then, does not want to try to speak a language until he knows it quite well. He is conscious of his pronunciation in it and deliberately tries to sound like an authentic speaker (1967, 678–80).

In the case of these multilingual Indians, we see that using a foreign language accurately has not only a pragmatic but also a cultural value, and the requirement of exogamy provides a strong motivational factor.

Having treated the first—and easier—of the two questions posed at the beginning of this paper, let us now examine the second one, that is, whether attaining linguistic accuracy is a legitimate and achievable goal of classroom foreign language instruction.

Much available research on accuracy in second language classroom environments suggests rather strongly that it remains an elusive goal even in so-called (and ill-named) immersion programs. Research on French immersion programs for anglophone Canadians seems to suggest that accuracy is nowhere near the levels predicted and at times claimed by its proponents.

Roy Lyster (1987), a French immersion instructor at the grade-eight level, reports what he calls surprise at the kind of French he was hearing in the classroom from anglophone students who had been in the early immersion program for eight years. His own observations failed to match claims made for the success of French immersion programs in terms of receptive skills and cultural sensitivity, which had been characterized as nearly native, even though the productive skills of writing and speaking did not reach nativelike levels. He cites several studies that document a lack of sociolinguistic competence due to a lack of contact with francophones (Harley, 1984), and a lack of grammatical competence, manifested in "an artificial language void of cultural relevance and riddled with serious errors in syntax, vocabulary and pronunciation" (Bibeau, 1984). Hammerly (1985) calls this artificial language of immersion students "faulty interlanguage" and a kind of "pidgin."

These classroom-based findings are strikingly similar to those reported by Schumann (1978) in *The Pidginization Process,* where factors such as social and psychological distance (for example, lack of contact with francophones), contribute to the imperfect and incomplete acquisition of the foreign language.

Lyster is not alone in questioning claims made for immersion programs. Hammerly points out that "the main problem [with invoking the arguments of Naturalistic Theory] is that the conditions that make natural language acquisition possible *cannot* be recreated in the second language classroom. . . . One condition absolutely essential to natural language acquisition, being surrounded by, and constantly interacting with, native speakers, will never exist in second language classrooms" (1985, 15).

Still looking at Canadian programs, Irène Spilka (1976, 549) reports that after six or seven years of a French immersion program, 52.26% of the sentences produced by early French immersion pupils in grade six were incorrect, as opposed to less than 7% (6.19%) for native-speaking French children of the same grade.

Looking at programs in the United States, Politzer (1980) studied the performance of anglophone students in a French/English bilingual school in San Francisco in which French was the language of instruction starting in kindergarten. He reports that on tests, which consisted of descriptions of a picture, "certain basic errors in French appeared to be relatively persistent even at the fifth grade" (after five years of immersion in French). He speculates that such persistent basic errors "may well represent a tendency to simplify French, to remove redundance and constitute . . . a step toward the creation of a 'pidgin' " (1980, 292). Cohen (1976) reports similar findings for Spanish immersion students. Politzer adds that "the evidence from [this study] makes it clear that those bilingual immersion programs in which children are **not** learning the FL from exposure to a peer group will not lead to acquisition of correct language patterns, if there is sole reliance on functional use. Some kind of formal language instruction is evidently needed to supplement a purely functional approach to acquisition of a second language" (1980, 293). He concludes that "even in the immersion type bilingual education in which there is a large peer group speaking the second language (e.g., English in the United States), language teaching does evidently make a difference . . ." (297).

Not to imply a cause and effect relationship, Tracy Terrell (1989) seems also to have concluded that some instructional intervention on the part of the foreign language teacher can indeed be helpful, not only to encourage learning but acquisition as well. He writes that "in addition to its function as a source for monitoring, explicit knowledge of the grammatical generalizations in the target language can be helpful to the learner in the acquisition process itself" (1989, 22). He suggests that "grammar instruction can facilitate the acquisition process as an advanced organizer, as a technique for providing input with multiple occurrences of the same meaning-form relationship, and to provide forms for monitoring" (23).

Terrell is concerned that reliance on "contextual strategies and guessing" may indeed render the available input more or less comprehensible, but provides no assistance to the learner/acquirer with the task of dividing up the input into meaningful units, especially at the morphological level. He gives the example of an instructor providing "good comprehensible input using Spanish past tense forms on numerous occasions without the students even attending to or acquiring Spanish past tense morphology at all" (24). A similar observation would be the instructor's use of subjunctive forms in Spanish, which the students would comprehend lexically, but without analyzing the morphology and perhaps even the syntax. Terrell suggests that "a reasonable hypothesis is that any information about how the input is organized might aid the learner in this segmentation process" (23).

Manfred Pienemann (1984) has also shown that even in conjunction with a natural *second* language acquisition process, carefully tailored formal instruction can aid, that is, enhance and even accelerate, natural acquisition. He notes that, "a given linguistic structure cannot be added through instruction to the learner's interlanguage at any desired point in time in his/her acquisitional career" (1984, 198), pointing out that "an L2 structure can only be learned through instruction if the learner's language is close to the point when this structure is acquired in the natural setting" (201). Subsequently, Pienemann discusses at length (207–209) crucial ways in which his findings are distinct from and incompatible with Krashen's $i + 1$ hypothesis. In support of Terrell's (and others') recognition that mere comprehension is not sufficient to ensure acquisition, Pienemann hypothesizes that often "the gap between comprehension and production [may] be more than one acquisitional stage. . . ."

These types of observations may at least in part account for the data that suggest that immersion students or others involved in putatively fertile acquisitionist/communicationist environments show good listening comprehension but comparatively poor speaking and writing skills. Students apparently learn and/or acquire each others' interlanguage with relative ease. In this respect, Terrell (1989, 25) observes that "if the learner has mislearned a rule or misapplied a rule, the output will be incorrect. Since it is probable that incorrect output is as easily acquired as correct output, approaches that rely heavily on monitored output activities will have to resort to strict error correction to avoid acquisition of the wrong forms."

It would seem, based on the research cited in this paper, that in spite of our best efforts we have not yet discovered a pedagogy that routinely produces second language users who are both fluent and accurate in their production of the target language. It may in fact be impossible to do so under the instructional conditions that we typically face.

Even accepting the possibility that the acquisitionist or communicationist position is theoretically correct or at least provides significant insight into some aspects of adult second language acquisition, it seems that in an institutional setting we cannot successfully create a true natural-acquisition environment.

The so-called immersion programs, which might be better labeled "very intensive programs," clearly take the learners further along in listening comprehension than do most other types of programs. The mere fact that they fail to produce genuine bilinguals should not be held against them; that is, it would be unwise to conclude as did Bibeau (1984) that immersion is a failure. At the same time, however, we must decide how concerned we as a profession should be about the apparent tendency of students in such programs, and even in other much less intensive ones, to acquire pidginized interlanguages.

It is at this point that theoretical pedagogy and reality meet face to face. Discovering a satisfactory answer to the question of pidginized interlanguage entails a long and difficult look at some fundamental questions for our profession. Who are our clients? What are their needs? Their expectations? Their intentions with respect to their proposed length of study? That is, are they planning only on meeting a foreign language requirement, are they intent on continuing beyond that level, or are their minds at least open to that possibility? Granted that everyone is different, can we make predictions about what methods, materials, techniques, and other considerations seem to be most promising in a global sense? What are our goals of instruction, and how have they been determined? How much time do we have available to reach whatever goals we set? In that time, what can we reasonably expect as the product of classroom instruction?

The answers to these questions will vary from institution to institution, and may depend on many unknown or uncontrollable factors. Nevertheless, these questions require answers if we are to proceed in any coherent and defensible fashion.

We can get an idea about what goals might be achievable by calculating at least a model version of time available. A typical university-level introductory language program that meets for fifty minutes, five days a week, for three fifteen-week semesters offers 187.5 hours of exposure to the target language, the equivalent of roughly 11.72 days in the real world, assuming that a typical day in a natural, acquisition-rich environment provides sixteen hours of exposure.

If we add two three-credit intermediate courses, we get seventy-five more hours for a total of 262.5 hours (16.4 days). The student who continues through a full undergraduate major in the language then takes twenty four upper-division units for three hundred additional classroom hours, or an additional 18.75 days. Thus, a complete university program, from the elementary level through an undergraduate major, in a typical program provides some thirty-five days, or roughly a month, in classroom contact with the target language. If we double this time to account for out-of-class contact with the language, through homework assignments, contact with native speakers, practice time in the language laboratory, and so forth, we can stretch the exposure to the equivalent of seventy days, that is, exactly ten weeks.

I should add that these calculations are superidealized. They assume that fifty minutes of quality exposure are available for each student in each fifty-minute class, that students in the classroom are as highly motivated to master the language as they would be if they were in a monocultural/monolingual environment that provided a target-language peer group, and further, that the type of instruction they are receiving is at least as conducive to acquisition as exposure in a natural, second language environment would be. Since none of these assumptions is likely to be true, students involved in our hypothetical program in fact have considerably less than the calculated ten weeks' exposure.

Viewed in this light, our position as foreign language educators seems to be desperate. That is, it would seem that no method, no set of materials, no pedagogical or curricular revolution can even theoretically make it possible for us to produce fluent, virtually bilingual adult users of other languages on the strength of instructional programs alone. I believe, however, that our position is desperate only when we myopically, and perhaps egocentrically, assume that producing functioning bilinguals is a legitimate and realizable goal of classroom instruction.

I feel quite certain that no one ever became bilingual uniquely on the strength of formal, instructionally based study. It seems to me that the fundamental goals of foreign language instruction are first, to help our students recognize the enormous benefits of learning other languages and second, to help them learn or acquire enough social, cultural, and linguistic ability to risk spending an extended period abroad. When we have a student at the point where he or she triumphantly announces, "I'm going to spend the summer in Mexico," or, "I've just been awarded an internship in West Germany," we can confidently acknowledge that we've done our job and fulfilled our mission as educators.

This perspective can translate into concrete objectives that we can strive toward in our admittedly limited opportunity to make a change in our students' lives. Of course, we must try to help our students establish rudimentary lexical and grammatical competence in the target language. But at least as important, we must also strive to provide experiences that encourage the development of communicative strategies as well.

Many of the linguistic tools needed for the development of strategic competence can be learned very early by beginning students as unanalyzed chunks, what Lily Wong-Fillmore (1976) calls "formulaic utterances." Her research (1976, 640) found that the "strategy of acquiring formulaic speech is central to the learning of language" even in a natural, acquisition-rich environment. Such chunks allow learners to establish at least limited management potential in a conversational setting, and also provide a data base for self-analysis and linguistic segmentation, which are so important to the acquisition process.

Even before the acquisition process has proceeded significantly, a student who knows, for example, how to get a native listener to "play back" his message to him can check the degree to which his intended message was received. This makes possible a series of successive approximations that greatly increases the chance of achieving successful communication, even given limited mastery of the target language. A student can also negotiate his way more successfully through a conversation if he knows how to ask his listener to slow down, repeat, restate and paraphrase, and so on. These are enabling skills in the context of second language acquisition, and contribute, albeit indirectly, to the acquisition process, assuming an appropriate milieu.

All of the preceding entails that we understand our role as *instigators*: instigators of a lifelong process of first foreign and later second language acquisition. In such a role, timing is everything. There is a time for formal instruction in a sheltered, classroom environment and a time for experiential learning in a natural, acquisition-rich environment. In the classroom, we must learn to recognize and then maximize the most productive instructional strategies in order to provide the best possible base for eventual foreign study. As foreign language educators, our mission is to launch as many vessels as we can, even as we recognize that we will not likely be there to see them when they arrive at their destination.

REFERENCES

Bibeau, Gilles. 1984. "No Easy Road to Bilingualism." *Language and Society* 12: 44–7.

Cohen, Andrew. 1976. "The Acquisition of Spanish Grammar Through Immersion: Some Findings After Four Years." *Canadian Modern Language Review* 32.5: 562–74.

Hammerly, Hector. 1982. *Synthesis in Second Language Teaching: An Introduction to Linguistics*. Blaine, Wash.: Second Language Publications.

———. 1985. *An Integrated Theory of Language Teaching and Its Practical Consequences*. Blaine, Wash.: Second Language Publications.

Harley, Birgit. 1984. "How Good Is Their French?" *Language and Society* 12: 55–60.

Lyster, Roy. 1987. "Speaking Immersion." *Canadian Modern Language Review* 43.4: 701–16.

Pienemann, Manfred. 1984. "Psychological Constraints on the Teachability of Languages." *Studies in Second Language Acquisition* 6.2: 186–214.

Polanyi, Michael. 1962. *Personal Knowledge: Towards a Post-Critical Philosophy.* New York: Harper and Row.

Politzer, Robert. 1980. "Foreign Language Teaching and Bilingual Education: Research Implications." *Foreign Language Annals* 13.4: 291–7.

Schumann, John H. 1978. *The Pidginization Process.* Rowley, Mass.: Newbury House.

Sorensen, Arthur P., Jr. 1967. "Multilingualism in the Northwest Amazon." *American Anthropologist* 69.6: 670–84.

Spilka, Irène. 1976. "Assessment of Second-Language Performance in Immersion Programs." *Canadian Modern Language Review* 32.5: 543–61.

Terrell, Tracy D. February 1989. "The Role of Grammar Instruction in a Communicative Approach." *Northeast Conference Newsletter.* 22–5.

Wong-Fillmore, Lily. 1976. "The Second Time Around: Cognitive and Social Strategies in Second Language Acquisition." Unpublished Ph.D. Thesis, Stanford University.

Chapter 4

The Foreign Language Classroom as a Place to Communicate

Bill VanPatten

The University of Illinois at Urbana-Champaign

INTRODUCTION

I take as my point of departure two major conclusions regarding research on communication.[1] The first is a definition of communication as it is generally used in discussions of communicative competence: communication is the interpretation, expression, and negotiation of meaning in a given context (based on Savignon, 1983). The second is how communicative language ability is acquired. Purely and simply, people learn to communicate by engaging in communication (Savignon, 1972; Rivers, 1987; Day, 1986). While tautological at first glance, this has rather profound and complex implications for the foreign language (FL) classroom if the goal of instruction is to develop some measure of communicative language ability.[2]

The implications of accepting that people learn to communicate by communicating are profound, because as a profession we must confront the baggage we have inherited from both grammar translation and audiolingual methodologies. *Real* teaching for communicative language ability has made us question the rationale and existence of concepts such as the grammatical syllabus, grammatical sequencing, mastery, bad habits/fossilization, mechanical drills devoid of meaning, translation exercises, and a host of others. However, as we attempted to move as a profession from audiolingual methodology to communicative language teaching, the transition was far from absolute or complete. Initially, those who modified their curricula at all did so by "slapping on" communicative practices to their grammatical syllabi. Communication and learning to communicate were seen as add-ons to the existing syllabus of language teaching. In addition, keeping in line with many of the then-prevalent beliefs, communicative ability was thought to obtain from a careful sequencing of mechanical to meaningful to communicative "drills."

Subsequently, we witnessed the development of contextualized grammar practices and most recently, we have seen the traditional grammar sequence dressed in functional jargon. Thus, the lesson that is actually intended to teach and drill the preterit tense in Spanish is now called "Learning to talk about single events in the past" and the lesson that is a pure exercise in manipulating relative pronouns is called "Linking two sentences together." Although these seem to be improvements in teaching for communication, a closer look at what is meant by such innovations and how they are used reveals that we are still basically trying to teach the traditional grammatical syllabus and get our students to learn grammar. The currently popular "conversation cards" are nothing more than discrete grammar practices, as revealed by the research of Kinginger (1990).[3] And, waving the red flag of fossilization, many continue to claim that communication should only happen after mastery of surface features of the language.

On the other hand, there are those who suggest that true teaching for communicative language ability would put communication at the center of both the syllabus and the classroom. That is, that only by abandoning the grammatical syllabus can one get a true focus on communication in the classroom. Instruction in grammar, independent of sequencing, is either questioned entirely (for example, Krashen and Terrell, 1983) or new roles for grammar and grammatical instruction are being sought (for example, Rutherford, 1987; Pienemann, 1985; Pica, 1985; VanPatten, 1987a and 1989).[4]

The implications of accepting that people learn to communicate by communicating are as complex as they are profound. We have learned much from research in second language acquisition, perhaps the most important idea being that the majority of people (for whatever reasons) never reach nativelike abilities in the second language. Complete mastery of the grammar of a language is a teacher's dream. What has been documented about acquisition is that grammatical structure and other features of language are acquired in piecemeal fashion, that even verb and pronoun paradigms are acquired in piecemeal fashion, that there are stages of acquisition for many features of syntax, that certain things must precede others, and that classroom learners take to the task of language acquisition many of the same processes that nonclassroom and child first language acquirers do (see VanPatten, 1986b and 1989, as well as the collection in Pfaff, 1987, for some discussion). In short, *there are cognitive and psycholinguistic constraints on the acquisition of grammatical structure, constraints that instruction cannot overcome (especially for early and intermediate learners).*[5] Important new concepts brought to light in second language research also include the role of meaningful input (that is, language the learner hears or sees and processes for meaning) and interaction with input (that is, the verbal and nonverbal activity in which a learner engages to process and respond to input).

With what we know at this point about second language acquisition, I would like to state up front my position about instruction: good teaching works *with* the natural properties of language acquisition to encourage them in the right direction. Under the heyday of audiolingualism, teachers were encouraged to guard against bad habits, avoid errors, and inhibit or eradicate a host of other psycholinguistic bogeymen and bogeywomen that were seen to be the result of letting learners do what comes naturally. (Of course, the goal was the difficult if not impossible goal of developing nativelike abilities for all learners.) For the sake of the average learner, it seems more appropriate that natural properties of language acquisition be channeled, not avoided. These natural properties need to be directed for the benefit of the learner, not squashed because they interfere with perfect learning of grammar for discrete point tests. Whether or not one adopts this particular view of the fit between teaching and acquisition,[6] the bottom line for teaching toward communicative language ability is that instructors must not have false expectations about the impact of instruction on learner output.

What seems to follow, then, is that communication in the classroom and the development of communicative language ability in general must take into consideration how language acquisition happens (or doesn't happen). How is it that an emphasis on communication and building communicative language ability considers stages of acquisition? The piecemeal nature of the acquisition of grammatical structure? The role of meaningful input? Interaction with input? And if communication is the expression, interpretation, and negotiation of meaning, are all three facets to be emphasized at all levels of instruction in equal proportion?

These are questions that I would like to explore in this paper. To begin, we must first sketch out some general stages of language acquisition from the learner's perspective.[7] From this perspective, I will outline one way in which communication can be realized in the classroom and how the development of communicative language ability can be encouraged.

ACQUISITION FROM THE LEARNER'S PERSPECTIVE

We can broadly (and very roughly) define the emergence of language during acquisition as consisting of three stages: early, mid, and advanced. As learners move from stage to stage, they add and drop certain processing and organizing strategies for getting and using language. In order to be an advanced learner, a person must have gone through the stages of being an early and a mid-stage learner; that is, one cannot begin acquisition with the processing strategies that advanced learners use.

Acknowledging the fact that there is no such thing as a clear-cut set of demarcation lines for progressing from one stage to the next, we might define early stage learning as heavily lexical. That is, it is the learner's "job" to get words and other units of language to express meaning and to find ways to combine these units together to express propositions. The learner's input processing mechanism, then, is dominated by a search for lexical items, chunks, and routines (that is, unanalyzed phrases such as *megusta* and *yocreoque*) and the means for expressing certain universal concepts such as tense and agency. Pienemann and Johnston (1985) have called this stage "presyntactic," suggesting that the syntactic units and the rules that govern them (for example, noun phrases and noun-phrase movement) of the target language are not even processed yet by a learner. (See

VanPatten, 1987b, for a more complete discussion of early-stage language development in learners.)

In mid-stage acquisition lexical processing continues (people are always learning words and routines), but mid-stage is clearly distinguishable from early stage by students' incorporation of the processing of morphology and some syntactic elements that are the less marked features of the language. In other words, chunks and units of language that were evident in the early stage begin to give way to (or at least coexist with) bits and pieces of morphology, canonical word order, and other grammatical features. (See Hyltenstam, 1987, and VanPatten, 1987b, for some discussion.)

The more advanced stages of acquisition build on previous stages. However, here we also see the acquisition of nonmeaningful and purely grammatical features of the language, in addition to the more marked features of the language, for example, adjective agreement in Spanish, use and distribution of certain relative pronouns, preposition stranding in English. The move to an advanced stage of acquisition takes considerable time and exposure to meaningful language.

While admittedly sketchy, this broad-stroke outline of stages of acquisition provides a basis for some discussion of what a curriculum might look like. As expressed earlier, I believe that instruction should channel the processes of language acquisition, not work at odds with them. How does stage of development affect what we do in the classroom?

A GLOBAL CURRICULUM[8]

Utilizing the three stages of acquisition just sketched, and taking into consideration the concepts of input, interaction, and the constraints on the acquisition of grammar, we might also think of the curriculum as consisting of early, mid, and advanced stages. The early-stage curriculum could be characterized by more emphasis on input and interaction with input than on output and mastery of grammatical forms.[9] That is, learners get and receive more "practice" hearing and seeing meaning-based language than they do in producing. As I will show, however, this does not mean that we advocate silent periods or even force them on the learners. Nor does it mean that we avoid any work on output (either written or spoken). (I will discuss grammar instruction in a later section.)

The intermediate stage of the curriculum would include many input-oriented activities of the early stage, but would begin to move learners toward more production. An example of this might be content language learning or information-based learning where learners get content/information from course materials (and the instructor!) but then have tasks that guide them in doing something with the information.

The advanced stage would move away from an emphasis on input as described here and would adopt a more focused skills development as learners' needs for language use become clearly defined. Thus, French for commerce, Spanish for legal purposes, literature courses, and the like, would all work on specific skills related to their own domains. (Note that even though output is encouraged at this stage, learners are still receiving and interacting with input in some way.)

What must be underscored here is that instruction in grammar, while appropriate at certain stages in different ways, is not the organizer of the curriculum, at least not in terms of sequencing materials. A communicative curriculum must be based on meaningful topics and/or functions of language. I will discuss the role of grammar and grammar instruction in a later section.

Before beginning the outline of one possible curriculum and before offering specific examples of classroom activities, it is important to remind ourselves to pay attention more to the framework of the curriculum than to the specific examples. What might be an appropriate topic or accepted function for one context (such as a university) may not be appropriate or may not work for another context (such as a high school). Topics, functions, and so forth may also vary depending on culture and the social context of acquisition (for example, Spanish versus American versus Japanese ways of talking about family). Finally, the linguistic differences that exist between languages, for example, between Russian and Spanish, are important to keep in mind. The point should not be lost that what is advocated here are not so much the specific examples as the general conceptual framework, that is, the move from interpretive to expressive communicative abilities and the move from processing input to processing output.

COMMUNICATION IN THE EARLY STAGES

It is appropriate now to discuss the communicative nature of this global curriculum. Given that the earliest stages of both acquisition and a global curriculum involve an emphasis on input and interaction with the input, it makes little sense *constantly* to push the learner to speak in a creative fashion. Nor does it make sense that the goal of every lesson or unit be to produce language. Since the learner's job at this point is to process input and get language, it seems more appropriate that communication on the part of the learner at this stage involve more of an *interpretation* of language. It is the instructor, the materials, reading texts, and other target sources of language that *express* most of the meaning in the earliest stages. Appropriate communicatively based activities, then, involve having the learners actively process and interpret language that they hear and see. The verbal output of learners is minimal, in a sense, though as we will see (for example, in Activities 3 and 4 below), learners can be encouraged to use "packaged" language for communicative purposes as well as for providing input to each other. In short, we do not prohibit output in the early stages of acquisition; we give it a more appropriate role for the beginning learner.

It might be useful to illustrate how this becomes reality in the classroom. Recalling that our curriculum is driven by topics, not by grammar, let us suppose that our topic is family. Within this topic, we might specify some longer range productive goals (for example, describing your or another's family, getting information from someone about his or her family) but more important, some shorter term goals (for example, understanding someone else's description, understanding others' questions about your family). We might establish some subtopics related to family that allow the learner to see and hear more language (such as, Do all family members get along? When should children become independent from their parents? How has the family changed over the years? How is the family conceived of culturally?) An instructor might begin the unit with a description of his or her family. However, it is not enough that the instructor talk *at* the students: he or she must also engage them in active interpretation and comprehension of the input. Thus, the learner *negotiates* meaning consonant with task and ability. Following is a sample scenario from an activity that I have done with first-day students in first semester Spanish. *All* talk and activities presented here are done in the foreign language. (The reader should understand that the instructor would have prepared visuals ahead of time):

Activity 1 (providing initial input)

Today we are going to talk about my family. I have a most interesting family (displays "My family" on board or overhead). Here is me. These are my parents. This is my father and this is my mother. Father . . . mother. My father's name is Bill. My mother's name is Juanita. They are divorced. This is my stepfather, Joe. My stepfather. And this is my sister . . . my only sister. Her name is Gloria (turns off overhead or covers visual).

Let's see what kind of memory you have. What is my father's name—Joe or Bill? (responses) What is my mother's name—Juanita or Gloria? (responses) Right. Gloria is my sister, not my mother. And do I have any brothers? (responses) No (shows visual again). All right, to summarize, my family consists of my father, Bill, my mother, Juanita, and my sister, Gloria. I have no brothers. Oh, I also have a stepfather, Joe. My parents have been divorced since 1972 (writes date on board). Now, that was easy, but here are some other family members (now reveals grandparents).

These are my grandparents. My grandparents. These are my maternal grandparents and these are my paternal grandparents. This man here, Dick, is my paternal grandfather. And this woman, Bridgitte, is my paternal grandmother. Grandfather . . . grandmother. But Bridgitte passed away many years ago; Bridgitte is dead (points to tombstone). These are my maternal grandparents. Domingo is my paternal grandfather . . . and Concepción is my maternal grandmother. Domingo passed away in 1985; Domingo is dead. Just to review, Dick and Bridgitte are my paternal grandparents and Domingo and Concepción are my maternal grandparents. Grandfather . . . grandfather . . . grandmother . . . grandmother. Both Bridgitte and Domingo are dead. By the way, Dick lives in Indiana and Concepción lives in California (removes or covers visual).

Ready for a real memory test? (Teacher shows new overhead, or distributes ditto.) In the left column are names; in the right column are relationships. You have two minutes to match the name to a relationship. (After two minutes, teacher calls time and "quiz" is reviewed with original drawing exposed; teacher engages in some light "conversation" in which students answer with one word, yes/no type responses, such as, "Did you know that I was half Mexican? How does your family compare to mine—do you have more brothers and sisters?")

Now, here is the real interesting part. (Reveals visual of extended family with aunts and uncles, some cousins, and so on. Instructor continues presentation using same format as before.)

The above is a sterilized presentation of input, that is, false starts, stops, and natural pauses and repetitions are not represented. It does not capture the natural interactions that occur between instructor and class. And the reader may not have the feel of how the instructor points to the persons in the visual and facilitates comprehension nor how the instructor would use intonational patterns and facial expressions. What is necessary to comprehend here is that the instructor's job is to *express* herself and convey meaning to the students to get them to attend to her speech for the information that it conveys. Also, students might raise hands and ask for a repetition or show with a facial expression that they have not comprehended something. They might laugh, show astonishment or react in some other nonverbal way. In other words, they would try to *negotiate* their interpretation of what the instructor is saying with whatever means they have. They would let the instructor know when they have understood something and when they haven't.

An important point to note is that in no case is the learner allowed to simply sit there. The instructor periodically questions the students about the meaning conveyed or relates a personal story. This accomplishes two things: it keeps the learners tuned in and it helps to negotiate more meaning (that is, instructors can tell what was effectively communicated and what was not). By questioning the content, by asking for verification of intended meaning, and by asking learners questions about themselves, instructors are assisting learners in interpreting meaning.

After this initial presentation, the instructor might continue using family descriptions in input as the basis for games, group work, surveys, and the like. Following are some examples:[10]

Activity 2

Listen to the description of the family provided. Then select the drawing that best matches what you heard.

Activity 3 (student "generated" input)

When your teacher says "Begin!" start looking for people in the class who respond "yes" to the questions below. When someone says "yes," ask him/her to sign the appropriate line. Remember: you cannot ask a person two questions in a row!
1. Do you have a brother-in-law? _____
2. Are all your grandparents alive? _____
3. Do you have an unmarried uncle? _____
and so on. (Note: when a student is approached, he/she is not allowed to look at his/her own paper but is to look at the other student and listen . . .)

The purpose of these activities is to provide more meaning-based input and to learn correctly to interpret the input. The activities are also tied to purposeful language learning: they all involve activities that build toward describing and/or interpreting a description of someone's family. Eventually, we can guide the students into giving and exchanging more information about each other through guided interchanges. For example, the following three-tiered activity has learners interacting with written input, producing minimal output (that is, the output is structured for them and they have been prepped with previous input-output practices in question-asking as well as provided with the model essay they are to write):[11]

Activity 4 (guided description-output-activity)

Pair up with someone whom you do not know well. Do this activity one step (paso) at a time.

Primer paso: read the following paragraph. Make a note of the type of information that is missing in each blank:

La familia de _____

La familia de mi pareja es _____ (1) _____ . En total son _____ , _____ padres y _____ hijo/a(s). Toda la familia vive en /Los padres viven en _____ .[12] Su padre tiene _____ años y su madre tiene _____ .

Sus hermanos asisten a _____ . Se llaman _____ y tienen _____ años, respectivamente. _____ es el/la mayor de la familia y _____ es el/la menor.

(1) = grande, pequeña, mediana

Segundo paso: formulate a series of questions that will help you obtain all the missing information so that you might construct a composite of your partner's family. It may help to write out the questions first. As you interview your partner, jot down all information given!

Tercer paso: after obtaining all information, write a short essay using the structure of the paragraph above, plugging in all the information you have gotten. You may need to make adjustments to suit the uniqueness of your partner's family. Feel free to ask any other questions and add to the paragraph if you like.

While learners are in a sense producing language, the focus is still on input: that is, language is provided for students to hear, read, and produce for each other. The tasks do not encourage "free" unstructured output but instead are purposeful tasks related to clearly definable goals that are do-able by the students for their general stage of acquisition and ability.

COMMUNICATION IN THE INTERMEDIATE STAGES

As opposed to the early-stage curriculum, the intermediate stage is marked by a move toward expressing one's own meaning within the confines of the classroom community. While learners are still getting input from teacher, texts, and other sources, there is at this stage a concerted effort to provide the learners with abundant opportunities for verbal output and negotiation.

What kinds of opportunities are these? How are they different from the more input-oriented activities of the early-stage curriculum? I suggest that the intermediate-stage curriculum should emphasize guided tasks in which information is exchanged between learners. These can be information gap activities, games that go beyond the word and sentence level, activities that involve the stringing together of discourse (such as those that involve narrating and describing events), and others. Examples of each follow.[13]

Activity 5 (information gap)

Homework: Learners are given a blank outline about animal intelligence and are divided into two groups. Group A receives one text and group B receives another text, both about animal intelligence. Each group reads its passage and fills in the outline leaving blank the places for which it does not have information.

In class: Learners pair up with someone from the other group. By asking and answering questions, the learners are to complete the outline. The next day, there is a quiz based on the information obtained. Eventually, learners use the information obtained to perform a written or oral synthesizing task that deals with a particular question that the class is "researching."

What is clear from the information gap activity is that real information is being exchanged, that is, A knows something that B does not and vice versa. Both A and B must express and negotiate meaning to arrive at a satisfactory conclusion to the task. (It is worth noting that learners are still receiving input via the texts they must process for information.)

Activity 6 (game that goes beyond the sentence and word level)

The instructor spills out onto the table ten items from a woman's purse and names each, for example, an airline ticket, a picture of someone, a napkin from a bar somewhere, a lipstick, and so on. The learners are instructed to act like detectives and deduce how all these items fit together, that is, who they belong to, what she did with them, what her personality is like, and so on. They are then to give a full account to the class. They may write out and practice their accounts before presenting them orally. (Note: learners are not allowed to read their accounts.) Subsequently, learners read a short story in which the principal character actually does this with a purse she finds on the bus. The class then compares and contrasts their conclusions with the characters. How and why are they similar or different?

In this particular activity, learners are involved completely in output that they themselves structure. Negotiation of meaning is not present. It can, however, be added by asking the rest of the class to take notes on the account and to ask questions, to argue and say, "No, I think . . . ," and so forth. The instructor may wish to model one version with different objects before allowing the class to strike out on its own. (Again, input is still present.)

Activity 7 (describing someone)

Class is divided into two groups. The instructor distributes photographs to each group: for each person in group A, there is someone else in group B who has the exact same photograph. Group A's task is to find the person in B with the same photograph by describing the person, for example, "Pardon me, I'm looking for someone. She is tall, has blond hair and is dressed . . . . Her eyes are blue . . . ." Person B responds: "Yes, she is right here," or "I'm sorry. I do not know her."

In this activity, person A is doing most of the self-expression and language use. Negotiation occurs depending on the rules that the instructor stipulates, for example, B cannot say anything until the end, putting all the expressive burden on A, versus B is allowed to interrupt at different points and say, "Pardon me, did you say blond hair?" or "Could you repeat that last description please?" thus helping A make her expression clearer and more accurate in terms of information.

COMMUNICATION IN THE ADVANCED STAGES

In the more advanced stages, we would hope that our FL learners are "turned loose" into the native speaking environment (for example, study abroad, field work). But given that even after study abroad FL learners return to classrooms in the case of language majors, what kinds of activities allow for expression, interpretation, and negotiation of meaning in literature, civilization, and other classes? As I have argued before (VanPatten, 1987a), we must recognize that even within the confines of literature and civilization courses students are still language learners and must be provided with opportunities to express, interpret, and negotiate meaning within the classroom community.

At the advanced stages of acquisition, activities based on communication might include debates and/or the acting out of scenes from a literary piece. Following are examples of such activities.

Activity 8 (debate)

We have just completed our reading of the novel El túnel. As you know, the principal character has killed the object of his desire, a woman named María, and has been incarcerated. If the character were North American, his attorney could claim in court that he is guilty by reason of insanity. Do you think such a claim is justifiable? Divide yourselves into those who do and those who don't. Once into groups, prepare your position and be prepared to explain and defend it. Here are some things that you will need to do in the library and at home as part of your defense:

1. Obtain a definition of insanity (as used by courts).
2. Review the novel thoroughly to find evidence to support your position.
3. Anticipate what the "other side" will argue and what evidence it will use, and prepare counterarguments.

You have this week plus the weekend to prepare. Come Monday with a five-minute opening statement ready to go. I will moderate and have my own questions to propose to each group.

Activity 9 (scenes)

If you have really understood the psychology of the characters in a literary work and you understand the author's intent in having them behave and speak in certain ways, you should be able to project their behavior(s) into novel situations. Imagine that you are Don Quijote. How would you react to the flirtations of someone other than Dulcinea? And if you were Sancho Panza, what might you tell the Don as his adviser and confidante? Three students will take the roles of Don Quijote, Sancho Panza, and a woman. The rest of the class will help to "direct" the scene by providing location and situation, and to provide feedback as to the appropriateness of the interactions. Are our classroom actors being faithful to the characters and motivations behind them?

As we conclude this section on curriculum, again cautionary remarks are in order. Rather than take the examples as ready-made recipes, the reader is encouraged to ask how in his/her particular context one might emphasize interpretation in the early stages and self-expression in the intermediate and advanced stages.

HOW GRAMMAR FITS INTO A COMMUNICATION-BASED CURRICULUM

For different reasons, there are those who would interpret a focus on communication in the classroom as being "antigrammar." That is, those who embrace communicative methodology and communicative curricula are often accused of not having a "concern for linguistic accuracy" or of disenfranchising our learners from nativelike abilities with the language. In a series of other publications (VanPatten, 1986a, 1986b, and 1988), I have argued against an extreme position for the role of linguistic accuracy and grammar teaching in the early and intermediate stages of a curriculum. I suggest that such a concern, in particular for early-stage learners, is a neo-behaviorist view of language acquisition and simply does not jive with what we know about the psycholinguistic underpinnings of these stages. I would hope, however, that a close reading would show that I do *not* eschew grammar and grammar instruction; rather, I seek to find its proper place in a communicative curriculum. Based on the curriculum I have just sketched, I have recently suggested what kind of grammar instruction is appropriate for each stage by asking the following question: what might be psycholinguistically appropriate at various stages of acquisition, that is, what can learners *make use of* at each stage of acquisition? (See VanPatten, 1989.)

First, let us consider some of the day-to-day approaches to grammar instruction that are consonant with a communicative focus. We will discuss five:

1. language notes
2. language appreciation
3. comprehension facilitators
4. structured input
5. grammar in context or structured output

The first, *language notes,* are straightforward comments about structural features of the FL. They serve to alert the learner that the FL has a particular feature. There is no practice (input or output) associated with them. Here is one example:[14]

> In the reading, you may have noticed *se* used with these verbs: *se pierden* (*perder* = to lose), *se mantienen, se transmiten, se manifiestan, se inicia.* This *se* is unlike the *se* of *se levanta* or even *se parece.* This use of *se* is called the "passive *se*" and is roughly equivalent to English "are lost," "are transmitted," "is initiated," and so forth. What do you think the following mean?
>
> 1. Las características heredadas se ven en los rasgos físicos.
> 2. Hoy día se estima todavía el trabajo pionero de Mendel.
> 3. Los factores genéticos que causan el cáncer no se conocen en el mundo científico.

The second type of grammatical instruction, *language appreciation,* is different from the first in that it involves more explanation, some short practices, and works best when students are allowed to see and hear the grammar item rather than produce it. The purpose of this kind of instruction is to give learners some conceptual control of a feature of the grammatical system. An example follows:[15]

> The following section is to help you with your ability to understand object pronouns when you see or hear them. While you may incidentally gain some expressive/productive ability with them, this is not the intended goal.
>
> **Los pronombres** (*Pronouns*)
>
> You have already learned what subjects and objects are (lesson 2) and you already know what a subject pronoun is. For example, what is the subject and what is the object of the verb *miran* in the following sentence?
>
> Los padres miran a los hijos.
>
> Right. *Padres* is the subject (parents are the ones doing the watching) and *hijos* is the object (the things being watched). What is the subject pronoun that corresponds to *padres*? Ellos, él, or nosotros?
>
> _____ miran a los hijos.
>
> Right again. *Ellos. Los padres* is the subject noun and *ellos* is the subject pronoun.

In Spanish (and English), not only are there subject pronouns, but there are also object pronouns:

The parents watch *them* (that is, the kids).
Los padres *los* miran (es decir, a los hijos).

This introduction is followed by step-by-step activities and explanations that lead the learner through all of the object pronoun system in Spanish. There is a *culminating* final activity, which is reproduced here:

Actividad A

Read the following passage to yourself. Then do the questions that follow.

Mis abuelos maternos son mexicanos y los quiero mucho. Viven en San José y cuando viajo a California, siempre los visito.
    Mi abuela se llama Concepción y es una persona muy especial. Tiene una habilidad psíquica (puede "ver" eventos del futuro y del pasado) pero no la usa con mucha frecuencia. Dice ques es un regalo de Dios y debe usarla con cuidado (care). Todos en la familia la admiramos mucho.
    Una vez la policía la llamó para pedirle ayuda con un crimen (un asesinato). Mi abuela tocó un objeto personal de la víctima y tuvo una "visión" del homicidio. Vio muy claro al asesino (sus ojos, color de pelo, etc.) y pronto la policía lo capturó. Mi abuela se convirtió en una celebridad de noche a la mañana (overnight).

Paso 1.
1. Select the title that best fits the passage.
    a. "Mi abuela: víctima de un crimen"
    b. "Por qué capturaron a mi abuela"
    c. "Un talento especial"

Select the best response based on what you read in the passage.
2. Mi abuela es una celebridad porque . . .
    a. la policía la investigó.
    b. un hombre la atacó pero ella pudo desarmarlo.
    c. ayudó a la policía.

3. Respeto de su poder psíquico . . .
    a. lo usa poco.
    b. no lo controla muy bien.
    c. no lo toma en serio.

4. ¿Qué describe mejor mis sentimientos hacia mi abuela?
    a. La critico por su locura (craziness).
    b. La quiero y la estimo mucho.
    c. No tengo reacción porque nunca la veo ni la visito.

Paso 2. Find the seven third-person object pronouns that occur in the passage and underline them. Then tell to what they refer. The first is done for you.

1. . . . . *los* quiero mucho   "los" refers to "mis abuelos" _____

2. _____

3. _____

4. _____

5. _____

6. _____

7. _____

You will encounter and learn more about various uses of object pronouns in Spanish in your course of study.

All of these particular grammar activities for language appreciation can be done outside of class, leaving more class time for interactive meaning based work.

The third kind of grammar instruction is called a *comprehension facilitator*. This is nothing more than a short, quick explanation of something with examples. The instructor uses this to provide students with a hook before listening or reading with the intended purpose that meaning might be more easily processed. An example follows:

> *Paso 1*. Read the selection at your own pace. Skip over any words that you cannot guess or seem unimportant. Note: in the first paragraph, almost all the verbs appear in the past tense. For example, *fueron separados* = they were separated. Since the paragraph is talking about two people, what do you think the following mean: *descubrieron? compraron?* You have not studied these verb forms and need not know them yet but it might help you to recognize that they are past tense forms while you read.

A fourth kind of grammar instruction is called *structured input*. In this kind of activity, the instructor (or materials) isolates one feature or subfeature of the FL and uses it systematically in the input so that form-meaning connections are easily made. Here is one example.[16] The student has just read what imperfect verb forms "mean" and is now given the opportunity to see them used and to interpret sentences in context before producing them. All sentences relate to the student's real life and contain mostly first-person singular verb forms:

Actividad B

How has your world changed? Which of the following were true for you as a child but are not true now? Which were true then and still are true now? The speaker on the tape will say each sentence for you. You may repeat it if you like.

	cierto de niño y falso hoy	cierto de niño y cierto hoy
1. Me gustaba dormir con una luz prendida.	☑	☐
2. No comía las verduras.	☑	☐

3. Tenía un amigo invisible.	☑ ☐
4. Tenía miedo a los perros grandes.	☑ ☐
5. Me levantaba temprano los sábados por la mañana para mirar la televisión.	☐ ☐
6. Yo era el centro del mundo de mis padres.	☐ ☐
7. No hacía muchas tareas (tasks) domésticas.	☐ ☐
8. Me llamaba por un apodo (nickname).	☐ ☐
9. Me gustaba hacer bromas (jokes).	☐ ☐
10. Pasaba mucho tiempo solo/a.	☐ ☐

The last type of focus on form to be discussed is *grammar in context* or *structured output.* Structured output activities put a grammatical item to *immediate* use for communicating about a given topic and/or performing a given function. Upon completion of the activity, learners may not have the item under output control, but they are using it during the activity. Normally, such an activity requires previous knowledge of the grammatical item but, in the case of a verb form and in other grammatical categories where there are multiple forms, only one form may appear in the output. Following is one example based on the imperfect to express habitual, repetitive events in the past for the first person singular.[17] Note that an activity of the structured input kind (previous activity) can lead into the structured output kind:

Para entregar

Actividad C

Here are some common everyday actions, events, and states. Create sentences that compare what you do now to what you used to do as a child. Bring them to class tomorrow.

Modelos: Hoy, manejo un carro. Pero de niño yo no manejaba.
Hoy no dependo de mis padres pero de niño dependía de ellos mucho.

1. estudiar español

_____

2. salir por la noche

_____

3. tener deudas (debts)

_____

4. pagar cuentas (bills)

_____

5. acostarme a las _____

_____

6. comprar la ropa

_____

7. dormir _____ horas

_____

8. gustarme el brocolí

_____

What is to be gleaned from these five different ways to focus on form is that the grammatical feature is never divorced from meaningful use. It always appears where learners either process input for meaning or are working at making output for meaning. Even language appreciation activities involve meaning in one way or another: there should be no mechanical drills unrelated to a topic with unreal people named John and Mary. Grammar instruction in a communicative curriculum, then, should always try to support the idea that meaning is encoded in grammatical features (as well as other features. But that is the point of other chapters in this volume.)

It should be obvious that some activity types are better suited for some grammatical items depending on stage of the curriculum, whether emphasis at the time is on input or output, how complex the grammatical items are, variations from one language to another, and so on. For example, all of these focus-on-form activities are appropriate for early-stage learners in one way or another. Caution is warranted, though, with structured output activities: if overused, they can become psycholinguistically unwieldy in that learners may come to think that they have to internalize all grammar for productive control. For more advanced learners, language notes, structured input, and comprehension facilitators might be of minimal use.

CONCLUSION

As the research outlined by Savignon (in this volume) suggests, in order to learn to communicate, learners must be engaged in communicating throughout the developmental process. And as the FL research on what happens during "communicative tasks" demonstrates (for example, Brooks, 1990; Kinginger, 1990), learners use their instructors and their past learning experiences as models. If their instructors are overly concerned with grammar and pieces of language, or give mixed messages about what is important during a given activity, learners will abandon true communication during such activities. If instructors themselves use language meaningfully and are constantly attempting to communicate with learners, then the learners in turn will attempt to communicate with each other when tasks with clear information goals are set up for them. It is only in the latter scenario that learners will actually focus on the interpretation, expression, and negotiation of meaning. In short, the acquisition of communicative language ability must begin with the instructor using language to interpret, express, and negotiate some kind of meaning with students.

What I have attempted to outline in this paper is how communication can happen in the classroom setting, given both the constraints and possibilities of the classroom. I make no claims in this paper that what I have outlined develops communicative competence in its broadest sense, that is, an ability that includes some element of cultural competence and sociolinguistic competence. I leave that for others to discuss (see Kramsch and Byrnes, this volume). As far as I can imagine, there will be little if anything incompatible with what I have suggested here. That is, cultural competence should begin with learning to *interpret* the cultural behavior of others rather than to produce it. I would advance the claim, however, that enough communicative ability can be developed by emphasizing communication exchange in the classroom that learners can subsequently get the cross-cultural and sociolinguistic competence from the native speaking environment, should they so choose. In other words, by providing opportunities to develop certain strategic and discourse competence as part of communicative language development, learners can get real firsthand input about the sociocultural dimensions of language use from native speakers in the real world.

Admittedly, this is just one way to interpret how the findings on communication and second language acquisition might help us structure our curricula. It is, as I see it, adaptable and flexible and does indeed work toward the common goal of developing learners' ability to use the second language for communicative purposes.

ENDNOTES

1. I would like to thank James F. Lee for some very insightful comments on an earlier version of this paper. His contribution to my professional endeavors (and my life in general) has been considerable. Nonetheless, the responsibility for content and language in this paper is mine.

2. It is important to recognize the term *some measure* rather than *total* or *nativelike* ability. It is doubtful that most learners can or ever do develop nativelike abilities.

3. For those who are not familiar with "conversation cards," these are cards distributed to groups of three students. One student takes on the role of listener, another the question-asker, and the third acts as moderator. The question-asker has a card with information in English that he/she is supposed to ask. The moderator has the target-language question written out. As the question-asker formulates the question, the moderator provides feedback as to the structural accuracy of the output. The question cannot be "asked" until the moderator approves of its formal accuracy. As noted by Kinginger, when engaged in such activity, the students realize that this is a discrete grammar practice and treat it as such. The question is never really asked, and the third student never really answers it. It appears that the goal of the activity from the *students'* perspective is to produce a structurally correct question, and *not* to initiate and sustain conversation.

4. Not all of the persons cited claim that the grammatical syllabus needs to be abandoned, but they (and others) do perceive the need to change the type of grammar instruction as well as the expectations of grammar instruction.

5. For a more complete discussion of these findings, see VanPatten (1986b) and VanPatten (1989).

6. There are those who would choose to ignore most if not all of the research on second language acquisition as unrelated to the foreign language context. What is being ignored by these authors is that psycholinguistically the processes do *not* change from context to context; only the quality and quantity of input received and the quality of interaction change. There is no reason, theoretical or empirical, to suppose that language learners process language differently depending on context. For more discussion of this, see VanPatten and Lee (1990) and several of the articles contained therein.

7. A discussion of the acquisition of grammatical structure is appropriate since most FL educators, materials, and instructors still view grammar as central to the classroom and we will never move beyond the grammatical syllabus and mastery of grammar until language acquisition as a phenomenon is comprehended by the profession as a whole.

8. This section of the paper is based on VanPatten (1987a). Much detail, especially concerning reading and writing, has been left out here and the reader is referred to this article for more complete information.

9. Some erroneously conclude that providing learners with meaningful input means "to talk at the learner." Nothing could be further from the truth. Interacting with input means that learners respond to the input and do something with it either verbally or nonverbally, whatever resources are available to them. They are also encouraged to attend to the input since they are being guided toward eventual output. Hopefully, this will become clear with the examples provided.

10. Based on activities in VanPatten *et al.* In progress.

11. Taken from VanPatten *et al.* In progress.

12. Not all the family may live together, so choose the appropriate expression.
13. These intermediate-stage activities are based on materials in VanPatten *et al.* In progress.
14. Taken from VanPatten *et al.* In progress.
15. Taken from VanPatten *et al.* In progress.
16. Taken from VanPatten *et al.* In progress.
17. Taken from VanPatten *et al.* In progress.

REFERENCES

Brooks, F. B. 1990. "Foreign Language Learning: A Social Interaction Perspective." *Second Language Acquisition–Foreign Language Learning.* Eds. B. VanPatten, and James F. Lee. Clevedon, U.K.: Multilingual Matters.

Day, R., ed. 1986. *Talking to Learn.* Rowley, Mass.: Newbury House.

Higgs, T. V., and R. Clifford. 1982. "The Push Toward Communication." *Curriculum, Competence, and the Foreign Language Teacher.* Ed. T. V. Higgs. Skokie, Ill.: National Textbook Co. 57–9.

Hyltenstam, K. 1987. "Markedness, Universals, Language Typology, and Second Language Acquisition." *First and Second Language Acquisition Processes.* Ed. C. Pfaff. Cambridge, Mass.: Newbury House. 55–78.

Kinginger, C. 1989. "Task Variation and Classroom Learner Discourse." Unpublished Ph.D. thesis, University of Illinois at Urbana-Champaign.

Krashen, S., and T. D. Terrell. 1983. *The Natural Approach: Language Acquisition in the Classroom.* Hayward, Calif.: Allemany Press.

Pfaff, C., ed. 1987. *First and Second Language Acquisition Processes.* Cambridge, Mass.: Newbury House.

Pica, T. 1985. "Linguistic Simplicity and Learnability: Implications for Language Syllabus Design." *Modelling and Assessing Second Language Acquisition.* Eds. K. Hyltenstam and M. Pienemann. Clevedon, UK: Multilingual Matters. 137–151.

Pienemann, M. 1985. "Learnability and Syllabus Construction." *Modelling and Assessing Second Language Acquisition.* Eds. K. Hyltenstam and M. Pienemann. Clevedon, U.K.: Multilingual Matters. 23–75.

Pienemann, M., and M. Johnston. 1985. "Factors Influencing the Development of Language Proficiency." Unpublished manuscript, University of Sidney, Australia.

Rivers, W. M., ed. 1987. *Interactive Language Teaching.* Cambridge, U.K.: Cambridge UP.

Rutherford, W. E. 1987. *Second Language Grammar: Learning and Teaching.* London: Longman Press.

Savignon, S. J. 1972. *Communicative Competence: An Experiment in Foreign Language Teaching.* Philadelphia: Center for Curriculum Development.

———. 1983. *Communicative Competence. Theory and Classroom Practice.* Reading, Mass.: Addison-Wesley.

VanPatten, B. 1986a. "The ACTFL Proficiency Guidelines: Implications for Grammatical Accuracy in the Classroom?" *Studies in Second Language Acquisition* 8: 56–67.

———. 1986b. "Second Language Acquisition Research and the Learning/Teaching of Spanish: Some Research Findings and Implications." *Hispania* 69: 202–16.

———. 1987a. "On Babies and Bathwater: Input in Foreign Language Learning." *Modern Language Journal* 71: 156–64.

———. 1987b. "X + Y = Utterance." Paper delivered at the Special Workshop, "Explaining Interlanguage Development," LaTrobe University, Melbourne, Australia, August.

———. 1988. "How Juries Get Hung: Problems with the Evidence for a Focus on Form in Teaching." *Language Learning* 38: 243–60.

———. 1989. "What Should Portuguese Language Teaching Do About Grammar?" *Proceedings of the National Conference on Portuguese Language Teaching and Testing.* Eds. K. Koike and A. Simoes. Austin, Tex.: University of Texas Press. 25–42.

VanPatten, B., and J. F. Lee. 1990. *Second Language Acquisition and Foreign Language Learning.* Clevedon, U.K.: Multilingual Matters.

VanPatten, B., *et al.* In progress. An Untitled First and Second Year Spanish Program. New York: McGraw-Hill Publishers.

Chapter 5

Theoretical and Pedagogical Problems of Separating "Grammar" from "Communication"

Nina Garrett
Cornell University

The relationship of the title of Section II of this book, "The Role of Instruction in Classroom-Based Foreign Language Acquisition," to the four chapters in it—reports on research on the role of communication and of grammar, and discussions of the implications of such research for the classroom—reflects the field's pervasive belief that in classroom language acquisition one of the major issues is the continuing debate that pits a focus on form against a focus on meaning. My mandate was to discuss the implications for the classroom of the research on the role of grammar undertaken within this debate. If I were to interpret that charge strictly, this paper would be a short one, since I shall argue that most of the research undertaken on this general heading, whether its conclusions are used to argue for or against a role for formal instruction, ought not to be taken to have any implications at all for our understanding of classroom foreign language acquisition.

This argument is based on several different kinds of problems in extrapolating theoretical significance or pedagogical guidelines from such research. The first level of difficulty lies in the question of generalizability from the particular focus of so many of the studies to the domain with which we are concerned, that of the adult classroom foreign language learner. The vast majority of studies investigating the relative value of a focus on meaning and a focus on form are of dubious relevance to our context because they are characterized by one or more of the following:

1. The acquisition they study is "mixed" in that it takes place both in classrooms and in the natural setting, so that it is impossible to be sure what forces are operating.

2. They focus on second language acquisition in children, whose cognitive capacities are much less developed than are those of our adult learners.

3. They explore the acquisition of English, a language which is markedly different from most of the other languages taught in our classrooms, in the paucity of its inflectional system and its nonadherence to many of the grammatical concepts represented by the Latinate grammars, which still rule our textbooks' terminology.

It should not be inferred that the validity of this research in its proper context is here being called into question, but its conclusions cannot validly be used as a basis for the theory or the pedagogy of our context. The authors of such studies are generally careful to indicate the limits on their generalizability, but they are routinely cited in the foreign language debate on the value of formal instruction.

Second, when studies along these lines are carried out on adults in the foreign language classroom, they typically represent a change from *second language acquisition* research to *pedagogical* research: they are designed to manipulate certain pedagogical variables and assess the effect of that manipulation on learners' language performance, with the object of using the results to motivate changing the pedagogy. The field of foreign language education is substantially in agreement on its goal, on the particular kind of language behavior that students are expected to learn—"communicative competence"—and pedagogical research experiments with manipulations of the pedagogical situation, which are hypothesized to help them learn it. This is appropriate if we assume that the classroom is a closed sphere within which pedagogical policy prescribes the goal, communicative competence is defined as the behavior we teach, and our theory of how language is learned is derived from research on how learners seem to behave on the basis of our teaching. Again, pedagogical research is certainly valid in its own right, but it is not of itself second language acquisition research, because its hypotheses are not rooted in second language acquisition theory.[1]

Even as pedagogical research, this kind of study is generally rendered highly questionable by the impossibility of establishing a testable distinction between an approach that does include some focus on form and one that does not. Proponents of both approaches substantially agree on the nature and function both of grammatical competence and of communicative competence, on the priority and greater interest of the latter, and on the desirability of having the acquisition of grammatical competence take place with as little overt or explicit focus on form as possible in the classroom.

Those who argue for *some* focus on form and those who argue against it do not in fact disagree very much as to the communicative importance of formal accuracy. The pro-grammar side feels that it is fairly important, but doesn't want to be accused of pedantry and elitism; the antigrammar side feels that it is not very important, but doesn't want to be accused of having no linguistic standards or encouraging "me Tarzan, you Jane" communication-by-whatever-means language learning. Their positions on teaching practice are also more similar than different: both sides believe that most class time should be spent on communicative activities. Given these similarities in the underlying belief structure and in the resultant lesson plans and classroom practice, it is hardly surprising that little of the research on this issue, as undertaken by proponents of either position, is generally accepted as valid enough to win over anyone of the other persuasion. Neither position constitutes a hypothesis that can be operationalized independently of the other. Part of the reason for the longevity of the debate, obviously, is that it is unresolvable.

Third, even within a solipsistically defined pedagogical domain, methodological comparisons are of questionable validity; there are simply too many uncontrollable variables—in the learners, in the design of the materials, which supposedly embody the methods, and especially in the teachers and what they actually do in the classroom. Good teachers (experienced, intuitive, fluent teachers) don't "teach by the book," either the language textbook or the methods book of their training; they elaborate, delete, innovate. It is impossible to pin down the method of good teachers—and we are surely not interested in research on poor ones.

The fourth and most serious problem with the research on the value of a focus on form, be the conclusions positive or negative, is the questionable significance of the data collected. Some of these problems with the data raise questions about the applicability of this research even to the other domains of SLA. For example, some studies report on the data of very small numbers of learners. Many of them aggregate the data from learners from a variety of native languages; even where the native language is common to the research group, aggregating data across learners obscures individual patterns of development to the point where the "average" data are meaningless.

But the fundamental problem with the data is that whether the measures of accuracy used in the particular study are discrete-point or integrative tasks, the data consist of the misproduction or nonproduction of particular morphemes or word-order patterns that appear obligatorily in "equivalent" utterances by native speakers of the second language, and the data analyses generate statements about the second-language linguistic rules that learners misapply or do not apply. In other words, these studies look at the learners' product, at the utterance itself, and they analyze it in terms of the structural rules that can be applied to native-speaker utterances.

These kinds of product data and their analysis tell us nothing about the *process* by which an individual learner constructs a particular utterance, the process by which he or she encodes meaning in words or grammatical form.[2] Such an approach ignores the fact that learners' overt misuse or lack of use of a grammatical form in the research task may not be an accurate reflection of their internal sense of grammaticality, as work by Bley-Vroman (1983), Andersen (1984), and Garrett (forthcoming), among others, strongly suggests. For one thing, learners' unconscious and idiosyncratic sense of what a given grammatical form is used for may not correspond to what it actually means for a native speaker of the target language, so that "erroneous" production of a structure may in fact be marking a quite different meaning. For another, even when learners have a relatively good idea of the meaning that the grammar is supposed to mark, they may mark it with lexical devices or with some other grammatical form to which the study is not sensitive. Finally, learners' production of a grammatical form is often *correct* for the wrong reasons, that is, their erroneous interlanguage rule may produce the correct form in certain environments, thus skewing the conclusions drawn from incorrect production. If we have no idea how the grammatical structure in question is operating *in the learner's mind* (as contrasted with *in the second language system*), we can hardly conclude from scores on its incorrect appearance or nonappearance anything of theoretical significance about learners' use of grammar, or any reliable guidelines about the effectiveness of instruction on that use.

At bottom, of course, questions about what data we need and how we should analyze them are basic questions of theory. A research paradigm contrasting the value of a focus on grammar with a focus on communication creates problems, which both derive from and contribute to a fundamental and pervasive confusion between the several related but different theories that are components of second language acquisition theory. The separation of form and meaning has its genesis in the notion of communicative competence, which has been considered to be the major theoretical construct in our field for nearly two decades now. But what is "communicative competence" a theory *of*?

To answer that we have to start by making clear distinctions between a number of different but related areas of theory that motivate research on language—theories accounting for language knowledge, language use, and language acquisition. A theory of *language knowledge,* an understanding of the relationship of form and meaning in an abstract system (competence, in the Chomskyan sense), is the province of linguistics, and in the olden days, when *knowledge of language* was the goal of FL education, it was straight linguistic theory on which our practice was based.

But we have changed our goal; now we want our students not just to have language knowledge but also to be able to use it. And here, I submit, is the heart of the problem: the term *use* refers to two phenomena, which are quite distinct but are almost never distinguished in SLA discussions. The sense in which it is most widely employed refers to interpersonal communicative language behavior; language is *used* to perform communicative functions. It is this sense that is invoked by familiar statements about using the rules of language, knowledge of language—grammatical knowledge—in communicatively appropriate ways. But the other sense in which we talk about using the rules of language is totally different: the rules of language, grammatical knowledge, are also said to be *used* in actual comprehension and production of utterances. In this sense *using language knowledge* is not a social but a psychological phenomenon, not interpersonal but inside the individual mind. These two senses are conflated when we talk about using the rules of language to communicate, because producing and comprehending language form the basis for communication, and that conflation has caused endless confusion, with those interested in studying each perspective misunderstanding those concerned with the other. Within SLA as a field, psycholinguists and sociolinguists tend to eye each other uneasily, each aware that the other's theories have an important role but unsure of how they complement or compete with each other. A comprehensive and rigorous theory of SLA must clearly address both phenomena separately and must establish principled relationships between them.

However, at this point we encounter a major obstacle, which is the conventional assumption that the grammatical rules of language are used *as a basis for* comprehension and production, the assumption that learners acquire competence and then use it in performance. Both sides in the debate agree on this; they disagree about whether that "underlying" competence can be acquired (efficiently or at all) without explicit formal instruction.

But in fact there is good reason to believe that it is really the other way around, that what a learner actually acquires is not bits of knowledge about how the abstract language system works, but mapping or processing ability. (Psychologists generally use processing to refer to an automatic and fully internalized ability, and since automaticity is problematic for classroom learners the term *mapping* will be used instead to refer to the forming of connections between language form, whether lexical or grammatical, and meaning or communicative function.) Mapping ability is acquired in the course of comprehending and producing specific meanings, and *knowledge* of language only develops as that ability becomes automatic and stable. In other words, performance is really the basis for competence. Chomsky himself has referred to a grammar as "the theory of the system of rules that a person possesses . . . *after having acquired a language*" (personal communication, reported in Steinberg, 1982) and to universal grammar "as a characterization of the genetically determined language faculty . . . as a 'language acquisition device' . . . that yields a particular language *through interaction with presented experience,* a device that converts experience into a system of knowledge attained" (Chomsky, 1985, 3) (emphasis added on both). What we actually acquire in the course of those interactions is the ability to use the mapping rules of our speech community, the held-in-common, collective-unconscious generalizations about what form represents what kind of meaning. Only after several years of first language acquisition, when the ability to produce and comprehend language has become essentially automatic, do children have intuitions about what is grammatical—only then do children have Chomskyan competence, or knowledge of language. Similarly, it is only after second language learners develop a systematic ability to map meaning onto form that they have stable intuitions. (Whether these are seen to be intuitions about the second language or about their own interlanguage is beside the point.) So it is not that language learners practice using linguistic rules until they internalize or automatize them; they practice mapping until the ability is so automatic that it generates the stable intuitions that represent their new knowledge. Using language in this sense requires the ability to make extremely complex associations between meaning on the one hand and lexical and formal features on the other.[3]

We must therefore discard our conventional ways of talking about learners using or internalizing linguistic rules, rules of grammar, as a *basis* for expressing meaning, and recognize that communication is based on the use of psycholinguistic rules, mapping rules.

Communicative competence, in its original strict sense, is part of, or an extension of, *knowledge of language,* represented not only by intuitions about what is grammatical but also by intuitions about what is appropriate. The difference between grammatical and communicative competence is relative; it can be thought of as residing in the kind of meaning that is conveyed through what used to be referred to as "optional" linguistic rules—not only semantic meaning, but also sociolinguistic, pragmatic, and discourse meaning. Both competences are kinds of language knowledge, and both result from the same kind of cognitive activity, meaning-form mapping.

Thus, the first domain of our theory and research must be the nature of language learner mapping. The second is the learner's knowledge of the second language; the knowledge is secondary to and dependent on the mapping, and neither the idiosyncratic mapping *nor* the learner's knowledge can be extrapolated from a linguistic analysis of the product, the learner's (erroneous) utterances. The third domain is then the ability to use language (that is, to make use of their ability to map all different kinds of meaning onto appropriate forms) in actual interpersonal communication. Here again we have routinely lumped together two phenomena, which must be understood as logically separate even though each can be investigated only in the context of the other. The ability to access the meaning-form connections held in memory, to process them automatically, and to articulate them in real-time discourse is one phenomenon; the ability to perceive correctly the demand of the communicative situation for a specifically appropriate meaning-form connection is the second. The first is cognitive, the second sociocultural. They are highly interdependent; the perceived demand of a communicative situation may generate either affective or cognitive stresses, which break down the ability to access the desired language, or a misunderstanding of the situation may lead to the successful accessing of an inappropriate utterance. The social use of language is theoretically and logically dependent on the psychological, and a theory of how language is "used" in the social sense is really culturally grounded discourse theory; it requires an understanding of the cultural norms of the second language society that goes well beyond the strictly linguistic.

The fourth area of theory and research is *language acquisition,* which refers to the changes over the course of time in learners' ability to map meaning onto form, in their ability to access these mapping rules in real time in communication, and in their ability to deploy them appropriately in response to the demands of the interaction. Again, simply describing the changes in the product, in learners' utterances, between time A and time B does not give us insight into the changes in the mapping, the operation of the cognitive mechanisms, or the cultural competence that underlies appropriateness.

From this perspective it is obvious that the theory of communicative competence (as developed in the work of Hymes, Labov, Firth, or Halliday, to name only a few linguists associated with the concept) is neither a theory of language processing nor a theory of language acquisition, but rather an extension of the theory of language knowledge. It grew out of the recognition that a description of the lexicon and the formal features of a language is not of itself adequate to specify or predict the kinds of meaning expressed and comprehended in communication. Most of the work in this area has been undertaken by sociolinguists, who have convincingly demonstrated and elaborated significant features of sociolinguistic meaning, features that systematically constrain, and are crucial to, the interpretation of formal features and of lexicon. None of us would challenge the claim that the enriched and extended concept of language knowledge that it offers is the one we want our students to have as a result of acquiring a second language. Theory and research demonstrating sociolinguistic, discourse, and pragmatic systematicity certainly provide essential consciousness-raising about the many subtle ways in which vocabulary and grammar convey many subtle kinds of meaning beyond the obvious referential ones.

But as Taylor (1988) painstakingly makes clear, the notion of communicative competence almost immediately lost its strict sense, and it rapidly collected those connotations that have continued to confuse the second language acquisition community. It has almost universally been understood to be a theory of language *ability*. Linguistic or grammatical competence refers not to ability, but to knowledge about grammaticality. Communicative competence does not mean ability to communicate; it means knowledge about appropriateness, which includes but is not limited to grammaticality. But the literature on communicative competence is not content with explaining this kind of knowledge; it also asserts both that communicative competence tells us how to use the rules of grammar, which equates it with processing ability, and that it *is* the ability to communicate appropriately as well as grammatically, which equates it with the ability to engage in communicatively appropriate behavior. The "explanations" of communicative competence thus conflate knowledge on the one hand with those two different kinds of ability on the other, and so the concept has become a strange hybrid.

It is easy to see how this hybridization came about: our pedagogical practice took place for years in a theoretical gap between the abstract knowledge of language and the cultural knowledge underlying communicative functioning, and we needed some theoretical handle on the complex issue of "language use." But a concept that encompasses too many quite different entities or processes cannot make a rigorous account of any of them. Advances in psycholinguistics, in cognitive science, and in cultural theory, as well as in sociolinguistics, pragmatics, and discourse theory, now allow us to see that all of these contribute in principled ways to—and are related to each other in principled ways within—the notion of language use.

But like biological hybrids, this hybrid theory of communicative competence is sterile; it has lost all theoretical rigor and cannot generate testable predictions for SLA research. If we use the term communicative competence in its original rigorous sense, it refers to a theory of language knowledge, not of acquisition; if we use it to connote ability or proficiency in interpersonal communication, it defines our pedagogical goal but is theoretically empty. Conflating these has prevented us from recognizing that the theory of communicative competence was never intended to tell us anything about speakers' mapping or processing of language, about their actual ability to express meaning in real time through choices of lexicon and grammatical form. Nor was it intended to generate hypotheses about the actual course of the acquisition of processing ability.

Unfortunately, in its adaptation to the pedagogical context, the original notion of communicative competence has undergone a still more serious sea change. In our justifiable efforts to raise our students' consciousness (as well as our own) about the way sociolinguistic, discourse, and pragmatic features govern meaning, we have allowed the assumption to develop that meaning can be separated from form and can be conveyed independent of it; indeed, in a great deal of the pedagogical literature, meaning is defined *in opposition to* grammatical form (we are told to "focus on meaning, not on form"), which leads to the assumption that meaning resides in lexicon and in discourse and speech-act markers. But meaning is not formless semantic expression; lexical items have crucial grammatical features, and many formal grammatical markings (phonology, morphology, syntax, suprasegmentals) have crucial semantic, sociolinguistic, discourse, and pragmatic meaning.[4] Every adult utterance has grammatical structure, whether or not it is overtly or correctly marked, just as every adult utterance has semantic, sociolinguistic, discourse, and pragmatic meaning, whether or not the utterer is aware of these or has any conscious grasp of the connections between these kinds of meaning and the forms that encode them. So to separate communicative meaning from grammar, to argue that it is possible to "use" language meaningfully without grammar, is to define "grammar" so narrowly as to distort the concept beyond all recognition.

For example, very little of this research makes any theoretically rigorous reference *either* to the semantics of grammar (cf. Wierzbicka, 1988, or Givón, 1984) *or* to the complex relationship between semantics, pragmatics, and syntax, *or* to work in psychology exploring cognitive mechanisms for processing meaning and form simultaneously and for organizing semantic or other associative networks.[5] (Koike's article (1989) on the transfer of L1 pragmatic constraints and the consequent impact on L2 syntax is an excellent counterexample to this lack.) Pedagogical research on the role of grammar in the FL classroom generally ignores the probability that the most automatic language processing in the adult learner is the syntacticization of grammatical relations, clause relationships, and universal but not cross-linguistically equivalent notions such as time and space. In the absence of connections to this kind of linguistic or psycholinguistic theory, our research on grammar has tended to use as data the production of an *ad hoc* set of unrelated morphemes, or of relatively simple and unambiguous phenomena like negation or interrogation, which short-circuits the potential for a significant two-directional relationship between classroom foreign language acquisition and other areas of language theory and research.[6]

The hard truth is that the blurring and politicization of the terms "competence," "communicative competence," "meaning," and "grammar" in foreign language education has resulted in a confusion that keeps us locked into unresolvable pedagogical issues and locked out of serious participation in theoretical discourse with linguists and psycholinguists. This is not to say that their theory should be ours, but only that we have not yet succeeded in developing a body of classroom foreign language acquisition theory rigorous and coherent enough to generate research data that could have serious implications for the classroom or could be taken seriously in the development of language acquisition theory generally. The relationship between linguistics and foreign language acquisition—as Charles Ferguson put it at the 1988 Georgetown Round Table—should not be routinely regarded as a unidirectional flow of wisdom, but we must take the initiative in setting a compelling agenda.

What then should be the specifications for such a theory and such a research agenda? We need to establish our own priorities for four kinds of theory about learner language—idiosyncratic form-meaning mapping, language knowledge, language use in speech acts, and language acquisition—that is, the acquisition of language mapping, which is central.

As regards meaning-form mapping, the work of psycholinguists like Slobin (1985) and MacWhinney (1987) provides a wealth of hypotheses as a starting point for the investigation of classroom mapping, especially as a corrective to our long-standing neglect of cognitive factors such as those stressed by McLaughlin (1987).[7] Psychological research suggests the important role played by individual variables, not only affective ones like motivation and anxiety but cognitive ones like learning style. Our theory of foreign language mapping has to recognize the ways all of these are constrained by the classroom situation, and by the fact that our learners are adults for whom one set of language mapping strategies is already fully automatic. Research must also preserve the integrity of data from individual subjects, since there is ample reason to believe that language processing is a highly individual matter, even among very similar learners in the same classroom situation; the object of study must be the details of the meaning-form associations forged by individual learners (cf., Garrett, forthcoming). To explore process rather than product, in psycholinguistic terms, we must look at underlying meaning, not just superficially at lexicon, politeness markers, and unrelated morphemes; we must consider not only what the words and forms produced by learners would mean as uttered by a native speaker, but what idiosyncratic meaning they may have in learner language, and why such idiosyncratic meaning-form connections are created by a learner. Research on language processing is not of itself research on acquisition, but acquisition can only be assessed by making testable predictions about the changes over time in the ability to create and to access form-meaning connections; a rigorous paradigm for investigating processing is essential to and must precede acquisition research. We need much longer-term studies than are common in classroom SLA, and broader ones as well, those that look at a wide range of typologically contrasted L1-L2 pairs.

As regards language knowledge, we have not yet given serious thought to the question of which approach to linguistic theory would be most useful to us—Chomsky's government and binding framework, or Bresnan's lexical functional theory, or Givón's functional typological analysis, to name the most obvious. In extending the notion of language knowledge to include communicative competence, we must develop our understanding of pragmatic and discourse factors, which has hitherto lagged behind our understanding of sociolinguistic ones.

The ways in which learners recognize those features of a second language interaction that call for communicatively appropriate as well as grammatical utterances call for precisely the more sophisticated understanding of discourse that underlies sociolinguistic variation, and are also dependent on the development of a relevant theory of cultural competence, and this domain is discussed in the papers by Kramsch and Byrnes (this volume).

Language acquisition per se can be assessed and understood only through research over time on individual learners' ability to create, access, and deploy form-meaning connections. A rigorous paradigm for investigating idiosyncratic mapping at any one point in time is therefore essential to and must precede acquisition research. The crucial importance of preserving individual data militates heavily against cross-sectional studies of acquisition, since the aggregation of data across learners inevitably confuses individual variation with acquisition patterns. We need much longer studies than are common in foreign language acquisition, and broader ones as well, which look at a wide range of typologically contrasted L1-L2 pairs.

In the long run, we might well find that research on SLA mapping would merge seamlessly with a qualitatively different kind of pedagogical study, so that we could ask what kind of learner, in what kind of language learning activity, makes what kind of use of what kind of pedagogical mechanism, be it special input, cognitive organizers, activities for automatizing learned knowledge, feedback of whatever kind. But hypotheses about pedagogical treatment are premature until we know a great deal more than we do now about second language mapping when pedagogical treatment is held stable.

Space does not permit me to go into the potential of the computer and interactive technologies for collecting unprecedented kinds and amounts of classroom second language acquisition data in testing such a body of theory, but I have discussed it in considerable detail elsewhere (Garrett, 1989 and forthcoming) and continue to regard it as the sine qua non of our agenda. The computer's ability to elicit and analyze the individual learner's interactions with language data as they take place in real time allows us to come closer to seeing into on-line processing of language than we can achieve with any other research method. Noblitt and Bland's presentation on learner use of lexical and grammatical data bases in the course of writing French compositions on the computer (this volume) supplies strong support for that claim.

What implications for the classroom can we derive from research suggesting that second language mapping by adult learners in the classroom context is psycholinguistically valid in its own right and that we can understand either learner knowledge or acquisition only if we understand the mapping first?

The first implication is that we must keep an open mind about how learners form grammatical concepts and what those concepts are. The fact that students do not learn communicative appropriateness from old-fashioned and simplistic rules of grammar is not of itself a valid basis for insisting that *concepts of grammaticality*—that is, an understanding of the interconnectedness of meaning and form—cannot and should not be taught in any other way. We cannot assume that when grammar is not mentioned in class learners will automatically, successfully, induce the foreign language's grammatical concepts from the input; we have to investigate what they actually do induce and why. It is worth remembering that when some twenty-five years ago audiolingual methodology suggested that because listening and speaking were primary we should teach for at least six weeks without letting students see the written form of the language, we discovered that they were making up their own idiosyncratic rules connecting sound and orthography, with sometimes long-term disastrous results. If we tell adult students with well-developed cognitive capacities (which they cannot simply turn off in the language classroom) simply to "listen for meaning" in the limited input they receive, they are certain to create their own idiosyncratic rules connecting meaning and form, with the same potential for disastrous results, because they have no alternative but to connect whatever forms are salient to them with meaning *as determined by their native language*. But different languages mark quite different concepts with their grammar as well as their lexicon; the forms "indirect object" or "subjunctive" do not express the same meaning across languages. We know that *cultural* presuppositions seriously limit learners' ability to make appropriate use of classroom language and cultural data to understand a foreign culture in its own terms because they interpret data in the conceptual framework of their own culture and its ways of signifying meaning (cf. Nostrand, 1989). We have every reason to suspect that the same thing will happen in their interpretation of grammatical input data.

We can choose from a wide range of options in *how* we make learners aware of grammatical form and its relationship to all different kinds of meaning; teachers can either use metalinguistic discussions as advance organizers or ways of summarizing and categorizing induced patterns, or avoid them by structuring classroom language use to make the patterns and their meaning and function accessible, discussing the patterns in other terms. We could let students do most of this kind of learning on the computer outside of class, if we had computer grammar materials designed on the basis of SLA theory.

And so the second implication (which strongly seconds Jarvis, this volume) is that we should focus our attention on research paradigms exploring interlanguage mapping of all kinds of meaning, and for the moment at least abandon standard attempts to evaluate methodology. At our present state of knowledge, a focus on SLA must be kept independent of pedagogical manipulation; we must keep methodological factors constant so that we can study learners' cognitive processing as we find it happening. The weak results of so many methods-comparison studies suggest that method makes very little difference in learning that can validly be separated from differences in teacher personality or individual learner characteristics. At the early stages of language learning, any reasonable method is likely to be as good as any other in the practice of a well-trained, experienced, personable, enthusiastic, and fluent teacher. (It may well be that the choice of method at the early stages will have a significant impact on the shape of later SLA, but so few of our learners reach advanced levels that we cannot yet undertake research testing that hypothesis.)

I hope I have succeeded in justifying my refusal to take seriously the implications for our classroom practice of most of the research cited in debates about the value of a "focus on form." Once we realize that the acquisition of the ability to create and use form-meaning connections is the central object of our concern it becomes clear that from this perspective we know almost nothing about natural second language acquisition in adults, let alone what natural SLA implies for the classroom. My point is not to claim that we know that we should teach grammar, but simply that almost none of our research so far has really focused on the question of what concepts, what meaning-form associations, our students themselves actually make out of classroom input of any kind, and that a deeper understanding of this aspect of learning is a prerequisite for research on pedagogical techniques for improving their ability to make the right ones. Because we have not yet established clear and workable distinctions between theories of language knowledge, language mapping and processing, language use in communicative functions, and language acquisition, we have not been able to generate testable hypotheses about individual classroom foreign language learners' processing and acquisition. Until we do so, research attempting to evaluate the relative efficacy of a "focus on form" and a "focus on meaning" goes on fueling a debate that is both formless and meaningless.

ENDNOTES

1. Since several of the papers presented in this volume have established different definitions of "second" as contrasted or equated with "foreign" language acquisition, the reference here should be made clear. I use "second language acquisition" (SLA) as the general term covering the acquisition of any language after the native one, whether in or out of the classroom, in or out of the community where the second language is the native one. "Foreign language acquisition" thus refers to a specific category of SLA, and the theory of this kind of acquisition must be related in principled ways to general SLA theory, though it may be very different in its particulars. I distinguish sharply between SLA theory/research and pedagogical theory/research.

2. The contrast between "process" and "product" is also ambiguous in SLA discussions. In some theorizing it is the "process of acquisition" that is the object of study, and its product is the learner's level of language ability at the point where the acquisition process halts. In contrast, from a psycholinguistic perspective the process under scrutiny is the "thinking," which connects form and meaning, also referred to as "mapping," and the product of this processing is the utterance itself. Some of the discussion during the conference seemed to indicate a confusion between these two senses.

3. This perspective on the acquisition of mapping ability and its relationship to language knowledge is not Chomsky's but represents my own understanding of language acquisition as buttressed by his statements.

4. In the language of a native speaker, of course, there is no straightforward one-to-one mapping of meaning onto form, though in learner language there may be (cf. Andersen, 1984).

5. See Wilga Rivers's paper, this volume, for a more detailed discussion of work in this area.

6. This research direction derives in part from the circumstance that SLA theory has been developed much more in the ESL than the FL context. Even though some significant work in SLA has by now been undertaken in French and Spanish, these languages (like English) have relatively limited inflectional systems (i.e., less obvious grammar) and are closely related to English. Speakers of any of these languages attempting to communicate in another can convey meaning relatively successfully with little "focus on form," by unconsciously allowing the mapping rules of their native language to operate, and that has allowed theorists studying the acquisition of these languages to slip into using the term "grammar" to refer simply to those meaningless little bits that matter only to pedants. This is not by any means to imply that all ESL research suffers from this slipshod notion of grammar; Rutherford's *Second Language Grammar* could well be considered required reading for foreign language teachers.

7. Proponents of communicative competence tend to stress the difference between seeing language as facts for knowing and seeing it as a tool for doing, and they tend to see "cognitive" as referring only to a concern for the former. This is much too narrow.

REFERENCES

Andersen, R. W. 1984. "The One-to-One Principle of Interlanguage Construction." *Language Learning* 34: 75–95.

Bley-Vroman, R. 1983. "The Comparative Fallacy in Interlanguage Studies: The Case of Systematicity." *Language Learning* 33: 1–17.

Bresnan, J., ed. 1982. *The Mental Representation of Grammatical Relations.* Cambridge, Mass.: MIT Press.

Chomsky, N. 1985. *Knowledge of Language.* New York: Praeger.

Garrett, N. 1986. "The Problem with Grammar: What Kind Can the Language Learner Use?" *Modern Language Journal* 70: 133–47.

———. 1989. "Computers in Foreign Language Teaching and Research." *Computing Across the Curriculum: Academic Perspectives.* Ed. W. H. Graves. McKinney, Tex.: Academic Computing.

———. Forthcoming. *In Search of Interlanguage: A Computer-Based Study of Second Language Acquisition.* New York: Peter Lang.

Givón, T. 1984. A Functional Typological Approach. Amsterdam: John Benjamins.

Koike, D. A. 1989. "Pragmatic Competence and Adult L2 Acquisition: Speech Acts in Interlanguage." *Modern Language Journal* 73: 279–89.

McLaughlin, B. 1987. *Theories of Second-Language Learning*. London: Edward Arnold.

MacWhinney, B. 1987. "Applying the Competition Model to Bilingualism." *Applied Linguistics* 8: 315–27.

Nostrand, H. L. 1989. "Authentic Texts and Cultural Authenticity: An Editorial." *Modern Language Journal* 73.1.

Rutherford, W. 1987. *Second Language Grammar: Learning and Teaching*. London: Longman.

Slobin, D. I. 1985. *The Cross-Linguistic Study of Language Acquisition*. Hillsdale, N.J.: Lawrence Erlbaum.

Steinberg, D. B. 1982. *Psycholinguistics: Language, Mind, and World*. London: Longman.

Taylor, D. S. 1988. "The Meaning and Use of the Term 'Competence' in Linguistics and Applied Linguistics." *Applied Linguistics* 9: 148–68.

Wierzbicka, A. 1988. *The Semantics of Grammar*. Sydney: Academic Press.

Learning Environments in Foreign Language Acquisition

Chapter 6

French Immersion and its Offshoots: Getting Two for One

Merrill Swain

The Ontario Institute for Studies in Education

INTRODUCTION

In the mid-1960s, one lone class in a school outside of Montreal embarked on an innovative second language teaching experiment. The purpose of the experiment was to improve the students' level of proficiency in French as a second language (FSL) relative to other students who were taught FSL in short daily periods of grammar-based lessons. The experimental class was referred to as the French "immersion" group because, throughout the school day, the teacher used only French. In other words, all classroom management and all instruction of content material took place in the second language.

That class happened to be a kindergarten class. The students in it continued in later grades to study at least part of their academic subjects in French. Over the years, offshoots from the original French immersion program have been started. They vary with respect to the age at which the students start the program, and the proportion of the school day devoted to instruction in French. What all these immersion programs have in common, though, is that substantive academic content is taught using the medium of the students' second language. Today in Canada, over 250,000 students are currently enrolled in some form of a French immersion program. And in both Canada and the United States, immersion now exists in a number of languages: Ukrainian, German, Spanish, Cree, Hebrew, and Japanese, to name just a few.

The French immersion programs in Canada have been extensively evaluated, and the purpose of this paper is to consider some of the research findings associated with the programs. The findings that will be discussed relate to the issue of whether one can have "two for one," that is, whether one can enhance second language learning without sacrificing content knowledge. In this context, two basic questions have been addressed:

1. How proficient do students become in their second language?

2. How knowledgeable are students about the content taught to them in their second language?

In order to understand the results obtained, particularly with respect to second language learning, recent research has begun to examine the nature of the teaching in immersion classrooms. Thus, an important third question is:

3. What teaching and learning processes account for the outcomes identified in question 1?

TWO IMMERSION OFFSHOTS

The discussion in this paper will concentrate on two offshoots of the original primary level French immersion program: one that begins with twelve- to fourteen-year-old adolescents, and one that is taught at the university level. The first has come to be known as *late* immersion, in contrast to the *early* immersion program which begins in kindergarten or grade one. The second has come to be known as a *sheltered* program, in contrast to one intended for native speakers of the target language.

Late Immersion

Late immersion begins at grade six, seven, or eight. Instruction in French may be for as much of the day as 100% or as little as 50%. During that time students take, for example, history, geography, mathematics, and/or science in French. Prior to entering the late immersion program, students will have had short (twenty to fourty minutes) daily periods of what, in Canada, are referred to as 'core' FSL classes for at least a year. Following the late immersion program, which may last for one or more years, students are usually able to take several subjects per year in secondary school in French if they so choose. (For more detailed descriptions of these programs, see Swain and Lapkin, 1982; Genesee, 1987).

French Skills In addressing the question of how proficient late immersion students become in French, there are several possible benchmarks. One can ask how well they do relative to students taking core FSL classes who, although they get much less exposure to French, nevertheless get more focused instruction *about* the language. Or one can ask how well late immersion students perform relative to immersion students who begin their program at a much earlier age. Or one can ask how well late immersion students perform relative to native speakers of French. Let us consider each of these comparisons in turn, at appropriate points in time.

The most appropriate time to compare late immersion students with core FSL students is immediately after the first year of the program when both groups have had similar FSL backgrounds, and what differs is the FSL program they have followed during the school year in question. The findings have been consistent across a number of studies (for example, Barik and Swain, 1976; Genesee, Polich, and Stanley, 1977): late immersion students do significantly better than core French students on all tests of French administered. For example, Genesee, Polich, and Stanley (1977) evaluated a late immersion program that began at grade seven. They report that at the end of grade seven, based on a standardized test of French achievement and on interviews with students where their comprehension, grammar, enunciation, rhythm and intonation, vocabulary use, and fluency were assessed, late immersion students were significantly better than core French students. Similarly, Barik and Swain (1976) evaluated a late immersion program that began at grade eight. Assessment of the students' French involved their reading, listening comprehension, and speaking skills. The late immersion students' scores were, again, significantly better than those of core French students.

Comparisons of late immersion students with immersion students who began at an earlier age—usually in kindergarten or grade one—are probably most appropriate to make as the students graduate from secondary school, when the time spent studying in French is as equivalent as possible given the nature of the two programs. Such comparisons suggest that there are surprisingly few differences between early and late immersion students in their French skills as they graduate from secondary school. Early immersion students do tend to show superior speaking skills, and less consistently, superior listening comprehension skills relative to late immersion students. However, in their ability to read and write in French, early and late immersion students appear to be similar. (Hart and Lapkin, 1989a, 1989b; Wesche, 1989). These findings are consistent with other recent research, which suggests that "older may be better," in the sense of being more efficient, in acquiring at least some aspects of a second language (see Swain and Lapkin, 1989).

To get some indication of these students' functional ability in French, it is useful to look at their results on the Canadian Public Service Commission Test. This is a test used by the Canadian federal government to assess the ability of its employees to function in designated bilingual positions. This test has three levels, A, B, and C, with C representing the highest level of proficiency. Each level of the test has a reading, writing, speaking, and listening part. Grade twelve immersion students in the Ottawa region were given levels A and B of the test (Morrison, 1981). The majority of students obtained level B. Many might have been able to function in French at level C but unfortunately, they were not given that level of the test. The description of levels is specific to the work environment. For example, for speaking, functioning at level B involves the following:

Oral Expression: This level implies the capacity to take part in a variety of verbal exchanges using a variety of sentence types (simple, compound and complex). The individual at this level would function optimally in a one-to-one interview, but should also be able to contribute to meetings and discussion groups. One would be able to convey the essentials of his/her line of reasoning. There would likely be difficulty in expressing nuances or in using specific vocabulary, idioms, and regional variants in their appropriate contexts. Grammar and pronunciation will often show mother tongue interference but will only occasionally result in misunderstanding. Hesitations of moderate length may be relatively frequent on general or work-related topics and would increase as one attempts to speak in detail on any specific subject matter.

Comparisons with native speakers of French have been made throughout the students' immersion schooling. Generally, the results have revealed a pattern whereby the scores of similar-aged francophones and late immersion students on listening comprehension and reading tests are close or similar; whereas on tests assessing speaking and writing skills, late immersion students' performance is significantly poorer than that of their francophone peers (Genesee, 1987; Hart and Lapkin, 1989a). For example, Hart and Lapkin (1989a) found that graduating late immersion students performed similarly to Quebec francophones on a listening comprehension and reading test, but not on a cloze test. The listening comprehension test consisted of three excerpts from radio broadcasts, similar to that which a student might hear in academic situations. The reading test involved three reading passages dealing with the exploration of space, bilingualism in the United States, and the French language. The cloze test was based on an extract from a journalistic essay on the proliferation of opinion polls. Students perceive their most serious weaknesses to be in the areas of grammar ("not being able to get things like verb tenses and prepositions right") and vocabulary knowledge ("not having the right words to write what you want to communicate"), which corresponds to test results (for example, Harley and Swain, 1984; Harley and King, in press).

The opinions and plans of a sample of immersion students as they graduate from secondary school have been polled (Hart and Lapkin, 1989a). Asked about the ease with which they could accomplish selected real-life activities in French compared to English on a four-point scale ranging from "just as easily" to "probably couldn't do it," late immersion students tended to respond with "a little more difficult." There were interesting differences noted, however:

> In general, students evidence, on average, less confidence in coping with activities removed from academic settings—telephoning a travel agent, having a job interview, writing a letter of complaint—than activities which are, at most, extensions of their school experience. The strongest indication of this pattern is the sharp contrast in ratings regarding two speaking activities—participating in a history class discussion and having a job interview. . . . The class discussion item . . . attracts the most positive ratings, the job interview item, the least positive (Hart and Lapkin, 1989a, 9).

An overwhelming proportion of late immersion students questioned planned to attend university after graduating from secondary school. Of those planning to attend university, about 80% of them said they wanted to take from a quarter to three quarters of their courses in French. A significant proportion (approximately 40% to 60%) of the late immersion students would "definitely" or "most likely" seek a job where they would use French, would accept a job that involved working totally in French, and would take an interesting job in an area where they would need French or everyday activities outside of work.

Thus, the late immersion experience appears to have achieved for its students significant second language learning in the four skill areas, particularly in listening comprehension and reading. The students, naturally enough, feel more confident about their ability to function in their second language in domains that are similar to, or extensions of, their academic environment. Furthermore, in general, the students wish to continue to learn and use French in future education and work settings.

Academic Achievement But what about the immersion students' mastery of the content taught to them using French as the language of instruction? Generally speaking, this question has been broached through the use of standardized tests of achievement given to the immersion students and to a comparison group of English-speaking students who have studied the subject in English, in which case the language of the test has been English; or to a comparison group of French-speaking students who have studied the subject in French, in which case the language of the test has been French.

The results associated with the mastery of content appear to be related to the subject and to the amount of prior core FSL instruction that the immersion students have had. Where late immersion students have had—as in Montreal and Ottawa—core FSL instruction each year through to the immersion year(s), the level of mastery of content taught in French by the late immersion students is similar to that attained by regular English-instructed students (Genesee, Polich, and Stanley, 1977; Stern *et al.*, 1976). If the amount of prior core FSL instruction is limited to only one year, however, short-term gaps in knowledge in some subjects, for example in science, have been noted (Barik and Swain, 1976).

In the province of Quebec, the Ministry of Education administers Secondary School Leaving Examinations in a number of subjects at the end of grade eleven. Late immersion students in Montreal who continued to take several course options in French after a one-year, late immersion program, obtained higher scores than those obtained by students attending French-medium schools throughout the province. These examinations include histoire, géographie, mathématiques, and dactylo. The interpretation of these results should be made cautiously owing to possible differences in the characteristics of students who make up the two populations (Genesee, 1987). However, in another study, Genesee (1976, 1977) compared a one-year, late immersion group at grade eleven with a group of English-speaking students, controlling for IQ. Both groups of students took Leaving Examinations in physics, chemistry, and history. The immersion group took the exams in French and the English group took the exams in English. Results of the comparisons showed the immersion group to be doing as well as the English group on all three exams.

Overall, then, the results suggest that late immersion students with several years of core FSL "backup" are able to master the content taught to them using French as the language of instruction.

The University of Ottawa Sheltered Program

On the surface, the main differences between the late immersion program and the sheltered program offered at the University of Ottawa is that the latter starts at an even later age, and it is less intensive. Both programs use the teaching of content subjects as the means for second language learning.

This section will focus particularly on the sheltered course in which "Introduction à la psychologie" was taught because that is the course that has been most extensively researched from a content learning and language learning perspective. In principle, however, any university subject holds the potential for similar adaptation (see, for example, Sternfeld, 1988).

In order to enter the sheltered psychology course, students must demonstrate an intermediate level of receptive proficiency in French (Brinton, Snow, and Wesche, 1989). These learners typically come from a school background of enriched—by, for example, student exchanges—core FSL. (A large portion of immersion graduates are beyond the proficiency range considered appropriate for being in the sheltered class (Wesche, 1985).) For these learners, the course is seen as an alternative to advanced second language courses and as a transition to being able to take courses intended for native speakers. To take the course, the students sign a contract. The contract requires them to do all the assigned reading in French and to attend at least 80% of all class sessions.

The course is taught twice weekly for one and one-half hours per class. The first fifteen to twenty minutes is taught by a second language instructor, while the rest of each class is taught by the psychology professor. The FSL instruction is intended to help students understand the readings and to prepare them for upcoming topics through, for example, the introduction of key vocabulary and concepts. Strategies for "polite interruption" or requesting restatement are taught. Specific language problems that students inquire about are dealt with, but there is no explicit teaching of grammar (Brinton, Snow, and Wesche, 1989).

Whether consciously or not, the psychology professor makes adjustments in his/her language use as compared to when native speakers of French are taugnt. Wesche and Ready (1985) have documented a number of these adjustments which include slower pace, more careful enunciation, more frequent and longer pauses, more explicitness and more redundancy of both form and content. (For a more complete description of the University of Ottawa program, see Brinton, Snow, and Wesche, 1989.)

French Skills The second language and content learning of three successive groups of students who have been enrolled in the sheltered psychology course have been studied (Edwards *et al.,* 1984; Hauptman, Wesche, and Ready, 1988). The examination of French language skills has not been as extensive as for late immersion students. Nevertheless, the results are interesting.

The progress made in French was examined in two ways. First, pretest French scores were compared with posttest scores to determine if significant gains had been made in the students' proficiency as a result of attending the sheltered psychology course. Second, posttest scores of the sheltered group were compared with those of students who had taken a regular, four-hour-per-week, advanced FSL class for a total of forty-five hours. The students in the advanced FSL classes came from within the same proficiency band as the students enrolled in the sheltered classes. (Nevertheless, comparisons of the two groups at the end of their respective courses took into account pretest differences through analysis of covariance.) The FSL advanced course emphasized receptive skills. Authentic text materials in both reading and listening are used. The written texts are taken from introductory university textbooks in the students' areas of concentration. The listening materials represent tasks that students would probably encounter in the university context (Hauptman, Wesche, and Ready, 1988).

French proficiency measures evaluated the receptive skills and included a listening comprehension test in which students listened to a tape-recorded radio interview and answered questions about it, a dictation test (scored to reflect listening comprehension), a translation test, which involved translating a short passage from the psychology text from French to English, and a cloze test based on a passage about world records.

Overall, the results show that the sheltered psychology students made significant gains in their receptive French skills as a result of attending the course. Thus, even though the exposure to French in the subject matter course was relatively brief—thirty-nine hours—these adult students were able to make significant progress in their understanding of French. Additionally, the gains in French proficiency of these students were comparable to those of students studying French in regular second language classes.

Academic Achievement How well did the students in the sheltered psychology course master the content they were taught? As it turns out, the same course was taught to native speakers of English using the same course outline and the same textbook, only in English. The end-of-semester multiple-choice exam was the same for both groups, and was bilingually presented. Comparisons were made between the grades obtained on the final psychology examination by the sheltered group and by the students who took the course in their native language. The comparisons showed that their grades were similar, providing evidence that students in the sheltered classes learn the subject matter as well as students taking the course in their first language (Edwards *et al.*, 1984; Hauptman, Wesche, and Ready, 1988).

The students in the sheltered psychology course received both an FSL credit and a psychology credit. It appears that they deserved this two-for-one reward.

CLASSROOM-BASED OBSERVATIONS

The goal of immersion programs has been to develop a functional level of proficiency in French that will permit students to continue their education in French or to fill jobs requiring bilingual skills. Sheltered courses are intended "to provide a transition between the second language classroom and the 'real world'" (Brinton, Snow, and Wesche, 1989). In the case of immersion programs, the development of all four skills is seen as important. In the sheltered program, emphasis has been placed on the development of receptive skills, on the assumption that the development of productive skills will follow suit (Krashen, 1985). In the case of immersion programs, however, we have seen that although the students attain levels of comprehension skills comparable to native speakers, their productive skills remain far from nativelike, particularly with respect to grammatical competence. In the case of students' improvement of speaking or writing skills as a result of the sheltered program, we simply do not know whether or not they improve: it is an issue that has not been investigated.

There are several hypotheses that have been put forward to suggest why the productive skills of the immersion students lag considerably behind their comprehension skills. One hypothesis is that once students have developed a level of proficiency that allows them to be understood by each other and their teacher, there is no social motivation to go beyond (Swain, 1978). Given that language is learned for communication, this hypothesis is likely to find some support. However, other hypotheses, based on the teaching methodology itself, have been proposed. For example, Harley and Swain (1984) hypothesized that in order to promote greater accuracy in the production of French by immersion students, there is a twofold need:

1. for the provision of more focused L2 input which provides the learners with ample opportunity to observe the formal and semantic contrasts involved in the relevant target subsystem . . . and

2. for the increased opportunity for students to be involved in activities requiring the productive use of such forms in meaningful situations (310).

Swain (1985) argues that there are at least two roles in second language acquisition that might be attributed to production (output), independent of input. One, as Schachter (1984) has suggested, is the opportunity it provides to test out hypotheses—to try out means of expression and see if they work. A second function is that *using* the language, as opposed to simply comprehending the language, may force the learner to move from semantic processing to morphosyntactic processing. As Krashen (1982) himself has said: "In many cases, we do not utilize syntax in understanding—we often get the message with a combination of vocabulary, or lexical information plus extra-linguistic information" (66). Thus, it is possible to comprehend input—to get the message—without a syntactic or morphological analysis of that input. The claim, then, is that producing the target language may be the trigger that forces the learner to pay attention to the means of expression needed to successfully convey his or her own intended meaning. Of course, if students are given inconsistent or no feedback regarding the extent to which their messages have successfully (accurately, appropriately, and coherently) been conveyed, output may not serve these roles.

It was with these ideas in mind that we decided to observe immersion classrooms to determine the degree to which these hypothesized needs were found.

Our observations were made in early immersion programs rather than late immersion programs. From informal observations and discussions with teachers, we know that, generally speaking, as grade level increases, there is more teacher talk and less student talk. This culminates, as Wesche and Ready (1985) observed, in the university-level, sheltered psychology class, with little interaction between students and the professor, who mostly lectured to the students. Thus, if the hypothesized needs are not present in the early immersion program, they are unlikely to be found at later grade levels.

The observations from early immersion classes were made in nine grade three and ten grade six classes in Ontario school boards (Swain and Carroll, 1987). These classes were each observed and tape-recorded for a full day, and the tapes were subsequently transcribed and analyzed from a number of different perspectives. Let me summarize some of our findings.

We found that teachers created few opportunities for systematically using contrasting forms and functions in their content teaching. Rather, teacher talk was spontaneously used in service of the content being taught. Consequently, for example, the use of different verb forms was extraordinarily skewed. Over 75% of the verbs used were in the present or imperative. Only about 15% of verbs used by the teachers were in the past tense, 6% in the future tense and 3% in the conditional. Of the 15% used in the past tense, about two-thirds were in the past indefinite and one-third in the imperfect. The use of the imperfect was almost completely limited to the verbs *avoir, être, faire,* and *vouloir.* Its use with action verbs was virtually nonexistent (Swain, 1988). Sorting out form and function on this basis would be difficult, and indeed, it is an enduring problem of the immersion students.

Another enduring problem is the students' use of *tu* and *vous,* which among early immersion students tends to be restricted to *tu* (Swain and Carroll, 1987). We counted the frequency with which *tu* and *vous* were used by the teachers and the functions they served. That is, we noted whether *tu* and *vous* were being used to signal grammatical information (singular or plural) or sociolinguistic information (familiar or formal/polite). As it turned out, *vous* and *tu* as *forms* were used about equally often. On average, each was used approximately once a minute by teachers. However, when we looked at the use of *tu* and *vous functionally,* the picture changed dramatically. There was on average less than one instance per day of the use of *vous* as a marker of politeness or deference (Swain, 1988).

These examples illustrate the absence of planned input focusing on problematic areas. Perhaps planned focused input is best accomplished in the French language arts part of the immersion curriculum—as an adjunct to content teaching. Such an adjunct model has been described at the university level by Brinton, Snow, and Wesche (1989), where "students are enrolled concurrently in two linked courses—a language course amd a content course—with the idea being that the two courses share the content base and complement each other in terms of mutually coordinated assignments" (16). In the immersion context, the adjunct course could supplant the type of grammar activities that we observed occurring, which mainly emphasized the learning of formal paradigms and categories (for example, conjugating verbs, parsing sentences, identifying object complements) and rules of written grammar (for example, verb agreement), rather than relating the forms to meaning in context (Harley, 1985).

Other observations illustrate the limited output of the students and the inconsistent feedback students receive based on that output. In our analysis of the data, we categorized each time students spoke without interruption according to the length of their utterances. The utterances were categorized as minimal (one or two words), phrase (adverbial, nominal, or verb), clause or sustained (more than one clause in length). We found that, excluding students' reading aloud, less than 15% of student utterances were sustained, that is, greater than a clause in length. Furthermore, a substantial portion of their utterances—40%—consisted of minimal one- or two-word responses to teacher initiations (Swain and Carroll, 1987). In reaction to their utterances, teachers, on average, corrected only 19% of the grammatical errors students made.

Teachers were not consistent about the corrections they made. For example in the same lesson, the teacher corrected the use of the auxiliary as shown in the first example, but ignored its incorrect use as shown in the second and the third examples.

1. S   J'ai venu te prendre.
   T   Pardon?
   S   Je suis venu.

2. S   J'étais très froid dehors, alors j'ai revenu dans la maison.

3. S   J'ai allé en haut.

There seems to be little sense in which students are pushed toward a more coherent and accurate production (comprehensible output) of French (Swain, 1985). When they are corrected, that frequently suffices and there is no further follow-up. In relatively long student turns, teachers rarely made corrections at all. For example, in one class, students were asked to summarize or read aloud what they had written about their favorite TV program. Over sixty-five grammatical errors were noted in this portion of the transcript. However, not one error was corrected.

The issue of error correction—or negative feedback—is an important one both theoretically and pedagogically. Pedagogically, the question is where error correction fits into communicative language teaching as it can severely disrupt the flow of communication. Theoretically, issues such as whether error correction can influence the path of language learning at all, and if so, whether its impact is restricted to specific kinds of linguistic knowledge, are at stake. Furthermore, one might ask if certain ways of correcting errors are more effective than others. For example, does it take "explicit hypothesis rejection" to effect change, or are indirect means, such as clarification requests and comprehension checks, equally as effective? (See, for example, Birdsong, 1988; Pica et al., 1988; Carroll et al., 1989). These are issues that future research will have to resolve.

In the meantime, it is clear that the immersion students are getting limited opportunities to speak in class, and when they do, the feedback they get is more likely to be content focused rather than language focused. This situation is due in large part to the implementation in our schools and universities of the typical transmission model of content teaching, where the teacher is seen as the provider of information and the students, the recipients (Goodlad, 1984). Other pedagogical models, such as cooperative learning (Kagan, 1986), are more learner-centered and interactive in nature, and thus maximize students' productive use of the second language. Experimentation with such models must be extended and carefully evaluated in our search to improve ways of getting two for one, that is, of integrating content and second language learning.

REFERENCES

Barik, H. C., and M. Swain. 1976. "A Canadian Experiment in Bilingual Education: The Peel Study." *Foreign Language Annals* 9: 465–79.

Birdsong, D. 1988. *Metalinguistic Performance and Interlinguistic Competence.* New York: Springer-Verlag.

Brinton, D. M., M. A. Snow, and M. Wesche. 1989. *Content-Based Second Language Instruction.* New York: Newbury House.

Carroll, S., Y. Roberge, M. Swain, H. Brasche, and M. Shechter. 1989. "The Effectiveness of Error Correction in Promoting Adult FSL Learning." Toronto: OISE/Modern Language Centre. Mimeo.

Edwards, H., M. Wesche, S. Krashen, R. Clement, and B. Krudenier. 1984. "Second Language Acquisition Through Subject-Matter Learning: A Study of Sheltered Psychology Classes at the University of Ottawa." *Canadian Modern Language Review* 41: 268–82.

Genessee, F. 1976. "Evaluation of the 1975–76 Grade 11 French Immersion Class. Addendum." Montreal: Protestant School Board of Greater Montreal.

———. 1977. "Departmental Leaving Examination Results: June 1977." Montreal: Protestant School Board of Greater Montreal.

———. 1987. *Learning Through Two Languages: Studies of Immersion and Bilingual Education.* New York: Newbury House.

Genesee, F., E. Polich, and M. Stanley. 1977. "An Experimental French Immersion Program at the Secondary School Level." *Canadian Modern Language Review* 33: 318–32.

Goodlad, J. I. 1984. *A Place Called School: Prospects for the Future.* New York: McGraw-Hill.

Harley, B. 1985. "Second Language Proficiency and Classroom Treatment in Early French Immersion." Paper presented at the FIPLV/Eurocentres Symposium on Error in Foreign Language Learning: Analysis and Treatment, Goldsmiths' College, University of London.

Harley, B., and M. L. King. In press. "Verb Lexis in the Written Compositions of Young L2 Learners." *Studies in Second Language Acquisition.*

Harley, B., and M. Swain. 1984. "The Interlanguage of Immersion Students and Its Implications for Second Language Teaching." *Interlanguage.* Eds. A. Davies, C. Criper, and A. P. R. Howatt. Edinburgh: Edinburgh UP. 291–311.

Hart, D. J., and S. Lapkin. 1989a. "French Immersion at the Secondary/Postsecondary Interface: Final Report on Phase 1." Toronto: OISE/Modern Language Centre. Mimeo.

———. 1989b. "French Immersion at the Secondary/Postsecondary Interface: Final Report on Phase 2." Toronto: OISE/Modern Language Centre. Mimeo.

Hauptman, P., M. Wesche, and D. Ready. 1988. "Second Language Acquisition Through Subject-Matter Learning: A Follow-Up Study at the Universtiy of Ottawa." *Language Learning* 38: 433–75.

Kagan, S. 1986. "Cooperative Learning and Sociocultural Factors in Schooling." *Beyond Language: Social and Cultural Factors in Schooling Language Minority Students.* Los Angeles: Evaluation, Dissemination and Assessment Center, California State University. 231–98.

Krashen, S. D. 1982. *Principles and Practice in Second Language Acquisition.* Oxford: Pergamon.

———. 1985. *The Input Hypothesis: Issues and Implications.* New York: Longman.

Morrison, F. 1981. "Longitudinal and Cross-Sectional Studies of French Proficiency in Ottawa and Carleton Schools. Ottawa: Research Centre, Ottawa Board of Education, Ontario.

Pica, T., L. Holliday, N. Lewis, and L. Morgenthaler. 1988. "Comprehensible Output as an Outcome of Linguistic Demands on the Learner." *Studies in Second Language Acquisition* 11: 63–90.

Schachter, J. 1984. "A Universal Input Condition." *Universals and Second Language Acquisition.* Ed. W. Rutherford. Amsterdam: John Benjamins. 167–83.

Stern, H. H., M. Swain, L. D. McLean, R. J. Friedman, B. Harley, and S. Lapkin. 1976. *Three Approaches to Teaching French.* Toronto: Ontario Ministry of Education.

Sternfeld, S. 1988. "The Applicability of the Immersion Approach to College Foreign Language Instruction." *Foreign Language Annals* 21: 221–26.

Swain, M. 1978. "Home-School Language Switching." *Understanding Second Language Learning: Issues and Approaches.* Ed. J. Richards. Rowley, Mass.: Newbury House. 238–51.

———. 1985. "Communicative Competence: Some Roles of Comprehensible Input and Comprehensible Output in Its Development." *Input in Second Language Acquisition.* Eds. S. M. Gass and C. G. Madden. Rowley, Mass.: Newbury House. 235–53.

——. 1988. "Manipulating and Complementing Content Teaching to Maximize Second Language Learning." *TESL Canada Journal* 6: 68–83.

Swain, M., and S. Carroll. 1987. "The Immersion Observation Study." *The Development of Bilingual Proficiency Final Report: Volume II—Classroom Treatment.* Eds. B. Harley, P. Allen, J. Cummins, and M. Swain. Toronto: OISE/Modern Language Centre. 190–341.

Swain, M. and S. Lapkin. 1982. *Evaluating Bilingual Education: A Canadian Case Study.* Clevedon, U.K.: Multilingual Matters.

——. 1989. "Canadian Immersion and Adult Second Language Teaching: What's the Connection?" *Modern Language Journal* 75: 150–59.

Wesche, M. 1985. "Immersion and the Universities." *Canadian Modern Language Review* 41: 931–35.

——. 1989. "Long-Term Outcomes of French Immersion Education." Paper presented at Second Language Research Forum, Los Angeles.

Wesche, M., and D. Ready. 1985. "Foreigner Talk in the University Classroom." *Input in Second Language Acquisition.* Eds. S. M. Gass and C. G. Madden. New York: Newbury House. 89–114.

Chapter 7

Foreign Language Development during a Semester Abroad

Robert M. DeKeyser
University of Pittsburgh

INTRODUCTION

It is a popular belief that a semester overseas can bring about a spectacular increase in foreign language skills. Classroom instruction is often equated with a large amount of grammar drills and vocabulary explanation, while residents in a foreign country are supposed to master the language through communication, with little conscious attention paid to structure. Many students, teachers, and program administrators echo these beliefs, whether they themselves have had such overseas experience or not. In other words, Stephen Krashen's (1982, 1985) ideas about the relative facility of learning as it takes place in many classrooms, as opposed to the dramatic effects of large amounts of comprehensible input in a stimulating and nonthreatening environment, seem to have a lot of intuitive appeal, even to those who have never read about his controversial dichotomy.

As a result, "mastery of a modern language has traditionally been perceived as the most direct educational benefit of study abroad" (Goodwin and Nacht, 1988, 16), even though, of course, it is only one of many arguments invoked to justify educational programs overseas.

In spite of the practical relevance of this issue for many thousands of students each year, research on foreign language teaching and learning has rarely focused on the transition from the classroom to the native-speaking environment and vice versa. Most research in applied linguistics has concerned itself either with academic learning and classroom achievement only or with acquisition in a native-speaking environment only, usually by immigrants or foreign workers.

EFFECT ON LINGUISTIC OUTPUT
IN PRODUCT TERMS

One can, of course, easily find a few dozen articles about the advantages of study abroad, but most of these are entirely speculative, or mere descriptions of the administrative setup, or studies about personal growth or affective variables such as attitudes toward the foreign country or motivation for further study of the language (see, for example, Bicknese, 1974a, 1974b; Hamers, 1984; Stitsworth, 1988; Tucker and Lambert, 1970). This paper will deal exclusively with language development.

Kaplan (1989) reports on how much French American students used during six weeks in France, and states that the students found they had made more progress in comprehension than in production, but does not look at any linguistic evidence. Diller and Markert (1983) report scores on the MLA Cooperative Foreign Language Tests of reading and grammar for fourteen students before and after a spring quarter in Germany. For reading, scores increased by a percentage ranging from 24% to 367%, with a mean of 121%. For grammar, gain scores ranged from 1% to 415%, with a mean of 62%. No attempt was made to pinpoint the exact nature of the improvement in linguistic terms, and there was no control group.

The only large-scale study, to my knowledge, that has ever looked at the contribution of overseas experience to foreign language skills—and that can be said to have involved control groups, even though it was not an experimental study—is John Carroll's (1967) study of 2,782 college seniors majoring in French, German, Italian, Russian, or Spanish at 203 institutions. The two variables that were the strongest predictors of students' listening scores were the amount of time spent abroad, and the age at which study of the language began. The effects of these two variables were independent from each other. The size of the effect varied somewhat depending on the specific language, and the absolute level attained varied, of course, with the number of years of study, but a fairly consistent pattern emerges from the data: a year of overseas study, on the average, brings students from around level two on the FSI speaking scale (limited working proficiency) to around level three (minimum professional proficiency). The effect of a summer course in the foreign country, or even just having toured around in it, is about half that size. The effects on skills other than listening are not reported in detail in the article available to me, but Carroll claims they are similar to the effects for listening.

Two German researchers (Moehle, 1984; Moehle and Raupach, 1983; Raupach, 1983, 1984, 1987) have done case studies documenting the speech of German college students of French and French college students of German. The results of these studies indicate that grammar, in terms of frequency of mistakes or length and syntactic complexity of sentences, did not change in any noticeable way as a result of several months spent in France by the German students. What changed was the speech rate (that is, the number of syllables per second increased), the number of pauses (decrease), and the length of the stretches of speech between pauses (increase) (Moehle, 1984).

For French learners of German, however, there was little change in these quantitative characteristics of speech after a stay in Germany, but their grammar improved "enormous[ly]," especially in inflections (Moehle, 1984). It is not clear whether this difference between the two types of learners was due to a lower proficiency of the French students at the beginning of the study or to the highly inflected character of German.

Raupach (1984) showed how the more fluent character of a German learner's French after a stay in France was largely due to her use of formulas, that is, standardized "fillers," "modifiers," and "organizers" (*bon, vraiment, c'est*), which freed the learners from having to resort to subsidiary hesitation strategies such as drawls and filled or unfilled pauses.

Raupach (1987) has argued at length that the quantitative differences between performance before and after the stay in France can be attributed to procedural learning and automatization resulting from practice. His use of the data is illustrative rather than systematic, however.

EFFECT ON LINGUISTIC OUTPUT IN PROCESS TERMS: MONITORING AND COMMUNICATION STRATEGIES

In order to investigate the influence of an overseas experience on how learners put their L2 knowledge to use during communication and how learners compensate for gaps in their knowledge, DeKeyser (1986) designed a comparative study of two groups. The first group consisted of seven American students participating in a six-month overseas program in Spain, who were observed during the fall quarter of 1984–85. They had all gone through the two-year basic course sequence at their home university, but some of them had skipped the first quarters because they had had the equivalent in high school. Their proficiency level was intermediate. The second group consisted of five students of the same university who were planning to study in Spain or Latin America in 1985–86; they were observed in their second-year, second-quarter Spanish classes in the United States during the winter of 1984–85. These students had taken the four preceding quarters of the course sequence (but most of the students had skipped the first quarter because they had had the equivalent in high school).

All subjects were volunteers. None of them had spent any substantial time in a Spanish-speaking country before. While these "convenience samples" were small and somewhat heterogeneous, they did present the advantage of having two groups with a substantial amount of shared classroom experience, one group having the overseas experience in addition.

To assess whether the two groups were comparable on a series of variables known to affect foreign language learning in general and monitoring in particular, the subjects were given the Modern Language Aptitude Test (Carroll and Sapon, 1959) and two questionnaires: one concerning attitude, motivation, and risk-taking, and one about attitude toward correctness.

The differences between the two groups regarding the control variables were quite small, and none of the t-tests for these five variables (language learning aptitude, attitude, motivation, risk-taking, attitude toward correctness) reached a significance level of alpha = 0.05. The two groups, then, were comparable for the purpose of this study.

At the beginning of the quarter the students took a Spanish grammar test dealing with the most important points of second-year grammar (the copula, the subjunctive, conditional clauses, relative clauses). The purpose of this test was to assess the learners' baseline grammar knowledge in a situation conducive to monitoring. The students of both groups were interviewed three times during the quarter, approximately at three-week intervals, with three goals in mind: collecting a sample of their Spanish under semicontrolled conditions, gaining information about their communicative and learning behaviors by means of a subset of questions geared toward these topics, and gaining access to their conscious thought processes during performance by means of a stimulated-recall session immediately following the interview.

Around the same time each interview took place, the students also participated in an experiment consisting of describing a picture to a native speaker, who had to copy the picture on the basis of the learner's descriptions.

The researcher regularly visited the students' classrooms in the United States as well as in Spain, and took fieldnotes about the students' interaction with the teacher. Furthermore, the group in Spain was observed in a variety of informal situations.

Monitoring

Because the frequencies of specific structures in the interviews and the picture descriptions were often too low for a valid comparison with the results for those structures on the grammar test, the comparison had to be limited to one of the four problems on the test: the use of the copula *ser/estar*.

The results on the grammar test were often far from perfect, for the copula as well as for the other structures, which means that some students simply did not have the knowledge to be monitored during oral performance (for details, see DeKeyser, 1990). For those students, however, who gave consistently correct answers for the *ser/estar* problem on the grammar test, the results for the oral tests were quite consistent as well, as is clear from the following three tables.

Table 1 shows the results for the use of the copula before a predicate noun (where *ser* is required) by those students in Spain who made consistently correct judgments on the corresponding part of the grammar test. As can be seen from the table, these students always used *ser* correctly during the oral tests.

Table 2 presents parallel data for the copula before an expression of location, where *estar* is required. While the data are somewhat less clear-cut in this case, the percentage of correct uses is very high, and varies between 80% (October) and 90% (November).

The frequencies in Table 3 pertain to the recordings for the students in the United States with consistent judgments on the grammar test for *ser/estar* before a predicate noun. The table shows that both students used *ser* with a high degree of consistency in the oral test. For the use of *estar* before an expression of location,

— *Table 1* _____

Frequencies for the Copula before a Predicate Noun
(Spain — students with consistent judgments)

	October		November		December	
	ser	estar	ser	estar	ser	estar
Student 1	18	0	12	0	10	0
Student 2	15	0	14	0	8	0
Student 7	8	0	7	0	11	0
Total	41	0	33	0	29	0

there were no students in the U.S. group with consistently correct answers on the grammar test.

To summarize, those students in Spain who made consistently correct judgments about the use of *ser* before a predicate noun always used it correctly in oral communicative tasks, and those who made consistently correct judgments about *estar* before an expression of location used it correctly in the vast majority of cases. The students in the United States with consistently correct judgments for *ser* before a predicate noun used it correctly in almost all cases. Students in both groups appeared to monitor their knowledge about *ser* and *estar* quite efficiently during oral communication, at least those students whose knowledge appeared to be solid on the grammar test.

The students' inconsistent judgments on other parts of the grammar tests were reflected in their choice of the default option where that was possible, that

— **Table 2** _____

Frequencies for the Copula before an Expression of Location
(Spain — students with consistent judgments)

	October		November		December	
	ser	estar	ser	estar	ser	estar
Student 2	0	2	2	4	1	6
Student 5	2	12	0	7	0	5
Student 6	5	14	1	14	2	8
Total	7	28	3	25	3	19

— **Table 3**━━━━━━━━━━━━━━━━━━━━━━━━━━━━━━━━━━━━

Frequencies for the Copula before a Predicate Noun
(U.S. — students with consistent judgments)

	January		February		March	
	ser	estar	ser	estar	ser	estar
Student 1	19	0	5	2	8	0
Student 5	5	0	12	0	12	0
Total	24	0	17	2	20	0

is, choosing *que* as relative pronoun or choosing the indicative after affirmative verbs of opinion, or in avoidance strategies and a variety of mistakes, where there was no clear default option, that is, in conditional sentences.

When students overseas were asked about differences in their learning or speaking since they had come to Spain, they never mentioned anything like the difference between consciously learning grammar in the United States and picking it up automatically in Spain. When asked more explicitly whether they agreed that language development abroad was largely automatic, they all rejected this idea. No evidence was found, then, to suggest that foreign language development in the native-speaking environment involves less monitoring than learning in the classroom context.

As no differences in degree of monitoring were found between the two groups, it comes as no surprise that no clear evolution during the stay abroad was found either. The only case where improved monitoring of a known rule was documented was for the use of *estar,* and even there the evidence was scant. In all other cases the numbers were too small to allow for comparison, or the students' usage was either completely consistent (for *ser*) or completely inconsistent (for conditionals) throughout the quarter.

Communication Strategies

What do learners do, at home and abroad, to supplement their insufficient knowledge of the foreign language during communication? In order to answer this question, we analyzed the data on the use of communication strategies in both groups, presented in Table 4.

A two-way analysis of variance revealed no significant difference between group and type of communication strategy ($F = 0.32$; $df = 7$; $p = 0.94$ and $F = 0.63$; $df = 7$; $p = 0.73$ for the picture descriptions and the interviews, respectively). While this lack of statistical significance may have been due to the small number of subjects ($n = 7$ for the Spanish group and $n = 5$ for the United States

— *Table 4*

The Use of Communication Strategies in Both Tasks for Both Groups

	Picture Descriptions		Interviews	
	Spain	U.S.	Spain	U.S.
topic avoidance, message abandonment	41 4.91%	57 6.64%	22 8.46%	8 3.17%
meaning replacement, overgeneralization	59 7.07%	68 7.92%	35 13.46%	37 14.68%
L1, literal translation, foreignizing	51 6.11%	45 5.24%	17 6.54%	45 17.86%
circumlocution	294 35.21%	222 25.84%	12 4.62%	6 2.38%
restructuring	58 6.95%	72 8.38%	49 18.85%	29 11.51%
confirmation request	262 31.38%	218 25.38%	103 39.62%	91 36.11%
appeal and indir. appeal	43 5.15%	81 9.43%	15 5.77%	13 5.16%
other	27 3.23%	96 11.18%	7 2.69%	23 9.13%
Total	835 100.00%	859 100.00%	260 100.00%	252 100.00%

The classification of communication strategies in this table and the next basically conforms to Faerch and Kasper's (1983) taxonomy. We expanded the category of appeal, however, to include the occurrences of indirect appeal. The latter category consists of instances where the learner does not explicitly ask the native speaker for the word corresponding to a concept or an English word, but indirectly encourages him to do so by saying "I don't know the word for this in Spanish," "what is this called again," and so on. By confirmation request we mean eliciting an evaluative reaction from the native speaker, sometimes explicitly by asking "Is that a word?" but usually implicitly by a question intonation on the word the learner feels uncertain about.

group), there is a further argument against the hypothesis of difference between the two groups: the biggest between-group differences in Table 4 are not the same for both tasks. In the picture descriptions, the most conspicuous differences are the frequency of circumlocution (higher in Spain), and that of appeal and indirect appeal (higher in the United States), whereas in the interviews the frequencies that stand out are those for L1-based strategies (higher in the United States) and restructuring (higher in Spain). Only the category "other" is more frequent in the

United States for both tasks (this is mainly due to the frequency of incorporation for the U.S. group).

In the case of circumlocution, the figures for the two tasks are not inconsistent; the evidence is simply too scant for the interview part. In the case of L1-based strategies and appeal/indirect appeal, the difference may have been brought about by the way the interlocutor was perceived: in the United States, most subjects knew the interviewer as a bilingual teacher, which was not the case in Spain; in the United States, the artist hired for the picture drawing tended to give more feedback to the students, and thus encouraged the strategy of appeal. No such explanation seems to hold for restructuring, however; it may be that students in Spain had learned to use this inconspicuous and nativelike strategy more frequently than the students in the United States but that the rigid requirements of the picture-description task kept them from using it efficiently.

At any rate, if there is a (not statistically significant) tendency for certain, strategies to have a different relative frequency in the Spanish group than in the U.S. group, this is due to the particular characteristics of the tasks and the interlocutors rather than to a developmental process in Spain. It is certainly not the case that the use of communication strategies changed drastically during the students' stay in Spain.

The next section will provide a closer look at individual differences in the use of strategies in order to show first, that the instruments and analyses used were adequate to point out meaningful differences where they did exist; and second, how important individual differences in the use of strategies were in determining the communicative efficiency of otherwise comparable students when they interacted with native speakers during their stay overseas.

Individual Differences

September 20, 3:30 P.M. The newly arrived American students sit down for a drink on one of the many terraces on the Plaza Mayor. The waiter comes to take the order. Paul asks what kinds of Spanish beer they carry and while the waiter recites a list of beer brands, Paul suddenly says "yes," meaning "that's the kind I want." As soon as the waiter leaves, Tim asks Paul: "Did you know that beer?" and Paul has to admit he did not. For fear of losing face, he faked native-like competence in his choice of beer, even though that meant that he did not know what kind of brew to expect. And Tim was stunned (Fieldnotes, September 20).

From hindsight, this little incident appears to have been a presage of Tim's and Paul's extremely different approaches to communicating in the foreign language. Throughout the quarter, Paul made every possible attempt to appear like a native speaker, while Tim almost purposely projected himself as a learner. In the following pages, we will see how these opposite attitudes pervaded many facets of these learners' communicative behavior, and how they can be explained by more general aspects of their personality.

Tim's speech was characterized by precision and meticulousness at the four traditional levels of linguistic description. At the phonological level, the most important features were a careful, sound-by-sound pronunciation, the somewhat superfluous effort to make the Castilian distinction between the interdental and the alveolar *s*, the exaggerated pronunciation of the single *r* (flap) as a double *r* (apical trill), a slow tempo, and an unnaturally rising and falling intonation, especially within word groups, which sometimes gave rise to comical effects, for instance, in a classroom conversation on November 12:

El esposo de Ferraro era un hombre ´`—muy simpático´`.

Tim's intonation and his pause after *hombre* made some students laugh, because it sounded like the sentence was finished (*Ferraro's husband was a man.*).

At the morphological level, there were quite a few hesitations about verb conjugation, and Tim made no effort to hide this. Instances such as *sal–saló–salé–salí* were not uncommon.

At the syntactic level, Tim's speech clearly stood out by his spontaneous use of more complex constructions (conditional sentences, relative clauses, comparative constructions) in a variety of situations, in contrast to the other students, who usually avoided them, even when the researcher tried to elicit such constructions in the interviews. But the lexical level was the most conspicuous of all. Tim had an extraordinary vocabulary, which he used spontaneously on all occasions. Sometimes he would use a series of synonyms, for example, *plenamen–claramente–obviamente* (picture description, Oct. 25) as if he were reading them from a dictionary. Some of the explanations of word meaning that he gave in answer to the teacher's questions sounded dictionary like. And indeed, for the first eight weeks or so, Tim always carried a heavy dictionary around, wherever he went. Later on he said he did not need it so much anymore. Furthermore, he did not let one occasion go by to ask the teachers in class for the meaning or the spelling of a word they had used, even to the point that teachers and fellow students became irritated.

Paul's speech was, in many ways, the opposite of Tim's. He spoke very fast, and often articulated very indistinctly. Unstressed vowels were reduced frequently, and final *-n* was hard to perceive. The intonation was very flat and the rhythm very irregular. While the researcher was working on a transcription of Paul's interviews, and taking notes on the irregular rhythm, Paul came into his room to give him another tape-recording, and said that, while listening to his tape, he had noticed he spoke "in blurts" (fieldnotes, Nov. 28). There were very few long, cumbersome hesitations in Paul's speech, but an extraordinary number of short pauses, often within word groups, even between articles and nouns, and so on.

Paul never drew attention to conjugation or other grammar problems in the way Tim did. Self-corrections were done very quickly and inconspicuously, as for a slip of the tongue in the native language, and Paul's indistinct articulation often made it difficult to hear whether he made the correct subject-verb or adjective-noun agreement.

One of the reasons why Paul seemed to get stuck less often than Tim was probably his more frequent use of restructuring. Table 5 shows thirty-nine instances of restructuring for Paul in the interviews and picture descriptions combined and only ten for Tim. Paul also seemed more prone to solving a communication problem by meaning-replacement or overgeneralizing a word (ten instances versus three for Tim) than by directly or indirectly appealing to the interlocutor (three instances versus eight for Tim). And many of Paul's relatively infrequent confirmation requests were more nativelike than the rising intonation on a doubtful word that was used by most learners most of the time. He regularly asked questions such as *sabes el tipo?* (do you know the kind?), *tienes la primera herramienta ahí?* (do you have the first tool there?), *es un instrumento para coger hojas, no?* (it's a tool to pick up leaves, right?), *sabes, tienes problemas?* (do you know, do you have problems?), *es mejor ahora?* (is it better [explained] now?). Because of these frequent comprehension checks, Paul did not have to show he had doubts about particular words, but could give the interlocutor the responsibility of signaling any problems he may have had.

These few aspects of Tim's and Paul's performance in Spanish fit into a more general frame of language behavior. Tim adopted a playful approach to the language, and treated it as an object, almost as a toy. He loved puns, and was

— Table 5 —————————————————————————

Communication Strategies Used by Tim and Paul in the Interviews and Picture Descriptions Together

	Tim	Paul
topic avoidance, message abandonment	5 3.94%	11 7.14%
meaning replacement, overgeneralization	3 2.36%	10 6.49%
L1, literal translation, foreignizing	9 7.09%	6 3.90%
circumlocution	47 37.01%	52 33.77%
restructuring	10 7.87%	39 25.32%
confirmation request	40 31.50%	27 17.53%
appeal and indirect appeal	8 6.30%	3 1.95%
other	5 3.94%	6 3.90%
Total	127 100.00%	154 100.00%

amazingly good at them in a language that, after all, he had not mastered very well yet. So big was the disparity between his limited proficiency in the language and his creative play on words that native speakers often did not get the joke, assuming Tim was simply confused. Examples of these puns are to be found in the researcher's fieldnotes (hereafter FN):

> While standing in line in the cafeteria, R. asks Tim.: *Qué más?* (What else?). Tim reacts by running over to a table, grabbing a jar of water and pouring it over his hand. When asked for an explanation of this peculiar behavior, Tim says: *Me dijiste "quemas"* (you told me "you're burning") (FN, Nov. 12).
> Over dinner R. asks Tim *¿Cuánto cuesta una red?* (How much does a [volleyball] net cost?), and Tim says *La mitad de una pared* (Half of [what a] wall [costs]; the Spanish word for *wall* sounds like *par-red,* pair-net) (FN, Nov. 5).

Sometimes Tim played this kind of joke when he *was* confused or did not understand:

> At the breakfast table, Tim is talking about the problems he is having with his razor. The Spanish are using the word *maquinilla* (electric razor). Apparently Tim does not know this word. He grabs the butter on the table and pretends to be shaving with it (Sp. *mantequilla* = *butter*) (FN, Oct. 4).

Besides making puns, Tim generally liked to play with words. On the second day in Spain, he was dancing down the stairs while singing a made-up song in Spanish; *con mucho gusto me introduzco* ("I'm pleased to introduce myself") (FN, Sept. 21). In the same vein, during a trip through southern Spain, Tim reacted to the Beatles' song "Yellow Submarine" being played on the bus by improvising Spanish lyrics (FN, Jan. 1). Later the researcher was told by one of Tim's relatives that Tim had written poetry in high school that had been published in a prestigious journal.

Paul, on the other hand, did *not* treat language as a toy, but more as a garment that was to make him look more like the natives. During numerous interactions with the researcher he always made two points: that whatever problem he experienced in Spanish was a problem he also had in English sometimes, and that he felt very comfortable interacting with the Spaniards, who often "did not realize he was a foreigner."

His high speech rate was the most obvious consequence of his attempt to appear nativelike. After eight weeks in Spain, however, Paul told the researcher that he was consciously trying to slow down during the interview, because a Spanish woman had told him that she could not understand him because he spoke too fast. He seemed to imply that he spoke too fast *for the Spaniards,* not for himself to be able to articulate well enough to be understood (FN, Nov. 14)!

Another aspect of nativelike speech that Paul adopted quickly was the use of fillers such as *pues, bueno,* and so forth. In a presentation of a few minutes in a history class toward the end of the quarter, he used *pues* three times, *y todo* six times, *bueno* six times, and *es que* ten times (FN, Dec. 5).

The difference in style between Paul and Tim was not without effect on the natives' appreciation of their respective proficiency. The researcher never asked the Spanish students what they thought about the performance of any of the learners, but they made spontaneous comments to him every once in a while.

Comments about Paul's speech were *only* positive, those about Tim's speech *only* negative:

> Paul speaks the best. (J. from V.; FN, Oct. 7)
> Paul has the best accent and speaks the best. (T. from V.; FN, Oct. 23)
> Paul manages well already. (J. L. from A.; FN, Oct. 28)
> Tim does not understand a thing. (J. from B.; FN, Oct. 25)
> A native speaker gives up trying to explain something to Tim and says to R.:
> "You understand Spanish better, don't you?" (FN, Nov. 24)

Ironically, the same day that J. L. told the researcher Paul "managed well already," Paul told the researcher he found J. L. impossible to understand (J. L. had indeed the worst articulation R. had ever heard from a native speaker). But apparently Paul had faked comprehension quite well!

Tim's and Paul's approaches to language were only part of a more general aspect of their personalities. Tim often behaved like a clown (some people called him *el payaso*), and he sometimes walked through the city hopping up and down as if he were alone in the world (a form of behavior that is not recommended in a provincial town such as the one where the students were staying). Paul was more concerned about his image, and easily became irritated at little aspects of daily life in Spain. The best way to summarize the difference in personality may be to say that Tim was much more spontaneous overall than Paul.

Conclusions about Communicative Processes Abroad

The main conclusion of this study is that the group differences were far less important than the individual differences. While students undoubtedly gained in fluency and expanded their vocabulary in Spain, they did not drastically change their monitoring behavior or their use of communication strategies. There were clear differences, however, within the overseas group, in monitoring style and in preference for certain communication strategies. These differences had a strong impact on the way the learners were perceived by the native speakers, and were consequently sought out or avoided for informal interaction.

The results of our study, then, do not suggest a strong dichotomy between learning language in the classroom and picking it up abroad, or between grammar and oral proficiency. If there was any gap, it was between the students' generally inconsistent judgments on a multiple-choice test, and the knowledge of grammar that may have been expected, taking into account that these students had success-fully taken six quarters of Spanish, and extensively dealt with the problems represented on the grammar test in class. What was lacking, then, was not so much the controversial interface between what was learned and what could be used for communication, but a thoroughly learned system that would allow students to perform consistently on any kind of grammar test, not just on a test with prototypical sentences in a format they are used to, and that could be drawn on during communication.

If people are to benefit maximally from a stay abroad, they need to be able to monitor inconspicuously and to use communication strategies that mask their problems instead of drawing attention to them. Only then will they be able to take full advantage of the two-way informal interaction that is an essential ingredient of the overseas experience, regardless of whether one takes the view that it is the comprehensible input that counts or the practice.

FURTHER PERSPECTIVES ON THE ROLE OF THE "SEMESTER ABROAD"

The studies cited at the beginning of this article presented quantitative and qualitative evidence for a strong influence of the time spent abroad on foreign language proficiency. The presentation above, however, showed that a stay abroad does not necessarily entail a radical change in communicative processes. If these processes are not strongly affected, why is it then that a stay abroad can make a big difference in proficiency?

One can easily list, of course, a number of obvious reasons. First, the sheer number of hours spent in the native-speaking environment provides a huge amount of comprehensible input for all students, and a sizeable amount of speaking practice for those who are willing to make an effort. Second, being in an environment where one can get many things done in the foreign language that could not be accomplished in the native language is a constant motivational boost. Third, students overseas, if they work at it, acquire at least some skill in managing truly informal interaction with multiple native speakers, an activity that is rare, if not nonexistent in the classroom.

There may also be, however, a number of less obvious reasons for the sometimes dramatic gains in proficiency gained after a stay abroad. These reasons are of a more fundamental psycholinguistic nature, and may, once they are better understood and documented than is the case now, give indications for how the classroom itself could be made to have some of the beneficial effects of a stay abroad. I will speculate on three such reasons here.

First, a semester in the native-speaking environment, following or combined with a (high) intermediate course with some focus on the explicit teaching of grammar, provides a prolonged opportunity for an ideal mix of focus on form and focus on meaning. Contrary to classroom learners, who receive very little input that would allow them to test hypotheses about the language, and contrary to the grammatically naive learners who do not know what aspects of the input to focus on, learners who do not know all the rules but know that there are problems with perfective/imperfective, indicative/subjunctive, and who know the basic principles motivating the choice between these forms, can fine-tune their knowledge by selectively paying attention to the relevant parts of the input. Richard Day's (Day and Frota, 1986) introspective study of his learning of Portuguese in Brazil certainly testifies to the importance of the interaction between what was learned in the classroom and what was present in the input, in the sense that a combination of these two elements was much more likely to lead to correct production than either of them alone. Furthermore, even when the student has not learned a rule, the sensitivity to form brought about by formal study will make him better prepared for noticing certain forms in the input; this may explain the interaction between instruction and informal practice that Nina Spada (1985, 1986) found for adult ESL learners: those who received the most form-focused instruction benefited the most from informal practice. Barbara Freed's (in press) findings that informal practice correlated most with progress on traditional tests of grammar and reading comprehension for students at the beginning level can also be interpreted in this way. In Michael Long's (1988) terms, a focus on *form* is important, not necessarily a focus on *forms*. And conversely, whereas formal learning provides a focus for the processing of input, daily input and interaction with natives provide a renewed interest in focusing on certain structures in formal learning contexts. Several of the students I observed in Spain, for instance, started begging for more discussion of the subjunctive after making a number of observations in their interaction with Spaniards; these were the same students who claimed they found grammar to be boring and irrelevant at the beginning of their stay abroad. This is nothing else, of course, than an application of the pedagogical principle that students learn better when what is being taught is presented as an answer to their questions.

Second, the fact that so many communicative contexts keep reoccurring during a stay abroad creates something like a natural communicative drill. There is focus on meaning, of course, each time the student buys fruit in the store, each time he asks his friends at the dinner table how they spent the afternoon, each time he agrees where and when to meet his new tennis partner, but the recurrence of these conversations makes them into an ideal form of comprehensible input, in the sense of what Merrill Swain (1985) described as good comprehensible input: because it is so comprehensible, it allows for focus on form. This focus on form then immediately carries over into active communicative practice.

Third, and maybe most important, when focus on form leads to the remembering of a word or phrase heard in the native-speaking environment, the memory is integrated into episodic memory (Tulving, 1983) as part of the memory of an event. And because any event is to some extent a synesthetic experience, the new linguistic item becomes part of what Earl Stevick (1981) has called a "well-integrated configuration" in long-term memory. The more sensory experiences the item is associated with, the easier it will be to retrieve. And the more that certain elements of the event are salient (faces, noises, emotions), the better the recall of the other elements in the event or episode will be (Craik, 1989). Needless to say, such multiple linking with sensory experiences is rare in the classroom, where every interaction takes place among the same people, between the same four walls.

Much of what has been said in the preceding pages is rather speculative, of course. There is a clear need for further study on the role of a stay abroad in foreign language development. All the studies done so far, including our own, have clear limitations, either by their very small number of subjects or by their restriction of the criterion measure to general assessments of proficiency. Further studies should try to link data on the linguistic product with data on psycholinguistic and sociolinguistic processes. They should not be limited to a simple pre-post design with or without a control group, but should be longitudinal, that is, follow the learners closely throughout their overseas experience, and integrate test data with more ethnographic data, paying due attention to individual differences. Because it is extremely difficult to find large and homogeneous samples for a study on this topic, it would be wise to capitalize on the advantages of intensive case studies first, and to compare the results of different studies later, rather than to try to establish statistically significant findings in separate studies.

One of the main issues to be addressed in future research will be the differential effect of experience abroad as a function of the students' level of achievement at the beginning of their trip. Ability profiles and personality traits will be other foci for such research.

REFERENCES

Bicknese, G. 1974a. "Study Abroad. Part I: A Comparative Test of Attitudes and Opinions." *Foreign Language Annals* 7: 325–36.

——. 1974b. "Study Abroad. Part II: As the Students See It: The Junior Year Abroad Reassessed." *Foreign Language Annals* 7: 337–45.

Carroll, J. 1967. "Foreign Language Proficiency Levels Attained by Language Majors Near Graduation From College." *Foreign Language Annals* 1: 131–51.

Carroll, J., and M. Sapon. 1959. *Modern Language Aptitude Test. Form A.* New York: Psychological Corporation.

Craik, F. 1989. "On the Making of Episodes." *Varieties of Memory and Consciousness. Essays in Honor of Endel Tulving.* Eds. H. Roediger and F. Craik. Hillsdale: LEA. 43–57.

DeKeyser, R. 1986. "From Learning to Acquisition? Foreign Language Development in a U.S. Classroom and During a Semester Abroad." Unpublished Ph.D. dissertation. Stanford University (UMI DA #87-00743).

——. 1990. "From Learning to Acquisition? Monitoring in the Classroom and Abroad." *Hispania.* 73: 238–47.

Diller, E., and A. Markert. 1983. "The Telescope Curriculum: An Oregon-Tübingen Experiment in First-Year German." *Unterrichtspraxis* 16: 223–29.

Faerch, C., and G. Kasper. 1983. "Plans and Strategies in Foreign Language Communication." *Strategies in Interlanguage Communication.* London: Longman. 20–60.

Freed, B. In press. "Language Learning in a Study Abroad Context: The Effects of Interactive and Non-interactive Out-of-Class Contact on Grammatical Achievement and Oral Proficiency." In *Proceedings of the Georgetown University Round Table 1990.* Washington, D.C.: Georgetown University Press.

Goodwin, C., and M. Nacht. 1988. *Abroad and Beyond. Patterns in American Overseas Education.* Cambridge: Cambridge UP.

Hamers, J. 1984. "L'Evolution des Attitudes Envers la Langue Seconde et l'Identité Culturelle Chez les Jeunes Québecois Francophones et Anglophones." *Canadian Modern Language Review* 41: 283–307.

Kaplan, M. 1989. "French in the Community: A Survey of Language Use Abroad." *The French Review* 63, 290–99.

Krashen, S. 1982. *Principles and Practice in Second Language Acquisition*. Oxford: Pergamon.

————— 1985. *The Input Hypothesis: Issues and Implications*. London: Longman.

Long, M. 1988. "Instructed Interlanguage Development." *Issues in Second Language Acquisition. Multiple Perspectives*. Ed. L. Beebe. Rowley, Mass.: Newbury House. 115–141.

Moehle, D. 1984. "A Comparison of the Second Language Speech of Different Native Speakers." *Second Language Productions*. Eds. H. Dechert *et al*. Tübingen: Gunter Narr. 26–49.

Moehle, D., and M. Raupach. 1983. *Planen in der Fremdsprache*. Frankfurt: Peter Lang.

Raupach, M. 1983. "Analysis and Evaluation of Communication Strategies." *Strategies in Interlanguage Communication*. Eds. C. Faerch and G. Kasper. London: Longman. 199–209.

—————. 1984. "Formulae in Second Language Speech Production. *Second Language Productions*. Eds. H. Dechert *et al*. Tübingen: Gunter Narr. 114–37.

—————. 1987. *Procedural Learning in Advanced Learners of a Foreign Language*. Duisburg: Universität Gesamthochschule Duisburg [L.A.U.D. Papers B 167].

Schmidt, R., and S. N. Frota. 1986. "Developing Basic Conversational Ability in a Second Language: A Case Study of an Adult Learner of Portuguese." *Talking to Learn. Conversation in Second Language Acquisition*. Ed. R. Day. Rowley, Mass.: Newbury House.

Spada, N. 1985. "Effects of Informal Contact on Classroom Learners' L2 Proficiency: A Review of Five Studies." *TESL Canada* 2, 51–62.

—————. 1986. "The Interaction between Type of Contact and Type of Instruction: Some Effects on the L2 Proficiency of Adult Learners." *Studies in Second Language Acquisition* 8, 181–200.

Stevick, E. 1984. "Memory, Learning and Acquisition." *Universals of Second Language Acquisition*. Eds. F. Eckman, L. Bell, and D. Nelson. Rowley, Mass.: Newbury House. 24–35.

Stitsworth, M. 1988. "The Relationship Between Previous Foreign Language Study and Personality Change in Youth Exchange Participants." *Foreign Language Annals* 21: 131–37.

Swain, M. 1985. "Communicative Competence: Some Roles of Comprehensible Input and Comprehensible Output in Its Development." *Input in Second Language Acquisition*. Eds. S. Gass and C. Madden. Rowley, Mass.: Newbury House. 235–53.

Tucker, R., and W. Lambert. 1970. "The Effect on Foreign Language Teachers of Leadership Training in a Foreign Setting." *Foreign Language Annals* 4: 68–83.

Tulving, E. 1983. *Elements of Episodic Memory*. Oxford: Oxford UP.

Chapter 8

Tracking the Learner in Computer-Aided Language Learning

James S. Noblitt and Susan K. Bland

Cornell University

The development of computer-aided language learning (CALL), with its capacity for creating an interactive learning environment, coincides with a national trend toward seeking ways to improve undergraduate education. Far from being a dehumanizing force in the educational process, the computer has assisted in devising methods that place an emphasis on individual learning through the use of information processing tools (see Noblitt, 1989). Language information of interest to researchers has face value for computer applications (see, for example, Evens *et al.*, 1987; Gass, 1987), and this suggests a changing relationship between theoretical and applied research. The computer offers a new environment for language study as knowledge is made available in different ways and in new forms. The interesting educational implications of this environment are thus more epistemological than technological.

Recent emphasis on communicative competence in foreign language learning has produced a great deal of professional interest in computer-aided, multimedia presentation of authentic materials. Many have commented on the fact that computerized learning environments encourage student interaction with rich data bases of tutorial and reference materials, and humanists are enthusiastic about computer applications that stress creativity by providing environments in which students may learn by doing (see Noblitt, 1990).

There has been less comment on the fact that the new technology also encourages the direct involvement of instructors in the learning process, chiefly by providing a record of student requests for information at the moment they are attempting to use the language as a means of expression. This previously inaccessible "window" into the information-processing styles of students not only permits evaluation of the effectiveness of instructional software, it provides an empirical basis for investigating the processing strategies used by students when investigating the relationship between form and meaning. Interesting questions about the teaching and learning process are raised as one investigates the implications of computerized collection of data for data base design, error analysis, and SLA research.

During the spring 1989 semester we sought to address these questions in a cooperative research effort.[1] We conducted a pilot study of first and second year learners of French who were attempting creative writing with a software system for foreign language learning called *Système-D* (Noblitt, Solá, and Pet, 1987, described in Noblitt *et al.*, 1986). The program is a fully supported and documented writing assistant for French. It combines a bilingual word processor with an interconnected set of language reference materials, including a bilingual dictionary, verb morphology, examples of usage, and supplementary information on structure, word families, and functional topics.

In order to investigate the use of language reference material by students while they were engaged in writing, it was necessary to devise a "tracking" utility, that is, a device for recording requests for information. Students had reported informally that rapid access to lexical information was a motivating factor in using French for creative writing. By tracking the learner's ongoing interaction with the computer during a composing task, we used *Système-D* primarily as a research tool to provide data on how students learn to write in French; but we also wished to see if we could explore the nature of the second language acquisition process itself.

INTRODUCTION

Beginning L2 learners often use what may be called a "lexical strategy" toward the target language. They assume that for every word in L1 there exists a one-to-one lexical match in L2. The extreme form of this view can be called the *naïve lexical hypothesis;* that is, a foreign language is simply an encoded form of the native language. As learners gradually become aware of the complex interaction of the syntactic, semantic, pragmatic, morphological, and phonological aspects of the lexical relationship between L1 and L2, they upgrade their hypotheses about the target language by exploring how the target language organizes meaning through its own lexical or grammatical devices.

Technological developments in the creation and management of large computerized data bases have opened up new possibilities in the field of applied lexicography (see Byrd *et al.*, 1987). There is increasing interest in exploiting computer-based research on language and the lexicon, especially as word processors, dictionaries, and spelling and grammar checkers have come into general use. Relatively little is known, however, about the educational implications of these new devices. We studied the potential of *Système-D* as an appropriate environment for exploring the language learning behavior of learners at the elementary and intermediate levels of formal instruction, since it offers an example of an "enriched" lexicon in which various types of linguistic information are represented in a relational data base. The program is based on what the authors have called the *interlex* concept, that is, a general-purpose program design, which applies insights from interlingual lexicography in creating associative bridges between two languages.

A lexical approach to L2 learning assumes that much of what the learner needs to know about L2 can be organized as lexical information (see Bland, 1987). Such an approach provides information about the target language that beginning students (not only linguists and lexicographers) can understand. As Garrett (1988) has pointed out, the conceptual structure of the program provides the possibility of exploring in depth the learner's mental conception of L2 as well as evaluating the learner's use of software.

Interest in the potential for computer-assisted research on second language acquisition—dubbed CARSLA by Garrett *et al.* (1989)—is growing as researchers explore the possibilities of the new technology for providing empirical data on the learning process (see, for example, Leech and Candlin, 1986; Smith, 1987). This research uses the computer as a tool for gathering and analyzing data on the nature of the psycholinguistic processing involved when students use their developing interlanguage systems to interact in a CALL environment. Studies such as Jamieson and Chapelle (1987) convinced us we could use the computer itself to explore the strategies used by language learners. The purpose of our pilot study was to extend CARSLA into the area of writing in a foreign language by tracking the language learner engaged in a composing task. We wished to know what use, if any, could be made of tracking information by students, instructors, and SLA researchers.

THE PILOT STUDY

Ten volunteer subjects used *Système-D* software to work on from two to five composing tasks that were assigned by their French instructors during the spring 1989 semester. A tracking system was designed to maintain records of the student queries made during the composing tasks. Key presses were recorded by the computer as students went back and forth from the word processor to the reference data bases. This provided detailed data on the words and phrases asked for (both successfully and unsuccessfully), the query language of choice (either French or English), the query type (such as requests for lexical, functional, or morphological information), and the query path from source (such as the editor) to target (such as the dictionary). This information, when compared to the actual student composition, permitted us to study the real-time processing strategies used by our students.

It should be noted that the design of the study favored those who were already familiar with computers, and indeed most of the volunteers felt somewhat at ease with the equipment. (Only one student wished to be included in the study in order to learn word processing.) We found that the uninitiated were easily discouraged by technical difficulties, and it was not easy to distinguish between language problems and equipment problems. In a more controlled study it will be necessary to differentiate more clearly the effects of lack of linguistic knowledge versus lack of ability to access freely the available data. We opted to report only on data base searches and not on failure to interact with the program.

OBSERVATIONS

The pilot study demonstrated that one may readily observe how students get information while they are engaged in a composing task at the computer. When tracking information is compared to the finished composition, it is possible to reconstruct a great deal about the process the learner went through to arrive at the finished product. We found the data to be extremely useful for at least three areas of application: enhancing the data base of learner reference material, providing both student and instructor with a basis for error analysis, and formulating developmental questions for further research on second language acquisition.

Enhancing the Data Base

Let us first consider the record of *no-finds* that we collected. No-finds are words or phrases not found by the student during a search for information. After sorting these queries and discarding mistakes (such as typos and other misspellings, which the learner can easily correct) we were able to identify potential gaps in the data base. We emphasize the word *potential* here because we have found that not every student query is necessarily appropriate for inclusion in a pedagogical data base.

On the basis of these questions, we determined a number of candidates for additions to the data base. These included lexical items such as *graduate, laboratory, downtown, symbol,* and *relevant,* primarily because the items were entailed by the kinds of writing assignments made, and appropriate French equivalents were available, even though these words did not appear in the original basic vocabulary lists. On the other hand, there were no-finds that were not added to the data base, such as *half-truth* and *make-believe.* Straightforward lexical equivalents in French are lacking for these words, and we decided that it was consistent with the pedagogical objectives of elementary instruction for the student to find a way to paraphrase within the basic vocabulary.

On the other hand, requests for specific examples of general categories, even though a particular example might be of low lexical frequency, seemed legitimate for creative writing at the elementary level. Expansions of hypernyms such as *animals, flowers,* or *musical instruments* were made available in a supplementary data base. Of great interest were no-finds that revealed a lack of cultural understanding, such as *Ivy League* and *square miles.* This type of query emphasized the need for classroom instruction on the relationship between cultural differences and translation equivalents in a foreign language.

Some no-finds allowed us to spot areas where our glossing was defective. For example, we added the English word *degree* for the French word *diplôme,* which had been glossed only as *diploma*. We added the sense of *opportunity* to the word *chance* in order to distinguish the French word *occasion* from *chance*, which had been glossed as *chance, luck*. The result was that the basic list of some four thousand French words was linked to over five thousand English equivalents. (Note that the reverse ratio is true for most bilingual glossaries, in which the foreign language entries outnumber those given in the native language.) We adopted the strategy of establishing a core vocabulary of French entries, then adding glosses based on basic English word lists and student queries. The computer program easily searched indexed data base files for the appropriate associated glosses.

Enhanced explanations in the grammatical notes attached to dictionary items were typically drawn from the data base of student misunderstandings. It is relatively simple to compare finished compositions with their corresponding query logs and to draw conclusions about what went wrong. For example, a student attempted to translate *would* as a lexical item in its habitual past sense use in English (I would go when I was young). Since it was only glossed in the conditional sense (I would go if I had time), the student was led to use the tense in the wrong context. A note for the past sense of *would* has now been added to its conditional sense. In another instance (prior to the pilot study), the lack of information distinguishing the reflexive and nonreflexive uses of the verb *étonner* led to an ingenious if incorrect attempt to offer the verb with both reflexive and nonreflexive pronoun attached! We added clearer examples to the data base.

Another type of student difficulty revealed in the query logs was the attempt to find information at the "wrong address." The important pedagogical issue here is the frequent gap between what students call something and what teachers (and textbooks) call it. For example, learners tend to look up words or phrases such as *none* or *each other* rather than grammatical concepts such as "negation" or "reflexive verbs." Even when a dictionary example of usage is provided, beginning learners frequently do not infer the necessary grammatical adjustments. As a result, we created more direct links between lexical entries and pedagogical explanations of related grammatical, semantic, or pragmatic issues. Function words, in particular, were linked to relevant grammar discussions. Direct linking means that the student does not need to know the metalinguistic terminology under which the information is categorized, but may get access to that information by simply pressing the Note button. For example, students may go from *none* to appropriate French equivalents and associated grammatical explanations of negation, or from *each* to *each other* to a grammatical explanation of reflexive verbs.

The hypertext relationship between what one is writing and the multidimensional space of relevant linguistic information makes it important not to have to categorize information as either grammatical or lexical. The new technology appears to offer a proper medium for storing language data in such a way that information may be retrieved without losing its inherent relational structure. For example, we link hypernyms (such as *couleur*) to their exemplars (such as *rouge, bleu,* and so on). We link function words (such as *en*) to their grammatical contexts (such as *en France, en partant,* and so on) and then to word families (such as *countries*) or discussions of grammar (such as "present participle"). The interesting point is that the links lead to the context of meaning the student is attempting to express. The tracking data indicate that foreign language information is explored to the extent that it bears on the task or point of interest at hand.

Error Analysis

The pilot study led to several important pedagogical considerations for the teacher. Data base queries, as has already been mentioned, can reveal misconceptions about how speakers of the target language view the world. It is thus possible to link the effort of self-expression to a learning experience about the target culture, to reinforce the notion that to be bilingual is to be, in part at least, bicultural. There is no need to rehearse here the fact that the general educational benefit of foreign language study lies exactly in this area. How can the computer-aided language learning environment assist in addressing the proper balance between form and content, between skill and knowledge, between training and education?

We came to the conclusion that tracking data, properly used, can assist both instructor and student in seeing the interplay between skill getting and skill using. It is important, however, not to create an atmosphere of impersonal, high-tech "snooping" on what the students are doing in the lab. We recommend giving the students a printout of the tracking data along with a copy of what they have written. Self-expression and creativity imply ownership on the part of the writer. Any sense of invasion of privacy would effectively discourage use of the instructional medium.

The query log is useful for the student as a way of keeping track of questions about the expression of meaning in the foreign language that have not been resolved. The intricacies of various paths through reference material that result in dead ends are often lost by the time a student completes a written composition with a conventional dictionary and grammar book. A query record enables students to keep track of their questions and hypotheses about the language learning process at the moment they were most interested in the information. It serves as a diagnostic tool for understanding problems with the language in the course of later conferences with the instructor, and it keeps track of lexical items that most need review before exams.

The instructor may compare compositions with query logs to see how forms of expression were arrived at, and it is possible to assess student involvement with the composition task by noting the number and quality of queries as well as time on task. As for content, however, our observation during the study was that the technological environment did little to improve the quality of writing if instructors did not assign topics that demanded self-expression. The increase in productivity that was observed with those using word processors did not mean an increase in the quality of writing unless students were invested in what they wrote. The instructor must face essential pedagogical questions: why are students interested in expressing themselves in a foreign language? What are they interested in saying that motivates learning?

Another useful feature of tracking is a record of category errors in searches. If students persist in expecting lexical equivalents for English words, it may be very productive to use an example from a particular student's search to illustrate how the target language uses a morphological device for accomplishing what is done lexically in the native language. A surprising number of students did not explore information in other data bases until the instructor pointed out its existence.

Another kind of information that is revealed in the query log is the willingness of the student to engage in the trial-and-error nature of the language learning process, to participate in the vital creative construction techniques of paraphrase and analogical formation. Consider, for example, the following query path taken by a student who wished to find a French word for *messy* in the bilingual dictionary:

Query	English	French	Result
1	messy		no-find
2	diorder		no-find
3	disorder		no-find
4		desordre	no-find
5		deordre	no-find
6		disordre	no-find
7	mess		no-find

After pursuing this apparently dead-end query path, the student used the expression *en desordre* in her composition.

We note two striking features of this path, which inform the teacher about the student's linguistic knowledge and learning strategies. First, the different attempts at spelling provide insight into the student's hypotheses about the French spelling system and its relation to English cognates. Second, the attempts at paraphrase demonstrate that the student has learned not to expect a direct translation from English into French. Since paraphrasing, guessing, and taking chances are all considered to be productive language learning strategies (see Brown, 1987), this query path offers very positive information about the student's learning behavior.

By contrast, some students complained that they "could never find what they wanted," but their query logs did not show evidence of attempts to paraphrase. This suggested that such students would greatly benefit from instruction in learning strategy, in which they are encouraged to paraphrase, guess, take risks, and so forth (see Omaggio, 1986, for examples of learning strategy exercises). Query logs thus provide the teacher with a great deal more information than is otherwise available from the composition alone. They open up the possibility of fruitful discussions with the student, based on a comparison of the query log and the composition, and they also suggest certain helpful instructional practices.

A substantial problem in the assessment of language learning behavior, as first pointed out by Schachter (1974), is the identification of what has been called "avoidance behavior," namely, the tendency by the learner to avoid certain difficult expressions or structures by substituting similar expressions or structures, which are simpler in form. It is often difficult for the teacher to determine what structures their students are avoiding; one may simply feel that the composition is stylistically flat or uninteresting. Interestingly enough, query logs provide empirical evidence for determining avoidance behavior. By comparing the query log with the composition, it is possible to see what information the student seems to ignore or avoid using. For example, a third semester student query log and composition revealed a search for the word *only,* which was glossed as *ne . . . que* in French, an expression which requires morphosyntactic adjustments. Despite this computer response, the student chose a simpler one-word expression, *seulement,* listed as an alternative below the *ne . . . que* entry. The choice turned out to be satisfactory in the context used, but it remains for the teacher to find out whether the student got the right answer for the wrong reason!

Developmental Questions

Finally, let us now turn to some of the theoretical and pedagogical issues raised by the data. First of all, the relative ease with which it is possible to collect data and locate gaps in the data base raises the issue of what the appropriate size of a data base should be for first and second year students. To what extent should the data base be restricted from the point of view of the languages in contact? We entered about forty-four hundred French items by comparing a number of lexical lists, principally the *Français Fondamental* and glossaries from college-level texts.[2] Additions were made from the field testing as described above, and we included expansions of hypernyms in the vocabulary data bases.

The inclusion of data bases for word families raises questions of prototypicality; the best exemplars for English *vegetables* (for example) do not necessarily match with the best exemplars in French for the translation equivalent *légumes.* Lists of related words invariably reflect a cultural point of view. Consider, for example, the items associated with English *bathroom* that fail to match with the French *salle de bain.* Similar problems are associated with drawing up a functional list of phrases. Eventually one is led to consider encyclopedic information and hypermedia presentation devices. We were impressed, however, with how much can be done with relatively simple technology when it is used as a complement to traditional instruction.

From the point of view of the curriculum, there are important questions concerning the appropriate time for the introduction of writing, the nature of composition topics, and the instructional costs for teaching students how to use the foreign language as a means of expression. Tracking appears to offer a way for interested instructors to evaluate in some detail the impact of their innovations, offering a window on the process of language learning and use. The transitional behavior of the language learner in upgrading interlanguage hypotheses appears to be amenable to in-depth study in a CALL environment.

An analysis of the types of words, phrases, and other information searched for suggests a typology of queries that represent different levels of sophistication for student hypotheses about L2. The present discussion is a pretheoretical classification of the behaviors we could observe. (See Bland *et al.*, in press, for further analysis and discussion of query types. She notes that error categories do not capture the behavior of students across all tasks, but that variation in query type occurs for different topics. The proficiency of the learner, at least at the levels we observed, is best assessed by functional domain rather than globally.)

1. *Token query*: an expectation of correspondence at word level. Evidence: high ratio of English queries, inflected rather than base forms (for example, *saw, plants, smaller, would*).
   Phrase query: an expectation of correspondence at phrase level. Evidence: English queries, compound forms (for example, *square miles, each other*).

2. *Type query*: an expectation of correspondence with base forms. Evidence: English uninflected queries (for example, *say,* where context of composition indicated *said*).
   Category query: an expectation of structural correspondence. Evidence: metalinguistic reference queries (for example, "subjunctive," "pronouns").

3. *Circumlocution*: an expectation of abstract semantic equivalent. Evidence: linked English queries (for example, *opportunity* to *chance* to *occasion*).
   Relexicalization: an expectation of associated types or subentries in L2. Evidence: high ratio of searching in French (for example, paraphrasing, browsing under French entry).

These query types appear to correspond with different levels of sophistication on the part of the learner when one compares tracking data to finished compositions. As mentioned earlier, however, more research is needed to distinguish clearly familiarization with the technology from actual language learning. (One of our subjects, a novice at word processing, was afraid to leave the editor portion of the program to perform lexical searches for fear of losing what had been typed!) In general, the quality of writing improves as students are less tied to one-to-one lexical matching behavior. Students move away from naive queries based on lexical items in English to more productive queries using base forms, grammatical concepts, paraphrases, and attempts at relexicalization (that is, creating meaning from the French point of view).

Other evidence for relexicalization might be found in a comparison of the percent of English dictionary look-ups versus French dictionary look-ups. Although we did not have enough subjects in the pilot study to offer significant quantitative measures or correlations with instructor evaluations, we did note striking differences in some raw statistics. The eight students in our second semester course had a mean score of 80% for English as the preferred look-up language. One student used English for 100% of the queries; another used English for only 48%. The study suggests that more extensive longitudinal studies of this nature should reveal more precisely how learners upgrade their hypotheses about the foreign language, and gradually progress toward relexicalization in the target language. A correlation with writing proficiency would offer a valuable psychometric tool.

CONCLUSION

The purpose of this brief report has been to discuss the benefits that we have seen for instructors of tracking the language learner in a computer-aided language learning environment. These benefits include the ability to enhance the data base so as to accommodate learner characteristics, the ability to document insights into error analysis, and the ability to formulate pedagogical and theoretical questions about the language learning process and CALL. The use of tracking data in conjunction with student consultation offers the teacher a new tool for studying student learning. In addition to suggesting the value of a learning environment that uses the target language as a vehicle for self-expression, it provides a means for working at the strategic rather than purely tactical level to teach students how to learn.

We made several observations about technology and its potential impact on data base enhancement. Tracking of queries permits the data base manager to get empirical information on what students consider useful information. A simple data-entry system permits local control of lexical content for special-purpose courses, such as foreign language for business, health, literary criticism, and so on. Electronic data bases can be continuously upgraded, if desired, and this represents a significant improvement over the way corrections and additions are made available in printed form.

We made a number of qualitative observations that we offer for what they are worth. Rapid, on-line access to information is judged to be far superior to manual dictionary searches, and some students are much more productive in the computer-aided environment. Students who do not enjoy conversational classes like having an alternative modality for success in the foreign language classroom and readily express themselves in written mode. Students who are invested in the content of their compositions are more open to formal corrections and are willing to rewrite in order to polish what they have written.

Tracking the student use of the data base helped us get a picture of the best form of assistance for the person who is in the process of writing. The learner who is concentrating on content is not receptive to an extended discussion on form, as that would interrupt the creative flow. On the other hand, quality information is needed to varying degrees for learners at different levels of mastery. The technology offers an interesting solution by making it possible to create relational data bases, which can be explored to the depth needed for appropriate information, with links to varying types of information. For example, our student may believe that there is a French word for *would*. The query is naive, but it is still possible to create links to the French morphological approach to making equivalent meaning. The student may decide whether to pursue the matter through a data base of examples or through a discussion of tense usage in the reference grammar. The basic idea is to offer increasing detail on demand, respecting the learner's need to balance information getting with the demands of expression. Properly employed, such devices should create an active learning environment and enhance our ability to use the classroom for higher-level discussions of content and textual cohesion.

ENDNOTES

1. The research was carried out in the Department of Modern Languages and Linguistics at Cornell University with the assistance of Professor Geri Gay, Director, Interactive Media Center, and research assistant Susan Armington. Jon Meltzer, a programmer with Professor D. Solá's Technology Transfer Project, provided the data base tracking utility. This research was supported by a Sears-Roebuck minigrant for instructional inquiry, administered by David Taylor-Way of the Cornell Center for Instructional Support, and by funds from the Interactive Media Center and the College of Arts and Sciences, Cornell University. We are grateful to all those who supported our efforts.

2. We were guided by studies such as Mitterand (1963), who says (15): *Dans une liste de mots rangés par ordre décroissant de fréquence, les cent premiers mots recouvrent 60% du texte dépouillé, quel qu'il soit; les 1000 premiers mots, 85%; les 4000 premiers, 97, 5% . . .*

REFERENCES

Bland, S. K. 1987. "A Lexical Approach to K2." Paper presented at the Conference on Grammar Teaching and Learning, Georgia State University, December 1987.

Bland, S. K., J. Noblitt, G. Gay, and S. Armington. In press. "The Naive Lexical Hypothesis: Evidence from CALL." *Modern Language Journal,* December 1990.

Brown, H. D. 1987. *Principles of Language Learning and Teaching.* 2nd ed. Englewood Cliffs, N.J.: Prentice-Hall.

Byrd, R., N. Calzolari, M. Chodorow, J. Klavans, M. Neff, and O. Rizk. 1987. "Tools and Methods for Computational Lexicography." Manuscript. Hawthorne, N.Y.: IBM.

Evens, M., T. Markowitz, T. Ahlswede, and K. Rossi. 1987. "Digging in the Dictionary: Building a Relational Lexicon to Support Natural Language Processing Applications." *IDEAL* 2: 33–44.

Garrett, N. 1988. "Review of Système-D." *Foreign Language Annals* 21: 161–65.

Garrett, N., J. Noblitt, and F. Dominguez. 1989. "Computers in Foreign Language Teaching and Research: A New Humanism." *Computing Across the Curriculum: Academic Perspectives.* Ed. W. Graves. EDUCOM Strategies Series on Information Technology. McKinney, Tex.: Academic Computing Publications.

Gass, S., ed. 1987. "The Use and Acquisition of the Second Language Lexicon." Special Edition of *Studies in Second Language Acquisition* 9.2.

Jamieson, J., and C. Chapelle. 1987. "Working Styles on Computers as Evidence of Second Language Learning Strategies." *Language Learning* 37: 523–44.

Leech, G. N., and C. N. Candlin. 1986. *Computers in English Language Teaching and Research.* London: Longman.

Mitterand, H. 1963. *Les Mots Francais.* Paris: Presses Universitaires de France.

Noblitt, J. 1989. "Technology and Language Learning." *Academic Computing* 4.2.

———. 1990. "Computing and Creativity." *CALL: Papers and Report.* Eds. M.-L. Craven, R. Sinyor, and D. Paramskas. La Jolla, Ca.: Athelstan.

Noblitt, J., D. Solá, and W. Pet. 1986. "Bilingual Word Processing." Proceedings of the 1986 IBM Academic Information Systems University AEP Conference "Tools for Learning," San Diego, April 5–8, 1986. 36–44.

———. 1987. *Système-D: Writing Assistant for French.* Boston: Heinle & Heinle.

Omaggio, A. 1986. *Teaching Language in Context.* Boston: Heinle & Heinle.

Schachter, J. 1974. "An Error in Error Analysis." *Language Learning* 24: 205–14.

Smith, W. F. ed. 1987. *Modern Media in Foreign Language Education.* Lincolnwood, Ill.: National Textbook Company.

Section **IV**

Foreign Language Acquisition Research Outside the United States

Chapter 9

European Research on Second Language Acquisition[1]

Christiane von Stutterheim
University of Heidelberg

INTRODUCTION

The teaching of a foreign language must try to make optimal use of the human language learning capacity—that species-specific capacity which allows us to learn our mother tongue and to extend this knowledge, with varying success, to other languages. This capacity, which changes and deteriorates generally with age, is still not well explored. One way to understand its nature and function would be through a careful and systematic examination of how people acquire a second language in different settings, both inside and outside the classroom. Many factors must be taken into account in such an investigation, such as the age of the learners, their motivation, their exposure to the target language, the structure of the languages involved, the typological relation between the languages involved, to mention but a few, and it will still surely take a long time before the principles of language acquisition, and more specifically of second language acquisition, are clarified.

In the following we will characterize, in a nutshell, what has been done and is being done in Europe in the field of second language acquisition (SLA) research.[2]

Within the limitations of a survey article, it is impossible to do justice to all projects and researchers; therefore we will try rather to highlight some points that we feel are particularly characteristic for the European branch of the field. In doing so we will concentrate on research on *second language acquisition* in the sense just mentioned. This does not mean that there are no other important lines of research pursuing different goals and using a different methodology. In particular, considerable work has been carried out in the field of applied linguistics. The number of projects and studies conducted under a pedagogical perspective by far exceeds work in SLA research.

The main issues in applied linguistics have been the general problems of the "what," the "when," and the "how" of language teaching (see James, 1980; for a survey, Bausch et al., 1989). The central topics addressed in this field relate to

1. the question of what constitutes optimal progression in the different linguistic domains (syntax, lexicon, and so on) and their interrelation;
2. the role of contrastive analysis in foreign language teaching;
3. the determination of suitable target norms for foreign language learners;
4. the analysis of communication strategies and the problem of contextualization of the second language;
5. methodological issues, such as "free" versus "guided" teaching (see Piepho, 1974; Hüllen, 1980; Cherubim 1980; Knapp-Potthoff and Knapp, 1982; *Handbuch der Curriculumforschung*, 1983; Bausch et al., 1984; Bausch et al., 1986; Bausch et al., 1989, among many others).

An interesting and important development in this field resulted from the recent extensive labor migration into the central European countries. As a consequence of this migration, large groups of immigrant children entered what were traditionally monolingual schools. This situation and the immense problems related to it motivated research on topics of the following kind:

1. the role of sociopsychological factors in FLA, resulting in different concepts of intercultural education;
2. the interrelation between the acquisition of linguistic competence and communicative competence;
3. the particular influence of the first language (in connection with errors observed in spoken and written language) (Müller, 1974; Meyer-Ingwersen et al., 1977; Neumann and Reich, 1980; Neumann, 1989; Stölting, 1980; Fthenakis et al., 1985; Apeltauer, 1987).

All in all, European research in foreign language acquisition closely resembles the work done in this field in the United States and Canada. Turning now to the topic proper, we will start with a brief historical outline of the field of second language acquisition research.

DEVELOPMENT OF SECOND LANGUAGE ACQUISITION RESEARCH

Until about fifteen years ago, there was little systematic research of the SLA process. The field was characterized by a number of mainly small studies of specific teaching and learning problems, most of them based either on classical contrastive analysis following Lado's work (see Raabe, 1976; Nickel, 1972a; the volumes edited by Fisiak, such as Fisiak, 1984) or on the analysis of learners' errors (see Nickel, 1972b; Kielhöfer, 1975; Kohn, 1980; Cherubim, 1980). This work was surely valuable and helpful for teaching. But there was no attempt to study and to characterize the acquisition process and its underlying principles as a topic in its own right. This situation changed in the early 1970s when several European researchers, first in Germany, then also in other countries (notably France and Holland), began larger research projects on how a second language is acquired in everyday communication, that is, without explicit teaching.

The most important of these are discussed below.

The Kiel Group

The key issue of this project, which was initiated by H. Wode, was the universality of the acquisition process across all types of acquisition and all languages. Empirical work concentrated on spontaneous SLA by children at different ages, with English and German as target languages. Data were collected longitudinally. Both the method and key issues were strongly inspired by work in first language acquisition research. In addition to studies in the area of phonology, the acquisition of particular morphemes was investigated in depth. The analyses covered negation, verb inflection, and question formation (Felix, 1978; Felix, 1980; Wode, 1981).

Comparing the results with patterns found in first language acquisition, Wode concluded that both types of acquisition processes can be explained by the same set of general developmental principles. He therefore assumed the two processes to be alike in that both groups of learners create their learner language system on the basis of the same cognitive strategies (for a discussion, see Felix, 1982; Klein, 1986).

The Heidelberger Projekt
Pidgindeutsch (HPD)

This project, which was initiated by W. Klein in 1973, studied the acquisition of German by adult Italian and Spanish immigrant workers who had acquired German without any language instruction. The data, which were collected cross-sectionally, were provided by forty-eight subjects representing different levels of linguistic competence. The focus of the analysis lay on the development of syntax. In order to describe the different syntactic systems of the learner languages without recourse to the target language norm, a variety grammar was developed using probabilistic weightings, which gave an adequate account of system-internal variation. The analyses led to detailed descriptions of the development of syntactic constituents (expansions of the different phrases) and the development of the rules relating to the order of syntactic constituents in the clause (focusing on verbal elements in main and subordinate clauses) (HPD, 1975; Klein and Dittmar, 1979).

One of the main goals of the HPD was to relate the results of the linguistic analysis to external sociopsychological factors; these were factors such as contact with Germans at work and in leisure time, duration of stay, and the external biological factors, such as age and sex. Although tendencies in the correlations were found, it turned out that a much finer descriptive instrument would be needed in order to take account of the individual clusters of external factors (see "Sociopsychological Factors in SLA," below).

The ZISA Project (Zweitspracherwerb italienischer [portugiesischer] und spanischer Arbeiter)

Similar to the HPD, data were collected from Italian, Spanish, and Portuguese workers (forty-five informants in a cross-sectional study, later supplemented by twelve longitudinal recordings). The project, initiated by J. Meisel, had two major aims: it set out first to describe the acquisition process in terms of developmental stages; and second, to relate the observed regularities to external factors. As with the HPD, the ZISA project focused on syntactic development, but used a different descriptive instrument. The syntactic systems of the learner languages were described on the basis of phrase structure rules in combination with a transformational component. Particular rules were identified in the analysis as indicative of the respective developmental steps (for a detailed description, see Clahsen, Meisel, and Pienemann, 1983).

The linguistic results obtained were then correlated with sociopsychological factors. The major finding was that maximal "integrative orientation" and maximal "segregative orientation" did not correspond to maximal versus minimal learning success, respectively. Since the instrument used for measuring these sociopsychological variables stood on a weak methodological footing, the conclusions were treated as an initial step only (see "Sociopsychological Factors in SLA," below).

The GRAL Group

In 1976, a number of French researchers in Paris and in Aix-en-Provence began to coordinate their work on second language acquisition under the name GRAL— "groupe de recherches sur l'acquisition des langues." The group's composition as well as the topics studied changed over the years; however, the following issues were of persistent concern:

1. the acquisition of specific structural properties of French, notably the word-order properties of the spoken language and the expression of temporal and spatial categories;
2. the development of metalinguistic awareness, as induced by confrontation with a different culture and a different language.

There was also a permanent interest in the application of SLA findings to the classroom (Giacomi and Véronique 1985).

Research in the Netherlands

The increase in non-native children in Dutch schools posed major problems for the educational system. This situation provided the practical impetus for a number of studies in the field of SLA. Most of these studies were concerned with the acquisition of a second language by immigrant children. As in the other projects reported above, the focus was placed on syntactic and morphological development in the learner language on one hand, and on the influence of social and psychological factors on the other hand (Appel, 1984; Lalleman, 1986).

This brief survey of the various projects across Europe indicates the increasing interest in SLA *in social context*. This was due to increasing labor migration within Europe. The central European countries were faced with the problems associated with large numbers of adolescent and adult foreign workers. These workers normally did not know the language, they received virtually no language instruction, and they had to learn the language, if they learned it at all, by everyday social contacts with the host—and often hostile—environment. These circumstances created a situation where the success and failure of the language learning process at an advanced age could be studied under conditions in which no particular teaching method was involved.

Research in the 1980s

The 1980s are characterized by three major developments. First, five research teams from five European countries began a large-scale, cross-linguistic longitudinal study of adult foreign workers in their respective countries. This project was funded by the European Science Foundation in Strasbourg and coordinated at the Max-Planck-Institute for Psycholinguistics in Nijmegen, Holland. It is about to be completed. Since it is the largest project on SLA in Europe and representative of one important branch of SLA research, we will focus on it below. There are also a number of projects, dealing with questions similar to the ESF project, such as Dittmar's project in Berlin (Dittmar and Terborg, 1988), Ramat's in Pavia (Ramat, 1988), and my own work (von Stutterheim, 1986).

Secondly, there are an increasing number of studies on several key issues of SLA such as transfer, communication strategies, and so on. There is no real common denominator in this work, although there was an overall tendency to shift the focus from product to processes (for general discussions, see Ellis, 1985, and Klein, 1986).

And third, there are a small number of studies inspired by recent work in theoretical linguistics, in particular Chomsky's notions of universal grammar (UG) and parameter setting. Studies carried out within this framework focus on the development of syntax with a special emphasis on those syntactic areas seen to be the touchstone for UG principles (for example, negation, word order in relation to the development of morphological marking). The actual positions put forward by the followers of this approach are divergent. Basically the following claims are found:

1. Principles of UG determine SLA in the same way as first language acquisition.
2. Only a subset of the UG principles can still be at work in SLA.
3. Principles of UG are not accessible for the second language learner (Clahsen and Muysken, 1986, 1989; Clahsen 1989; Jordens, 1987).

Since these studies cannot be seen as characteristic of the field in Europe but rather as an extension of the work done on this topic in the United States, we will not go into further detail here.

Let us conclude this bird's eye view on the European scene by mentioning five features, which we take to be typical of the work carried out there:

1. Research focuses on second language acquisition through everyday contacts with the social environment.
2. Research is generally based on very comprehensive data bases where ecological validity is felt to be particularly important: as much as possible, attempts are made to obtain recordings of authentic interaction between learners and native speakers, rather than data from laboratory experiments.
3. The perspective taken is that of the learner: how does the learner, with her given learning capacity, her particular motives and her available knowledge, in particular her L1 knowledge, process the input offered to her by the social environment? How does the learner make use of the acquired linguistic knowledge?
4. The dominant methodological perspective is that of the "interlanguage." It is assumed that the language of the learner at any point is systematically guided by certain principles, as is the transition from one variety to the next in the course of development.
5. Many projects have a strong focus on the "cognitive or conceptual component," that is, rather than looking at how certain forms, such as inflectional morphology or word order, appear, researchers analyze how certain concepts, for example, time, space, possession, modality, are expressed over time.

So far we have broadly sketched that course of development in the field which resulted in what one could regard as a European perspective, if—given the heterogeneous picture of the field—it makes sense at all to talk about a European perspective. We will now come to a more detailed description of a number of selected studies.

SELECTED STUDIES

In struggling to find some way between a comprehensive but inevitably superficial description of the whole field, and a highly selective but more thorough presentation of only a few studies, we have decided in favor of a compromise. First we will give a rather detailed description of a group of closely interrelated studies and then we will briefly summarize further studies on special topics.

Concept-Oriented Studies

General Questions The studies we will concentrate on below have taken a functional or concept-oriented view of SLA. They approach the form-function relation in language from the side of the function (Pfaff, 1987). The assumption is that an L2 system can more adequately be described if the *content* to be expressed is taken as the starting point of the analysis. Learners do not acquire lexical fields and syntactic paradigms in their own right; learners acquire instead the means for referring to people, space, time, events, and so forth. In the case of the adult L2 learner, most of these conceptual categories do not have to be learned. What have to be learned are the specific ways and the specific means for expressing them.

We assume that the way in which the learner attempts to enrich her repertoire, as well as the use made of the linguistic means available at a given time, depends, partly at least, on the conceptual categories that the learner seeks to encode. Hence we may gain some insight into the "logic" of the acquisition process, and into the organization of learner languages, by looking at the way in which specific concepts such as temporality, and modality are expressed at various stages of the acquisition process.

Two aspects of language learning can thus be analyzed within one frame: the *linguistic system* that the learner has at her disposal at a given time, and the *use* of this system for meeting communicative demands. Empirically, we cannot study linguistic systems without getting involved with language use. And the learner, too, acquires the linguistic system in the context of language use.

One of the goals of studies like the ESF project was to gain insight into principles underlying the interrelation between functional demands and the development of the linguistic system. This goal was pursued by looking at how specific conceptual categories such as time, space, and modality are expressed; the following questions in particular guided the analyses.

1. What devices does the learner have at her disposal for representing categories of a conceptual domain, such as time, and how do they develop? What are the major factors determining the course of acquisition, and where, when, and how does the first language feature in the process?

   The concept-oriented approach allows for the integrated analysis of different linguistic systems (grammar, lexicon, pragmatic devices); development can therefore be traced in a way that comes closer to what is "really happening," as compared to analyses focusing on only one structural area, such as grammatical tense, for example (von Stutterheim and Klein, 1987).

2. A second group of questions is related to principles of language use. How does a learner express a given concept in discourse, and how do different expressive devices interact at subsequent levels of language competence? In what contexts are particular forms used? Do particular discourse types with their inherent structural properties constitute a determining factor for regularities of language use, and thereby trigger the acquisition of particular forms? One would, for example, expect modal expressions to play a more important role in argumentation than in descriptions, time reference to be more important in narratives than in argumentation, and so forth.

Let us now turn to some specific studies.

Setting of the Studies As mentioned above, all projects paid special attention to the ecological validity of the material analyzed. Therefore, all studies are based on extensive empirical data, where elicitation was carefully planned. We will briefly outline the setting of the ESF project since this group used the most elaborate techniques (Perdue, 1984, and the *ESF Final Report, Vol. I–VI,* 1988). The study is cross-linguistic, with ten different source-language/target-language pairs (SL/TL pairs); data collection was longitudinal and included regular monthly interviews with subjects (eight per language pair), as well as participants' observation of their social environment. The longitudinal data were completed by cross-sectional studies of control groups of second language learners, and groups of native speakers exposed to similar discourse situations.

Data collection was organized in three nine-month cycles. This meant that similar activities relating to specific research topics were initiated by all the SL/TL pairs at roughly the same time and these topics and activities were repeated twice, in roughly the same order, in two subsequent cycles.

The elicitation techniques chosen resulted in a combination of controlled and uncontrolled data. Spontaneous speech was elicited in the context of different communicative tasks (narratives, descriptions, instructions). Experiments were carried out in which the content to be verbalized was provided by some external source (film, role-play).

The transcribed and segmented tape recordings formed the basis for detailed case studies.

A Few Results In our discussion we will concentrate on the research area of temporality. Results are taken from studies by Klein (1983, 1986), von Stutterheim (1986), and the ESF group (in particular, Bhardwaj, Dietrich, and Noyau, 1988).

The goal of the studies on temporal reference in learner languages is to analyze the temporal structure of pieces of discourse and take this as the basis for the description of the linguistic means of the respective learner language at different levels of language competence. The result will give insights into the functioning of the devices on one hand, and the course of acquisition on the other. It was said above that the perspective taken in these analyses attempted to follow that of the learner. We will briefly illustrate this.

Put yourself in the situation of a learner who has a very poor command of a language, but who nevertheless wants to relate something that happened. You will find you have a limited repertoire of elementary words, no inflected forms, hence no way of marking tense and aspect. For the expression of temporal concepts you will have no more than a few adverbials. What you will probably do is locate the overall event in time, for example, by a date, and then present the events in chronological order without having to refer to temporal concepts again. The temporal structure of the narrative will probably be understood by the listener.

The result will certainly be a rather poor story in that there is little freedom in deviating from the event-line. Still, even with a very small linguistic repertoire a lot can be achieved by making use of contextual implications and pragmatic principles such as the "principle of chronological order," for example. The acquisition of aspectual marking would greatly extend your expressive means, however. You would, for instance, be able to introduce background material of different kinds. This is indeed the order in which development proceeds. In order to illustrate this, let us look at two examples of early learner language discourse. They represent the level at which the temporal structure of a piece of text is to a large extent conveyed implicitly. The hearer has to infer temporal relations from the inherent semantic properties of the reported events, from the order in which they are presented, and from world knowledge.

1. 1.1. ich heiraten
   I marry
   1.2. komm Deutschland arbeiten
   come Germany (to) work

In this example we conclude from the temporal semantics of the verb *to marry,* which has an inherent temporal boundary, that the event in 1.2. follows the event reported in 1.1.

2. 2.1. viel arbeiten ich bin jetzt
   much work I am now
   2.2. nicht mehr deutsch lernen
   not more German learn
   2.3. alles vergessen
   everything forget

In this case, we understand the three facts as contemporaneous because both 2.1. and 2.2. refer to temporally unbounded states. Simultaneity, however, is not explicitly marked but will be inferred from the semantics of the entire set of utterances (for example, verb + indefinite quantifier in object position, "to work much").

Such a system, effective as it may be, constrains the speaker considerably. Therefore, the next step, the acquisition of aspectual marking, can be seen as motivated by the need to gain more freedom in constructing complex temporal structures. Aspectual marking enables the speaker to integrate events and suspend their inherent aspectual properties (for example, *to last* [unbounded] versus [*has*] *lasted* [bounded]; *to leave* [bounded] versus *leaving* [unbounded]). Thus, every acquisition step leads to the extension of communicative competence in particular areas, and changes the balance between the different expressive devices. The more lexical and grammatical devices the learner has at her disposal, the less she has to rely on context, that is, on pragmatic devices and inferencing.

We will now have a closer look at the acquisitional sequences of the lexical and grammatical means for reference to time.

The acquisition sequences found for temporal expressions show similar patterns across subjects for the early phases. First, a system of adverbial expressions is acquired, the development of which follows the internal logic of the conceptual categories involved.[3] Expressions for basic temporal concepts are picked up first (*now, then, always* [for durative aspect], *finish/over* [for perfective aspect], date adverbials). The learner languages might differ as to the particular target language items chosen for the expression of these basic concepts, but the functions covered by the devices are the same. They enable the speaker to cover the basic functions of locating and relating (in one direction) events in time.

The expansion of the adverbial system can be regarded as a differentiation process of the basic concepts. For temporal location it always starts in the domain of pastness and then moves on to the domain of the future. That is, different degrees of pastness will be expressed earlier than different degrees of future. In the course of this differentiation process, categories of the source language come into play. Conceptually more complex temporal expressions (such as *already, yet*) exhibit language specific clusters, which might be subject to processes of interference.

For marking temporal relations, expressive devices for referring to the relation "following-in-time" are acquired first (for example, *then, after*); then, and often much later, lexical devices are acquired for the expression of the "before" relation. Explicit reference to simultaneity comes comparatively late, if at all. So far, this sequence has been observed without exception for all learners of all the languages studied.[4]

The first step in the acquisition of *grammatical* devices for expressing temporal concepts, that is, verbal tense/aspect-marking, can be said to be similar across learners with different source languages. The first marked verb forms, contrasting with the unmarked infinitive or stem, have aspectual meaning. This meaning, which for some languages does not correspond to the target language norm, can be derived from the use of these forms in discourse. The marked forms do not fulfill a locating function (this can and often has to be done more precisely by adverbial expressions); rather, they express a relative value, "perfective versus imperfective," thus indicating whether an event has to be seen as temporally bounded or unbounded (see below for an example).

Means for expressing both sides of the opposition can be found in learner languages. Most of the learners pick up forms for marking the perfective aspect (some kind of past participle).

> Regardless of the tense/aspect properties of the languages involved, the first clear morphological marking in this domain concerns the existence or non-existence of a right boundary of the matter time. (ESF, *Final Report VI*, 1988, 508).

Only a few learners "choose" means for expressing the imperfective first (for example, by using auxiliary + infinitive/stem). The two variants are both suited for establishing temporal relations between events. They merely differ as to which side of the opposition is represented by a marked form.

It is interesting to trace how morphological rules are actually acquired in an unguided learning process. In the case of the marking of a right boundary (some kind of perfective marker), the following steps have been found:

1. First, past participles occur as "rote forms" of verbs; these have an inherent perfective meaning (e.g., *gefunden/found*). The learner has not yet recognized the morphological structure.
2. Next, a formal opposition between the participle and an unmarked form appears. The learner acquires a rule with respect to a limited number of verbs.
3. The next step is the extension of the rule to all verbs. At this level, however, the perfective category is still selectively marked in discourse.
4. A further step is needed to reach the target language rule, the obligatory marking of temporal categories on the verb. This might imply a change or extension of the semantics of that particular form, for example, the move from an aspect system to a tense system[5] (see von Stutterheim 1986).

The basic aspectual system, which seems to be the same for all the specific target and source languages involved, is then extended language specifically. In the languages studied, the first tense forms used refer to the conceptual opposition past-nonpast; then differentiation within the category "past" occurs, and much later—in many cases never—a form for reference to future will be acquired. With regard to the sequence in which linguistic forms for these functions are acquired (for example, analytic versus synthetic; within the synthetic paradigms, infinite forms of the main verb versus auxiliaries + infinite verb forms), two groups of factors seem to be most influential. The first comprises such notions as saliency of the TL forms in the input, their frequency, the consistency of the paradigms, and their phonological properties. But second, it could also be shown that "the typological features of the respective (source) languages which determine the distribution of grammaticized semantic information" (ESF, *Final Report VI,* 1988, 517–18) also affect the acquisitional process.[6]

To illustrate the importance of typological features, we might consider conjunctions. Conjunctions as a syntactic category are quite complex in that they involve particular syntactic constraints for the respective syntactic construction. For the acquisition of conjunctions, the source language seems to play an important role. If the two languages, SL and TL, exhibit a similar pattern, like *quand/cuando* in French and Spanish, then this construction will be acquired fairly early. If, however, SL and TL show a maximal contrast in this domain, like German and Turkish (which does not have temporal conjunctions), a Turkish learner of German will acquire temporal conjunctions very late.

Looking at transfer phenomena, one has to bear in mind that transfer can become useful only where principles and means used in the source language are seen to be compatible with the general principles holding in the learner language. Given the fact that early learner language systems are characterized by pragmatic rather than by syntactic rules, transfer may increase when learner languages develop toward the target language norm, and there are more grounds for the recognition or assumption of source language/learner language/target language compatability (for a detailed analysis of transfer phenomena in the domain of word order, see Carroll, in press). However, cross-linguistic analysis in the ESF project has shown that transfer can become important, even at a very early level, but then it will affect the selection of a particular formal device for representing a given category.

Let us sum up the main results. The acquisition of expressive devices in one particular conceptual domain (for example, time, space) is partly determined by the internal notional structure of this domain. Another determining factor is given by the particular discourse function covered by the respective expressive devices. The acquisition of a syntactic rule does not take place in one step. The stepwise integration of such a rule into the learner language will be determined by specific semantic properties, pragmatic needs, and also formal properties of the devices in question. Transfer does not occur at an early level of the acquisitional process; later it can constitute one component in the construction process of the learner language system.

Some Further Research Domains

Transfer Transfer analyses, as they are carried out today, differ considerably from the traditional transfer or error analysis in the behavioristic tradition. "The conceptualization of transfer within the framework of creative learning and acquisition" (Kohn, 1986, 21) has led to a new perspective on this phenomenon. Here transfer is no longer seen from the point of view of certain L1-related structural properties of the learner language, but rather as a process that operates at two different levels: at the level of knowledge or competence and at the level of production or performance (Sharwood Smith, 1986). Accordingly, the goal of the research was not merely to describe phenomena due to transfer in the second language. The aim was rather to uncover the psycholinguistic processes that underlie transfer and the patterns behind the productivity of these processes, given that transfer seems to show up unsystematically across different linguistic domains and across aquisitional stages.

In recent years numerous studies have been carried out to investigate cross-linguistic influence in different domains of language competence, ranging from phonology to discourse phenomena (see Dechert and Raupach, 1980, 1989; Kellerman and Sharwood Smith, 1986; Kellerman, 1987; Ringbom, 1987). In contrast to the research discussed above, most transfer studies are based on experimental data, a methodological framework, which is—as Kellerman argues (1986, 35)—"indispensable if certain research questions are even to be formulated, let alone answered."

Within this perspective the processes of transfer are treated as a subtype of the many psycholinguistic processes that, in their entirety, constitute the whole system of language comprehension and production. Therefore, the studies of transfer should give us particular insights into language processing mechanisms in general. Research on cross-linguistic influence is therefore taken to be relevant for general linguistic theories and vice versa. For example, the theory of markedness, models of prototypicality, government and binding theory, (see Kellerman and Sharwood Smith, 1986).

Communication and Interaction In SLA   Although most of the studies in SLA research focus on the learner and different aspects of the functioning of her linguistic system, there are also studies that take the learner as a speaker/hearer who has to fulfill a given communicative task. Again we find a faceted picture of different aspects of L2 communication (for example, Dietrich, 1982; Long, 1982; Rath, 1983; Auer, 1983; Auer and di Luzio, 1984; Kutsch and Desgranges, 1985). One line of research developed around the notion of communication strategy. Taking empirical studies as their base, different taxonomies of communication strategies have been developed for the description of the phenomena found. They include—sometimes under different labels—strategies such as avoidance, reduction, circumlocution, transfer, and word coinage.

Faerch and Kasper (1983, 1984) have suggested a taxonomy which they characterize as based on a "psycholinguistic definition," (see Faerch and Kasper, 1984). They distinguish two basic strategies, rooted in different types of behavior.

> Avoidance behaviour manifests itself in *reduction stragegies,* whereas achievement behaviour underlies *achievement strategies* (Faerch and Kasper, 1984, 48).

These two groups are then further subclassified into a number of strategies, such as word coinage, code-switching, substitution for achievement strategies, and formal and functional reduction for reduction strategies.

Faerch and Kasper contrast their taxonomy with what they call "interactional definitions" of communication strategies. They argue that the latter definition cannot account for "strategic behaviour in other types of communication (e.g., in writing) and the existence of covert strategies" (1984, 61).

The problem related to this kind of work lies in the many *ad hoc* solutions necessary in order to account for the large variety of empirical phenomena.

Kellerman (1989), in a critique of the existing taxonomies, calls for a change of levels from the surface to the underlying psychological processes. On the basis of experimental work, he suggests tracing all the different strategies back to two basic compensatory strategies: the conceptual strategy and the core strategy. He also claims that these strategies are not restricted in application to the second language learner, but belong to the general linguistic competence of any speaker (see also Faerch and Kasper, 1984).

This assumption has important implications for language teaching. Whereas other studies have suggested teaching communication strategies (for example, Willem 1987), it would follow that the teacher could instead exploit this ready-made resource in second language acquisition. Progress in this controversy will demand more carefully controlled empirical work and cooperation at a theoretical level across the traditionally separated fields of L1, L2 acquisition and "normal" language production.

Sociopsychological Factors in SLA The growing interest in studying the role of sociopsychological factors was triggered by the "new group of second language learners," the immigrant workers and their families (see "Development of Second Language Acquisition Research," above). Concepts such as psychological, social, and cultural distance, or integrative versus instrumental motivation—as developed in Gardner and Lambert (1972) or in Schumann's pidginization theory (1978)—became relevant for an adequate analysis of the learning conditions of this particular group of learners (for a discussion of these factors, see Klein 1986, 35ff).

The weakness of the early studies on this topic was caused by the fact that the instrument for measuring these social and psychological factors was simply too global. As a result, correlations were found between, for example, the amount of contact, the degree of integrative motivation, and language proficiency. But these correlations gave at best, an overall picture of which factors are relevant. They cannot account for the (non-)achievement of the individual learner, which is always determined by a particular constellation of sociopsychological factors. As a consequence, researchers moved into a more detailed analysis of small groups of subjects. Let us look at two examples.

Lalleman (1986) could show that for her group (Turkish children in Holland) there was a "weak relationship . . . between language proficiency [LP] and social distance [SD] and between proficiency and cultural distance [CD] in the following sense: the higher the LP the smaller the SD/CD. It turned out that there was no relationship between language proficiency and psychological distance" (185). She argues that negative attitudes do not follow from social and cultural distance. Social and cultural distance turn out to be more relevant for the SLA process because they determine to some extent the degree of contact, that is, the amount of exposure to the target language.

In a recent study on the acquisition of German by Greek children, Kuhs (1989) carried out a detailed analysis of the correlation between the level of language proficiency and several sociopsychological factors (amount and quality of contact with the target language, attitude toward the target and source language, balance between the two attitudes, linguistic self-confidence in the target language). It turned out that there was no clear correlation between these factors and the variable "language proficiency." Kuhs then looked at different domains of linguistic competence (lexicon, syntax, orthography) and correlated them separately with the sociopsychological factors. This analysis yielded much clearer tendencies with respect to some of the correlation pairs.

All the studies mentioned seem to point in the same direction. Global correlations are of little help; they may even be misleading. In order to carry out reliable work in this field, the investigation has to be very fine-grained. Only then can the respective weight of the different factors be teased out—given the fact that any one learner will exhibit a different cluster of potentially relevent factors.

CONCLUSION

As we have seen, the picture of second language acquisition research in Europe is by no means uniform. If anything can be called a predominant perspective, it is the functional view described in the section above on Concept-Oriented Studies. These studies have yielded a number of important insights into the acquisition process.

Might the foreign language teacher benefit from studying these results? Is the situation really as bad as one has to conclude from Klein's statement?

> Anyone who claims that second language instruction must be arranged in a particular way on the evidence available from linguistics or neurophysiology or any other science, displays a measure of naivity if not presumption (1986, 55).

Looking at the course of development in natural language acquisition in one area, as we have done for temporality, everybody will agree that the "learner's way" cannot provide a model for language teaching. Taking the learner's sequence as a model for progression would mean that one would have to teach "wrong language" at some point, and this is certainly not reasonable.

A scientifically founded model for language teaching, making claims about the "what," "when," and "how" of the teaching process, cannot be derived from studies on natural L2 acquisition—at the moment. In the long run, however, we will gain a better understanding of the process of language acquisition, and consequently better ways of intervening in these processes.

ENDNOTES

1. I would like to thank Mary Carroll, Wolfgang Klein, and Katrin Lindner for their helpful comments on earlier versions of the paper.

2. Unfortunately there is no consistent terminology in this field. As in several other studies, I will distinguish between SLA and foreign language acquisi-

tion or learning (FLA). The first term is used for referring to the type of unguided language acquisition that usually implies that the learner is acquiring the language within a community speaking this language; FLA, on the other hand, is used in relation to guided language acquisition where the learner does not have contact with the second language outside the classroom. Of course there are cases in which both types of acquisition co-occur, for example, in the case of the immigrant children (see *Handbuch Fremdsprachenunterricht,* 1989).

3. See Becker, Carroll, Kelly (eds.), 1989, who found that the acquisition of devices for reference to spatial concepts also follows a pattern starting with "basic" conceptual categories with elaboration following a systematic way.

4. This parallels the results obtained in studies on temporality in first language acquisition (for example, Flores-d'Arcais, 1979). Although one might be tempted by the striking similarities between L1 and L2 acquisitional patterns, one should not jump to conclusions regarding the underlying processes. One argument, which runs counter to the assumption of identical processes in L1 and L2 acquisition, is that the parallelisms observed in the data hold only for very early phases.

5. For a discussion of the complicated semantic structure of the English and German present perfect, see Klein (1989).

6. For a detailed analysis of the intricate interplay of these two, sometimes counteracting factors, see ESF, *Final Report,* p. 510ff.

REFERENCES ————————————————————————

Apeltauer, E. 1987. *Gesteuerter Zweitspracherwerb: Voraussetzungen und Konsequenzen für den Unterricht.* Munich: Hueber.

Appel, R. 1984. *Immigrant Children Learning Dutch: Sociolinguistic and Psycholinguistic Aspects of Second-Language Acquisition.* Diss. Dordrecht: Foris.

Auer, J. C. P. 1983. *Zweisprachige Konversationen: Code-Switching und Transfer bei italienischen Migrantenkindern in Konstanz.* Arbeiten des Sonderforschungsbereiches 99. Universität Konstanz.

Auer, P., and A. di Luzio, eds. 1984. *Interpretive Sociolinguistics: Migrants-Children-Migrant Children.* Tübingen: Gunter Narr.

Bausch, K. R., H. Christ, W. Hüllen, and H. J. Krumm, eds. 1984. *Empirie und Fremdsprachenunterricht. Arbeitspapiere der 4. Frühjahrskonferenz zur Erforschung des Fremdsprachenunterrichts.* Tübingen: Gunter Narr.

————. 1989. *Handbuch Fremdsprachenunterricht.* Tübingen: Francke.

Bausch, K. R., and F. G. Königs, eds. 1986. *Sprachlehrforschung in der Diskussion. Methodologische Überlegungen zur Erforschung des Fremdsprachenunterrichts.* Tübingen: Gunter Narr.

Becker, A., M. Carroll, and A. Kelly, eds. 1989. *Reference to Space.* Final Volume, ESF-Report. Strasbourg: Nijmegen.

Bhardwaj, M., R. Dietrich, and C. Noyau, eds. 1988. *Temporality.* Final Report, ESF-Projekt. Strasbourg: Nijmegen.

Carroll, M. In press. "Word Order in Instructions in Learner Languages of English and German." To appear in *Linguistics,* special vol.

Cherubim, D., ed. 1980. *Fehlerlinguistik: Beiträge zum Problem der sprachlichen Abweichung.* Tübingen: Niemeyer.

Clahsen, H. 1989. "The Comparative Study of First and Second Language Development." Unpublished paper. Universität Düsseldorf.

Clahsen, H., J. M. Meisel, and M. Pienemann. 1983. *Deutsch als Zweitsprache: Der Spracherwerb ausländischer Arbeiter.* Tübingen: Gunter Narr.

Clahsen, H., and P. Muysken. 1986. "The Accessibility of Universal Grammar to Adult and Child Learners: A Study of the Acquisition of German Word Order." *Second Language Research* 2: 93–119.

———. To appear. "The UG Paradox in L2 Acquisition." *Second Language Research.*

Dechert, H. W., and M. Raupach, eds. 1980. *Towards a Cross-Linguistic Assessment of Speech Production.* Frankfurt/M.: Lang.

———. 1989. *Transfer in Language Production.* Norwood, N.J.: Ablex.

Dietrich. R. 1982. "Selbstkorrekturen: Fallstudien zum mündlichen Gebrauch des Deutschen als Fremdsprache durch Erwachsene." *Zweitsprachenerwerb.* Eds. W. Klein and J. Weissenborn. Göttingen: Vandenhoeck und Ruprecht. 120–49.

Dittmar, N., and H. Terborg. 1988. *Modality and Second Language Learning: A Challenge for Linguistic Theory.* Ms., University of Berlin.

Ellis, R. 1985. *Understanding Second Language Acquisition.* Oxford: Oxford UP.

European Science Foundation Project. 1988. *Final Report I–VI.* Strasbourg: Nijmegen.

Faerch, C., and G. Kasper, eds. 1983. *Strategies in Interlanguage Communication.* London: Longman.

Faerch, C., and G. Kasper. 1984. "Two Ways of Defining Communication Strategies." *Language Learning* 34.1: 45–63.

Felix, S. W. 1978. *Linguistische Untersuchungen zum natürlichen Zweitsprachenerwerb.* Munich: Fink.

Felix, S. W., ed. 1980. *Second Language Development: Trends and Issues.* Tübingen: Gunter Narr.

Felix, S. W. 1982. *Psycholinguistische Aspekte des Zweitspracherwerbs.* Tübingen: Gunter Narr.

Fisiak, J., ed. 1984. *Contrastive Linguistics: Prospects and Problems.* Berlin: Mouton Publishers.

Flores-d'Arcais, G. B., and J. Joustra. 1979. "The Expression of Temporal Order in Descriptive Language." *The Italian Journal of Psychology* 6.3: 203–23.

Fthenakis, W. E., A. Sonner, R. Thrul, and W. Walbiner, eds. 1985. *Bilingual-Bikulturelle Entwicklung des Kindes: Ein Handbuch für Psychologen, Padagogen und Linguisten.* Munich: Hueber.

Gardner, R. C., and W. E. Lambert. 1972. *Attitudes and Motivation in Second-Language Learning.* Rowley, Mass.: Newbury House.

Giacomi, A., and D. Véronique, eds. 1985. *Acquisition d'une Langue Etrangère: Perspectives et Recherches.* Tome 1/2. Actes du 5e Colloque International, Aix-en-Provence 1985. Université de Provence.

Hameyer, U., K. Frey, and H. Haft, eds. 1983. *Handbuch der Curriculumforschung.* Eds. K. Frey and H. Haft. Heinheim, Basel.

Heidelberger Forschungsprojekt 'Pidgin-Deutsch.' 1975. *Sprache und Kommunikation ausländischer Arbeiter: Analysen, Berichte, Materialien.* Kronberg/Ts.: Scriptor.

Hüllen, W., ed. 1980. *Understanding Bilingualism. Forum Linguisticum* 27. Frankfurt: Lang.

James, C. 1980. *Constrastive Analysis.* Harlow: Longman.

Jordens, P. 1987. "Neuere theoretische Ansätze in der Zweitspracherwerbsforschung." *Studium Linguistik* 22: 31–65.

Kellerman, E. 1986. "An Eye for an Eye: Crosslinguistic Constraints on the Development of the Lexicon." *Crosslinguistic Influence in Second Language Acquisition.* Eds. E. Kellerman and M. Sharwood Smith. New York: Pergamon Press. 35–48.

———. 1987. *Aspects of Transferability in Second Language Acquisition.* University of Nijmegen.

———. 1990. "Compensatory Strategies in Second Language Research: A Critique, a Revision, and Some (Non-) Implications for the Classroom." To appear in Memorial Volume for Claus Faerch (Title to be announced). Eds. R. Phillipson, E. Kellerman, L. Selinker, M. Sharwood Smith, and M. Swain. Clevedon, U.K.: Multilingual Matters.

Kellerman, E., and M. Sharwood Smith, eds. 1986. *Crosslinguistic Influence in Second Language Acquisition.* New York: Pergamon Press.

Kielhöfer, B. 1975. *Fehlerlinguistik des Fremdsprachenerwerbs: Linguistische, lernpsychologische und didaktische Analyse von Französischfehlern.* Kronberg/Ts.: Scriptor.

Klein, W. 1983. "Der Ausdruck der Temporalität im ungesteuerten Zweitspracherwerb." *Essays on Deixis.* Ed. G. Rauh. Tübingen: Gunter Narr. 149–68.

———. 1986. *Second Language Acquisition.* Cambridge: Cambridge UP.

———. 1989. *Time in Language.* Ms. Max-Planck-Institute for Psycholinguistics. Nijmegen, Holland.

Klein, W., and N. Dittmar. 1979. *Developing Grammars: The Acquisition of German Syntax by Foreign Workers*. Berlin, Heidelberg, New York: Springer.

Klein, W., and J. Weissenborn, eds. 1982. "Zweitsprachenerwerb." *Zeitschrift für Literaturwissenschaft und Linguistik* 45. Göttingen: Vandenhoeck und Ruprecht.

Knapp-Potthoff, A., and K. Knapp. 1982. *Fremdsprachenlernen und -lehren: Eine Einführung in die Didaktik der Fremdsprachen vom Standpunkt der Zweitsprachenerwerbsforschung*. Stuttgart: Kohlhammer.

Kohn, K. 1980. *Kontrastive Syntax und Fehlerbeschreibung*. Kronberg/Ts.: Scriptor.

———. 1986. "The Analysis of Transfer." *Crosslinguistic Influence in Second Language Acquisition*. Eds. E. Kellerman and M. Sharwood Smith. New York: Pergamon Press. 21–34.

Kuhs, K. 1989. *Sozialpsychologische Faktoren im Zweispracherwerb: Eine Untersuchung bei griechischen Migrantenkindern in der Bundesrepublik Deutschland*. Tübingen: Gunter Narr.

Kutsch, S., and I. Desgranges. 1985. *Zweitsprache Deutsch-Ungesteuerter Erwerb: Interaktionsorientierte Analysen des Projekts Gastarbeiterkommunikation*. Tübingen: Niemeyer.

Lado, R. 1957. *Linguistics Across Cultures: Applied Linguistics for Language Teachers*. Ann Arbor, Mich.: UMP.

Lalleman, J. A. 1986. *Dutch Language Proficiency of Turkish Children Born in the Netherlands*. University of Amsterdam.

Long, M. H. 1982. "Adaption an den Lerner: Die Aushandlung verstehbarer Eingabe in Gesprächen zwischen Muttersprachlichen Sprechern und Lernern." *Zweitsprachenerwerb*. Eds. W. Klein and J. Weissenborn. Göttingen: Vandenhoeck und Ruprecht. 100–19.

Meyer-Ingwersen, J., U. Neumann, and W. Kummer. 1977. *Zur Sprachentwicklung türkischer Schüler in der Bundesrepublik*. Kronberg: Scriptor.

Müller, H., ed. 1974. *Ausländerkinder in deutschen Schulen: Ein Handbuch*. Stuttgart: Klett.

Neumann, U. 1989. "Zweitsprachenunterricht Deutsch." *Handbuch Fremdsprachenunterricht*. Eds. K. R. Bausch, H. Christ, W. Hüllen, and H. J. Krumm. Tübingen: Francke. 69–72.

Neumann, U., and H. H. Reich. 1980. *Türkische Kinder-deutsche Lehrer: Probleme im Unterricht. Erklärungen und Hilfen*. 3rd ed. Düsseldorf: Schwann.

Nickel, G. 1972a. *Reader zur Kontrastiven Linguistik*. Frankfurt: Athenaum.

———. 1972b. *Fehlerkunde: Beiträge zur Fehleranalyse, Fehlerbewertung und Fehlertherapie*. Berlin: Cornelsen-Velhagen and Klasing.

Perdue, C., ed. 1984. *Second Language Acquisition by Adult Immigrants: A Field Manual*. Rowley, Mass.: Newbury House.

Pfaff, C. W. 1987. "Functional Approaches to Interlanguage." *First and Second Language Acquisition Processes*. Ed. C. W. Pfaff. Rowley, Mass.: Newbury House. 81–102.

Pfaff, C. W., ed. 1987. *First and Second Language Acquisition Processes*. Rowley, Mass.: Newbury House.

Piepho, H. E. 1974. *Kommunikative Kompetenz, Pragmalinguistik und Ansätze zur Neubesinnung in der Lernzielbestimmung im Fremdsprachenunterricht*. Düsseldorf: Pädagogisches Institut.

Raabe, H. (Hrsg.) 1976. *Trends in Kontrastiver Linguistik*. Tübingen: Gunter Narr.

Ramat, A. G., ed. 1988. *L'Apprendimento Spontaneo di una Seconda Lingua*. Bologna: Il Mulino.

———. 1988. *L'Italiano tra le Altre Lingue: Strategie di Acquisizione*. Bologna: Il Mulino.

Rath, R., ed. 1983. *Sprach- und Verständigungsschwierigkeiten bei Ausländerkindern in Deutschland: Aufgaben und Probleme einer Interaktionsorientierten Zweispracherwerbsforschung*. Frankfurt/M.: Lang.

Ringbom, H. 1987. *The Role of the First Language in Foreign Language Learning*. Clevedon, U.K.: Multilingual Matters.

Schumann, J. H. 1978. *The Pidginization Process*. Rowley, Mass.: Newbury House.

Sharwood Smith, M. 1986. "The Competence/Control Model, Crosslinguistic Influence and the Creation of New Grammars." *Crosslinguistic Influence in Second Language Acquisition*. Eds. E. Kellerman and M. Sharwood Smith. New York: Pergamon Press. 10–20.

Stölting, W. 1980. *Die Zweisprachigkeit jugoslawischer Schüler in der Bundesrepublik Deutschland*. Wiesbaden: Harrassowitz.

von Stutterheim, C. 1986. *Temporalität in der Zweitsprache*. Berlin: de Gruyter.

von Stutterheim, C., and W. Klein. 1987. "A Concept-Oriented Approach to Second Language Studies." *First and Second Language Acquisition Processes*. Ed. C. Pfaff. Rowley, Mass.: Newbury House. 191–205.

Willem, G. 1987. "Communication Strategies and Their Significance in Foreign Language Learning." *System* 15: 351–64.

Wode, H. 1981. *Learning a Second Language*. Tübingen: Gunter Narr.

Chapter 10

Trends in European SLA Research and Some Implications for the American Foreign Language Classroom

Thom Huebner

San Jose State University

INTRODUCTION

Any discussion of the implications of European efforts in second language acquisition (SLA) research for foreign language (FL) classrooms is doubly difficult: first because SLA research in Europe, as in North America, has burgeoned over the past two decades to the point that a comprehensive review in a paper of this sort is just not possible and any attempt to do so would surely offend those whose research would of necessity not be mentioned; and second, foreign language teachers have for years attempted to reconcile sometimes conflicting proposed implications of research in linguistics, psychology, and second language acquisition with what seems to work in classroom practice. Yet the close relationship that we like to believe exists between the what and how of learning on one hand and teaching on the other dictates a constant articulation of issues between those whose primary concern is in teaching and those for whom acquisition is the main interest.

Although European and North American efforts in second language acquisition have followed parallel paths to a large extent, they differ in interesting ways. Attempts have been made periodically to bring these two communities together: the AILA-sponsored Neuchâtel Colloquia (1973–78), the European North American (EUNAM) conferences in 1981 (see Andersen, 1984) and 1982 (Pfaff, 1987), the Georgetown University SLA-TESOL Summer Institute conference in 1985, and the Bellagio conference in 1987 have attempted to bring together researchers across the two continents for their mutual benefit. In addition, a number of reviews of European SLA research are now available to English reading audiences (such as Wode, 1981; Nichols and Meisel, 1983; Perdue, 1984; Noyau and Véronique, 1986).

In the following section, I will attempt to highlight some aspects of SLA research that to my mind appear fruitful, and which have been given more emphasis in Europe than in North America. Specifically, I will discuss some aspects of the European Science Foundation project not mentioned in von Stutterheim (this volume). Finally I will offer a few concluding remarks, some perhaps obvious, others more speculative, on the application of these findings for foreign language pedagogy.

EUROPEAN SLA RESEARCH: A PERSONAL PERSPECTIVE

In its early years, second language acquisition research in Europe, as in the United States, was influenced by contrastive analysis approaches to language teaching and learning. Sometimes the U.S. influence was direct, as in the case of the Center for Applied Linguistics-supported contrastive analysis projects for Serbo-Croatian-English, Hungarian-English, Polish-English, and Romanian-English, from which many good contrastive grammars have resulted. In other cases, particularly in the French literature, the influence of contrastive analysis was less strongly felt (Noyau and Véronique, 1986). Nevertheless, from the 1960s through the early 1970s, approaches to second language acquisition research in Europe, influenced by structural linguistics, contrastive analysis, and error analysis, paralleled directions taken in the United States.

As has been pointed out (for example, von Stutterheim, this volume), much of SLA research in Europe continues to run parallel to that of the United States. However, several forces contributed to research emphases in Europe, which have been less influential in the United States. Among these was Corder's (1967, 1981) notion of learner systems as "idiosyncratic dialects" with their own standards of grammaticality determined by the learner's stage of development. The articulation of this notion, later labeled "interlanguage" by Selinker (1972), has often been cited as the beginning of contemporary SLA research in the United States. The Neuchatel Colloquia (1973–78) and the influence of creolists (for example, Andersen (1977, 1978) were forces that freed many European researchers from the bounds of formal structuralist schools (Noyau and Véronique, 1986) and contributed to a focus on process. Finally, in a departure from the dominant patterns found in North America, the large influx of guest workers drew the attention of European sociolinguists to the phenomenon of second language acquisition, especially untutored SLA.[1]

These forces, I believe, have contributed to the examination of second language acquisition within the historical and social context in which it occurs. Rather than attempting to establish SLA as a developing discipline separate from "parent disciplines" of linguistics and psychology and supported by an infrastructure of educational programs and advanced degrees on the topic, the tendency has been toward viewing SLA as one facet of a larger epiphenomenon of language contact, acquisition, change, and loss. The Kiel project (Wode 1974, 1976, 1979) included comparative data from first language acquisition (both German and English), second language acquisition (German L1/English L2; English L1/German L2), pidgins and creoles, to identify developmental sequences in the linguistic structure of learner utterances. The HPD project (Heidelberger Forschungsprojekt *Pidgin-Deutsch* 1976, 1978; Klein and Dittmar, 1979), focusing on syntax and the development of function words as correlated with social factors among guest workers in Germany, found proficiency in German related to such variables as intensity and age upon arrival. Muysken's (1980) study of Moroccans learning Dutch in Amsterdam illustrates the relation between experiences of discrimination, attitudes toward the target speech community, and L2 acquisition level. Papers from the Second Neuchatel Conference on Bilingualism (Lüdi, 1986) point up the close relationship between L2 acquisition and evolving bilingualism, highlighting the need for second language researchers to look at the whole verbal repertoire of the second language learner and to take into account discourse structures found in learner varieties. Papers in Giacomi and Véronique (1986), comparing learner varieties with diachronic change and the evolution of pidgins and creoles, emphasize the influence of the learner's position relative to different social norms and the characteristics of SLA data collection processes on the linguistic features found in learner productions.

From this perspective, individual variation in learner varieties is examined less from the Labovian perspective of style shifts due to attention to speech[2] than as a necessary synchronic manifestation of the diachronic evolution of grammatical competence in a second language (Ellis, 1985). Among empirical studies, Hyltenstam's (1977, 1978) early cross-sectional and longitudinal studies were among the first to employ implicational scaling, an analytic technique widely used in sociolinguistics, to suggest a regular route of acquisition of certain aspects of Swedish syntax, independent of knowledge of first language and consistent with typological universals. Unlike the morpheme studies dominating SLA research in the United States in the 1970s, whose findings of a common order of acquisition of selected English morphemes form much of the theoretical basis for popular second and foreign language instructional approaches in the United States, psycholinguistic explanations for observed acquisition orders have been offered. For example, the studies of the ZISA project (Meisel 1975a, 1975b; Meisel *et al.*, 1979; Pienemann, 1980; Clahsen, 1980) suggest that the word-order rules required for standard German can be located along a developmental dimension, which all learners of German as a second language must pass through if their language is to approximate that of the target group: adverb-fronting, particle to end, inversion of subject and verb, adverb to final in verb phrases, and verb to final position in embedded clauses. Furthermore, the acquisition of the word-order rules at each successive stage can be ranked according to their cognitive complexity and explained by psycholinguistic principles similar to Slobin's operating principles.[3]

Following a linguistic tradition dating back to the Prague School and perpetuated in Europe by linguists such as Bühler, Firth, Beneviste, Jakobson, Halliday, and Firbas, SLA research on that continent has also reflected a greater functional (as opposed to formal) orientation toward language structure than corresponding work in the United States.[4] In this respect, two different but complementary approaches emerge. The first starts with an identification of observable surface markers (that is, morphemes or lexical items) and ascribes semantic or pragmatic functions (predication, identification, deictic reference to person, time, space, and so forth) to them. The second identifies instances of reference to semantic and pragmatic notions and traces the evolving linguistic means employed to express them (Trévise and Porquier, 1986). Thus, de Vries (1981) examines the thematic structure (that is, order of old and new information) in the Dutch of Turkish informants. Pfaff (1987) looks at the changing functions of determiners and pronouns among Turkish learners of German. Extra and Mittner (1984) include a section on spatial reference. The evolving means for marking of temporal reference has been studied for German (von Stutterheim and Klein, 1987; Meisel, 1987) and French (Trévise, 1987; Véronique, 1987).

Detailed attention to linguistic form is also reflected in the approach to the treatment of input and interaction. The nature of input to second language learners and of interaction among native and non-native speakers has long been a focus of second language acquisition research both in North America and in Europe. Much of that research has been motivated by the development of conversational analysis (Sacks, Schegloff, and Jefferson, 1974), classroom discourse (Sinclair and Coulthard, 1975), and Krashen's input hypothesis. The tendency has been to develop taxonomies of conversational adjustments made in native speaker/non-native speaker (NS-NNS) interaction that contribute to comprehensible input (for example, Long, 1985), and to determine the kinds of interactional tasks that most favor these adjustments (for instance, Pica et al., 1989).

An alternative approach, found more commonly in European than North American research,[5] is one concerned with the communicative intent of utterances in NS-NNS interactions and the interpretation of them shaped by linguistic and nonlinguistic knowledge. Thus, Trévise and Heredia (1984) illustrate how a limited command of French verbal tense morphology leads to a greater reliance on extralinguistic use for the interpretation of utterances, which in turn results in misunderstandings both ways. Becker and Perdue (1984) show that it is not just the lack of linguistic means that give rise to misunderstandings, but also the uses to which those forms are put and the assumptions one holds regarding the roles of the interactants in the discourse. But conversational adjustments can, as microanalyses (cf. Gumperz, 1982) of NS-NNS discourse strategies reveal, also contribute to the development of the learner's L2 lexical, syntactic, and discourse systems (cf. Py, 1986; Giacomi and Vion, 1986; Perdue, 1987).

The focus on intent and interpretation, and on the linguistic and extralinguistic cues signaling them, has inevitably led to an interest in the metalinguistic activities involved in the acquisition process. Studies of both guided and unguided second language acquisition suggest that conscious conceptualization and metalinguistic activity on the part of the learner is always present in one form or another in acquisition. Furthermore, learners' linguistic productions may differ considerably from their metalinguistic verbalizations, even in tutored contexts (Berthoud, 1981; Giacobbe and Lucas, 1982). Any attempt to understand descrepancies between students' linguistic and metalinguistic productions must take into account both the sources of the metalinguistic knowledge and the learners' attitudes toward both the target language norms and the social structure within which those norms operate (Véronique and Faïta, 1982; Mittner and Kahn, 1982).

Each of these research trends can be seen in the work of the European Science Foundation Project, *Second Language Acquisition by Adult Immigrants* (cf. Perdue, 1984).

THE EUROPEAN SCIENCE FOUNDATION PROJECT: GOALS AND INTENT OF PROJECT

The European Science Foundation project set out to examine the developing untutored learner varieties of five European languages by the speakers of six source languages for a total of ten TL-SL pairings. The goal of the study was to characterize language-specific versus generalizable phenomena in the acquisition process. More specifically, the project attempted to determine both *how* (that is, in what order, at what speed, and to what extent) elements of the TL are acquired and to *explain* the acquisition process in terms of cognitive-perceptual factors, propensity, and exposure. By looking at acquisition in untutored settings, the focus of investigation is on the acquisition of communicative competence. This differs from tutored learning in that it doesn't necessarily involve the learning of grammar rules of the kind presented in classrooms. From a North American perspective, perhaps the most unique aspect of this multinational study is its attempt to relate the development of communicative competence to the development of grammatical competence.

In order to do this, the project employed a qualitative approach to data collection and analysis as a first step for diachronic understanding of (NS-NNS) interaction and second language development. Native speaker performance of specific genre types and interactions found in naturally occurring situations were collected and analyzed. This led to the development of elicitation strategies designed to tap the learners' linguistic means for expressing the semantic and pragmatic notions inherent in these situations and the learners' strategies for coping with the task when linguistic means were lacking: narratives for reference to participants; events and temporal notions; "stage directions" to elicit means for spatial reference; role plays for evidence of misunderstandings.

The ethnographic influence is seen in its emphasis on triangulation and the collection of secondary as well as primary data. Selinker (1985–1986) refers to the collection of learner utterances through the kinds of elicitation tasks mentioned above as *primary data*. But the ESF project also collected taped reactions to these tasks, in which learners make explicit their communicative intent. To these data, Selinker applies the term *secondary*. These secondary data serve several purposes:

1. They help ensure mutual understanding.
2. They reveal the learner's attitude toward the language being learned.
3. They provide additional text types for analysis, texts with perhaps greater attention to linguistic form.
4. They provide evidence for the relationship between metalinguistic and meta-cognitive knowledge on one hand, and linguistic performance on the other.

In analyzing these data, the project employs a top-down approach, beginning with the larger discourse structure of the text in question. It focuses on how the learner "applies his restricted repertoire of lexical items and grammatical rules in order to communicate, and how these repertoires interact with more general communicative skills, such as particular non-verbal means and specific discourse techniques" (Perdue, 1984). This implies, of course, the impossibility of studying acquisition without looking at NS-NNS interaction.

One task faced by learners is to segment the stream of speech into units, to which they must assign meaning or function. That the native speaking interlocutor performs a facilitative function in this process has often been observed: articulate clearly, stress important words, topicalize, use either/or questions, and so forth (for example, Long, 1983). However, cross-linguistic microanalyses of specific NS-NNS interactions highlight the role of this facilitative input in the acquisition of specific aspects of linguistic competence. Perdue reports, for example, that in the development of anaphoric systems, "learners of Dutch clearly perceive appropriate strong-form pronouns before clitic pronouns, and learners of French need time to analyze—thus spend time in misunderstanding—the pre-verbal clitic-auxiliary complex, which indeed first turns up in their production as a verbal prefix trace" (Perdue, in press, 9).

But the learner is far from a passive participant in this process. Repetitions and restatements in interviews illustrate how language practice and language acquisition are always accompanied by epi- and metalinguistic activities (the first type implying a lower level of consciousness and formalization; cf. Giacomi and Véronique, 1986). These activities and their corresponding competencies are revealed spontaneously when problems arise. This, along with the form of the accompanying linguistic data and an educated guess as to the intent of the utterance through controlled elicitation techniques, can give useful hints as to the effect of misunderstandings and communication breakdowns on the learners' existing linguistic system and on the process of acquisition of linguistic and communicative competence—more probably than grammaticality or preference judgments on a number of constructed sentences.

Lack of understanding results in a potential tension between the need to learn and the need to keep the conversation going. Learners' repetition of key words (Voionmaa, 1984; Allwood and Abelar, 1984) in the NS's utterance serves a double function: it allows a "'second go' at the utterance while isolating the item which cannot be associated with a meaning" (Perdue, in press, 11).

One side effect of such a metalinguistic side-sequence, however, is the disruption of the discourse. An alternative is to employ a wait-and-see strategy, providing only back-channeling, (Yngve, 1970; or in the language of the ESF Feedback Report, *narrow feedback* [NFB]) to indicate that "yes, I am listening," in hopes that greater context will contain clues to unlock the mysteries of meaning.

The strategies that learners employ in doing this vary, not only among individuals but also over developmental time and across discourse types, as Vion and Mittner's (1986) taxonomy of repetitions and their description of two learners' use of these repetitions illustrate. Similarly, while occurrence of back-channeling among informants to the project remains high over the period of language acquisition studied, it is hypothesized that the development is from a stage where narrow feedback occurs "unaccompanied by other information to a stage where NFB serves to initiate, structure or conclude other types of information" (Allwood, 1988).

From this perspective on SLA, evidence supports the view that manifestations of linguistic awareness are not random and play an important role in the acquisition process. Learners consciously wrestle with the problem of matching linguistic input to their own existing representations of the target language. The report on the process of the developing lexicon (Broeder *et al.*, 1988) cites examples of Slobin's (1978) "spotlight effect," in which the learners single out from the NS input individual lexical items and successively attempt to apply their own word-formation rules until they produce what they believe the word should be. Only then is the word accepted as what the NS had already said.

Having isolated lexical items from the stream of input and assigning meaning to them, the learner is also faced with the task of using these items in production. The learner's lack of target language morphology makes an analysis of these productions in terms of syntactic constructs, such as grammatical case and tense, for example, meaningless. Nevertheless, cross-linguistic comparisons of early learner utterances produced in narrative retellings illustrate the systematicity inherent in early learner varieties, regardless of source or target language. The learner appears to express semantic and discourse-pragmatic relationships using initial hypotheses consisting of some core principles (Corder, 1981).

With respect to narrative retellings, at the very earliest stages, learner productions are characterized by considerable variability, both across individuals and within any given text. It is the interlocutor who structures the collaboratively produced retellings through questions, which form the thematic content of the narrative propositions. Informants provide the focused information through one-word or one-phrase answers. The topic-focus structures formed through these question and answer sequences are soon echoed in the topic-focus structures that informants incorporate into extended texts.[6]

Analysis of a series of retellings across learners and over time suggests that as learners begin to produce more extended discourse, almost all produce a basic learner variety, which respects a set of phrasal, semantic, and pragmatic constraints. A phrasal constraint is one that governs general word order (for example, NP1-V-NP2). A semantic constraint governs the assignment of case properties (for example, controller first). Pragmatic constraints govern the topic-focus information structure of utterances (for example, focus last).

Synchronic variations from these constraints are for the most part systematic and a function of the domain of language use. In narrative retellings, for example, deviation from the NP1-V general word-order constraint is pragmatically governed: to signal a shift in one or more of the referential domains of temporality, location, and participant.

With new linguistic demands, continued target language input, and previous linguistic knowledge, grammatical acquisition can be seen as an attempt to overcome these constraints and to ascribe functions for newly isolated lexical items in the target language input. At this point, what is isolated for analysis is often the result of perceptions shaped by knowledge of one's first language. Still, development is variable, even among learners with the same source language. Thus, in the Punjabi-English data, M's use of participial forms (Bhardwaj, 1988) and R's use of anaphoric forms (Huebner, 1989) illustrate the influence of source language temporal categories and discourse organization, respectively, on learner productions.

Nevertheless, target-language–specific structures begin to emerge. This can be illustrated by the development of pronominal systems cross-linguistically. Although learners developed anaphoric systems to varying degrees of complexity and completion, the following generalities are consistent with the findings of an earlier individual case study (cf. Huebner, 1983, 155–74):

1. Definitely referring NPs are acquired before overt pronouns.
2. Singular pronouns are acquired before plurals.
3. Nominative pronouns are acquired before oblique pronouns.
4. Animate referring pronouns are acquired before inanimate pronouns.

This can be seen as a function of the basic constraints in connected text: maintenance of reference to animate controllers in the first NP position.[7]

However, real-life interaction demands that controllers (that is, agents as opposed to patients) must sometimes be placed in focus, while participants already established in the discourse are referred to in controlled (that is, patient) roles. In English, maintenance of reference to a controlled participant can be accomplished through unstressed accusative pronominal forms in postverbal direct object position. While this structure violates the "focus last" constraint, it preserves the basic phrasal constraint (NP1-V-NP2). The result is a more tightly integrated distribution of topic and focus information across the structure of the utterance (Huebner, 1983). The expression of the equivalent information in French requires a preverbal clitic anaphoric form. Clitic pronouns, once acquired, are associated with left- and right-dislocated NPs, resulting in a new target-language–specific pattern type: (NP)-pro-pro-V-(NP) (Perdue, in press, 22).

IMPLICATIONS

Implications of research in second language acquisition for classroom pedagogy must be approached with extreme caution. Perhaps a natural reaction is to assume that if one can identify a common sequence for the acquisition of structures in a second language, then the next step would be to incorporate into the design of a syllabus the presentation and practice of these structures in the order in which they are acquired. The ESF data do not propose developmental stages as explicitly as those proposed for German word-order rules described by Meisel, *et al.* (1979). But even if they did, Long's (1985) critique of Pienemann's (1985) "teachability hypothesis"—the sequencing of grammatical syllabi to reflect developmental stages in the acquisition of those word-order rules—would apply equally to any such proposal here. One cannot assume that it is practical or even possible to group students by acquisitional stage. Even if it were possible, not all students at the same stage would necessarily be ready for instruction in the structure on the same day. Finally, there is no guarantee that students at the same acquisitional stage for one structure or set of structures would be at the same stage for other structures.

In fact, the data cited above on NS-NNS interaction would seem to support the position that teacher rough-tuning in the form of communicative interaction facilitates acquisition. On the other hand, the strong evidence of metalinguistic activity among even second language acquirers in untutored settings suggests that there is a place for a focus on form in the second or foreign language classroom.

The data from the ESF project strongly suggest, however, that acquirers even at relatively early stages can produce extended texts, albeit imperfect ones. Different types of text call for the use of specific linguistic devices: means for introducing and maintaining reference to participants and for temporal sequencing of events in narratives, for example. Thus, the inclusion of learner-produced extended texts of various kinds—even at the earliest stages of foreign language learning—would appear to be compatible with the development of both communicative and linguistic competence. Whether the high output demands placed on students by the production of such texts would in the long run result in premature fossilization remains an empirical question.

Another area in which the European research into SLA might have implications for the foreign language teaching profession is that of assessment. While proficiency-based instruction and evaluation have received support from many researchers and practitioners alike, several questions have been raised about the efficacy of teaching for and testing oral proficiency, particularly at the elementary and intermediate levels. With specific reference to the ACTFL/ETS Provisional Proficiency Guidelines, some have accused that test of focusing on discrete points of grammar rather than on a more global measure of communicative competence (Savignon, 1985). Others have found the functions listed as criteria to be a diverse collection of grammatical tasks, whose low level of abstraction is not generalizable from one activity to the next (Kramsch, 1986). A top-down analysis of the semantic and discourse-pragmatic categories elicited in the oral proficiency interviews might provide a better picture of what specifically test-scorers are responding to.

Finally, the European Science Foundation project has provided the field with an enormous amount of cross-linguistic data on adult second language acquisition within a consistent theoretical and methodological framework. Nevertheless, those data are limited to untutored adults learning European languages. Application of this framework to tutored settings of various kinds would contribute in some measure to our understanding of the effects on the acquisition process of explicit focus on language through presentation and practice in school contexts. Furthermore, an examination of the acquisition of languages typologically distant from European languages would shed light on the universality of the core constraints that appear to govern the acquisition of communicative and grammatical competence in the ESF project.

ENDNOTES

1. Wode (1981) notes that studies of naturalistic L2 learning date back to Kenveres (1938) and Tits (1948), but the first such studies using modern linguistic techniques were those of Ravem (1968, 1970, 1974).

2. See Beebe (1988) for a review of this perspective.

3. Variable performance in other aspects of the TL morphology (that is, deletions, optional permutations, and the degree of expansion of a sentence) are determined "by socio-psychological factors which reflect the learner's attitudes towards the learning task, the target language and the target society" (Nichols and Meisel, 1983, 80).

4. See, however, Huebner (1983), Kumpf (1983), and Sato (1985) for some North American exceptions.

5. A notable exception to the North American research in this area is that of Varonis and Gass (1985).

6. That early learner productions reflect topic-focus organization of information content has long been observed; cf. Huebner (1983).

7. See also Pfaff (1987); the data and analysis in this paper were first reported at the second EUNAM conference in Göhrde, West Germany, in August 1982.

REFERENCES

Allwood, Jens, ed. 1988. *Second Language Acquisition by Adult Immigrants, Final Report, Volume 11: Feedback.* Strasbourg: European Science Foundation.

Allwood, Jens, and Yanhia Abelar. 1984. "Lack of Understanding, Misunderstanding, and Adult Language Acquisition." *Studies in Second Language Acquisition by Adult Immigrants.* Eds. Guus Extra and Michele Mittner. Tilburg: Tilburg University.

Andersen, Roger. 1977. "The Impoverished State of Cross-Sectional Morpheme Acquisition Accuracy Methodology." *Working Papers on Bilingualism* 14: 47–82.

———. 1978. "An Implicational Model for Second Language Research." *Language Learning* 28: 221–82.

————, ed. 1984. *Second Languages: A Cross-Linguistic Perspective*. Rowley, Mass.: Newbury House.

Becker, Angelika, and Clive Perdue. 1984. "Just One Misunderstanding: A Story of Miscommunication." *Studies in Second Language Acquisition by Adult Immigrants*. Eds. Guus Extra and Michele Mittner. Tilburg: Tilburg University.

Beebe, Leslie M. 1988. "Five Sociolinguistic Approaches to Second Language Acquisition." *Issues in Second Language Acquisition: Multiple Perspectives*. Ed. L. M. Beebe. New York: Newbury House.

Berthoud, Anne-Claude. 1981. *Activité Metalinguistique et Acquisition d'Une Langue Seconde: Etude des Verbes Deictiques Allemands*. Bern and Frankfurt: Peter Lang.

Bhardwaj, Mangat Rai. 1988. "Chapter Three: TL English." *Second Language Acquisition by Adult Immigrants. Final Report. Vol V: Temporality*. Eds. M. Bhardwaj, R. Dietrich, and C. Noyau. Strasbourg: European Science Foundation.

Broeder, P., G. Extra, R. von Hout, S. Stromquist, and K. Voionmaa, eds. 1988. *Second Language Acquisition by Adult Immigrants, Final Report, Volume III: Processes in the Developing Lexicon*. Strasbourg: European Science Foundation.

Clahsen, Harald. 1980. "Psycholinguistic Aspects of L2 Acquisition." *Second Language Development: Trends and Issues*. Ed. S. Felix. Tübingen: Gunter Narr Verlag.

Corder, S. P. 1967. "The Significance of Learners' Errors." *International Review of Applied Linguistics* 5: 161–70.

————. 1981. *Error Analysis and Interlanguage*. Cambridge: Oxford UP.

Ellis, Rod. 1985. "Sources of Variability in Interlanguage." *Applied Linguistics* 6: 118–31.

Extra, Guus, and Michele Mittner, eds. 1984. *Studies in Second Language Acquisition by Adult Immigrants*. Tilberg Studies in Language and Literature 6. Tilberg: Tilberg University.

Giacobbe, J., and M. Lucas. 1982. "Métalangue des apprenants *ser et estar*." In *Acquisition d'une langue étrangère II*. Ed. A. Trévise. Paris: Presses Universitaires de Vincennes. 111–27.

Giacomi, A., and D. Véronique, eds. 1986. *Acquisition d'une Langue Etrangère: Perspectives et Recherches*. Aix-eu-Provence: Service des Publications de l'Université de Provence.

Giacomi, Alain, and Robert Vion. 1986. "Metadiscursive Processes in the Acquisition of a Second Language." *Studies in Second Language Acquisition* 8: 355–68.

Gumperz, John J. 1982. *Discourse Strategies*. Cambridge: Cambridge UP.

Heidelberger Forschungsproject *Pidgin-Deutsch*. 1976. *Arbeitsbericht III: Untersuchungen zur Erlernung des Deutschen durch ausländische Arbeiter*. Germanistisches Seminar der Universität Heidelberg.

Huebner, Thom. 1983. *A Longitudinal Study of the Acquisition of English*. Ann Arbor: Karoma Press.

———. 1989. "Establishing Point of View: The Development of Coding Mechanisms in a Second Language for the Expression of Cognitive and Perceptual Organization." *Linguistics* 27: 111–43.

Hyltenstam, Kenneth. 1977. "Implicational Patterns in Interlanguage Syntax Variation." *Language Learning* 27: 383–411.

———. 1978. "Variation in Interlanguage Syntax." *Working Papers* 18. Department of General Linguistics, Lund University.

Klein, Wolfgang, and Norbert Dittmar. 1979. *Developing Grammars: The Acquisition of German Syntax by Foreign Workers*. Berlin: Springer-Verlag.

Kramsch, Claire. 1986. "From Language Proficiency to Interactional Competence." *Modern Language Journal* 70: 366–72.

Kumpf, Lorraine. 1983. "A Case Study of Temporal Reference in Interlanguage." *Proceedings of the Los Angeles Second Language Research Forum, Vol 2.* Eds. C. Campbell *et al.* Los Angeles: UCLA Department of English.

Long, M. 1983. "Linguistic and Conversational Adjustments to Non-native Speakers." *Studies in Second Language Acquisition* 5: 177–93.

———. 1985. "A Role for Instruction in Second Language Acquisition: Task-Based Language Training." *Modelling and Assessing Second Language Acquisition.* Eds. Kenneth Hyltenstam and Manfred Pienemann. San Diego: College-Hill Press.

Lüdi, Georges, ed. 1986. *Devenir Bilingue/Parler Bilingue; Zweisprachig Werden/ Zweisprachig Sprechen; Getting Bilingual/Speaking Bilingual*. Tübingen: Gunter Narr.

Meisel, Jurgen M. 1975a. "Der Erwerb des Deutschen durch ausländische Arbeiter: Untersuchungen am Beispiel von Arbeitern aus Italien, Spanien und Portugal." *Linguistische Berichte* 38: 59–69.

———. 1975b. "Ausländerdeutsch und Deutsch ausländischer Arbeiter: Zur möglichen Entstehung eines Pidgin in der BRD." *Zeitschrift fur Literaturwissenschaft und Linguistik* 18: 9–53.

———. 1987. "Reference to Past Events and Actions in the Development of Natural Second Language Acquisition." *First and Second Language Acquisition Processes.* Ed. C. Pfaff. Cambridge, Mass.: Newbury House.

Meisel, J. M., H. Clahsen, and M. Pienemann. 1979. "On Determining Developmental Stages in Natural Second Language Acquisition." *Wuppertaler Arbeitspapiere zur Sprachwissenschaft* 2: 1–53.

Mittner, M., and G. Kahn. 1982. "Réflexions sur l'Activité Metalinguistique des Apprenants Adultes en Milieu Naturel." *Acquisition d'une Langue Etrangère II.* Ed. A. Trévise. Paris: Presses Universitaires de Vincennes.

Muysken, Pieter. 1980. "Attitudes and Experiences of Discrimination: The Speech of Moroccan Foreign Workers in the Netherlands." *Proceedings of the 1980 Antwerp Sociolinguistics Symposium*. Ed. K. Deprez. Ghent: Story Scientia.

Nichols, Howard, and Jurgen M. Meisel. 1983. "Second Language Acquisition: The State of the Art (With Particular Reference to the Situation in West Germany)." *Language Development at the Crossroads: Papers from the Interdisciplinary Conference on Language Acquisition at Passau*. Eds. S. W. Felix and H. Wode. Tübingen: Gunter Narr Verlag.

Noyau, Colette, and Daniel Véronique. 1986. Survey Article. *Studies in Second Language Acquisition* 8: 245–63.

Perdue, Clive. 1987. "Real Beginners, Real Questions." *S'Approprier une Langue Etrangère*. Eds. H. Blanc, M. le Douaron, and D. Véronique. Paris: Didier Erudition.

———. In press. "Cross-Linguistic Comparisons: Organizational Principles in Learner Languages." *Cross Currents in Second Language Acquisition and Linguistic Theories*. Eds. T. Huebner and C. A. Ferguson. Amsterdam: John Benjamins.

Perdue, Clive, ed. 1984. *Second Language Acquisition by Adult Immigrants: A Field Manual*. Rowley, Mass.: Newbury House.

Pfaff, Carol. 1987. "Functional Approaches to Interlanguage." *First and Second Language Processes*. Ed. C. Pfaff. Cambridge Mass.: Newbury House.

Pfaff, Carol, ed. 1987. *First and Second Language Processes*. Cambridge, Mass.: Newbury House.

Pica, T., L. Holliday, N. Lewis, and L. Morgenthaler. 1989. "Comprehensible Output as an Outcome of Linguistic Demands on the Learner." *Studies in Second Language Acquisition* 11: 63–90.

Pienemann, Manfred. 1980. "The Second Language Acquisition of Immigrant Children." *Second Language Development: Trends and Issues*. Ed. S. Felix Tübingen: Gunter Narr Verlag.

———. 1985. "Learnability and Syllabus Construction." *Modelling and Assessing Second Language Acquisition*. Eds. Kenneth Hyltenstam and Manfred Pienemann. San Diego: College-Hill Press.

Py, Bernard. 1986. "Making Sense: Interlanguage's Intertalk in Exolingual Conversation." *Studies in Second Language Acquisition* 8: 343–53.

Ravem, Roar. 1968. "Language Acquisition in a Second Language Environment." *International Review of Applied Linguistics* 6: 175–85.

———. 1970. "The Development of Wh-Questions in First and Second Language Learners." *University of Essex Language Center Occasional Papers* 8: 16–41.

Sacks, H., E. Schegloff, and G. Jefferson. 1974. "A Simplest Systematics for the Organization of Turn-Taking in Conversations." *Language* 50: 696–735.

Sato, Charlene Junko. 1985. "The Syntax of Conversation in Interlanguage Development." Diss., UCLA.

Savignon, Sandra J. 1985. "Evaluation of Communicative Competence: The ACTFL Provisional Proficiency Guidelines." *Modern Language Journal* 69: 129–33.

Selinker, Larry. 1972. "Interlanguage." *International Review of Applied Linguistics* 10: 83–100.

———. 1985–86. Review article: "Attempting Comprehensive and Comparative Empirical Research in Second Language Acquisition. A Review of *Second Language Acquisition by Adult Immigrants.*" Part One in *Language Learning* 35: 567–84. Part Two in *Language Learning* 36: 83–100.

Sinclair, J. McH., and R. M. Coulthard. 1975. *Towards an Analysis of Discourse: The English Used by Teachers and Pupils.* London: Oxford UP.

Slobin, Dan Isaac. 1978. "A Case Study of Early Language Awareness." *The Child's Conception of Language.* Eds. A. Sinclair, R. Jarvella, and W. Levelt. Berlin: Springer.

Trévise, Anne. 1987. "Toward an Analysis of the (Inter)language Activity of Referring to Time in Narratives." *First and Second Language Acquisition Processes.* Ed. C. Pfaff. Cambridge, Mass.: Newbury House.

Trévise, Anne, and Christine de Heredia. 1984. "Les Malentendus: Efforts de Loupe sur Certains Phenomènes d'Acquisition d'une Langue Etrangère." *Communiquer dans la Langue de l'Autre.* Eds. C. Noyau and R. Porquier. Paris: Presses Universitaires de Vincennes.

Trévise, Anne, and Remy Porquier. 1986. "Second Language by Adult Immigrants: Exemplified Methodology." *Studies in Second Language Acquisition* 8: 265–75.

Varonis, Evangeline M., and Susan M. Gass. 1985. "Miscommunication in Native/Nonnative Conversation." *Language in Society* 14: 327–44.

Véronique, D., and D. Faïta. 1982. "Solicitations de Données Syntaxiques Auprès d'un Groupe de Travailleurs Maghrèbins." *Encrages* 8/9: 47–66.

Véronique, Daniel. 1987. "Reference to Past Events and Actions in Narratives in L2: Insights from North African Workers' French." *First and Second Language Acquisition Processes.* Ed. C. Pfaff. Cambridge, Mass.: Newbury House.

Vion, Robert, and Michele Mittner. 1986. "Activité de Reprise et Gestion des Interactions en Communication Exolingue." *Langages* 84: 25–42.

Voionmaa, K. 1984. "En Studie av Lexical Overforing hos Vuxna Sprakinlarare." *Proceedings of the Fourth Scandinavian Conference on Bilingualism.* Eds. E. Wande *et al.* Uppsala: University of Uppsala.

von Stutterheim, Christiane, and Wolfgang Klein. 1987. "A Concept-Oriented Approach to Second Language Studies." *First and Second Language Acquisition Processes.* Ed. C. Pfaff. Cambridge, Mass.: Newbury House.

Vries de, J. 1981. "Een taalontlokkingsgesprek met buiten landse arbeiders." *Toegepaste Taalwetenschap in Artikelen* 10: 104–31.

Wode, Henning. 1974. "Natürliche Zweitsprachigkeit: Probleme, Aufgaben, Perspektiven." *Linguistische Berichte* 32: 15–36.

———. 1976. "Developmental Sequences in Naturalistic L2 Acquisition." *Working Papers on Bilingualism* 11: 1–31.

———. 1979. "Operating Principles and 'Universals' in L1, L2, and FLT." *International Review of Applied Linguistics* 17: 217–31.

———. 1981. *Learning a Second Language: An Integrated View of Language Acquisition.* Tübingen: Gunter Narr Verlag.

Yngve, Victor. 1970. "On Getting a Word in Edgewise." *Papers from the Sixth Regional Meeting of the Chicago Linguistics Society.* Chicago: U. of Chicago Press. 567–77.

Chapter 11

Some Comparative Reflections on Foreign Language Learning Research in Europe and the United States

Albert Valdman

Indiana University

INTRODUCTION

Difference in Teaching Context

A comparison between two objects presupposes a common frame of reference. Unfortunately, so different are the settings in which foreign language learning research is conducted in Western Europe and in the United States that the comparative enterprise is fraught, if not with perils, at least with great difficulty.

Ferguson and Huebner (1989) have underscored the marginal role foreign language instruction plays in American education and the special constraints that this marginality places on its delivery in schools and universities. The dominance of TESOL specialists in second language acquisition (SLA) research, which these authors note, stems not only from the close historical links between that field and linguistics, but also from the level and type of language instruction in which they are engaged. Applied linguists in TESOL programs train overseas students (and increasingly, instructors) enrolled in (or teaching in) regular university programs. Although the proficiency of ESL students differs widely, it is generally relatively high, and some of the problems with which ESL specialists deal differ little from a qualitative point of view from those of instructors engaged in mother-tongue development. In contrast, because of the short instructional sequences that characterize foreign language (FL) instruction, the bulk of learners are located at the lower end of the proficiency spectrum. As a consequence, the range of research concerns that can be addressed within FL programs is relatively much narrower than those of ESL programs, and, as we shall see, of European FL programs.

Because FL instruction is accorded a major role in the European educational curricula, even secondary school programs offer researchers a range of student proficiency, interests, and motivation much broader than those generally found in American universities. For example, in Denmark all pupils enroll in English classes beginning in the fifth year; they begin the study of German in their seventh year; and they must select a third language, which they study during their last three years of secondary schooling. Most students enrolled in European university courses in commonly taught languages are advanced learners demonstrating proficiency levels superior to those attained by American FL majors.

Because of the status of English as the dominant language of international communication, the teaching of that language in Western Europe differs mainly from that of ESL in America only in that the latter is taught in a target language-speaking environment. Consequently, research concerns and opportunities may be expected to be comparable. With the establishment of English as the dominant language of international communication, the traditional threefold distinction between mother tongue, second language, and FL breaks down. As Arditty and Coste (1987) remark, in a large number of societies the notion of mother tongue either is not a useful one from an educational perspective or cannot be easily characterized. Instead, it is preferable to identify which language varieties function as primary educational media, as major regional or international vehiculars, as in-group vernaculars, and so forth. The status and functions of a language, that is, whether it is valorized or not, used as a medium of communication, employed as a tool for the transmission of knowledge, or simply studied as a school subject, determine in large part the learning context, and these distinctions may be expected to constitute major variables. In light of these considerations, it is clear that, because of significant differences in the learning context both in the United States and in Western Europe, a clear distinction must be drawn between research on the learning of English and that of other languages.

Taxonomies of SLA Research

By the very nature of the object it seeks to describe and analyze, the locus of foreign language learning (FLL) research is in the classroom. Two proposed taxonomies focus on the content of what is being observed. Faerch and Kasper (1985) classify this type of research under three perspectives: educational, psycholinguistic, and discourse. The last type applies various methodologies of discourse analysis to classroom discourse; the psycholinguistic perspective is concerned with processes of learning, with the relationship of input to intake and ultimate product of learning, and with changes from one stage of learning to another; the educational approach, which is the dominant educationist tradition of American FLL research, investigates the effect of various external variables on the product of learning. More useful for the comparison attempted here are two partially intersecting taxonomies proposed by French SLA and FLL researchers. Jo Arditty and Daniel Coste (1987) identify three perspectives, which they order developmentally and, at least tacitly, rank hierarchically in progressive order: structural, psycholinguistic, and sociolinguistic. The structural linguistic perspective gives priority to the analysis of systems in contact as a means of predicting, if not the course of learning, at least the problem areas. The psycholinguistic perspective focuses on learners' interlinguistic productions and the respective effects of the L1, the L2, and universal categories and processes. The sociolinguistic perspective, inspired by the ethnography of communication and conversational analysis, is centered on the observation of learners' interactions with various social partners.

Henri Besse (1986), recognizing that in the classroom context observation and experimentation cannot be dissociated from pedagogical intervention, offers a three-way classification based on the interaction between these three activities. Type 1 research limits itself to the simple observation of product (for example, error analysis), and cannot pretend to be either empirical or scientific, that is, to predict certain products from the effects of certain variables. Type 2 research provides some correlation between product and learning variables. The fact that it involves some control of input variables leads to conflicts of interest when the investigator also wears the hat of supervisor of instruction or classroom teacher, but this type of research may comprise two phases: one in which observation and pedagogical intervention proceed as the instruction unfolds, and another where observation and analysis are based on collected products, such as audio or video recordings. Type 3 research is the only one that may claim to be properly scientific since, although it may aim to provide some principled basis for positive pedagogical intervention, it is detached from the teaching situation. Because this type of research requires maximal control of input variables and the context of learning, it generally focuses on narrowly defined linguistic or communicative features. Besse adds that to qualify as scientific, FLL research must be replicable and, to be truly significant, it must be longitudinal rather than cross-sectional.

It would be both presumptuous and unrealistic for me to attempt to undertake an exhaustive comparative review of American and West European FLL research. I will limit myself to some reflections about major differences, some of which derive from the divergences in learning environment adumbrated above. I will describe general trends, focusing on those in Europe, since they are likely to be the least familiar to an American audience, and examine a small number of representative case studies. As was indicated, studies bearing on the tutored learning of English will be eliminated from consideration because of the special place that English holds in the educational system by virtue of its role as the major language of international communication. Finally, my association with a teaching program in French and my links with French colleagues and institutions explain why I will deal mainly with research on the learning of French as an FL.

MAJOR TRENDS

Dominant Models

It is not unfair to say that in the United States FLL research tends to follow, with a lag of several years, research orientations in ESL, just as the latter adopts theoretical constructs and methodologies dominant in L1 development research. Since few of the ESL studies (but see Schuman, 1978 for a signal exception) have dealt with incipient learners, there has been a great disparity between the proficiency levels of those whose learning was being observed. On the other hand, in the United States both FLL and SLA investigators have limited their observations to learning in the special environment of the classroom, and they have not generally observed the use of the target language in naturalistic situations.

The influences on European FLL research have been more diverse. The oldest strand, comparable in its aims and methodologies to American ESL, is represented by the teaching of the national language to technicians and other advanced learners speaking a variety of native languages; witness the impact of the CREDIF and of the CRAPEL (the Centre de Recherche et d'Applications Pédagogiques en Langue at the University of Nancy, which has specialized in the self-directed instruction of French as an SL and of English as an FL) on applied linguistics in France. Another important current is formed by enunciative theory and its associated emphasis on epilinguistic and metalinguistic activities in FLL, centering in the program in English linguistics at the University of Paris VII (see below). But the most recent powerful theoretical and methodological thrust stems from the observation of naturalistic learning and use of the target language by newly arrived immigrants and migrant workers at low levels of proficiency within the European Science Foundation project (Klein and Perdue, 1986). Focusing first on psycholinguistic issues, particularly the expression of basic semantic notions such as spatial reference and temporality in incipient interlanguage, this strand of research has moved on to the characterization of interactive discourse and broad sociolinguistic issues. Finally, the fact that several naturalistic studies of incipient FLL have been undertaken in the multilingual setting of Switzerland has introduced into discussions about FLL such topics as code-switching and code-mixing. The European research on the development of linguistic and communicative skills on the part of immigrants, together with the multilingual setting in which that research has been carried out, have led to questioning of the validity of the traditional distinction between mother tongue and second language acquisition, on the one hand, and native-native (*endolingual*) and native-foreigner (*exolingual*) communicative interactions, on the other hand.

Research Approaches

For American FLL researchers, Besse's Type 3 research, associated with a psycholinguistic perspective, ranks as the most highly valued category. This has led to a predilection for narrow-focus studies, which address highly specific questions within particular theoretical perspectives. For example, Krashen's five hypotheses (1981) provide a common theoretical frame of reference. Given the constraints of classroom FLL in the United States and professional pressures for quick publication of results, these are necessarily cross-sectional studies, the results of which Besse rightfully views as tentative until they can be verified by longitudinal research. At best, these studies yield results that require replication under a variety of comparable situations before valid conclusions can be extrapolated. At worst, they fail to make any significant contribution to the understanding of the processes underlying the nature of FLL. Both types of outcome will be illustrated with reference to recent studies.

A fundamental issue in American FL learning that periodically reappears, particularly when theoretical perspectives undergo reorientation, is that of the usefulness of explicit grammatical analysis for the acquisition of communicative ability. This obviously is linked to the issue of the contribution to acquisition (in Krashen's sense) of overt attention to form. Observing that both proponents of explicit approaches (McLaughlin, Omaggio, Rivers) and opponents (Krashen, Terrell) have failed to marshal adequate empirical support, Virginia Scott proposes to construct an experiment that will settle the issue.

She identifies two morphosyntactic structures of French presumably difficult to learn (the use of the subjunctive and relative pronouns) and then sets out to construct two distinct conditions for the presentation of the target features, one that would qualify as implicit and the other as explicit. The implicit condition is fulfilled by embedding the target features in an oral text. The explicit condition is met by providing learners with formal explanations of the target features. The relative efficacy of each of the two contrasting conditions is measured by comparing the performance of learners following each of the two treatments on a common set of pre- and posttests. On the basis of the results, Scott claims a "clearly . . . superior performance of students exposed to explicit grammar teaching strategies" (1989, 18).

Although superficially this research appears to observe all the canons of controlled experimentation, it is debatable whether the crucial variables, the traits that distinguish implicit and explicit grammatical presentations, are adequately distinguished and whether the evaluation of linguistic performance is meaningfully measured. Let us consider the latter question first. In light of the type of linguistic performance that proponents of the two opposite views have assumed as the desired outcome of instruction, namely, the ability to communicate in naturalistic conditions, the performance tasks devised by Scott are trivial and/or inappropriate. The writing task consists of filling in the blanks in isolated sentences. The oral task, which requires the subject to respond to personalized questions by using the target features, hardly qualifies as communicative. However, the most artificial aspect of the study is the attempt to observe the durable effect on learning of the two pedagogical treatments. These were administered to learners for a total of sixty minutes during a two-week period.

With regard to the distinction between implicit and explicit strategies for the presentation of grammar, it is not obvious that embedding the target features in ten-minute narratives presented during six consecutive class meetings constitutes enriched input. That type of procedure does not ensure that learners will attend to the critical semantic and formal features of the selected target grammatical structures. The most glaring weakness of Scott's definition of the grammatical variable, however, is the superficial and atheoretical nature of the grammatical analysis (as compared to those of Flament-Boistrancourt, 1986 and Lantolf, 1988; see below) and its lack of relevance to a teaching program that aims at imparting a minimal level of communicative ability. Her analysis of the so-called complex relative pronouns identifies only one critical feature, the level of determinacy of the antecedent, but it fails to contrast definite and indeterminate antecedents. Most important, it fails to distinguish among the various discourse functions served by these complex relative pronouns. From a discourse perspective, what is central about these function words is not their invariant indeterminate referent but the function of the types of clauses in which they occur and their relationship to other function words.

Bill VanPatten's more sophisticated and more controlled study dealing with a related issue, the relationship between conscious attention to input and intake in the development of interlanguage (1990), nonetheless demonstrates the limitations of Type 3 psycholinguistically oriented FLL research. To test the claim that simultaneous processing of meaning and form can occur only if comprehension is automatized, thus releasing attention to form, he administers comprehension tasks under three main conditions to students learning Spanish as a FL, who possess various degrees of mastery in the language. The comprehension task involves extracting information from a three-minute recorded sample of the target language while focusing exclusively on the content or while attending either to lexical or grammatical information. The latter concerns grammatical features that are claimed to be lacking in semantic function: agreement for third person plural marked by affixation of -n or the use of the definite determiner la. The results indeed support the hypothesis, but despite its elegance and tight control, inherent problems of validity limit its relevance to the question posed. Does listening to a single three-minute excerpt constitute a significant listening comprehension task, and does the identification of a single lexical item (inflación) represent a significant instance of attending to lexical form? In sum, the study, conducted by one of the ablest young FLL researchers in the United States, points up the dilemma of researchers in the field as they bravely attempt to navigate between the Scylla of lack of rigorous control of variables and the Charybdis of extrapolation from experimental classroom conditions to naturalistic conditions.

In comparison, European FLL researchers favor psycholinguistically oriented studies fitting Besse's Type 2. Although many of these studies share design features found in American research, the concern is less for the demonstrable statistical significance of results than the identification of psycholinguistic processes that orient the development of learners' interlinguistic systems. As will be seen from the studies discussed below, the questions explored are generally broader. The loss of control is compensated for in part by the greater validity of the data amassed and their closer approximation to actual FLL tasks.

SPECIFIC ISSUES

Linguistic Models

Chomskyan models have exerted a less profound influence on research in the area of morphosyntax in Europe than in the United States. One indigenous model that deserves special mention is *enunciative theory,* first put forward by E. Benveniste (1966) but developed within a foreign and second language learning perspective by A. Culioli, one of the leading specialists of English linguistics in France. Culioli has never expounded his theory in readily accessible publications, and it can be extracted only from dissertations and articles dealing with morphosyntactic problems of English, which his disciples have written. Its application to problematic uses of the progressive construction (*be* + *-ing*) will serve to illustrate it (Holec, 1976). The traditional analysis of that construction as a marker of the progressive (inchoative) aspect fails to account for many so-called stylistic uses, such as *You will be forgetting your name next!* or *When she said she took the money, she was lying.* For H. Adamczewski (1974), these so-called marginal uses provide the key to an understanding of the basic function of the feature in communicative interactions. He claims that the English progressive is the *trace* of the presence of the *enunciator* in the *enunciative act.* To relate this notion to generative grammar terms, one might say that the utterance *When she said she took the money, she was lying* contains an implied performative (that is, the enunciator claims with regard to *X* that she is lying). In other words, the utterance is, as it were, filtered through the enunciator who takes the responsibility for its truth value. The pedagogical advantage for communicative FL teaching of a model such as enunciative theory that relates surface structure to pragmatics without the postulation of several layers of deep structure is evident. The enunciation model also harmonizes well with the Piagetian view of language as a cognitive activity and of language acquisition in constructivist terms.

Deep-Level Analysis of Interlanguage

Although they do not eschew universalist sources for interlinguistic features (see, for example, Chaudenson, Valli, and Véronique, 1986), European FLL researchers are more likely than their American counterparts to account for them by transfer from the L1. However, they do not view transfer as operating in the positivistic manner assumed by early contrastive analysts (that is, by the transfer of highly specific surface features), but more abstractly by the interpretation of L2 surface features in terms of L1 subsystems. D. Flament-Boistrancourt's study of relativization in Dutch learners of French (1986) is exemplary in this regard and contrasts with J. Lantolf's interesting comparison of the use of a related syntactic feature by FL learners and native speakers of Spanish (1988).

Flament-Boistrancourt observes that Dutch advanced learners of French (university students up to the master's level) do not consistently distinguish between clausal and NP antecedents in relative phrases serving as prepositional objects. In other words, whereas they generally insert the indeterminate pronoun *ce* in subject or direct object position (for example, *Elle arrive toujours en retard au cours, ce que le professeur ne remarque jamais*), they do so sporadically (from 50% to 10%) in prepositional object position (for example, *Elle arrive toujours en retard, ce dont le professeur se moque*). One explanation for this difference in interlinguistic performance lies in the direction of Kennan and Comrie's Noun Phrase Accessibility Hierarchy (NPAH) (1977): the prepositional object relative clauses are lower in the NPAH implicational hierarchy. But Flament-Boistrancourt also accounts for the disparity between the near-perfect distinction between clausal and NP antecedents at the upper end of the NPAH and the sporadic distinction at the lower end by reference to the students' L1 system. For subjects and direct objects, Dutch matches up with French in providing different relativizers for NP and clausal antecedents in subjects or direct objects (*die* or *dat* versus *wat*, as opposed to *qui* or *que* versus *ce qui* versus *ce que*), but it does not for prepositional objects. In the case of the latter the difference in relativizers (*wie* or *waar,* as opposed to *dont* versus *ce dont* in French) correlates not with the syntactic nature of the antecedents (NP or sentential) but with the animacy feature of the antecedent: + or − human. In other words, the source for the learner's interlinguistic rules is not only syntactic but semantic as well.

In contrast, J. Lantolf attempts to measure the development in interlanguage of syntactic complexity by referring only to universal syntactic implicational hierarchies, the NPAH and the Sentence Complement Hierarchy. The latter postulates an implicational order between medial, initial, and final sentential complements. For example, in Spanish, initial sentential complements (*El que no se casaran le mató*) are marked with respect to final sentential complements (*Ella dijo que él era inteligente),* and would be expected to be acquired late. Indeed, Lantolf shows that, on the one hand, FL learners show few types of relatives located at the lower end of the NPAH (prepositional objects, possessives, and comparatives) and, on the other, that they seldom use initial sentential complements.

The systematic and wholistic nature of interlinguistic restructuring is explored from a different perspective in H. Andersen's (1986) study of the frequency of pronoun usage by Danish high-school learners of French for whom it is the third foreign language (following instruction in English and German). She analyzes patterns of use in terms of a functional hierarchy (subject, object, oblique object) and a higher-level semantic distinction, + human versus − human. She notes invariance of pronoun usage, that is, adherence to target language norms for + human but variability with overgeneralization in the direction of the masculine for − human. That is, learners are likely to correctly distinguish gender (or more probably sex) in [*le monsieur . . . il dit*] or [*la dame . . . elle dit*] than in [*le soleil . . . il/elle brille*] or [*la lune . . . il/elle brille*]. Of course this system of pronominalization also reflects the wider generality of semantically based gender distinction systems.

The Observation of the Development of Syntactic Machinery

An inherent weakness of much interlinguistic research is its use of standard adult formal speech as a reference, rather than vernacular speech employed in situations comparable to those of elicited interlinguistic samples. This faulty frame of reference, which G. Hazaël-Massieux (1986) labels a *supranorm,* leads to exaggerating the deviance of interlinguistic productions with respect to vernacular native speech. Although interlinguistic performance clearly attests to a *linguistic deficit* (Klein and Perdue, 1986), evidenced by the reduction of the content of the message and/or the reorganization of the message by use of pragmatic resources, this appeal to supranorm tends to exaggerate the putative deficit and minimizes the level of syntactic development attained by learners.

The decision by members of European Science Foundation project teams to consider the learners' communicative performance as self-sufficient and their interlanguage autonomous and adequate to meet their linguistic needs has enabled them to demonstrate the interplay of pragmatic and syntactic resources to express basic semantic categories, such as spatio-temporal relation, temporality, or such speech acts as argumentation. These studies have stimulated FLL researchers to look at classroom interactions from the same perspective (Grandcolas and Soulé-Susbielles, 1986).

In contrast, American FLL researchers generally tend to filter interlinguistic data through the categories of normative grammars. As a consequence, they fail to reveal the learner's novel ways of assigning new meanings to target language forms and marking target semantic distinctions in creative ways. In an otherwise noteworthy study of the expression of past tense by intermediate-level university learners of French, M. A. Kaplan (1986) starts from grammatical forms: the contrast between the imperfect tense indicating "a condition or habitual ongoing action in the past" and the compound past (passé composé) designating "a completed past or change of state," instead of from instances of student references to past events or states irrespective of the linguistic means marshaled by them. Although she concludes that the learners seemed to have developed an interlinguistic system in which unmarked forms (present indicative), expressing nonperfective aspect, contrast with the passé composé, expressing perfective aspect, she fails to take into account the fact that the marked member of the tense pair, the passé composé, also expresses a variety of meanings. Examining data collected from young French schoolchildren, A. Bentolila (1983) points out that in interactive discourse the passé composé functions as a completive, whereas in narratives it serves as a punctual. Compare:

1. Quoi, tu n'a pas encore rangé tes affaires?
   You mean to tell me you haven't yet straightened out your things?
   Regarde Stéphane, il a rangé toutes ses affaires.
   Look at Stéphane, he straightened out his things.

2. A Noël mon père il est rentré à la maison avec plein de cadeaux qu'on lui avait donnés à son travail.

At Christmas my father came back home with a lot of toys that they had given him at work.
Oui, il avait un chien, il a sauté dans un cerceau avec du feu.
Yes, he had a dog, it jumped through a flaming hoop.

A. Culioli's enunciative theory would provide a more satisfactory analysis of the various values taken on by these two verbal forms. Also inviting an analysis where the point of view of the enunciator plays a crucial role are uses of the imperfect for modulation: *Qu'est-ce qu'il vous fallait?* or *Qu'est-ce que vous vouliez?* ("What do you wish?"), the typical opener by shopkeepers when greeting customers.

In sharp contrast to Kaplan's more conventional approach are studies by D. Véronique (1986) and G. Kiss (1989) focusing on the structure of interlinguistic tense and aspect systems of learners of French. Although these are naturalistic studies not readily comparable to Kaplan's classroom research, they do show how the insightful analysis of learner productions embedded in a communicative context are more likely to reveal processes of foreign language learning than quantitative analyses of interlinguistic productions of groups of learners. Véronique looks at narratives produced by incipient learners in which the plot is woven with the aid of an unmarked verbal form, which, interpretable as a sort of aorist, is backed up with the adverbial *après*, and in which background circumstances are expressed by the presentative *y en a*:

3. Parce que moi [ātre] la France; y en pas [de] passeport, y en pas de rien. Après [lātre] la France, [lepase] la douane. Après [leparti] l'autoroute. Y en pas de sous, y en pas de rien. Après, y en a le stop. Après [levEny] les gendarmes
   Because I entered in France; there isn't any passport, there isn't anything. After I entered France, I went through customs. After I left the superhighway. There isn't any money, there isn't anything. After, there is hitchhiking. After there came the police.

Rather than tabulating errors in the use and the morphology of the imperfect and the passé composé, G. Kiss attempts to postulate an interlinguistic system by the examination of narratives made by a Hungarian adolescent learner of French. He shows that the function of interlinguistic forms cannot be accounted for only by general factors (transfers from the learner's L1 or previously learned L2s, saliency of morphological marking, and so forth) or by isomorphic interlinguistic relationships between linguistic forms and semantic notions, for example, the use of the present tense for imperfective and the passé composé for perfective. Instead, in interlinguistic performance the relationship between form and meaning is highly variable and highly context-dependent. Thus sentences 4 and 5 contain seemingly random errors in tense selection:

4. Quand Daniel **arrivait** à Paris, il **a fait** beau. = Quand Daniel est arrivé à Paris, il faisait beau.
   When Daniel arrived in Paris, the weather was nice.

5. Quand Daniel arrivait, François et ses parents ont finissé le dîner. = Quand Daniel est arrivé, François et ses parents avaient fini le dîner.
   When Daniel arrived, François and his parents had finished their dinner.

These are explainable by the imperfective meaning carried by the verb *to arrive*, which triggers the use of a contrasting form to carry the durative meaning in 4 and the use of the passé composé to express anteriority in 5, which triggers the use of the imperfect to express the perfective. As Kiss stresses, statistical tabulations of morphological accuracy and semantic and pragmatic appropriateness in the use of the imperfect and the passé composé in his subject's interlinguistic productions would fail to reveal the coherent relationships he has worked out between the L2 grammatical machinery he controls and the semantic and pragmatic demands of the communicative task in which he is engaged.

Exolingual and Endolingual Interaction: Current Sociolinguistic Perspectives

In prefacing a special issue of *Studies in Second Language Acquisition* on native-speaker reactions to approximative systems, Alison d'Anglejan (1983) declared, "It is only more recently that researchers whose main concern is the study of second or foreign language learning and teaching have raised their sights beyond the speaker and the code to include the social dimensions surrounding the acquisition and the use of the non-native language."

In view of the profound differences that exist in the total cultural and social context of foreign language instruction between the United States and Western Europe, it would be surprising if the new research domain delineated by d'Anglejan would be viewed and treated in the same way on both sides of the Atlantic.

If we include the field of English as a foreign language, sociolinguistically oriented research has been both more varied and more massive in the United States, and the direction of influence has been clearly from west to east. It would therefore be difficult to perceive fundamental theoretical and methodological differences. But, from the more limited frame of reference I have set for this paper, the differences are more clearly perceptible. The most salient difference I have been able to identify stems from the limited educational role that foreign language instruction plays in the United States and from the low levels of proficiency attainable under conditions of severely limited contact between the learner and situations of meaningful and communicative use of the target language. As a result, like their teaching colleagues, American FL researchers have focused on linguistic form rather than use, and they have tended to compare the proficiency and the communicative performance of learners with that of highly complexified formal modes of native speech.

One obvious example is oral proficiency testing. The original developers of the oral proficiency interview technique took as the explicit target norm the performance of literate educated native speakers. Though it is only implicit, that norm also serves as the template for the ACTFL version of the oral proficiency interview. But this reference to the well-formed speech of monolinguals has also dominated a very productive current of excellent experimental research. I am referring specifically to studies conducted in the 1970s and 1980s of native speaker reactions to the deviant speech of foreign learners.

Studies designed to determine the effect of errors at various levels of language structure (phonology, grammar, vocabulary) or of specific structural features on comprehension of the message on the basis of native speaker reactions were first conducted in the teaching of English as a foreign language (Burt, 1975; Johansson, 1975, 1978). Ervin (1977) was the first to apply this methodology to foreign language learning, although his more immediate objective was to compare ratings of comprehensibility on the part of three different categories of judges: naive native speakers of Russian, native Russian teachers of Russian to American learners, and American teachers of Russian. Druist (1977) and Guntermann (1977) applied this methodology to the observation of Spanish speakers' reactions to American learners' errors. Guntermann extracted errors in spoken Spanish produced by American Peace Corps volunteers in El Salvador. These errors were incorporated into speech samples produced by other Americans and presented to families with whom the Peace Corps volunteers had lived during their in-country training. Robert Politzer (1978) conducted a more controlled experiment in which 146 German teenagers were asked to compare six types of errors with each other. In addition to level of structure affected, Politzer examined the effect of several native judge characteristics: age, sex, and level of schooling.

French has been the language of predilection for native-speaker reaction studies, perhaps because the French are reputed to be particularly sensitive to foreigners' errors. Ensz (1976) adapted the methodology of Wallace Lambert and his associates in having native listeners react to five guises representing American learners of the language. Piazza (1980) investigated French secondary school students' reactions to six different structural categories of written and oral errors produced by a single American learner. The errors were judged on the basis of comprehensibility and level of irritability induced. Magnan (1982) conducted a similar study, but she returned to Politzer's concerns by also examining the effect of age and social class membership on judgments; younger speakers, most of them from the lower socioeconomic class, were less tolerant of gender errors. As did Ervin, Magnan compared the native speakers' reactions to reactions of various types of American teachers of French.

Viewed from the normative perspective of traditional foreign language teaching, interlanguage represents the attempt by a foreign learner to communicate while exhibiting only partial and deficient control of the target language. The numerous studies of native speakers' reactions to foreign learners' errors imply a view of *exolingual* (native–non-native) communication in which the burden is placed on the weaker partner. It is assumed that his or her deviations from properly formed standard target language usage will cause misunderstandings and irritation. But if, instead, one views interlanguage as an autonomous and self-sufficient idiosyncratic system with internal coherence and integrity (Corder, 1971), one is obliged to consider exolingual communication as involving collaborative negotiation of meaning. If one assumes further that, like *endolingual* (native-native) communication, exolingual communication is governed by Gricean principles and maxims, it requires an attempt on the part of the more competent native partner to reduce inequalities and to adjust to the linguistic deficiencies of the foreigner (Py, 1986). It is this perspective, issuing directly from the interlanguage hypothesis, that has been adopted by several teams associated with the European Science Foundation immigrant adult language acquisition project. Rather than focusing narrowly on the effect of native speakers' input and feedback on learners' intake, these researchers (Giacobbe and Cammarota, 1986; Flament-Boistrancourt, 1987; Vasseur, 1987) attempt to deduce the role of conversational interaction in the construction of interlinguistic grammars and the elaboration of interlinguistic lexicons.

Particularly noteworthy in this regard is the work of the Neuchâtel group, who observe FL acquisition in a naturalistic context (Py, 1986; Py and Alber, 1986; Oesch-Serra, 1989). Although that orientation is outside of the narrow scope set for this contribution, it is likely to have a profound influence on European classroom FL research, and thus deserves discussion. Because the Neuchâtel researchers work in the multilingual Swiss context, they are led to reinterpret features of exolingual interaction, traditionally stigmatized as dysfunctional (code-switching and code-mixing), as devices used by the participants to negotiate meaning and to manage communication. This type of research necessarily requires the minute analysis of conversational exchanges within the framework of the ethnography of speaking. For example, Oesch-Serra observed complex bilingual-diglossic interactions involving French, Standard German, and Swiss German in a Basel market. The interactions are complex, not only because the participants may choose from three different linguistic codes, but also because they interact at the same time as friends and vendor-customer. As they perform a commercial transaction, two of the participants—the native French vendor and the diglossic Swiss-German–Standard-German-speaking customer—narrate important recent events in their daily lives. Code-switching and code-mixing serve interactional, discursive, and more narrowly linguistic needs: they contribute to the more precise communication of meaning, the highlighting of topics, and the saving of face. From a different perspective, the participants alternate between an endolingual (here, more specifically, bilingual) and an exolingual mode of conversational interaction depending on whether the focus is on language use or language acquisition. The following two excerpts will illustrate the complexity of the interaction.

Ursula, a diglossic Swiss-German–Standard-German speaker, is buying food from her friends, Pierre and Annie, a Swiss-French-speaking couple who are vendors at the Basel market. In a German-speaking context Pierre uses the dialect, whereas his wife prefers the standard variety. As the commercial transaction unfolds, Annie is talking about the grade she received in an evening course and her children's reaction to the grade given her:

6. U   alors je prends encore un *zweihundert . . . oder so.* je sais pas. mets dedans
       then I'll take yet another two hundred more or less I don't know. Put in

A die Kinder sie haben soviel gelacht . . .
   the children they have so much laughed . . .

                              hesch freud gha?
                              Were they pleased?
A aber es ist so sch/schwer jetzt. c'est vraiment difficile jetzt tu vois
   but it's really difficult now   it's really difficult   now you see
A un six. c'est mon *zeugniss*
   a six. that's my report card

The interlocutors are in a bilingual (and also diglossic) mode, with switches between French and German (either the dialect or the standard variety). Code-switching serves both discursive and interactional functions, and the code-mix *zeugniss* reflects the fact that Annie is studying in Basel and is more likely to use the German term rather than its French equivalent *bulletin de notes*.

The exolingual mode manifests itself clearly in the next excerpt. To remedy a lexical gap in French Ursula switches to German. When Annie requests a repair, Ursula saves face by providing a French paraphrase after Pierre has provided her the French term needed for the repair. Note that both Annie and Pierre indicate to her that the repair has been properly accomplished:

7. U elle veut devenir *Geigenbauerin* pour le moment . . . pour ça il faut pas aller
      she wants to become instrument maker for now . . . for that it's not necessary to go
   A   qu'est-ce que c'est
                                                    what's that
   P   ah bon
                                                    oh yes
   U au gymnase   luthier. c'est luthier? *Geigenbauerin* celle qui fait les violons
      to high school instrument maker it's—   the one who makes violins
   A   ah!   ah oui
                                            oh.   *oh yes*
   P   luthier   ouais
          instrument maker   *yeah*
   U elle a dit. alors *dann werde ich Tierwär/wärterin.* tu sais ceux qui
      then she said. then I'll become veterinarian. you know those who
   A   ja
                                            yes
   U soignent les animaux
      take care of animals

The inclusion of complex bilingual situations where participants move back and forth between endolingual and exolingual interaction reduces the distinction between these two types of communicative situations, and it links to FL teaching types of mother tongue education where school children need to master a variety distinct from their vernacular. One domain of sociolinguistics where mother tongue education and FL teaching concerns merge is that of the establishment of suitable target norms. Valdman (1989) points out that the speech of native speakers varies with regard to degree of planning in response to social and contextual factors and that it is oriented toward alternative norms depending on speakers' sociopsychological orientations. This multitarget norm model makes the choice of any particular native norm as the target for foreign learners too restrictive. Instead, dynamic pedagogical norms need to be devised that can be modified as the learner's proficiency develops.

CONCLUSION

Although, as is the case for its American counterpart, Western European FLL research has been greatly influenced by trends and models in the field of ESL, it shows significant differences. Whereas American FL research tends to be product-oriented and experimental, European research is more likely to focus on the process of learning. It also favors observation of language use in interactional situations rather than evaluation of relative mastery of specific structural features. In the analysis of products of FLL, American researchers tend to adhere to traditional linguistic models and categories that operate with relatively superficial phenomena divorced from pragmatics. In contrast, Europeans refer to a wider variety of grammatical models, some of which, such as enunciation theory, take into account directly the specific circumstances under which language is used. Because their linguistic models start from deeper semantic notions and pragmatic intentions, European FLL researchers are less likely to favor extreme innatist views, and though they accept the centrality of restructuring in the formation of interlinguistic grammars and lexicons, they interpret it as involving significant, albeit very indirect, transfer from the learner's L1 or previously learned L2s. Transfer is likely to be more complex in Western Europe, where students either study more than one foreign language, or come to the FL class with previous bilingual or multilingual language use experience. Also, because European FL sequences are longer than those in the United States, it is easier to conduct longitudinal experimental or observational research. For example, in assessing attrition in the learning of French, Weltens, Van Els, and Schils (1989) had the opportunity of selecting students who had studied the language at the secondary school level for four hundred to six hundred hours. As Besse (1986) points out, to be properly scientific and significant, research in FL learning must be both replicable and longitudinal rather than cross-sectional in nature.

It should not be concluded from these remarks that Western European FL research is necessarily superior to that conducted in the United States. But just as our colleagues in Western Europe have been influenced and stimulated by research conducted in the field of ESL, so would American researchers benefit from keeping in touch with SLA and FLL research conducted by European colleagues, especially that of French and Swiss French teams, whose results are unlikely to appear in English-dominated international journals. The highly specific context of FL instruction in this country, especially the overt and covert objectives, shape and constrain the type of research that may be undertaken. For example, the strong emphasis on well-formed, formal, and highly standardized speech reflects a deeply ingrained though covert preference for language analysis. This dominant current in American FL teaching accounts for the tendency for researchers to focus on superficial grammatical features, which bear little resemblance to those of evolving interlinguistic systems that reflect the psycholinguistic processes underlying actual learning.

REFERENCES

Adamczewski, H. 1974. "BE + ing Revisited." *Linguistic Insights in Applied Linguistics.* Eds. S. P. Corder and E. Roulet. Brussels: AIMAV, and Paris: Didier.

Andersen, H. 1986. "L'Acquisition et l'Emploi des Pronoms Français par des Apprenants Danois." *ALE* 1: 25–44.

Arditty, J., and D. Coste. 1987. "Rapport: Interactions." *SALE* 15–22.

Bentolila, A. 1983. *Temps et Aspect en Français. Application au Discours de l'Enfant.* Port-au-Prince: Centre de Linguistique de l'Université d'Etat d'Haïti.

Benveniste, E. 1966. *Problèmes de Linguistique Générale.* Paris: Gallimard.

Besse, H. 1986. "Présentation: Apprentissage Guidé." *ALE* 2: 633–46.

Burt, M. 1975. "Error Analysis in the Adult EFI Classroom." *TESOL Quarterly* 9: 53–63.

Chaudenson, R., A. Valli, and D. Véronique. 1986. "The Dynamics of Linguistic Systems and the Acquisition of French as a Second Language." *SSLA* 8: 277–92.

Corder, S. P. 1971. "Idiosyncratic Dialects and Error Analysis." *International Review of Applied Linguistics in Language Teaching* 9: 17–160.

d'Anglejan, A. 1983. Introduction to special issue. *SSLA* 5: vii–ix.

Druist, J. 1977. "Grammatical Patterns in the Spoken Spanish of Bilingual Teenagers." Paper presented at the Annual Queens College Conference on Bilingualism and Second Language Teaching and Learning, New York.

Ensz, K. Y. 1976. "French Attitudes Toward Speech Deviances of American Speakers of French." Diss. Stanford University, Stanford.

Ervin, G. L. 1977. "A Study of the Use and Acceptability of Target Language Communication Strategies Employed by American Students of Russian." Diss. Ohio State University, Columbus.

Faerch, C., and G. Kasper. 1985. Introduction. *Foreign Language Learning under Classroom Conditions.* Eds. C. Faerch and G. Kasper. *SSLA* 7: 131–33.

Ferguson, C., and T. Huebner. 1989. "Foreign Language Instruction and Second Language Acquisition Research in the United States." *NFLC Occasional Papers.* 1–9.

Flament-Boistrancourt, D. 1986. "L'Interlangue Est-Elle un Système Réellement Autonome? Quelles Relations Entretient-Elle avec L1 et L2? Le Modèle

Chomskyen d'Acquisition, Sous-Jacent à l'Hypothèse de l'Interlangue, Est-Il Adéquat?" *ALE* 1: 71–84.

———. 1987. "Quelques Aspects du Rôle de l'Interaction Dans la Constitution d'Une Interlangue." *SALE* 63–71.

Giacobbe, J., and M. A. Cammarota. 1986. "Un Modèle du Rapport Langue Source/Langue Cible." *ALE* 1: 193–210.

Grandcolas, B., and N. Soulé-Susbielles. 1986. "The Analysis of the Foreign Language Classroom." *SSLA* 293–308.

Guntermann, G. 1977. "An Investigation of the Frequency, Comprehensibility and Evaluational Effects of Errors in Spanish Made by English-Speaking Learners in El Salvador." Diss. Ohio State University, Columbus.

Hazäel-Massieux, G. 1986. "La Créolisation: Est-Elle un Phénomène Limité dans le temps? L'expression du futur en Guadeloupe." Communication au V Colloque International des Etudes Crèoles, in *Etudes Crèoles* IX, 1: 114–26.

Holec, H. 1976. "Les 'Colloques' de Linguistique Appliquée de Neuchâtel (1972–75) I: Enonciation et Fonction de Communication." *Bulletin CILA* 49–55.

Johansson, S. 1975. "Papers in Contrastive Linguistics and Language Testing." *Lund Studies in English* 50.

———. 1978a. "Studies of Error Gravity: Native Reactions to Errors Produced by Swedish Learners of English." *Gothenburg Studies in English* 44.

———. 1978b. "Problems in Studying the Communicative Effects of Learners' Errors." *SSLA* 1: 41–52.

Kaplan, M. A. 1986. "Developmental Patterns of Past Tense Acquisition Among Foreign Learners of French." *Language Learning: A Research Perspective*. Eds. B. VanPatten, T. R. Dvorak, and J. F. Lee. Cambridge, Mass.: Newbury House. 52–60.

Keenan, E. L., and B. Comrie. 1977. "Noun Phrase Accessibility and Universal Grammar." *Linguistic Inquiry* 8: 63–99.

Kiss, G. 1989. "Le Cas des Grammaires Distantes: L'Acquisition des Temps du Passé par un Hungarophone." *Le Français dans le Monde* (Numéro Spécial—"Et la Grammaire"). February-March 1989. 75–83.

Klein, W., and C. Perdue. 1986. "Comment Résoudre une Tâche Verbale Complexe avec Peu de Moyens Linguistiques?" *ALE* 1: 307–30.

Krashen, S. 1981. *Second Language Acquisition and Second Language Learning*. Oxford: Pergamon Press.

Lantolf, J. 1988. "The Syntactic Complexity of Written Texts in Spanish as a Foreign Language: A Markedness Perspective." *Hispania* 71: 933–40.

Magnan, S. 1982. "Native Speaker Reaction as Criterion for Error Correction." *ESL and the Foreign Teacher: Report of Central States Conference on the Teaching of Foreign Languages*. Ed. A. Garfinkel. Skokie, Ill.: National Textbook Co. 30–45.

Oesch-Serra, C. 1989. "Gestion Interactive et Complexification du Discours: Les Séquences Narratives en Conversation Exolingue." Paper delivered at the Septième Colloque International, "Acquisition d'Une Langue Etrangère: Perspectives et Recherches." Aix-en-Provence, June 1989, 15–7.

Piazza, L. 1980. "French Tolerance for Grammatical Errors Made by Americans." *The Modern Language Journal* 64: 422–27.

Politzer, R. L. 1978. "Errors of English Speakers of German as Perceived and Evaluated by German Natives." *The Modern Language Journal* 62: 253–61.

Py, B. 1986. "Making Sense: Interlanguage's Intertalk in Exolingual Conversation." *SSLA* 8: 353.

Py, B., and J. Alber. 1986. "Interlangue et Conversation Exolingue." *ALE* 1: 147–65.

Schuman, J. 1978. *The Pidginization Process: A Model for Language Acquisition.* Rowley, Mass.: Newbury House.

Scott, V. 1989. "An Empirical Study of Explicit and Implicit Teaching Strategies in French." *Modern Language Journal* 73: 14–22.

Valdman, A. 1989. "The Problem of the Target Model in Proficiency-Oriented Language Instruction." *Applied Language Learning* 1: 33–51.

VanPatten, B. 1990. "Attending to Form and Content in Input: An Experiment in Consciousness." *SSLA* 12: forthcoming.

Vasseur, M. T. 1987. "La Collaboration Entre les Partenaires Dans les Echanges Entre Locuteurs Natifs et Apprenants Etrangers: Formes, Développements et Variations." *SALE* 32–43.

Véronique, D. 1986. "Reference to Past Events and Actions in Narratives in L2: Insights from North African Workers' French." *First and Second Language Acquisition Processes.* Ed. C. W. Pfaff. Cambridge, Mass.: Newbury House. 252–72.

Weltens, B., T. J. M. Van Els, and E. Schils. 1989. "The Long-Term Retention of French by Dutch Students." *SSLA* 11: 205–16.

_____ Section V___

The Acquisition of
Cultural Competence

Chapter 12

The Order of Discourse in Language Teaching

Claire Kramsch

University of California at Berkeley

Twenty years after the post-structuralist revolution in language teaching, researchers and practitioners are pausing to take stock. In Germany, Piepho is heralding the "post-communicative revolution" in language teaching (Piepho, 1989); in the United States, foreign language educators are looking beyond the early proficiency guidelines to postproficiency trends.

The road is not as easy as it seemed. Goals on which there seemed to be a consensus are more elusive than ever. In fact the very language used to describe these goals has proved treacherous; words such as *interaction, communication, authentic texts, individualized instruction,* either have been trivialized or have proliferated like professional viruses beyond recognition. Inflationary rhetoric and the uncautious transfer of research terminology into education have not only elicited the misunderstandings we know about the uses of the ACTFL guidelines (see, for example, Lee and Musumeci, 1988; MLJ Readers' Forum, 1988), they have generated among many foreign language teachers a distrust of language that should indeed make us pause, precisely because our business is language study.

This malaise in our professional language is only one aspect of a malaise that relates to what I will call, echoing Foucault, the order of discourse (Foucault, 1970). The notion of discourse in language teaching, born with Widdowson within the push for communication, has not had the role it should have had in subsequent public discussions. Second language acquisition research, as Edmondson notes (forthcoming), has been interested mainly in linear phenomena of turn-taking in conversation according to a cause-and-effect notion of interaction. Teachers and publishers have followed this "weak" interpretation of discourse. They have renamed discourse competence *sociocultural* competence, reducing it to the appropriate use of social politeness formulae and conversational management strategies.

The linguistic definition of discourse we have been using up to now, roughly that of "language in use in social contexts," has misled teachers into separating language from the conceptual schemata that language creates, the conceptual terrain in which knowledge is formed and produced through language. And indeed, discourse is not simply what is said per se, nor even, according to Ellis's definition (1986, 141), the procedures used for checking on uptake or comprehension, or the interactional sequences within conversation, but all the rules and categories of language use that organize our thoughts and our experience and that are so taken for granted, so much assumed as a constituent part of our cognitive system and therefore of knowledge, that they remain unvoiced and unreflected. These aspects of discourse, which concern ethnographers and anthropological linguists, have been excluded until now from language teaching research.

I will first try to stake out the procedures of exclusion that research and practice have imposed on themselves in relation to three aspects of the current discourse on communicative language teaching: focus on the learner, negotiation of meaning, and authentic contexts. I will then argue that the only way to bring about the changes that we aim for in foreign language education is to reintroduce the order of discourse into public awareness.

FOCUS ON THE LEARNER

Despite the best intentions to center foreign language teaching on the learner, the profession still operates under the assumption of an ideal unitary, unidimensional learner, individualistic in its purposes and needs, undivided in its intentions. This view is not only a reflection of a whole educational philosophy; it is also handed down from traditional speech act theory, itself inspired by Chomsky's ideal speaker. As Mary Louise Pratt remarks in her outspoken article on the ideology of the speech act, "speech act theory, in at least some of its dominant versions, supposes the existence behind every normal speech act of an authentic, self-consistent essential subject, a true self, which does or does not hold the intention that the other is supposed to recognize," does or does not know or want to give the answer to the question (Pratt, 1981, 8).

Of course, we know that learners vary. We know the effect that different types of literacy acquired at home can make on the way learners perceive and respond to questions (Sato, 1982; Heath, 1983); we recognize that there are gender differences in students' attitudes to language (Börsch, 1982) and in their use of language in social settings (Treichler and Kramarae, 1983); we have been shown the role that general educational background can play in the academic display of communicative competence (Cummins, 1983). Yet learner variables are seen as accounting only for learners' successes or failures; they have not put in question the (unitary) core of what should be taught and learned in language classes. Foreign language teachers still view it as their responsibility to give their students only the linguistic wherewithal to function appropriately in another speech community. They don't feel they have the obligation or even the time to teach academic literacy skills, alternative socialization skills, or sociocultural awareness of the students' native culture. They focus on the learner, but theirs is a truncated view of the learner.

Let me add that this narrow view is not only due to the paucity of SLA research in this area. It is true, as Swaffar pointed out recently, that "research too often looks at the learner without considering the learner variables" (Swaffar, 1989, 309) and that we need much more research on the ethnography of second language learning. But the paucity of ethnographic studies is in itself symptomatic of a lack of involvement in discourse phenomena in language acquisition.

The principles of exclusion I mentioned for the learner have been applied also to the notion of *speaker*. Speakers are taken for monolithic entities that ask for information, formulate excuses and complaints, express opinions and beliefs. These unified speakers act according to the Gricean principle of cooperation, which states, "Make your contribution such as is required, at the stage at which it occurs, by the accepted purpose or direction of the talk-exchange in which you are engaged." (Grice, 1975). Grice elaborates this principle with the four well-known maxims: be brief, be true, be relevant, be clear.

It is little wonder that foreign language learners have difficulty conforming to this ideal speaker type. When asked a seemingly innocuous question at the beginning of a lesson, such as, "Qu'est-ce que vous avez fait ce week-end?" they already stall and stutter: how much does the teacher want to know? does she really want to know how I spent my weekend? how relevant is it to a lesson on the passé composé? and then, which speaker persona should I put forth? A standard American self ("I studied, played football, and went to the movies"), a nonstandard self ("Well, er, I really didn't know what to do with myself . . ."), an institutional French learner self who will dutifully construct a weekend occupation out of the freshly learned vocabulary, or a French fictional self ("I murdered my brother, raped my sister, and drowned the cat")?

The Cross Cultural Speech Act Realization Project, conducted by an international team of linguists and reported on recently by Blum-Kulka, House, and Kasper (1989), started out with a universal view of speech acts. Its goal was to study the different linguistic realizations of the two speech acts, request and apology, across seven different languages and language varieties: German, British English, American English, Australian English, Danish, Hebrew, and Canadian French. It was to examine the value and function of politeness or deference in speech act realization and the universality of politeness phenomena across languages and cultures. They did find some marked cross-cultural differences in the selection, distribution, and realization of various pragmatic and discourse functions (for instance, Hebrew speakers tended to phrase their requests more directly than German speakers, German speakers seemed to use more listener's feedback in conversation than did British English speakers). However, more interesting, the results showed that differences in speech act realization were not accounted for by national factors alone, but that national factors interacted strongly with the way speakers perceived the situation: all the languages studied varied their mode of speech act performance by situational factors.

For instance, Juliane House's comparison of the realization of the marker *please* and the equivalent German marker *bitte* shows that the initial global assumption of cross-linguistic differences in the use of please/bitte had to be substantially refined (House, 1989). House had originally organized her variables according to six criteria of contrastive pragmatics: dominance, familiarity, right of requester to make the request, degree of obligation to comply with the request, likelihood of compliance, and degree of difficulty involved in making the request.

She pretty soon realized, however, that all these criteria interacted with the perception by the subjects of the value of the situation. If the situation was one that included a high obligation to comply with the request, a low degree of difficulty in performing it, and a strong right to pose that request, such as service encounters or bureaucratic exchanges, participants perceived that situation to be a *standard situation*. By contrast, if the obligation of the requestee to comply was relatively low, the request relatively difficult to make and if the requester had relatively low right to make the request, such as between personal acquaintances, the situation was perceived to be *nonstandard*.

Standard situations elicit more frequent use of please/bitte than nonstandard ones. For instance, in a standard encounter with a taxi driver, the question of the driver, "Where to, please?" is acceptable, but that question would sound odd in the nonstandard situation of a guest taking a fellow-guest home. Likewise, a policeman can ask, "What's your name, please?" but a party-goer should not use *please* to ask the name of another party-goer over cocktails. So please/bitte is not primarily a universal politeness marker, as was originally thought, but a situational marker.

House analyzed the behavior of native and non-native speakers of British English and of German in two situations: in the first, a student asks his roommate to clean up the kitchen, which the latter has left in a mess the night before; in the second, a policeman asks a driver to move her car. German speakers and German learners of English seemed to perceive both the kitchen and the policeman situations to be standard situations, licensing the use of the imperative with please/bitte; so to the roommate they would say, "Räum bitte die Küche auf/please clean up the kitchen," and as a policeman they would say to the driver, "Fahren Sie bitte weiter/move your car please"; by contrast, British English speakers would use much greater indirectness and no *please;* they would say to their roommate, "Do you think you could clean up the kitchen?" and to the driver of the car, "Would you move your car, Ma'am?" seemingly giving both situations a nonstandard value.

Of course the notion of standard and nonstandard itself varies according to cultures, which prompts Wolfson, Marmor, and Jones to remark, "Just as different cultures divide the color spectrum into noncorresponding or overlapping terms, so the repertoire of speech acts for each culture is differently organized" (Wolfson, Marmor, and Jones, 1989, 180). They go on to quote Coulmas: "The question of how a given communicative function is verbally realized in another speech community must always be conjoined with the question of how this function itself is defined by the members of the community in question and what status it has in the framework of its overall communicative pattern" (Coulmas 1981, 70).

Studying American English discourse patterns, Wolfson (1988) observed that middle-class Americans, too, differ in their speech behavior according to whether their relationship with their interlocutor is well-defined or whether it is open for definition or redefinition. The more status and social distance are seen as fixed, the more likely it is that people will know what to expect of one another and the less likely they are to run the risk of doing themselves social damage. Thus, intimates, status-unequals, and strangers all have in common a well-defined standing, whereas nonintimates, status-equal friends, coworkers, and acquaintances have a more fluid, ill-defined standing vis-à-vis the speaker. The phrase "Let's have lunch together sometime," said to a status-equal nonintimate acquaintance, is meant as the possible opening in a negotiation that may lead to a true social commitment. As we know, the social value of such an invitation by white, middle-class Americans is often misinterpreted by foreigners, who find its vagueness extremely frustrating and see it as a typical example of American insincerity.

So research in pragmatics points strongly to the importance of the situation, the context, as codeterminant of a person's intentions and appropriate behavior. It is not the *function* of expressing politeness in a foreign language that is most difficult for a foreigner, but understanding a *notion* of politeness that might be different from one's own. Up to now we have thought it was enough to give students the relevant linguistic structures, in order for them to function appropriately by expressing an alleged universal notion of politeness with foreign words. Now we have to realize that this will not do and that we also have to initiate learners to another way of "being in the world" (Becker, 1984).

NEGOTIATION OF MEANING

The exclusionary procedures observed in the definition of the learner/speaker have been at work also with respect to the basic tenet of communicative language teaching: negotiation of intended meanings. Not only learning and speaking, but the notion of communication itself has been predicated on a unique, original, creative individual exchanging and clarifying the meanings he or she clearly intended, according to Gricean principles.

And yet, we know that this is too schematic a view. The mouths of our students are filled with the words of others, or as Bakhtin would say "Language is . . . populated—overpopulated—with the intentions of others" (Bakhtin 1981, 294, quoted in Cazden, 1989). Their dialogues, their role-plays, their compositions, are full of invisible quotes from their surrounding public discourse: the media, commercials, childrens' books, policitcal rhetoric, literature. As the anthropological linguist A. L. Becker remarks, "Each person is an overlay of prior texts, which can be examined (introspectively) in a single human being (for unquestionably that overlay is different for each of us) or in a culture (since, just as unquestionably, the prior texts we have access to are far more numerous than those we individually remember)" (Becker, 1984, 218).

In the classroom these invisible quotes take on the appearance of errors in grammar and vocabulary. The American student of German who starts the sentence, "Ich mag . . . challenges" and asks the teacher, "Miss, how do you say *challenge* in German?" doesn't realize that his difficulty is not a missing vocabulary item, but a whole way of viewing the world. Whereas German culture considers difficulties as *Hindernisse* (obstacles), *Aufgaben* (tasks), *Probleme* (problems) or even *Schicksale* (destinies), American culture, born from a different history, values obstacles as tests of strength, things or events to be surmounted, overcome, beaten, and won, as on a football field. The American student first has to be sensitized to the ideological value of the word *challenge* in his/her own culture: the pioneer spirit of white America's beginnings, the inflation of the word in the last ten years, when entrepreneurship is praised to the point where even such catastrophes as the oil spills in Alaska are called "environmental challenges" by the media, and when the official term for such personal tragedies as physically handicapped persons is now "the physically challenged."

So when the student writes the following sentence: "Ich mag Herausforderungen aber diese Klasse ist lächerlich" (I like challenges, but this class is ridiculous)—meaning, "I like to study hard and to do difficult homework, but this course requires so much work that it is not fun anymore"—the teacher has to clarify the nature of the cross-cultural miscommunication. The prevalent sports metaphor in American English implies that an obstacle is first welcome as a test of strength until it is so overwhelming that it becomes ridiculous, that is, unfair competition. One then has a reason to refuse to compete and to leave the field, but not to put the obstacle in question. For a German speaker, such a metaphor cannot be applied to a learning task; one would speak, rather, of *Aufgabe,* or task, duty, responsibility.

Challenge versus task, environmental challenge versus environmental catastrophe, physical challenge versus human tragedy: two radically different world views expressed through language.

Not only is our students' discourse filled with invisible quotes, but so is the discourse of the profession itself. Just look at such phrases as *true* communication, *authentic* materials, *natural* approach, learners' *needs,* even words such as *interaction* and *negotiation of meaning*—the success of these phrases or concepts is due in no small part to the fact that they echo American political ideology (Polanyi, 1989). This ideology values the straightforward and the natural, by contrast with the artful and artificial; it believes that an individual is entitled to have needs, that these needs should be met, and that there is no problem that cannot be solved by honest, dispassionate, and rational (that is, unemotional) negotiation.

In an article entitled "The Politics of Politeness: Social Warrants in Mainstream American Public Etiquette," Thomas Kochman remarks that there is a political character to mainstream American public protocols of which mainstreamers are not aware. Examining in particular the concept of negotiation, he notes that it is based on the following basic beliefs: "there are multiple sides to an issue; no side has a monopoly on the truth; the more firmly one side believes that it is right, the less likely it is to be flexible enough to acknowledge the truth of the other side's position and to agree to [compromise]. Moreover, to the extent that one side is angry or emotional, its perspective on matters is likely . . . to be distorted." In Kochman's analysis, this social etiquette acts as a socializing agent: "it promotes mainstream American communication and discredits that of other social or cultural groups." It discredits in particular "presentations that are argumentative, confrontational, and emotional; presentations that reflect or display the degree to which an individual believes in what he/she says; or presentations that might rely upon force of individual personality or verbal skill in order to succeed . . ." (Kochman, 1984, 203).

Whoever has tried to teach students a different discourse style in conversation (more aggressive interruption patterns, greater verbal display, stronger confrontational positions, different patterns of indirectness) knows, from the sometimes virulent resistance encountered, how political and ideological such social practices are.

In a 1989 paper in which she examines the contributions of the Bakhtin circle to the notion of communicative competence, C. Cazden compares the different views of Hymes and Bakhtin on the matter:

> From the beginning Hymes has argued against the Chomskyian notion of a homogeneous speech community, and for recognition of diverse ways of speaking any single language. But in his portrayal of a "community as an organization of diversity," the images of co-existence seem peaceful, and individual shifting among language varieties seems painless unless access to the conditions necessary for their acquisition has been denied. For Bakhtin, the images are more of conflict than of co-existence—not only because of the external positioning of any speaker in the social structure, but because of the ideological marking of speech genres and words.

She adds, "Perhaps it would be fair to say that in Hymes's writings on communicative competence, the significant social problem is that of acquisition, and the conditions of interaction and the attitudes of identification that influence it. Whereas for Bakhtin, who writes less of acquisition, a significant phenomenon is the intra-individual heterogeneity—and potential conflict—among whatever varieties have been acquired" (Cazden, 1989, 122). Although Hymes sees himself as coming from a Marxist tradition, it is true that his work, with its greater emphasis on access than on conflict, reflects the way social issues are framed in the United States.

So, to go back to our previous example, negotiating the meaning of the German word *Herausforderung* would entail not eliminating the differences or even coming to a compromise between two opposed conceptions of *challenge,* but understanding fully the political passions that people attach to their world views and the power of the myths that nourish their imaginations.

Research and practice in SLA have excluded intra- and interlearner conflict. Our very notion of negotiation of meaning is based on a mainstream view of social behavior that our non-American students might not share and that the foreign culture might not warrant. In so doing, we have limited the discussions about two important notions to which I will now turn: context and authenticity.

AUTHENTIC CONTEXTS

When we view learners as socially constituted subjects, context is not just the backdrop against which a person speaks, but rather, context and subject continually mutually determine each other. We have always known this, and yet we act as if authenticity were attached to the authentic self, rather than being the result of forces that are at play in the situation.

When we use videotapes to show foreign behaviors and customs, their truth does not lie in the veracity of the slice of life ("that's how native speakers talk, behave, and so forth"), but in the way these speakers do what they do because of the social context that they create and respond to. If taught as a series of fragments of behavior with no links to any religious, historical, literary, or artistic context, such authentic videos are used in quite an inauthentic manner. Authenticity is not in the text, nor is it in the individual, but rather it is constitutive of the social and political conditions in the production of discourse.

Even the prefabricated dialogues of textbooks are authentic when viewed as the product of writers and publishers within a given educational and commercial situation (Kramsch, 1988).

The reasons for the general reluctance to teach language itself as a form of discourse are many. Discourse, as social practice, focuses on the extreme relativity of meaning and on the endless inter- and intralearner variation in language learning; it is thus unsettling for students in search of rules of speech and norms of behavior. It stresses particulars rather than universals of language acquisition; it is thus troublesome for teachers who have to teach different groups of different learners at different times of the day. It touches issues of social class and personal styles; it is therefore a sensitive subject in classes where learners come from different social and ethnic backgrounds. But the major reason why discourse has not found its full place in syllabi and guidelines is that discourse is not decontextualized knowledge; it is context itself.

One principle of educational policy is to teach decontextualized or at least context-reduced skills. Children learn to read and write by abstracting from the immediate surrounding context, thus gaining the power to manipulate various contexts through verbal control. But discourse—it is so tied to the competence, expressive agenda, rhetorical strategy, and functional goals of the speaker; the phatic ties of the speaker to the hearer; the indexical ties to the setting, the participants, and other dimensions of the speech event, with its structure emerging only in the course of its performance—discourse should be resistant to extraction from context. And yet textbooks now feature conversational gambits and sociolinguistic markers to be learned as items of vocabulary; authentic materials are used for behavioral training. By being taught as text, discourse has been decontextualized and is now taught according to structuralist principles of language learning.

Admittedly, this is not the whole picture. We have in fact recontextualized the foreign discourse, but into another culture—the culture of the American classroom: communication strategies are practiced in group interaction, grammatical exercises are "contextualized" by a one-sentence situational lead-in, authentic materials are used as a springboard for discussing larger cultural issues. Nevertheless, two constraints have been implicitly imposed on this recontextualization. Foreign discourse is now being observed, practiced, and discussed from an American cultural perspective and through American educational values. This is unavoidable to be sure; but isn't the role of education to help students decipher the rules and conventions in the production of educational discourse, too?

If we want to recapture the order of discourse in all its dimensions, we have to make learners and teachers conscious of its conditions of production throughout the foreign language curriculum: from the dialogues of their first-year textbooks to their literature, civilization, and history courses. I would like therefore to suggest a metaphor for a three-pronged, cross-cultural approach to the teaching of language as discourse. I will call these respectively the *container,* the *collage,* and the *montage* metaphors of language teaching. They are not ordered here according to developmental sequence or importance hierarchy. Each prong should be activated at every step of a learner's acquisition of language in an educational system.

CONTAINER — COLLAGE — MONTAGE: ASPECTS OF THE DEVELOPMENT OF CROSS-CULTURAL DISCOURSE COMPETENCE

Container

The first form of sensitization to discourse could be expressed through the container metaphor. A container is a receptacle for the storage and transportation of goods; as such it might be a suitable metaphor for the reception and transmission of knowledge. As in fairy tales, the learner-hero receives from a benevolent helper a magic box, a pot or a bottle that fills up with a life-saving substance when the magic words are uttered. Our professional language is very much influenced by this container metaphor: we speak of *learning content,* of *input and output,* of *learning outcomes, modes of delivery, target culture,* and we encourage our students to *retrieve* and *process information* by using specific communication strategies. We teach them also those gambits in conversation or magic etiquette *formulae* that can open for them the doors to social acceptability in face-to-face interactions.

There is one problem, however, with the container metaphor in language learning. Like the conduit metaphor, it is predicated on a reductionist view of human communication. Although facts and cultural information are necessary for communication, human relations and human understanding do not occur by using the correct magic formula or by applying the right cultural piece of information.

What we need is a metaphor that captures the relational nature of discourse, the complex and difficult negotiation of meaning that a student has to engage in to make sense of the social and cultural reality that the language both reflects and creates.

Collage

The plastic arts could provide us with a better metaphor, that of collage, that is, the juxtaposition of *papiers collés* or seemingly disconnected elements, to make a meaningful whole, analogous to the meaningful context that two interlocutors strive to create through a common language. A collage-type pedagogy orders grammatical, lexical, and cultural facts in such a way that they yield a deeper social meaning: syntactic structures are connected with speakers' intentions, vocabulary items are linked to the values attached to the corresponding concepts. Let me take an example.

When vocabulary items such as *work, vacation,* and *family,* are used in social contexts, they become loaded with what Galisson calls "charge culturelle partagée," culturally loaded concepts that have acquired a given meaning through their use across a variety of contexts at various times in history: slogans and statistics, pamphlets and posters, novels, poems, and newspaper articles (Galisson, 1987). Foreign learners of the language need help reconstructing this collage of contexts, and some textbooks offer precisely that. For example, *Sichtwechsel,* by Hog, Müller, and Wessling (1984), attempts to convey, by means of a collage of travel brochures, private letters, publicity ads, and literary texts, what a German speaker means by a good (*tolle*) or a lousy (*miese*) vacation. More recently, computer-assisted interactive videodiscs and hypertext technology permit extensive use of the collage principle for learning language in various contexts of use (Kramsch, 1989).

However, a collage approach cannot avoid the inherent subjectivity in the choice of cultural events and in the perspective of their presentation. For example, one of the favorite topics of textbooks written in France or Germany for the teaching of French and German as a second language is indeed that of leisure or vacation, such as in French, "Que faites-vous pendant vos loisirs?" and in German, "Wie verbringen Sie Ihre Freizeit?" This topic has a high priority on the list of potential topics of conversation in the two countries. But the very choice of this topic is for American students of moderate interest only, since the concept of leisure or vacation does not belong to public discourse as it does in Europe. For North American high school and college students, the question "How do you spend your vacations?" is often even irrelevant, since having a job during the summer and during the year is not only a financial necessity but an essential ingredient of one's self-image. Thus, the symbolic value of vacation is different in different countries and so is its importance as a topic of conversation.

Furthermore, although the collage principle strives to make sense of the social context of language in use, it cannot fully achieve its goal if it does not apply itself to both the foreign culture and the cultural context of the learner. Otherwise, we have not helped our students understand contexts of use, without which they cannot function satisfactorily, even as tourists.

So we have to supplement the container and the collage metaphors by a third one, taken this time from a cinematic technique: montage.

Montage

If the most important thing about the container was the information it contained (such as pragmatic functions and their realizations) and the most important thing about the collage was the thematic links between bits of information (such as the very notions of politeness, vacation, work, and play), the essence of montage is in the cutting or editing. Distance, focus, angle, movement, point of view provide the *mise-en-scene* or space. Sequence, slow or fast motion, flashback, flashforward, and dissolve provide the time. Together, time and space give a filmic event depth and meaning. The choice of techniques is determined by the critical eye of the filmmaker (in the Greek meaning of *kritein,* to cut), who decides when to cut where and how. The European term *montage* implies less the trimming process or "editing down" suggested by the American word, but rather a building action, a working up from the raw material.

How does this principle apply to language teaching? A montage metaphor captures the fact that in language teaching, foreign reality is constructed along two axes: a horizontal and a vertical. On the horizontal axis, present-day cultural phenomena are confronted in both cultures; on the vertical axis, each culture's phenomena are linked to their development over time. The selection of place and time is precisely the responsibility of the teacher. A pedagogy that is intent on illuminating contexts of language use, as seen both from the perspective of the native speaker and from that of the learner, would have to consider the following steps.

First, one would want to make the context of reference of the learner explicit, as in the *challenge* example mentioned above. As teachers, we have to develop an ear for such confrontative discourse phenomena. We know how to recognize grammatical or phonological errors, we know less how to recognize cultural breakdowns in communication. Any community of learners contains a multiplicity of voices that unavoidably come into conflict with one another, given the variety of our students' backgrounds, personal experiences, and individual personalities. Through them speak the voices of a given society and of given segments of that society. Our role as teachers is to bring these voices and the voices from the target culture to the fore, and identify and illuminate the border regions by placing them in their proper context. Rather than merely to lecture students on the culture and the history of the foreign country, it might be preferable to use occurrences of cultural inappropriacies in their own foreign discourse to make them aware of different discourse styles.

Next, one would have to place the learners' frame of reference and the foreign cultural world view in their respective horizontal and vertical contexts. Discussion of the former would have to include the institutional discourse of the classroom. We could profitably extend to foreign language teaching what Les Perelman says about the teaching of writing: "The most effective way to teach students how to write in all the institutional contexts they will encounter is to teach them the basic strategies for uncovering the rules that govern discourse in any particular context" (Perelman, 1986, 478), in particular the institutional discourse of academic prose, multiple-choice tests, and the rules for the display of oral proficiency in a classroom setting.

In the final analysis, a montage pedagogy requires foreign language teachers themselves to be "border people," at the intersection of different languages and cultures, and to reflect critically on their and others' forms of discourse. By becoming ethnographers of their own classroom, teachers can be the participant observers that can bring about change in their very object of study (see, for example, Ulichny, 1989).

CONCLUSION

Recent research in ethnography and cross-cultural pragmatics is offering the unique opportunity to combine the pragmatic and the cultural aspects of language in use and to link them to a broader definition of discourse than the one under which we have been operating until now. This broader definition includes not only speech functions and the systematics of turn-taking in conversation, but the very notions that govern discourse as a social activity in the presentation and transmission of knowledge.

By focusing on perceptions, beliefs, and social values, we make the task of the researcher inordinately more complicated. But teachers have a different responsibility. As communicative language teaching is examining its major concepts, in particular that of the natural and the authentic, and as the importance of the teacher is being reaffirmed, we want to avoid going back to an exclusive focus on linguistic form. The question is not whether metalanguage is necessary or not, but how to introduce metadiscursive consciousness at all levels of the curriculum. The reliance of language teachers on linguistic research to offer all the answers has often obscured the fact that social and political awareness is essential if they want to teach not only language *in* discourse but language *as* discourse.

REFERENCES

Bakhtin, Mikhail. 1981. *The Dialogic Imagination.* Austin, Tex.: University of Texas Press.

Becker, A. L. 1984. "Toward A Post-Structuralist View of Language Learning: A Short Essay." *An Epistemology for the Language Sciences. Language Learning.* Ed. A. Z. Guiora. Detroit, Mich.: Wayne State Press. 217–20.

Blum-Kulka, Shoshana, J. House, and G. Kasper, eds. 1989. *Cross-Cultural Pragmatics: Requests and Apologies.* Vol. XXXI of *Advances in Discourse Processes.* Ed. Roy O. Freedle. Norwood, N.J.: Ablex.

Börsch, Sabine. 1982. *Fremdsprachenstudium-Frauenstudium?* Tübingen: Stauffenberg Verlag.

Cazden, Courtney. 1989. "Contributions of the Bakhtin Circle to Communicative Competence." *Applied Linguistics* 10.2: 116–27.

Coulmas, Florian. 1981. "Poison to Your Soul: Thanks and Apologies Contrastively Viewed." *Conversational Routine: Explorations in Standardized Communication Situation and Pre-Patterned Speech.* The Hague: Mouton.

Cummins, James. 1983. "Language Proficiency and Academic Achievement." *Issues in Language Testing Research.* Ed. J. Oller. Rowley, Mass.: Newbury House. 108–29.

Edmondson, Willis. Forthcoming. "Some Ins and Outs of Foreign Language Classroom Research." *Foreign Language Research in Cross-Cultural Perspective,* Eds. K. de Boot, R. Ginsberg, and C. Kramsch. Utrecht: Benjamin.

Ellis, Rod. 1986. *Understanding Second Language Acquisition.* New York: Oxford UP.

Foucault, Michel. 1970. *Order of Discourse.* London: Tavistock.

Galisson, Robert. 1987. "Accéder à la Culture Partagée par l'Entremise des Mots à Charge Culturelle Partagée." *Etudes de Linguistique Appliquée* 67: 119–40.

Grice, H. P. 1975. "Logic and Conversation." *Speech Acts.* Vol. 3 of *Syntax and Semantics.* Eds. P. Cole and J. Morgan. 41–58.

Heath, Shirley Brice. 1983. *Ways with Words.* Cambridge: Cambridge UP.

Hog, Martin, B. D. Müller, and G. Wessling. 1984. *Sichtwechsel: Elf Kapitel zur Sprachsensibilisierung.* Stuttgart: Klett Verlag.

House, Juliane. 1989. "Politeness in English and German: The Functions of *Please* and *Bitte*." *Cross-Cultural Pragmatics: Requests and Apologies.* Eds. S. Blum-Kulka, J. House, and G. Kasper. Vol. XXXI of *Advances in Discourse Processes.* Ed. Roy O. Freedle. Norwood, N.J.: Ablex.

Kochman, Thomas. 1984. "The Politics of Politeness: Social Warrants in Mainstream American Public Etiquette." *Meaning, Form and Use in Context: Linguistic Applications.* Ed. D. Schiffrin. Georgetown University Round Table (GURT 84). 200–9.

Kramsch, Claire. 1988. "The Cultural Discourse of Foreign Language Textbooks." *Toward a New Integration of Language and Culture.* Ed. Alan Singerman. Middlebury, Vt.: Northeast Conference.

———. 1989. "Media Materials in the Language Class." *Contemporary French Civilization* 8.2: 325–45.

Lee, James, and Diane Musumeci. 1988. "On Hierarchies of Reading Skills and Text Types." *Modern Language Journal* 72.1: 173–87.

MLJ Readers' Forum. 1988. *Modern Language Journal* 72.1: 450–57.

Perelman, Les. 1986. "The Context of Classroom Writing." *College English:* 471–79.

Piepho, Eberhard. 1989. "Die postkommunikative Revolution." Paper presented at the XIth Internationaler Deutschlehrertagung, Vienna, August.

Polanyi, Livia. 1989. *Telling the American Story: A Structural and Cultural Analysis of Conversational Storytelling.* Cambridge, Mass.: MIT Press.

Pratt, Mary Louise. 1981. "The Ideology of Speech Act Theory. *Centrum* 1: 5–18.

Sato, Charlene. 1982. "Ethnic Style in Classroom Discourse." *On TESOL 81.* Eds. M. Hines and W. Rutherford. Washington, D.C.: TESOL.

Swaffar, Janet. 1989. "Competing Paradigms in Adult Language Acquisition." *Modern Language Journal* 73.3: 301–14.

Treichler, Paula, and C. Kramarae. 1983. "Women's Talk in the Ivory Tower." *Communications Quarterly* 31.2: 118–32.

Ulichny, Polly. 1989. "Exploring a Teacher's Ptractice: Collaborative Research in an Adult ESL Reading Class." Unpublished dissertation. Harvard University, Graduate School of Education.

Wolfson, Nessa. 1988. "The Bulge: A Theory of Speech Behavior and Social Distance." *Second Language Discourse: A Textbook of Current Research.* Ed. J. Fine. Norwood, N.J.: Ablex. 21–38.

Wolfson, Nessa, Thomas Marmor, and Steve Jones. 1989. "Problems in the Comparison of Speech Acts across Cultures." In *Cross-Cultural Pragmatics: Requests and Apologies.* Eds. S. Blum-Kulka, J. House, and G. Kasper. Vol. XXXI of *Advances in Discourse Processes.* Ed. Roy O. Freedle. Norwood, N.J.: Ablex.

Chapter 13

Reflections on the Development of Cross-Cultural Communicative Competence in the Foreign Language Classroom

Heidi Byrnes

Georgetown University

INTRODUCTION

A bedrock assumption of our profession is that foreign language teaching promotes cross-cultural understanding. Whether knowledge about the target language culture or cultures is the focus or only a by-product in programs that have other emphases, we have always assumed that any L2 learning would inherently work toward the goal of building up students' cross-cultural competence.

In our own time that goal is, in fact, stated clearly, and culture and language are explicitly taught together (Singerman, 1988). The rallying point behind the rejoining of language and culture in teaching is an emphasis on communication. On one hand, a communicative focus may amount to nothing more sophisticated than the desire that learners be able to use the foreign language, rather than know of and about its structural and lexical characteristics. On the other hand it may reflect a significant extension of the profession's scope: a shift from a precisely delimited interest in the linguistic knowledge base that a native speaker accesses during performance, to an interest in a whole range of knowledge bases, which one presumes underlie language in use. For this kind of communicative competence, linguistic competence is but one aspect, others being discourse, strategic, and sociolinguistic competence (Canale and Swain, 1980).

Whatever the motivation for an emphasis on language usage and use, the inclusive frame of reference is culture, not language. For example, rather than giving inordinate attention to the phonologically and syntactically correct production of speech, instruction is intended to help students grasp the social and cultural circumstances and consequences for their use of language. Ideally, students should understand which variant forms are appropriate within which contexts, the meanings they carry within those contexts and, by extension, the meanings that might be conveyed if any conventions were violated intentionally or accidentally.

Thus, a focus on the total communicative event inherently recognizes the primacy of cultural phenomena in the use of any language as a system for communicating meaning. Applying this insight to the foreign language situation, an emphasis on communication posits that, for learners to be communicatively competent in another language, they must not only be cross-linguistically but also cross-culturally competent.

BACKGROUND OBSERVATIONS

In teaching practice, two main strands toward the development of such a comprehensive communicative competence in another language have arisen. Both of them assume that the pivotal unit of investigation, and therefore of instruction, is the situated text rather than the decontextualized sentence. The first strand concentrates on oral situated texts, singling out interactive speaking ability, that is, communication strategies and the pragmatics of interactive, negotiated language use, as its central concern. The second strand deals primarily with written situated texts and works toward enhanced reading comprehension, toward a better sense of features of textuality, and toward a better understanding of how written texts can and do convey meaning. The pedagogical incorporation of both oral and written discourse into the foreign language classroom is predicated on the assumption that the deeper meanings of a text can be derived only through an understanding of its textuality. By carefully attending to textual coherence in the widest sense, to the stated, presupposed, and implied meanings, learners are, at the same time, accessing the cultural foundations of a text and therefore of the speech community as a whole. Overt textuality that is observable in various linguistic features, as well as covert textuality that relies on shared background knowledge, operate only on the basis of configurations of meaning, which are inherently culturally derived. As Swaffar states, "to the degree that an information pattern reflects textual coherences, it reflects cultural implications as well" (1986, 75).

Given this kind of understanding of the workings of language, the key questions are whether, to what extent, and how instruction can aid adult foreign language learners in a classroom setting, outside the target language culture and with only limited time on task, in uncovering these underlying cultural presuppositions and implications through the medium of classroom oral discourse and active engagement with texts.

In theory, both types of texts are inseparably grounded in cultural constructs and thus should offer equally valid avenues toward building up learners' cross-cultural competence. Yet they differ markedly from each other in the manner in which they allow the foreign language learner to access the underlying cultural reality and also in the degree to which such access is likely to take place in the typical L2 classroom.

In an era when emphasis on communication is in many cases equated with an emphasis on speaking, it is reasonable to expect a discussion on the development of cross-cultural communicative competence to focus on the development of oral language abilities in the classroom. However, I propose a focus on written texts for the following reasons.

First, central issues involved in the development of cross-cultural communicative competence are more easily exemplified with written texts than with oral texts, and probably more easily exemplified in comprehension than in students' own production. Second, I question the degree to which cross-cultural communicative competence, as it pertains to the spoken L2 can be addressed at all within the confines of most instructed L2 learning, and in particular, L2 learning in the American educational system (Kramsch, 1988).

It is important to remind ourselves that, even under the best of circumstances, foreign language instruction has only the most tenuous of C2 cultural moorings: it lacks the social reality that defines the C2 culture. In attempting to remedy that deficiency, instruction runs a serious risk of becoming stilted and inauthentic in its own ways. A forced C2 culture connection, for example, in terms of subject matter, role assignments, conversational behaviors, is a violation of the very culture-language connection that is being professed. As a consequence, L2 instruction inherently is in danger of trivializing the impact of culture, of tending to emphasize universals, of building on a sense of all humans being alike, of playing to the "global village" syndrome. In so doing it may actually reassert cultural uniqueness, even cultural superiority, as learners are struggling to become someone they cannot be.

But beyond that we must acknowledge the learners' processing limitations. For many, gaining a usable appropriate level of linguistic competence, with its most easily recognized requirement being that of internalizing a new grammatical and lexical system, rather exhaustively describes their efforts at acquiring another language. Given the enormous processing demands made on the learner, the current emphasis on oral language in the foreign language classroom runs a noteworthy risk of resulting in shallow functionalism, particularly at the beginning stages of language learning, which comprise the bulk of all instruction. In its format and in its content, instruction does not reflect the cultural differences that underlie diverse linguistic systems: it simply superimposes L2 language structures on C1 cultural realities as they are shaped in classrooms. As stated before, the classroom may in fact be incapable of such reflection, both because of the nonaccessibility of the C2 cultural reality and the tenacity of C1 frames of reference.

Thus, the decision to focus this chapter on written texts and the comprehension of these texts is an indication of certain analytical and situational limitations inherent in the American foreign language classroom. Perhaps this emphasis also points to the need for teachers to balance oral and written texts as they teach toward cross-cultural communicative competence.

THE NOTION OF CROSS-CULTURAL COMMUNICATIVE COMPETENCE

Given past skirmishes about the concept of competence as contrasted with performance (see Garrett, this volume) and also about the meaning of the concept *culture* (Allen, 1985), it is worth inquiring what one would accept as indicators of cross-cultural communicative competence in our learners. Indeed, it is worth asking in this context what constitutes cultural competence at all.

Before I venture a cautious reply, some further questions are intended to sketch out the range of options and opinions. Do we envision an appreciation of the achievements of the target language culture—big *C* culture, and on what basis would such achievements be judged? Or are we more inclined to take everyday little *c* culture, "patterns for living" as Brooks (1968) called them, as getting at the essence of the L2 culture? Would we be satisfied if learners could gain a heightened cross-cultural awareness, an awareness of the limitations and the range of options for our own culturally derived acting and being, or do we look—even if far down the path—toward having them become indistinguishable from native speakers? If so, what kinds of native speakers might these be? That is, what norms of culture are we aiming at? Whose interpretation of the essence of that culture will guide us in our decision-making process, both in terms of selection and in terms of presentation? Or is it more realistic to expect students to acquire a basic store of interrelated areas of factual knowledge about the other culture or cultures, as contrasted with differentiated awareness of discourse-analytical features, particularly features of conversational style (Tannen, 1981, 1984; Byrnes, 1986)? Beyond an assessment of past events, how do we project the concept of culture into the future; that is, how stable or how changeable do we take cultural features to be?

Whatever the answers, the following points seem crucial:

1. The charge of defining the essence of cross-cultural communicative competence becomes one of finding ways of dealing with the vexing problems of norm and variation, of finished product and dynamic, unstable process, of social construct and individual construction, of internal coherence and validity and external relativism and arbitrariness for cultural phenomena.

2. Any definition constitutes an extrapolation from performance to underlying competence.

3. Of necessity, the definition will be a statement in terms of idealized goals. It will bypass the cross-cultural shortcomings that learners are likely to exhibit for a very long time, just as their interlanguage grammar requires years of continuous adjustment.

4. Finally, instruction toward cross-cultural communicative competence is less concerned with getting learners to perform in highly specific ways than with having them conduct themselves within a range of possibilities that are accepted and acceptable within the C2 cultural reality.

Within the range of behaviors acceptable in the C2, the L2 learners will face additional constraints. They will have to meet the particular expectations that C2 communicative partners hold of non-native speakers. These are based on complex perceptions that L2 speakers have vis-à-vis the learners' C1 culture, and initial judgments of the non-native speaker's speech performance. At the same time the L2 learners must be able to maintain that understanding of themselves which they consider to be essential for their persona. That is, there may be critical reasons for maintaining, at a certain point, a C1-derived frame of reference, even if it contradicts C2-derived conventions and beliefs. That frame of reference must be permitted to remain valid, irrespective of whether the learners are still striving to adopt C2-derived ways of being and acting or whether they are unable or unwilling to adopt them and adapt further. Hopefully the resultant behavior will be recognized as a possible, though a marginal, individual variant within the C2.

Within these essentially negative superordinate specifications of the construct of cross-cultural communicative competence, one might characterize it as twofold: first, a competence that derives from knowledge of a wide range of synchronic and diachronic facts about the other culture. Among them would be its ways of organizing public and private life, time and space, its history, its artistic and scientific achievements, its institutions, its modes of social stratification, its myths about its past and its dreams for the future; second a competence that manifests itself in an awareness of the rules of language use, both oral and written, as they mark a given culture.

Both sets of competencies are intricately and inseparably tied to each other within the framework of culture. And both sets of competencies are essentially ideals that will not be achieved in a lifetime of work with the second language and culture, and can be no more than introduced within the confines of the foreign language classroom.

SOME PEDAGOGICAL IMPLICATIONS OF THE NEW PARADIGM

What conclusions are we to draw for instructors teaching and learners acquiring cross-cultural communicative competence in the second language classroom?

First, we must acknowledge a basic dilemma. Patrikis (1988) phrases it in the following fashion: "On the one hand, we must act as if observation and representation were immediate—without the distorting intermediaries of our experience and pre-conceived notions. On the other hand, we must act as if we were sharply cognizant of the persistent difficulties of interpretation. We must be able to make statements, and we must comprehend the shortcomings of those statements. We must be creative and critical at the same time" (1988, 23).

But we must also believe that there is a way out of this dilemma in the foreign language classroom, namely through one of the most basic ways of dealing with the world, that of comparison (Müller, 1980, 1983). By stimulating students to reflect on their expectations vis-à-vis the C2 culture on the basis of their C1 frame of reference, by seeing these expectations confirmed, disconfirmed, modified as they deal with L2 texts, by having them speculate on what must be true in and for the other culture for certain statements to be possible—whether these statements pertain to C2 or to C1 realities—both aspects can be accomplished, the uncovering of one's own belief system as well as the gradual building up of the other.

Thus, perhaps the most important conclusion is that the prospects for having learners make significant inroads in the development of cross-cultural communicative competence are sobering, nevertheless substantive. Key impediments exist in the acquisition of even the factual side of cross-cultural competence, not to mention the interactional side mandated within the new language use and creation paradigm (Swaffar, 1989). By the same token, within these constraints, written texts seem to be particularly valuable in helping learners develop cross-cultural communicative competence.

The remainder of this paper will address both aspects, limitations as well as possibilities.

The Constraint of Viewing C2 Phenomena through a C1 Framework

One of the most noticeable innovations of current communicative approaches to language teaching is the incorporation of authentic texts, whether spoken or in print. These texts reflect not only a heightened sensitivity to suprasentential linguistic features and the realization that meaning transmission occurs at the level of text within a social and cultural context; authentic texts are also taken to be the best way of "getting into the culture," its facts, beliefs, values, modes of behavior, without the interpretive bias of an outsider reporting on the culture.

We easily forget, however, that the same interpretive bias, namely, the C1 frame of reference, is just as likely to persist in reading as we know it to exist in L1 writing about the C2 culture. While we have essentially banished that kind of text from the L2 classroom, deeming it to be inherently flawed in terms of cultural sensitivity, we have not taken the necessary additional step, that of recognizing that L2 readers, in the act of constructing a meaningful interpretation for the L2 text about the C2 culture, must be expected to engage in the same kind of projection that influences writing in L1 about the C2 culture. In other words, what appears, on the surface, to be one of the strong features of authentic L2 texts, their representation of C2 cultural reality without explanatory or evaluative remarks, may be totally ignored or missed by the apprentice foreign language reader.

Indeed, much of recent reading research (Bernhardt, 1984; Carrell, 1984) concentrates on the insidious strength of C1 reader schemata, partly putting into question the laudable intention that underlies the selection of many an L2 text, namely, its cultural authenticity. When, in addition, this desirable authenticity is deemed to be enhanced by uniqueness of cultural reference, we are raising even higher the obstacles to meaning-construction by the second language learner.

To give an example, for better or worse, the depth of the experience of war is a unique feature of German literature, indeed the entire German social consciousness. It seems reasonable to demand that learning German means, to some extent, learning about this aspect of German culture. By contrast, most American learners have little understanding for and sometimes little patience with the defeatist vision of war in the linguistically rather accessible postwar German literature. Lacking a cultural predisposition for such texts, they find even the most manageable comprehension tasks from the standpoint of language decoding among the most unmanageable tasks from the standpoint of meaning construction.

One might interject that helping learners bridge such gaps is precisely the role of the cross-culturally aware foreign language instructor, and in principle that proposition is undisputed. However, in language classes as in literature classes, the hoped-for discussion or heightened cross-cultural awareness among students all too often runs aground due to the tenacity of individual learners' C1-derived ways of understanding the world.

Perhaps here, as in our conceptualization of comprehensible input in language learning, the "i + 1" phenomenon, this time applied to cultural distance, can illustrate the point. Particularly in the lower levels of instruction, when form-related difficulties are most disruptive of the construction of meaning, it may well be that demands on learners for an additional shift, away from their experientially based ways of interpreting phenomena, must be carefully monitored. Not only are unaccustomed ways of framing reality likely to be unmanageable in themselves, even if all linguistic forms were well known, but lack of the correct cultural frame of reference operates totally against the very heart of modern language teaching with authentic texts: encouraging students to guess creatively at formal features on the basis of the strength and validity of the background knowledge they can bring to the learning task.

Two suggestions come to mind for alieviating this disparity between the well-motivated demand for the use of authentic texts and learners' propensity to understand these texts from within their own cultural reality.

First, to capitalize on reader schemata, we might begin with L2 texts that are not too remote from learners' cultural experience or can relatively easily be brought into that category through advance work—and much of reading pedagogy tends in that direction. In this context, some degree of cultural proximity is not to be confounded with an illusory, bland universality of culture or with a watering down of the demand that students must confront cultural otherness. While the charge of unacceptable timidity and, consequently, of marginal returns in terms of a progression toward cross-cultural competence might arise, second language pedagogy must acknowledge the consequences of the dual burden placed on beginning students: unfamiliar language plus unfamiliar culture. Very likely, some compromise will have to be found between our desire to confront students with other value and belief systems and their need to be able to draw mentally on a presumably intact and valid system of background knowledge. For learners, the presumption of such validities must hold to a significant extent, allowing them to compensate for their restricted L2 linguistic repertoire.

Second, we might work with L2 texts that deal with an aspect of C1 that presumably is familiar to the learners. This approach recommends itself highly for the following reason: a text that on the surface appears to be a mere reiteration of known information in the garb of the L2, suddenly opens a door through which the glaring light of culturally motivated judgments can hit the student, perhaps for the first time. Our learners are generally affectively invested in the American interpretive tradition, if not to say ideology. Thus, texts dealing with such phenomena as extensive job experience during the high school years, frequent job changes throughout one's working life, the hiring and firing practices of small as well as large companies, afford a splendid opportunity for reaching them at an emotional and intellectual depth that discussion of topics peculiar to the C2 can rarely offer, precisely because they are the least-known factor in the equation.

The Constraint of Lack of Factual Knowledge

As the discussion above implies, learners typically lack a whole range of facts, synchronic and diachronic, about the C2 culture and often lack such knowledge even about their own culture. Thus, instead of insisting merely on L2 authentic texts on C2 culture as the best way in the foreign language classroom to work toward cross-cultural competence, we may well have to consider an entire progression that would include treatment of a specific topic in terms of L1 texts about C1; L1 texts about C2; L2 texts about C1; and ultimately, L2 texts about C2.

This progression suggests coordination with other subject-matter areas in the learners' curriculum for the first two stages, and such cooperative ventures might become one way for language instruction to work itself out of curricular irrelevance and perceived intellectual marginality. However, given the difficulties inherent in horizontal articulation across disciplines, not to mention students' tendency to compartmentalize their learning, it might even be preferable to have these texts assigned by the foreign language teacher as relatively undidacticized homework. Without the need for coordination with colleagues, the foreign language instructor would be free to select topics on the basis of the availability of suitable textual material in all the forms recommended. Under ideal circumstances initial texts could be both L1 and L2 texts dealing with C1 culture, to be followed, in reverse, by L1 and L2 texts treating the same general topic in C2 culture. Most important, by having students read texts in any of the suggested configurations, the foreign language classroom could send a crucial signal that an involved language learner is an involved explorer of the cultural reality that supports and maintains that language.

The Constraint of Scope and the Question of Validity

The previous suggestion, that the foreign language classroom must strive to incorporate linguistically diverse texts that arise from varying cultural realities but share a topical focus, is not based merely on the recognition of linguistic and cultural processing difficulties, which are particularly restrictive for beginning learners. It is really motivated by much graver issues. Among them are the problem of restricted selection, or scope, and its concomitant problem of restricted generalizability or validity for our cultural teaching.

First, foreign language instruction increasingly understands that serious culture teaching is not to be equated with the need to present a comprehensive view of the other culture— high culture and low culture, as we have come to call it. More recent discussion is also beginning to despair of the smorgasbord approach—a bite from the educational system, a nibble from the political organization tray, a weekend sharing the leisure time activities of a "typical" family, a chat with the intellectual giants of the culture—all occuring side by side without any connection, as though they could be neatly separated from each other and were not themselves subject to changes or variant forms, both synchronically and diachronically.

Instead, the challenge seems to be to overcome the severe shortcomings inherent in a situation that demands a hopelessly truncated presentation of the other culture. To my way of looking at it, such counterbalances are available only if the profession agrees that the processes and strategies for developing cultural awareness are ultimately more important than the details of the product. Within the American educational establishment and its back-to-basics movement, process advocates have not fared particularly well, making this dangerous ground to tread on. A process approach might also be an unacceptable suggestion within foreign language circles. In general, if cross-cultural competence is at issue at all, it is expressed and assessed in terms of knowledge of isolated facts.

But there is a dangerous capriciousness inherent in asking learners, or for that matter teachers who face certification, to prove their cultural competence through factual litanies, such as who lived when and where, who elects whom for what length of time, where one can find the most beautiful example of architectural style X, and who presents what kinds of flowers to whom on what occasion. Of course, these facts can be accurate, perhaps even useful bits of information. But without any anchoring in a network of synchronic and diachronic adjacencies and trajectories and, more important, without a preliminary assignment within a hierarchy of constructs (Kelly, 1963), knowledge of such facts might well represent everything from irrelevance to cultural wonderland.

This brings me to the second point, that of generalizability. Perhaps a stance of "less is more" is vulnerable to reductionism, but, given past experience, an exemplary in-depth treatment of a few topics, broadly related to each other, is likely to yield a greater harvest for the development of cross-cultural competence than a wide casting of the nets. In other words, a paring down of the scope with an attendant shift in methodological approaches from a product to a process orientation might well result in the kind of validity for the enterprise of teaching language and culture that we have often lacked, the validity that derives from an ability to deal with the C2 culture in the future. Instruction would have achieved its goals if it had enabled learners to assign new cultural phenomena correctly—whether newly encountered by the learner or newly developed within the culture—to coordinate or superordinate constructs (Kelly, 1963). This is a capability no amount of recitation of cultural facts can engender, but one that must be developed if "new" issues are not to be categorized as unbelievable, weird, or perhaps not noticed at all.

Returning to the previous suggestion of a mosaiclike clustering of a variety of texts, I envision this collection as deliberately incorporating different perspectives, different advocacies and intentions, and different textual genres (see also Müller, 1983). In addition, it must be accompanied by the honest admission to the learners that even this variety represents judgments, which the instructor brought to bear on the selection process.

Permit me one example. The women's movement in industrial societies has many surface similarities. Underneath these, however, are buried substantive differences that allow glimpses into respective overriding belief systems, systems of role assignments, expectations of individual and social responsibilities, and pervasive myths about women's identities. The recent court decision about a woman who was not promoted to full partnership in a law firm because of her unfeminine ways is just one example of American expectations. The increased attention in the American press to the issue of wife-beating might be another. If such texts are coupled with German texts looking at the status of American women, such as one entitled "They Are Fighting Grandma's Battles" (Kokott-Weidenfeld, 1986), a literary text like Gabriele Wohmann's short story "Komm Donnerstags" ("Come on Thursdays"), and perhaps documentation of legal initiatives as well as entrepreneurial successes of women in both cultures, then a host of challenges to received wisdom are likely to occur.

Initially, a single L2 text about the C2 culture might well be perceived as representing nothing more and nothing less than an instantiation of the issue that is an acceptable variant in the C1 culture as well. Thus, even with a high percentage of women in the American work force, the choice by a woman to stay home to raise her small children is certainly part of American reality. Consequently, the German story's mother, who stays at home with her nursery-school-age son is unlikely to be noticed as anything unusual. But the heroine in Wohmann's story really did not *choose* the option to stay home with her child; she lives in a society where she is *expected* to go that route and in fact has never contemplated any other solution. The ability to differentiate between a unique instantiation and a generalizable feature of the C2 culture is likely to develop only in conjunction with a variety of texts, in this case other German texts about the role and place of women. Only then can learners work toward assigning to one and the same surface phenomenon, which might exist in both cultures, a different cultural valuation.

The introduction of a thematically connected mosaic of texts that explores a theme in different languages and cultures was initially motivated by learners lacking factual and linguistic knowledge. It has now become motivated as a critical way to enhance learners, differentiated cross-cultural competence.

The Constraint of Immediacy of Judgment

I previously referred to the persistence of a C1 cultural frame of reference and have characterized it, among other things, as an ability or inability to note other phenomena. However, the concern is not merely with attention or inattention to a certain aspect of the C2 culture on the part of a cultural apprentice. It is really a matter of the inherently judgmental aspect of any cultural frame of reference.

In cautioning against an overburdening of learners with issues that are too removed from their own experiential background, one is not advocating material that lacks intellectual content and challenge and, thus, ultimately, value judgments. On the contrary—overextension of the learners' reach deserves serious consideration precisely because intellectual provocation is a continuous educational goal. But for intellectual growth to occur, the intellectual challenge inherent in a different configuration must first be noticed at all, and it must have some reasonable chance of allowing learners to shift previously held notions. All too easily powerful pulls occur, which result either in a negating of differences into a turgid sameness or an upgrading of differences into ready judgments of weirdness and ultimately of inferiority of the C2 culture. Neither one of these consequences contributes anything to intellectual growth.

The Constraint of a Mismatch of Form and Function

As my final point in discussing the need to relate facts to each other rather than to learn them in isolation, let me point to some problems with that very designation. Since we are dealing with cultural competence within the context of language teaching, I draw on two key concepts in linguistics to illustrate the dilemma, namely, the concepts of form and function.

In structural linguistics these terms have traditionally been used to arrive at units of analysis for the expression side of language and the meaning side of language, Their noncommensurateness, that is, a given formal representation serving a diversity of functions, and, conversely, a specific function finding numerous formal realizations, has been a staple of linguistic investigation.

Transferring both the concepts and their characteristic noncommensurateness to the task of developing cross-cultural competence in our learners can open numerous fruitful avenues of exploration:

1. What we designate as facts in a cultural context can pertain to both formal realization and functional value. We might say that the use of the word *house*, as in "let's meet at my house," spoken by a student, designates the residence

in its functional value, not necessarily in its formal realization: the student is likely to be renting a room or perhaps a small apartment. But in a phrase such as "the sale of houses has dropped considerably," we are referring to the formal realization of a place of residence, presumably a single detached house.

Given that we subconsciously operate from a functional perspective and generally expect only a very narrow band of specific manifestations, it is likely that we will stumble when our expectations are not met. We thus arrive at judgments about the inappropriateness of disparate ways of behaving, but rarely realize the relativity of the entire function-form unit that is embedded in our minds. The fact that the function of residing someplace should be firmly connected with a single house, is very much an American cultural phenomenon. It motivates an assessment that considers the fact that a large share of the German population lives in rental units to be a deviant, deprived state of affairs.

By extension, our ability to note phenomena for which we have no ready functional assignment is limited, and reassignment of form features to functions other than those to which we have become accustomed is cumbersome, even unsettling.

2. The interrelationship, at times nonseparability, in our consciousness of both function and form can easily be demonstrated. For an American, the function of transportation is most closely associated with the form of transportation by car, or perhaps plane. By contrast, the expectations of what formal manifestations the universal need for transportation is likely to take in other cultures can be vastly different, even in highly industralized counties, that is, public transportation by train, bus, streetcar, or subway.

3. A given function can have *marked* or *unmarked* representations. The designation of marked or unmarked is a shorthand way of determining what is expected within a culture and what is marginal, even downright unacceptable. Judging from the mix in the crowds one sees in the nation's airports, travel by plane has essentially become a nonmarked behavior, as is the use of personal cars. For many Europeans, however, travel by plane within the boundaries of their own countries would be highly marked behavior, while the nonmarked behavior for long-distance travel is likely to be use of a private car or public transportation.

4. Differences in what are considered unmarked and marked representations of a given function are often what characterizes subgroups of a culture. New York Jewish conversational style is one example of such a unifying and at the same time separating set of behaviors (Tannen, 1981). Here we find that the same insight can serve not only cross-societal, cross-cultural understanding, but can enhance intrasocietal cross-cultural understanding as well.

5. The membership of formal manifestations for a given function will vary among cultures. Conversely, this means that certain features of form will be assigned to different functions. For instance, the feature of shaking hands is part of the central, unmarked manifestations of exchanging greetings among

German adults. As an observable phenomenon, handshakes also exist in the American cultural context. But they would be marked aspects of the exchange of greeting, and would generally be assigned with the functional cluster of official business dealings and, therefore, a degree of formality. Thus, the analysis of German greeting behavior as being formal is the result of superimposing an American functional assignment on German behavioral manifestations.

6. Comparability between cultures is more likely at very high levels of functions or constructs, rather than at lower levels. However, even major constructs are ultimately defined only in terms of their constitutive manifestations, a fact that may actually render them noncomparable. For instance, what might be deemed a universal construct, for example, the need for security and predictability, has manifestations in American culture that put it within the sphere of the individual's options and responsibilities, (for example, the right of private citizens to own weapons, the individual's obligation to make plans for his financial future during the years of retirement), while for the German context its manifestations have a strong social component (for example, national health and retirement plans, long-range government sponsorship of benefits programs). This leaves open the question whether these two constructs are at all to be compared.

In the end, teaching toward cross-cultural competence might perhaps be no more and no less than fostering in learners a willingness to uncouple the value judgments inherent in the near-automatic functional assignment of a certain formal feature that result from successful socialization in one's own culture. Whether such detachment can be achieved depends on numerous factors, many of which are beyond the capabilities of the classroom, perhaps even beyond the malleability of cultural adults.

In any case, students should be expected to develop over an extended period of time some of the understandings that were mentioned above, slowly arranging the puzzle pieces of cultural insights into a coherent whole. Initially, such a "cultural coherence" is probably personal, even idiosyncratic. But, ultimately, it will have to stand up to the coherence demands of the C2 culture, even when learners are familiar with only limited topics and limited evidence within these topics. To meet these demands, learners will continually have to pose the following question: what must be the ideational and practical world of the other, individual or society, for a certain behavior to be deemed possible, acceptable, believable? The discovery procedure, the process itself, becomes the core of learners reaching toward and our teaching toward cross-cultural competence.

REFERENCES

Allen, Wendy W. 1985. "Toward Cultural Proficiency." *Proficiency, Curriculum, Articulation: The Ties that Bind.* Ed. Alice C. Omaggio. Middlebury, Vt.: The Northeast Conference.

Bernhardt, Elizabeth B. 1984. "Toward an Information Processing Perspective in Foreign Language Reading." *Modern Language Journal* 68: 322–31.

Brooks, Nelson. 1968. "Teaching Culture in the Foreign Language Classroom." *Foreign Language Annals* 1: 204–17.

Byrnes, Heidi. 1986. "Interactional Style in German and American Conversations." *Text* 6.2: 189–206.

Canale, Michael, and Merrill Swain. 1980. "Theoretical Bases of Communicative Approaches to Second Language Teaching and Testing." *Applied Linguistics* 1.1: 1–47.

Carrell, Patricia A. 1984. "Evidence of a Formal Schema in Second Language Comprehension." *Language Learning* 34: 87–112.

Kelly, George A. 1963, 1955. *A Theory of Personality*. New York: W. W. Norton.

Kokott-Weidenfeld, Gabriele. 1986. "Sie fechten Omas Kämpfe aus." *Rheinischer Merkur/Christ und Welt* 43.

Kramsch, Claire J. 1988. "The Cultural Discourse of Foreign Language Textbooks." *Toward a New Integration of Language and Culture*. Ed. Alan J. Singerman. Northeast Conference Reports. Middlebury, Vt.: The Northeast Conference.

Müller, Bernd-Dietrich. 1980. "Zur Logik Interkultureller Verstehensprobleme." *Jahrbuch Deutsch als Fremdsprache*. Eds. Alois Wirlacher, *et al.* Band 6. Heidelberg: Julius Groos. 102–19.

———. 1983. "Begriffe und Bilder: Bedeutungscollagen zur Landeskunde." *Zielsprache Deutsch* 2: 5–14.

Patrikis, Peter. 1988. "Language and Culture at the Crossroads." *Toward a New Integration of Language and Culture*. Ed. Alan J. Singerman. Middlebury, Vt.: The Northeast Conference. 13–14.

Singerman, Alan J., ed. 1988. *Toward a New Integration of Language and Culture*. Middlebury, Vt.: The Northeast Conference.

Swaffar, Janet K. 1986. "Reading and Cultural Literacy." *The Journal of General Education* 38.2: 70–84.

———. 1989. "Curricular Issues and Language Research: The Shifting Interaction." *ADFL Bulletin* 20.3: 54–60.

Tannen, Deborah. 1981. "New York Jewish Conversational Style." *International Journal of the Sociology of Language* 30: 133–39.

———. 1984. *Conversational Style: Analyzing Talk Among Friends*. Norwood, N.J.: Ablex.

Wohmann, Gabriele. 1979. *Komm Donnerstags*. Darmstadt: Luchterhand.

Section VI

The Acquisition of Literacy Skills

Developments in Second Language Literacy Research: Retrospective and Prospective Views for the Classroom

Elizabeth B. Bernhardt

The Ohio State University

INTRODUCTION

The past several years have experienced an incredible surge of interest in second language literacy. Since 1976 approximately 350 articles have been published on second language reading in major journals devoted to second language teaching and learning, such as *Language Learning, Studies in Second Language Acquisition,* and the *Modern Language Journal*. Approximately two hundred articles have been published on the second language writing process in comparable journals. Of all these articles, approximately 30% could be termed research contributions, that is, articles that explicate empirical data collected on second language readers and writers in the process of reading and writing. It is interesting that in this same period of time, the number of book-length collections on reading and writing processes has also increased substantially. In the past half-decade, an average of two to three volumes a year has appeared. These volumes include teaching-oriented texts, such as *Teaching Second Language Reading for Academic Purposes* (Dubin, *et al.,* 1986) and *Richness in Writing: Empowering ESL Students* (Johnson and Roen, 1989) and texts containing collections of studies, such as *Research in Reading English as a Second Language* (Devine, *et al.,* 1987) and *Writing Across Languages: Analysis of L2 Text* (Connor and Kaplan, 1987).

There are many reasons for this surge of interest. The tremendous increase in the number of learners who must receive content instruction in schools and universities in a language that is not native to them accounts for some of the sudden interest. In addition, generalized concepts of communicative language teaching have helped place emphasis on the written word: some argue, for example, that written materials provide "comprehensible input" (Krashen, 1981) as well as "comprehensible output" (Swain, 1985); others argue that the principal convenient and accessible source of authentic language materials (that is, written materials) must be tapped (Byrnes, 1988). Moreover, literacy research in general has acknowledged an interest in the cross-cultural encoding of information and, therefore, has brought further attention to second language reading and writing. Finally, the nature of written words—their time-independent nature versus the time-dependent nature of spoken language—has made research in the area of written language more manageable and less susceptible to attacks on validity and reliability than research on spoken language.

Clearly, the success of a research area cannot be measured by its quantity or by its trendiness, but rather, only by its quality. That is, a research area must be assessed according to the insights that it brings to a particular dimension of second language acquisition (in this case reading and writing) as well as to the whole of second language acquisition research. The first charge of this paper is to take a retrospective measure of second language literacy research in order to isolate its contributions to the knowledge base of the second language teaching-learning process as well as to understandings of that process within foreign language classrooms. Retrospection provides the backdrop as well as the explication for what the research area became and how it influenced and continues to influence instruction. The second charge of this paper is prospection. Prospection provides a look into the future in order to explicate how the research area will influence instruction and evolve relative to it. The prospective view of research is perhaps the most valuable, because it is used to improve instruction.

READING-WRITING RELATIONSHIPS

A relatively new line of research in first language literacy is termed *reading-writing relationships*. In fact, this line of research is considered to be "in its infancy" (Fillion, 1985, 79). This research thrust developed as a reaction to "the tendency to study particular skills and acts in isolation, apart from each other, and often apart from their significant use" (79). In other words, it was born of a belief among language educators that skills and functions of language are not separate phenomena. In fact, research-based definitions of reading and writing indicate that the only sensible way of viewing the two processes is to look at them as complementary. Tierney and Pearson (1985) make the point:

> We believe that at the heart of understanding reading and writing connections one must begin to view reading and writing as essentially similar processes of meaning construction. Both are acts of composing. From a reader's perspective, meaning is created as a reader uses his background of experience together with the author's cues to come to grips both with what the writer is getting him to do or think and what the reader decides and creates for himself. As a writer writes, she uses her own background of experience to generate ideas and, in order to produce a text which is considerate to her idealized reader, filters these drafts

through her judgments about what her reader's background of experience will be, what she wants to say, and what she wants to get the reader to think or do (1985, 63).

In taking this constructivist approach to both reading and writing, Tierney and Pearson provide an interesting perspective that unifies the two skills and inhibits the isolationist tendencies alluded to above by Fillion. This perspective also provides a convenient organizing principle for an analysis of reading and writing research in second language. The following sections of the paper use this perspective, first, for its organizational capacity and second, for its potential for providing insight into the second language teaching-learning process.

READING-WRITING RELATIONSHIPS IN SECOND LANGUAGE

The first paragraph of this paper provides documentation that there is quantitatively more second language reading research than there is second language writing research. This general commentary on the research base directly parallels first language literacy research, in which there is clearly far more reading research than writing research. Concomitantly, there are more *strands* of reading research than writing research. For convenience, then, nine strands of the second language reading research base will be used as suborganizing categories in this examination of research in reading and writing in a second language. Each strand in reading will include a discussion of the extent to which it parallels a facet of the writing research base.

This paper is not meant to be a comprehensive literature review to the extent that it reviews each study in reading and writing research in depth. The intent of the first section of the paper is to provide an overview of the generalized findings in second language literacy research. Tables are provided that categorize both reading and writing studies according to the research strands and each study included in the analysis is listed in the bibliography for the reader interested in the specific details of individual studies or strands of research. The latter section of the paper then speaks to research directions within foreign language classrooms.

Word Recognition

Nine studies listed in Table 1 comprise the data base in second language word recognition investigations. Findings from these studies are fairly consistent. Several studies find that processing speeds are dependent on fluency as well as familiarity with orthography. Others find evidence supporting phonological

— Table 1 _____

Research Studies in Second Language Reading (*continued*)

Word Recognition	Background Knowledge	Text Structure
Brown & Haynes, 1985	Adams, 1982	Carrell, 1984a
Favreau & Segalowitz, 1982	Alderson & Urquhart, 1988	Cohen *et al.*, 1979
Favreau, *et al.*, 1980	Campbell, 1981	Davies, 1984
Hatch, *et al.*, 1974	Carrell, 1983	Davis, *et al.*, 1988
Hayes, 1988	Carrell, 1987	Flick & Anderson, 1980
Haynes, 1981	Carrell & Wallace, 1983	Perkins, 1987
Koda, 1987	Connor, 1984	Stanley, 1984
Meara, 1984	Hudson, 1982	Steffensen, 1988
Walker, 1983	Johnson, 1981, 1982	Urquhart, 1984
	Lee, 1986a	
	Mohammed & Swales, 1984	
	Nunan, 1985	
	Olah, 1984	
	Omaggio, 1979	
	Parry, 1987	
	Perkins & Angelis, 1985	
	Steffensen, *et al.*, 1979	
	Zuck & Zuck, 1984	

Oral/Aural Factors	Syntactic Factors	Cross-Lingual Processing Strategies
Bernhardt, 1983	Barnett, 1986	Barrera, *et al.*, 1986
Connor, 1981	Bean, *et al.*, 1980	Bernhardt, 1986
Devine, 1981, 1984	Bhatia, 1984	Block, 1986
Ewoldt, 1981	Blau, 1982	Carrell, 1984b
Grosse & Hameyer, 1979	Guarino & Perkins, 1986	Clarke, 1979, 1980
		Cziko, 1978, 1980

Table 1

Research Studies in Second Language Reading (*continued*)

Word Recognition	Background Knowledge	Text Structure
Hodes, 1981	Jarvis & Jensen, 1982	Dank & McEachern, 1979
Muchisky, 1983	Olshtain, 1982	Douglas, 1981
Nehr, 1984	Robbins, 1983	Elley, 1984
Neville & Pugh, 1975	Strother & Ulijn, 1987	Groebel, 1980
Reeds, *et al.*, 1977		Irujo, 1986
Romatowski, 1981		Kendall, *et al.*, 1987
Tatlonghari, 1984		McDougall & Bruck, 1976
		MacLean & d'Anglejan, 1986
		McLeod & McLaughlin, 1986
		Padron & Waxman, 1988
		Perkins, 1983a
		Rigg, 1978
		Roller, 1988
		Sarig, 1987
		deSuarez, 1985
		Wagner, *et al.*, 1989

Metacognitive & Affective Factors	Testing	Instruction
Fransson, 1984	Allen, *et al.*, 1988	Barnett, 1988
Hosenfeld, 1977	Baldauf, *et al.*, 1980	Bensoussan & Ramraz, 1984b
Neville, 1979	Bensoussan & Ramraz, 1984a	Bialystok, 1983
	Bensoussan *et al.*, 1984	Brown, *et al.*, 1984
	Brown, 1985	Cooper, 1984
	Henning, 1975	Cowan & Sarmad, 1976
	Hock & Poh, 1979	Elley & Mangubhai, 1983
	Homburg & Spaun, 1982	Feldman, 1978
		Groebel, 1979

— **Table 1** ──────────────────────────────

Research Studies in Second Language Reading (*continued*)

Word Recognition	Background Knowledge	Text Structure
	Kamil, *et al.*, 1986	Hill, 1981
	Lee, 1986b	Hosenfeld, 1984
	Lee & Musumeci, 1988	Kleinmann, 1987
		Laufer-Dvorkin, 1981
	Markham, 1985	Lutjeharms, 1985
	Mott, 1981	Narayanaswamy, 1982
	Mustapha, *et al.*, 1985	O'Flanagan, 1985
	Perkins, 1984	Pederson, 1986
	Perkins & Brutten, 1988	Pugh, 1977
		Taglieber, *et al.*, 1988
	Propst & Baldauf, 1979	Tang, 1974
	Shohamy, 1984	VanParreren & Schouten-VanParreren, 1981
	Sim & Bensoussan, 1979	Williams, 1981

factors in word recognition; that is, second language readers frequently attend to graphemic features that may override attention to meaning or syntax.

These word-recognition studies lend themselves to generalizability to the extent that they employ similar research designs and data collection techniques—principally reaction-time measures and error-rate analyses. However, these studies lose generalizability to the extent that they do not describe the proficiency levels of their subjects, use both single-word and full-text stimuli, and for the most part, define subject groups *generically* rather than explicitly stating the word-recognition behaviors exhibited by individual subjects from various language backgrounds. No parallel research strand in writing *per se* seems to have been attempted. Certainly how learners learn to "write" characters or ideographs would fall under this category.

Background Knowledge

Several recent studies have revealed the importance of background knowledge within the comprehension process in a second language. This finding parallels the results of a preponderance of first language studies. The background knowledge studies listed in Table 1 may be subdivided into several categories for discussion. First, there are those studies that have examined cultural background and have blocked subjects within experimental designs according to ethnic background. Second, there are studies that have examined "topic knowledge" background, generally blocking on that particular variable along with proficiency level. Third, a number of training studies have investigated the manner and type of background knowledge that might be given to readers in order to increase comprehension.

Although the studies most often find a statistical main effect for background knowledge, there are a number of problems with them. The first problem is the reliability of many of the findings. Several studies have generated a different pattern of findings depending on the *language* of performance—either native or second. All studies involving ESL readers have, to this point, asked their readers to demonstrate comprehension in English. Data suggest that the findings of these studies are inherently biased against actual comprehension abilities and are skewed by subjects' second language writing abilities. A second problematic feature concerns the cultural compatibility of the pictures used in several of the studies to enhance comprehension and the readers' understanding of the pictorial representations. The pictures used in the studies were Western in nature and, consequently, place an added cultural burden on the comprehenders. Finally, and rather characteristically, the studies generically grouped non-native readers of English into proficiency levels without considering orthographic or cultural background variables. With these caveats in mind, however, the studies reveal a remarkable consistency in the impact of prior knowledge on the comprehension scores generated.

Interestingly, much has been debated about the nature of topics in second language writing. The discussion surrounding topic production has focused on how to make appropriate and fair topics for students. In so doing, however, McColly suggested that appropriate writing topics are ones with which ". . . students are deprived of something to say" (1970, 153). As a result, topics for compositions have become virtually "topicless." Additional studies have highlighted that students' criteria for selecting writing topics may not be the *topic* itself but rather the *length* of the question or topic and its position on the list of topic options. Shorter topics and those positioned near the top of the list tend to be favored.

Despite the consistent findings regarding the impact of background knowledge on reading comprehension, and despite the considerable discussion in writing regarding topic, little empirical research has been conducted in this critical area of writing.

Text Structure

Seven studies (Table 1) have investigated the manner in which texts are configured and the impact of that configuration on second language readers' comprehension. Another study, in contrast, looked at the converse: whether L2 readers can mentally configure a structure in the texts they are reading. All of the studies find that second language readers are sensitive to particular organizational patterns, such as a comparison-contrast or an inductive-deductive format.

Two facets of the text structure studies serve as caveats. The first key factor is that few of the studies used naturally occurring texts. Rather, the studies manipulated texts in order to test the impact of the manipulations on understanding. Hence, the role of text structure in naturalistic settings remains relatively unclear. Second, since so little is known about text patterns across cultures, a real understanding of the impact of different text types within different subject groups is equally opaque.

In fact, second language writing research lends insight into precisely this point: work has been conducted in second language writing regarding contrastive rhetoric. This strand of research stems from Kaplan's (1966) arguments that texts are configured in culturally specific ways. Kaplan argued that the structure of texts reflected the logical thought patterns of particular ethnic groups, some conceiving the world in a linear fashion; others in a more circular way.

Indeed, though Kaplan's ideas were attacked due to the writing samples he used and their length, the question of rhetorical structure and its impact on the learning of second language writing is undeniable. In fact, a number of studies listed in Table 2 indicate that reliance on native language rhetorical patterns is a significantly inhibiting factor in learning to write in a second language. The implications of these data are that learning to write in a second language means acquiring a different way of sequencing and structuring information in a text.

A subset of this research strand is the rhetorical structuring of particular *kinds* of discourse: scientific texts versus an essay format in the humanities, for example. This subset underlines that text structure is not generic to a particular

---

▬ Table 2 ━━

Research Studies in Second Language Writing

Background Knowledge	Text Structure	Initial Writing Development
Tedick, 1988	Connor, 1987a	Edelsky, 1982, 1983
Winfield & Barnes-Felfeli, 1982	Doushaq, 1986	Hudelson, 1983, 1984a, b
	Eggington, 1987	Saville-Troike, 1984a, b
	Grabe, 1987	
	Kaplan, 1966, 1987	Urzua, 1987
	Ostler, 1987	

— **Table 2** ————————————————————

Research Studies in Second Language Writing (*continued*)

Syntactic/Semantic Factors	Cross-Lingual	Testing
Adjemian & Liceras, 1984	Eggington, 1987	Carlson & Bridgeman, 1986
Cooper, 1976	Hinds, 1987	Connor, 1987b
Flahive & Snow, 1980	Hu, *et al.*, 1982	Gaies, 1980
Kameen, 1979	Jones, 1982, 1983	Kaczmarek, 1980
Krashen, *et al.*, 1978	Lay, 1982	Mullen, 1980
Lantolf, 1988	McKay, 1984	Perkins, 1980, 1983b
Mazurkewich, 1984	Mohan & Lo, 1985	Santos, 1988
Vann, 1979	Raimes, 1985	
	Scarcella, 1984	
	Scott & Tucker, 1974	
	Takala, *et al.*, 1982	
	Urzua, 1987	
	Zamel, 1982, 1983, 1985	

Instruction
Cumming, 1983
Harvey, 1987
Hendrickson, 1980
Keyes, 1984
Knepler, 1984
Raimes, 1979, 1983, 1985
Robb, *et al.*, 1986
Spack & Sadow, 1983
Stokes, 1984
Taylor, 1981
Zamel, 1976, 1987

language community, but is unique to particular "discourse communities" (Purves and Purves, 1986).

Oral-Aural Factors

A number of studies have investigated the relationship between second language learner competencies in reading and listening as well as learner sensitivity to the phonological system of the second language. Studies listed in Table 1 group into three categories. The first concerns the relationship between oral reading ability and comprehension; the second examines the facilitation of reading comprehension through listening comprehension; and the third group of studies probes the necessity of a phonological base for reading comprehension to occur.

The relationship between oral reading ability and reading comprehension in a second language is problematic. Some studies indicate that second language readers produce oral reading errors similar to those of native language readers. Others find patterns dissimilar to these studies and claim that variations in oral reading are not predictable on the basis of language background. Finally, in this series is a study that indicates that oral reading consistently impedes comprehension for second language readers. This study casts doubt on the appropriateness of using oral reading for any investigation of the comprehension process as well as on the findings of the former studies. Inconsistent results are also found in the studies investigating the relationship between reading and listening, some finding a fairly strong correlation, others finding none.

The inconsistent and problematic results in these studies reflect a much debated and unresolved issue in first language reading. Some researchers argue that phonological concepts are necessary for the development of reading skills (for example, Gough, 1972). Others argue, however, that it is the act of reading itself that facilitates the development of phonological awareness (Goodman, 1970, 1973). Clearly, the second language studies provide data to support both sides of this issue. One resolution of the dilemma may be that some phonological awareness is indeed necessary, *but* that phonological awareness may not have to be an accurate approximation of the second language's sound system—merely an approximation of *some* sound system.

The related strand of second language writing research concerns initial writing development in children. The reading and writing studies are linked because they focus on children as subject groups and indicate that reading and writing competencies are directly related to oral vocabulary and oral story-telling ability. Additionally, several studies of second language writing indicate that second language children, just as do native language children, "invent" spellings, particularly in English, according to how words sound.

Second language writing research, however, does not completely parallel the reading research in this domain, since researchers have analyzed much more complex factors than merely phonological elements regarding children's writing development. In particular, examinations of children's second language writing ability have contributed to an understanding of the influence of first language knowledge on the development of second language writing proficiency. In fact, because this influence has been documented through careful case studies conducted by several researchers, it has a much more credible knowledge base than the parallel area in second language reading.

Syntactic Factors

Relatively few second language reading studies have investigated the impact of syntactic knowledge on the ability to understand text. This lack of data is surprising on two counts. First, second language classrooms tend to expend a significant amount of time in the instruction and practice of syntactic structures. Second, materials are developed principally according to readability formulae that are clearly measures of syntactic complexity.

The studies in syntax are characterized by three research categories. The first category examines second language readers' understanding of the referencing system in text. The second group investigates syntax at the sentence level and beyond. Several studies in this second category find that increases in syntactic knowledge impact differentially on comprehension as general language proficiency increases. Other studies provide data parallel to much L1 data (Pearson, 1975), that is, that the syntactic complexity of text can actually aid comprehension even for lower proficiency learners. In other words, simplified syntax does not necessarily lead to a simpler comprehension task. Finally, a third category provides evidence that parallel translations can aid in the acquisition of syntactic patterns.

The types of experimental task used in these studies and the variety of methodologies employed make the comparison and contrast of findings rather difficult. First, some studies used multiple-choice testing. The limitations of multiple-choice tests, with respect to passage dependence versus passage independence, as well as their tendency to lead the reader toward an answer rather than providing an actual measure of understanding, are well-known. Second, some studies used cloze tests. Recent research regarding cloze testing casts doubt on the findings of studies that use it as a measure. Third, the different nature of the subject groups further compounds the difficulty in the development of research generalizations regarding syntax. Subject groups from different language backgrounds may have generated different patterns of findings and yet these patterns are masked by the generic subject groupings. Fourth, investigators tend not to discuss issues of comparative syntax. Finally, the topic of the texts and subjects' knowledge of the topics used are rarely noted. Hence, it is frequently unclear whether syntax is the key variable or whether it is confounded with topic knowledge.

The area of syntax in second language writing research may be considered either very broadly or rather narrowly. In the broad sense, a number of studies employing error analyses that have provided psycholinguistic evidence about second language acquisition are included (Table 2). But these studies used writing as an elicitation task rather than as a communicative act (for example, Lantolf,

1988). Thus, when writing is defined in a narrow sense as a written communication task that needs syntactic support, there has been little empirical investigation.

Cross-Lingual Processing Strategies

A number of second language reading studies have compared and contrasted reading strategies within particular second languages (intralingually), while others compared and contrasted strategies across the native and second languages (interlingually). They are listed in Table 1.

This area of second language research provides complementary as well as contradictory evidence. The intralingual processing studies generally indicate that second language reading skill acquisition is developmental. Developmental data parallel a well-established research tradition and data base in first language research.

Some interlingual studies find evidence of both transfer and interference, while others indicate that first language processing behaviors tend to *dominate* throughout the development of reading proficiency in a second language. Transfer and interference data parallel a long-running debate in second language acquisition research in general. The extent to which first language strategies facilitate acquisition and the extent to which they impede acquisition—in the case of second language reading skills—remains unclear.

Unfortunately, a synthesis of this research area, too, is extremely troublesome. Many of the studies, for example, employed either oral reading or cloze testing methodologies. The dubious nature of these procedures for revealing information about the comprehension process makes generalizations difficult. Perhaps more problematic, though, in any attempt to compare and contrast, is the variability in texts, in language background (both culturally and orthographically), and in the proficiency levels of subjects.

A parallel strand of research exists in second language writing. A number of studies listed in Table 2 have indicated that first and second language writers use similar composing processes. Other second language writing studies have detected differences according to proficiency level in both the composing and revision stages of writing. Lower-level writers usually attend to low-level features and local errors such as spelling and syntax and do not attend to how their message is communicating with their audience, as high proficiency writers do. Of course, this area is not unassailable. Some researchers indicate that consistent comparisons have not been made between and among writers. In addition, they maintain that definitions of proficiency level are unclear and inconsistent. Thus, interpretation of data must be made with the utmost caution.

Metacognitive Factors

Table 1 lists reading studies involving metacognition—the conscious awareness of cognitive processes. These studies find that good readers attend to meaning, read in phrases, and persevere through texts, and that an oral command of a language is requisite for second language reading comprehension. Such studies have had considerable impact on what is believed about learners' reading behaviors. Problematic is the very limited number of subjects within the studies, as well as the interview techniques used for data collection. There is a parallel dearth of writing studies.

Testing

The testing literature consists of a number of thrusts. The first thrust involves the use of first language school-based standardized tests for second language readers. A second area investigates the efficacy of the cloze procedure and miscue analysis as assessment devices. A third area has focused on the efficacy of the ACTFL Guidelines for Reading. The studies that focus on standardized tests indicate that such measurements tend to be biased against second language readers. Better predictors of achievement seem to be cloze test results. The studies focusing specifically on cloze tests, however, seriously question the validity of the cloze procedure as a reading assessment device. The miscue analysis studies present similar concerns. Although some find an increase in the quality of oral reading errors as readers progress through a text, others find no relationship between oral reading errors and comprehension. The studies focusing on the guidelines find them to be a wholly inappropriate framework for L2 reading assessment.

This area is probably the most important area of second language reading research at present. Until reliable and valid measures of second language comprehension abilities are developed, the entire area of second language reading research will remain uncertain. The studies listed in Table 1 underline the importance of the testing issue: there are fifteen instances of the use of cloze testing; twelve instances of the use of oral reading and miscue analysis; and fifteen instances of the use of recall, many of which do not indicate the language of recall or the manner in which recalls were scored. In summary, almost 50% of the second language reading research base needs to be viewed with the utmost caution, considering the dubious nature of the data collection and analysis procedures. This, of course, is not to argue that the other studies employed appropriate data collection procedures. The validity of their data-collection devices has simply not been investigated.

Studies regarding the assessment of second language writing have focused primarily on scoring devices. Scoring devices such as the length of T-units and how such T-units should be defined in addition to wholistic scoring measures are included in the research studies in Table 2. On a more global scale, studies investigating native speaker reactions to non-native compositions find that content errors are more disturbing than language errors. In addition, a new vein of research reveals how different approaches to the evaluation of students' written work can take into account the processes employed by students when composing texts. To date, however, scant research has been done to determine optimal assessment measures for second language compositions.

Instruction

Second language reading studies grouped under the general heading of instruction focus on one of two topics. One group discusses and provides data on course designs that facilitate reading achievement. The other group of studies focuses specifically on instructional strategies and materials.

The first group finds particular curricular designs facilitative of reading comprehension. Among these designs are different grouping strategies, various distributions of native and target language instruction in reading, and types of materials and exposure to reading materials available to learners. The second group finds particular instructional strategies in reading to be useful; these strategies include types of comprehension cues, inductive and deductive teaching strategies, open-ended questioning strategies, instruction in intensive reading strategies, training in memorization, questioning with reading texts removed, non-translation techniques, and training in think-aloud strategies.

These instructional-evaluative studies reflect a "what worked for our program" spirit. They do provide some insights into curricular design. As a whole, however, they do not describe contextual variables in enough depth to advise and seriously inform the field on questions of generalized curricular directions and methodologies.

Similar statements can be made regarding the research into appropriate instruction in second language writing. A number of researchers have investigated the use of journals, free writing, peer response to second language compositions, and the use of computers as instructional techniques. In addition, analyses of teachers' correction strategies indicate that teachers are inconsistent and rarely make corrections relevant to the communicative thrust of a piece of writing. These studies, listed in Table 2, are vulnerable to the same comments made about second language reading studies: they reflect descriptive data on what worked, and yet they are not designed in such a way as to allow substantive conclusions to be drawn from them.

READING-WRITING RELATIONSHIPS REVISITED

In second language literacy research, there is minimal overlap in the research strands focused on either reading or writing. *Or* is an important word in this discussion. There are essentially no studies that attempt to document or investigate the link between reading and writing in the same manner that this link has been studied in first language literacy research. In other words, second language research has perceived reading and writing as being essentially different dimensions of the composing process.

There are a number of reasons for this perception. The first reason involves the actual psycholinguistic make-up of first language learners versus second language learners. First language learners are placed in schools for the explicit intention of learning to read and write. This learning takes place simultaneously and the processes, merely by merit of their being placed together in the school curriculum, inevitably become in the learner's view two sides of the same process. In addition, an important distinction is that first language learners are generally at the stage of "learning to read" and "learning to write."

Second language learners, in contrast, with the exception of some bilingual learners, essentially have to "read to learn" and "write to demonstrate learning." Harkening back to the initial pages of this paper, it is clear that the increase in interest in second language literacy stems from adult learners who have to learn to use a second language functionally. In fact, many of these learners have already achieved a high degree of literacy in their first language. They do not need, therefore, to learn to read or to write as first language learners do.

Yet distinctions between first and second language learners are not simply psycholinguistic in nature. There are also differences in the reasons why second language learners become literate in a second language. In other words, the nature of the goals and the use of second languages is different from the nature of the goals in first language literacy. Both second and foreign language learners need to be able to read second language texts with comprehension: second language learners need to be able to gather information from a variety of fields in the second language, and foreign language learners need to be able to understand literary and cultural materials in the foreign language. These groups do not have, however, comparable needs in writing. Only second language learners who are competing in instruction with first language learners have to be able to write with the same facility with which they read. In the foreign language curriculum, however, although writing is indeed a curricular component, learners are not required to compose texts at the same level as native speakers. For the most part, when foreign language learners do compose in the second language the target audience recognizes that the composition is written by a foreign language writer and reads it principally for the *language use* in it, rather than for the *content*.

Even though there is little acknowledgment of second language reading-writing relationships, there seem to be some consistent findings in both reading and writing research. One such consistency is that the knowledge of the topic of either reading or writing seems to be an important variable. In what ways it is important, that is, whether it is facilitative, detrimental, or noise in the system, is still ambiguous. Another consistency is in the area of text structure. If readers can follow an author's structure, their comprehension scores increase. If writers acquire a second language discourse structure, their compositions improve. A third consistency is found in the area of cross-lingual text processing and text composing strategies. This area finds both similarities and differences between the development of text processing and composing in both first and second language— again, findings fraught with ambiguities.

PROSPECTIVE VIEWS FOR THE
FOREIGN LANGUAGE CLASSROOM

The reason these findings in L2 reading and writing research are so ambiguous may not be in the nature of the processes themselves, but rather in the nature of the research designs utilized. In fact, a consistent theme across all of the research strands in both second language reading and writing is that generalizability is practically and theoretically impossible, since the subjects in the studies are portrayed generically, the topics for either the reading or writing tasks are rarely mentioned, and the reading and writing tasks given second language learners have genuine validity and reliability problems.

In general, this is a sad commentary on second language reading and writing research. When there is no unified research emphasis, no research tradition that tempers and molds research designs, and little exchange among researchers who have a firm sense of previous findings and of the nature of, if not a command of, a number of languages, the development of a *potpourri*—used in both its English and its French sense—is inevitable. Until L2 researchers begin to use cleaner, more viable research methodologies, procedures, and analytic techniques, knowledge about literacy in a second language will remain speculative.

The above discussion of different facets of second language literacy research points to serious methodological limitations. These limitations are found generally in a lack of explicit description of subject groups, in sketchy descriptions of language proficiency, and in having confounded reading and writing abilities. In addition, a majority of second language literacy studies have failed to acknowledge the different linguistic and social backgrounds of subjects. The importance of such acknowledgment is underlined when considering that subjects from Western and non-Western cultures, with different educational backgrounds, with different expectations of literacy, and with first languages that have a wide array of textual and orthographic structures, are all placed in one group termed *second language readers or writers*. In addition, these readers or writers are rarely characterized by their expertise, their topic knowledge, or their background—all factors that research would indicate are critical toward understanding the cognitive and social processes of literacy skill development.

There may be a number of reasons for the failure of researchers to adequately detail their subject groups. One of these reasons may well be underdeveloped research skills. Yet a more fundamental reason may be the inability of researchers to cope with a multitude of languages. As Ferguson and Huebner (1989) point out:

> The TESOL profession has been an important locus of American research in second language acquisition, a fact largely responsible for the existence of a generation of American SLA specialists who do not themselves speak a second language . . . . Researchers do not necessarily need to have personal experience with the phenomena they want to investigate; . . . but it is at least worth noting that many American SLA researchers have little or no FL competence . . . (1989, 2).

While Ferguson and Huebner (1989) may be correct in their assertion that researchers do not need to have personal experience with the phenomenon they are investigating, it is incumbent upon researchers that their own deficiencies not place subjects at a disadvantage and thereby skew the data. This situation is nowhere more true than when subjects must use the second language to demonstrate understanding of that second language. Researchers consistently argue that subject groups are so heterogeneous that it is impossible to collect data without a *lingua franca*. This argumentation reveals the advantages of the foreign language classroom as an excellent forum for data collection and for the appropriate analysis of second language literacy skills.

There are three principal advantages to foreign language classroom research that enable a much more substantial and reliable data base in second language literacy to be generated. First of all, data from the foreign language classroom are not confounded with extraneous input sources. That is, researchers can provide confident and unambiguous information about the types of material learners have been exposed to, including vocabulary and structural frequency, as well as topic and discourse features. In a second language situation, with subjects from throughout the world, there is practically no way of knowing or gathering this information. Second, data from foreign language classrooms are collected from basically homogeneous groups. Foreign language groups tend to be from the same linguistic as well as cultural backgrounds. These characteristics eliminate the confounding variables found in many second language literacy studies, which override the experimental treatment and tend to either diminish or inflate the main effects. A third advantage links back to the comments by Ferguson and Huebner (1989) and involves language itself. Research in foreign language classrooms enables elicitations in the mother tongue. It also involves researchers who generally have intimate knowledge of the language and culture that the subjects are learning, as well as an intimate knowledge of the subjects' first language.

Ultimately, using foreign language classrooms for research purposes will facilitate the development of a more coherent, valid, and reliable reading and writing research base. Until such a research base exists, however, there can be little confidence in the instructional strategies and myths passed on about reading and writing to generation after generation of foreign language teachers.

REFERENCES

Adams, S. J. 1982. "Scripts and the Recognition of Unfamiliar Vocabulary: Enhancing Second Language Reading Skills." *Modern Language Journal* 66: 155–9.

Adjemian, C., and J. Liceras. 1984. "Accounting for Adult Acquisition of Relative Clauses: Universal Grammar, L1 and Structuring the Intake." *Universals of Second Language Acquisition*. Eds. F. R. Eckman, L. H. Bell, and D. Nelson. Rowley, Mass.: Newbury House. 101–18.

Alderson, J. C., and A. H. Urquhart. 1988. "This Test Is Unfair: I'm Not An Economist." *Interactive Approaches to Second Language Reading*. Eds. P. C. Carrell, J. Devine, and D. E. Eskey. Cambridge: Cambridge UP. 168–82.

Alderson, J. C., and A. H. Urquhart, eds. 1984. *Reading in a Foreign Language*. New York: Longman.

Allen, E. D., E. B. Bernhardt, M. T. Berry, and M. Demel. 1988. "Comprehension and Text Genre: Analysis of Secondary School Foreign Language Readers." *Modern Language Journal* 72.2: 163–72.

Baldauf, R. B., Jr., R. L. T. Dawson, J. Prior, and I. K. Propst, Jr. 1980. "Can Matching Cloze Be Used With Secondary ESL Pupils?" *Journal of Reading* 23: 435–40.

Barnett, M. 1986. "Syntactic and Lexical/Semantic Skill in Foreign Language Reading: Importance and Interaction." *Modern Language Journal* 70: 343–49.

Barnett, M. A. 1988. "Teaching Reading Strategies: How Methodology Affects Language Course Articulation." *Foreign Language Annals* 21.2: 109–19.

Barrera, B. R., G. Valdes, and M. Cardenes. 1986. "Analyzing the Recall of Students Across Different Language-Reading Categories: A Study of Third-Graders' Spanish-L1, English-L2, and English-L1 Comprehension." *Thirty-Fifth Yearbook of the National Reading Conference*. Eds. J. A. Niles and R. V. Lalik. Rochester, N.Y.: The National Reading Conference.

Bean, W. T., T. C. Potter, and C. Clark. 1980. "Selected Semantic Features of ESL Materials and Their Effect on Bilingual Students' Comprehension." *Twenty-Ninth Yearbook of the National Reading Conference*. Eds. M. Kamil and A. Moe. Washington D.C.: National Reading Conference.

Bensoussan, M., and R. Ramraz. 1984a. "Helping the Poor to Help Themselves: A Quantitative Re-Evaluation of the Outcomes of an Advanced Reading Comprehension Program in English as a Foreign Language." *System* 12: 61–6.

———. 1984b. "Testing EFL Reading Comprehension Using a Multiple-Choice Rational Cloze." *Modern Language Journal* 68: 230–39.

Bensoussan, M., D. Sim, and R. Weiss. 1984. "The Effect of Dictionary Usage on EFL Test Performance Compared With Student and Teacher Attitudes and Expectations." *Reading in a Foreign Language* 2: 262–76.

Bernhardt, E. B. 1983. "Three Approaches to Reading Comprehension in Intermediate German." *Modern Language Journal* 67: 111–15.

———. 1986. "Cognitive Processes in L2: An Examination of Reading Behaviors." *Research in Second Language Acquisition in the Classroom Setting*. Eds. J. Lantolf and A. Labarca. Norwood, N.J.: Ablex.

Bhatia, V. K. 1984. "Syntactic Discontinuity in Legislative Writing for Academic Legal Purposes." *Reading for Professional Purposes: Studies and Practices in Native and Foreign Languages*. Eds. A. K. Pugh and J. M. Ulijn. London: Heinemann Educational Books.

Bialystok, E. 1983. "Inferencing: Testing the 'Hypothesis-Testing' Hypothesis." *Classroom Oriented Research in Second Language Acquisition.* Ed. H. Seliger and M. Long. Rowley, Mass.: Newbury House.

Blau, E. K. 1982. "The Effect of Syntax on Readability for ESL Students in Puerto Rico." *TESOL Quarterly* 16: 517–28.

Block, E. 1986. "Comprehension Strategies of Non-Proficient College Readers." *Thirty-Fifth Yearbook of the National Reading Conference.* Eds. J. A. Niles and R. V. Lalik. Rochester, N.Y.: The National Reading Conference.

Brown, J. D. 1985. "A Norm-Referenced Engineering Reading Test." *Reading for Professional Purposes: Methods and Materials in Teaching Languages.* Eds. K. Pugh and J. M. Ulijn. Leuven, Belgium: Acco.

Brown, J. D., C. Yongpei, and W. Yinglong. 1984. "An Evaluation of Native-Speaker Self-Access Reading Materials in an EFL Setting." *RELC Journal* 15: 75–84.

Brown, T. L., and M. Haynes. 1985. "Literacy Background and Reading Development in a Second Language." *The Development of Reading Skills.* Ed. T. H. Carr. San Francisco: Jossey-Bass.

Byrnes, H. 1988. Personal communication, November.

Campbell, A. J. 1981. "Language Background and Comprehension." *Reading Teacher* 35: 10–14.

Carlson, S., and B. Bridgeman. 1986. "Testing ESL Student Writers." *Writing Assessment.* Eds. K. L. Greenberg, H. S. Wiener, and R. A. Donovan. New York: Longman. 126–52.

Carrell, P., and B. Wallace. 1983. "Background Knowledge: Context and Familiarity in Reading Comprehension." *On TESOL 82.* Eds. M. A. Clarke and J. Handscombe. Washington, D.C.: TESOL.

Carrell, P. T. 1983. "Three Components of Background Knowledge in Reading Comprehension." *Language Learning* 33: 183–207.

———. 1984a. "Evidence of a Formal Schema in Second Language Comprehension." *Language Learning* 34: 87–112.

———. 1984b. "Inferencing in ESL: Presuppositions and Implications of Factive and Implicative Predicates." *Language Learning* 34: 1–21.

———. 1987. "Content and Formal Schemata in ESL Reading." *TESOL Quarterly* 21.3: 461–81.

Chiste, K. B., and J. O'Shea. 1988. "Patterns of Question Selection and Writing Performance of ESL Students." *TESOL Quarterly* 22.4: 681–84.

Clarke, M. A. 1979. "Reading in Spanish and English: Evidence From Adult ESL Students." *Language Learning* 29: 121–50.

———. 1980. "The Short Circuit Hypothesis of ESL Reading: Or When Language Competence Interferes with Reading Performance." *Modern Language Journal* 64: 203–9.

Cohen, A., H. Glasman, P. Rosenbaum-Cohen, J. Ferrar, and J. Fine. 1979. "Reading English for Specialized Purposes: Discourse Analysis and the Use of Student Informants." *TESOL Quarterly* 13: 551–64.

Connor, U. 1981. "The Application of Reading Miscue Analysis to the Diagnosis of English as a Second Language Learners' Reading Skills." *Reading English as a Second Language: Moving From Theory.* Eds. C. W. Twyford, W. Diehl, and K. Feathers. Bloomington, Ind.: Indiana University School of Education.

———. 1984. "Recall of Text: Differences Between First and Second Language Readers." *TESOL Quarterly* 18: 239–55.

———. 1987a. "Argumentative Patterns in Student Essays: Cross-Cultural Differences." *Writing Across Languages: Analysis of L2 Text.* Eds. U. Connor and R. B. Kaplan. Reading, Mass.: Addison-Wesley. 57–71.

———. 1987b. "Research Frontiers in Writing Analysis." *TESOL Quarterly* 21.4: 677–96.

Connor, U., and R. B. Kaplan, eds. 1987. *Writing Across Languages: Analysis of L2 Text.* Reading, Mass.: Addison-Wesley.

Cooper, M. 1984. "Linguistic Competence of Practiced and Unpracticed Non-Native Readers of English." *Reading in a Foreign Language.* Eds. J. C. Alderson and A. H. Urquhart. London: Longman.

Cooper, T. C. 1976. "Measuring Written Syntactic Patterns of Second Language Learners of German." *Journal of Educational Research* 69: 176–83.

Cowan, J. R., and S. Sarmad. 1976. "Reading Performance of Bilingual Children According to Type of School and Home Language." *Language Learning* 26: 353–76.

Cumming, A. 1983. "Teachers' Procedures for Responding to the Writing of Students of English as a Second Language." Paper presented at the 16th Annual Canadian Council of Teachers of English Convention, Montreal, Quebec, Canada, May, 1983.

Cziko, G. A. 1978. "Differences in First- and Second-Language Reading: The Use of Syntactic, Semantic, and Discourse Constraints." *Canadian Modern Language Review/La Revue Canadienne des Langues Vivantes* 34: 473–89.

———. 1980. "Language Competence and Reading Strategies: A Comparison of First- and Second-Language Readers." *Language Learning* 30: 101–16.

Dank, M., and W. McEachern. 1979. "A Psycholinguistic Description Comparing the Native Language Oral Reading Behavior of French Immersion Students With Traditional English Language Students." *Canadian Modern Language Review/La Revue Canadienne des Langues Vivantes* 35: 366–71.

Davies, A. 1984. "Simple, Simplified and Simplification: What Is Authentic?" *Reading in a Foreign Language.* Eds. J. C. Alderson and A. H. Urquhart. London: Longman.

Davis, J. N., D. L. Lange, and S. J. Samuels. 1988. "Effects of Text Structure

Instruction on Foreign Language Readers' Recall of a Scientific Journal Article." *Journal of Reading Behavior* 22.3: 203–14.

Devine, J. 1981. "Developmental Patterns in Native and Non-Native Reading Acquisition." *Learning to Read in Different Languages.* Ed. S. Hudelson. Washington, D.C.: Center for Applied Linguistics.

———. 1984. "ESL Readers' Internalized Models of the Reading Process." *On TESOL '83.* Eds. J. Handscombe, R. Oren, and B. Taylor. Washington, D.C.: TESOL.

Devine, J., P. L. Carrell, and D. Eskey, eds. 1987. *Research in Reading English as a Second Language."* Washington, D.C.: TESOL.

Douglas, D. 1981. "An Exploratory Study of Bilingual Reading Proficiency." *Learning to Read in Different Languages.* Ed. S. Hudelson. Washington, D.C.: Center for Applied Linguistics.

Doushaq, M. H. 1986. "An Investigation Into Stylistic Errors of Arab Students Learning English for Academic Purposes." *ESL Journal* 5.1: 27–39.

Dubin, F., D. Eskey, and W. Grabe, eds. 1986. *Teaching Second Language Reading for Academic Purposes.* Reading, Mass.: Addison-Wesley.

Edelsky, C. 1982. "Writing in a Bilingual Program: The Relation of L1 and L2 Texts." *TESOL Quarterly* 16: 211–28.

———. 1983. "Segmentationandpunc.tu.a.tion: Developmental Data From Young Writers in a Bilingual Program." *Research in the Teaching of English* 17: 135–56.

Eggington, W. G. 1987. "Written Academic Discourse in Korean: Implications for Effective Communication." *Writing Across Languages: Analysis of L2 Text.* Eds. U. Connor and R. B. Kaplan. Reading, Mass.: Addison-Wesley. 153–68.

Elley, W. B. 1983. "The Impact of Reading on Second Language Learning." *Reading Research Quarterly* 19: 53–67.

———. 1984. "Exploring the Reading Difficulties of Second Language Learners and Second-Languages in Fiji." *Reading in a Foreign Language.* Eds. J. C. Alderson and A. H. Urquhart. London: Longman.

Elley, W. B., and Mangubhai, J. 1983. "The Impact of Reading on Second Language Learning." *Reading Research Quarterly* 19: 53–67.

Ewoldt, C. 1981. "Factors Which Enable Deaf Readers to Get Meaning From Print." *Learning to Read in Different Languages.* Ed. S. Hudelson. Washington, D.C.: Center for Applied Linguistics.

Favreau, M., and N. S. Segalowitz. 1982. "Second Language Reading in Fluent Bilinguals." *Applied Psycholinguistics* 3: 329–41.

Favreau, M., M. K. Komoda, and N. S. Segalowitz. 1980. "Second Language Reading: Implications of the Word Superiority Effect in Skilled Bilinguals." *Canadian Journal of Psychology/Revue Canadienne de Psychologie* 34: 370–80.

Feldman, D. 1978. "A Special Reading System for Second Language Learners." *TESOL Quarterly* 12: 415–24.

Ferguson, C., and T. Huebner. 1989. *Foreign Language Instruction and Second Language Acquisition Research in the United States*. Washington, D.C.: NFLC.

Fillion, B. 1985. "Writing, Reading, and Learning." *Contexts of Reading*. Eds. C. N. Hedley and A. N. Baratta. Norwood, N.J.: Ablex.

Flahive, D. E., and B. G. Snow. 1980. "Measures of Syntactic Complexity in Evaluating ESL Compositions." *Research in Language Testing*. Eds. J. W. Oller, Jr., and K. Perkins. Rowley, Mass.: Newbury House.

Flick, W. C., and J. I. Anderson. 1980. "Rhetorical Difficulty in Scientific English: A Study in Reading Comprehension." *TESOL Quarterly* 14: 345–51.

Fransson, A. 1984. "Cramming or Understanding? Effects of Intrinsic and Extrinsic Motivation on Approach to Learning and Test Performance." *Reading in a Foreign Language*. Eds. J. C. Alderson and A. H. Urquhart. London: Longman.

Gaies, S. J. 1980. "T-Unit Analysis in Second Language Research: Applications, Problems and Limitations." *TESOL Quarterly* 14: 53–60.

Goodman, K. S. 1970. "Behind the Eye: What Happens in Reading." *Reading: Process and Program*. Eds. K. S. Goodman and O. S. Niles. Urbana, Ill.: NCTE.

———. 1973. "Psycholinguistic Universals of the Reading Process." *Psycholinguistics and Reading*. Ed. F. Smith. New York: Holt, Rinehart and Winston.

Gough, P. B. 1972. "One Second of Reading." *Language By Eye and Ear*. Eds. J. F. Kavanaugh and I. G. Mattingly. Cambridge, Mass.: MIT Press.

Grabe, W. 1987. "Contrastive Rhetoric and Text-Type Research." *Writing Across Languages: Analysis of L2 Texts*. Eds. U. Connor and R. B. Kaplan. Reading, Mass.: Addison-Wesley. 115–37.

Groebel, L. 1979. "A Comparison of Two Strategies in the Teaching of Reading Comprehension." *English Language Teaching Journal* 33: 306–9.

———. 1980. "A Comparison of Students' Reading Comprehension in the Native Language With Their Reading Comprehension in the Target Language." *English Language Teaching Journal* 35: 54–9.

Grosse, C., and K. Hameyer. 1979. "Dialect and Reading Interferences in Second Language Perception and Production." *Die Unterrichtspraxis* 12: 52–60.

Guarino, R., and K. Perkins. 1986. "Awareness of Form Class as a Factor in ESL Reading Comprehension." *Language Learning* 36: 77–82.

Haddad, F. 1981. "First Language Illiteracy–Second Language Reading: A Case Study." *Learning to Read in Different Languages*. Ed. S. Hudelson. Washington, D.C.: Center for Applied Linguistics.

Harvey, T. E. 1987. "Second-Language Composition Instruction, Computers and First-Language Pedagogy: A Descriptive Survey." *Foreign Language Annals* 20.2: 171–75.

Hatch, E., P. Polin, and S. Part. 1974. "Acoustic Scanning and Syntactic Processing: Three Reading Experiments: First and Second Language Learners." *Journal of Reading Behavior* 6: 275–85.

Hayes, E. B. 1988. "Encoding Strategies Used by Native and Non-Native Readers of Chinese Mandarin." *Modern Language Journal* 72.2: 188–95.

Haynes, M. 1981. "Patterns and Perils of Guessing in Second Language Reading." *On TESOL '83*. Eds. J. Handscombe, R. Oren, and B. Taylor. Washington, D.C.: TESOL.

Hendrickson, J. M. 1980. "Error Correction in Foreign Language Teaching: Recent Theory, Research, and Practice." *Readings in English as a Second Language*. Ed. K. Croft. Cambridge, Mass.: Winthrop. 153–73.

Henning, G. H. 1975. "Measuring Foreign Language Reading Comprehension." *Language Learning* 25: 109–14.

Hill, J. K. 1981. "Effective Reading in a Foreign Language: An Experimental Reading Course in English for Overseas Students." *English Language Teaching Journal* 35: 270–321.

Hinds, J. 1987. "Reader versus Writer Responsibility: A New Typology." *Writing Across Languages: Analysis of L2 Text*. Eds. U. Connor and R. B. Kaplan. Reading, Mass.: Addison-Wesley. 141–52.

Hock, T. S., and L. C. Poh. 1979. "The Performance of a Group of Malay-Medium Students in an English Reading Comprehension Test." *RELC Journal* 10: 81–7.

Hodes, P. 1981. "Reading: A Universal Process." *Learning to Read in Different Languages*. Eds. S. Hudelson. Washington, D.C.: Center for Applied Linguistics.

Homburg, T. J., and M. C. Spaun. 1982. "ESL Reading Proficiency Assessment: Testing Strategies." *On TESOL '81*. Eds. M. Hines and W. Rutherford. Washington, D.C.: TESOL.

Hosenfeld, C. 1977. "A Preliminary Investigation of the Reading Strategies of Successful and Nonsuccessful Second Language Learners." *System* 5: 110–13.

———. 1984. "Case Studies of Ninth-Grade Readers." *Reading in a Foreign Language*. Eds. J. C. Alderson and A. H. Urquhart. London: Longman.

Hu, A., D. F. Brown, and L. B. Brown. 1982. "Some Linguistic Differences in the Written English of Chinese and Australian Students." *Language Learning and Communication* 1: 39–40.

Hudelson, S. 1983. "Roberto and Janice: Individual Differences in Second Language Writing." Paper presented at the Conference of the National Association for Bilingual Education, San Antonio, Tex., April 1983.

———. 1984a. "Kan Yu Ret and Rayt en Ingles: Children Become Literate in English as a Second Language." *TESOL Quarterly* 18: 221–38.

————. 1984b. "Developing Writing Abilities in a Second Language." Paper presented at the Ohio Conference of Language and Literacy for the Culturally Different Child, Columbus, OH, December, 1984.

Hudson, T. 1982. "The Effects of Induced Schemata on the 'Short Circuit' in L2 Reading: Non-Decoding Factors in L2 Reading Performance." *Language Learning* 32: 1–32.

Irujo, S. 1986. "Don't Put Your Leg in Your Mouth: Transfer in the Acquisition of Idioms in a Second Language." *TESOL Quarterly* 20: 287–304.

Jarvis, D. K., and D. C. Jensen. 1982. "The Effect of Parallel Translations on Second Language Reading and Syntax Acquisition." *Modern Language Journal* 66: 18–23.

Johnson, D. M., and D. H. Roen, eds. 1989. *Richness in Writing: Empowering ESL Students*. New York: Longman.

Johnson, P. 1981. "Effects on Reading Comprehension of Language Complexity and Cultural Background of a Text." *TESOL Quarterly* 15: 169–81.

————. 1982. "Effects on Comprehension of Building Background Knowledge." *TESOL Quarterly* 16: 503–16.

Jones, C. S. 1982. "Composing in a Second Language: A Process Study." Paper presented at the Sixteenth Annual TESOL Convention, Honolulu, HI, May, 1982.

————. 1983. "Some Composing Strategies of Second Language Writers." Paper presented at the Colloquium on Learner Strategies at the Seventeenth Annual TESOL Convention, Toronto, Canada, March, 1983.

Kaczmarek, C. M. 1980. "Scoring and Rating Essay Tasks." *Research in Language Testing*. Eds. J. Oller and K. Perkins. Rowley, MA: Newbury House, 151–59.

Kameen, P. 1979. "Syntactic Skill and ESL Writing Quality." *On TESOL '79*. Eds. C. Yorio, K. Perkins, and J. Schachter. Washington, DC: TESOL. 330–42.

Kamil, M. L., M. Smith-Burke, and F. Rodriguez-Brown. 1986. "The Sensitivity of Cloze to Intersentential Integration of Information in Spanish Bilingual Populations." *Thirty-fifth Yearbook of the National Reading Conference*. Eds. J. A. Niles and R. V. Lalik. Rochester, NY: The National Reading Conference.

Kaplan, R. B. 1966. "Cultural Thought Patterns in Intercultural Education." *Language Learning* 16: 1–20.

————. 1987. "Cultural Thought Patterns Revisited." *Writing Across Languages: Analysis of L2 Text*. Eds. U. Connor and R. B. Kaplan. Reading, MA: Addison-Wesley. 9–21.

Kendall, J. R., G. Lajeunesse, P. Chmilar, L. R. Shapson, and S. M. Shapson. 1987. "English Reading Skills of French Immersion Students in Kindergarten and Grades 1 and 2." *Reading Research Quarterly* 22.2: 135–59.

Keyes, J. R. 1984. "Peer Editing and Writing Success." *TESOL Newsletter Supplement No. 1: Writing and Composition* 18: 11–12.

Kleinmann, H. H. 1987. "The Effect of Computer-Assisted Instruction on ESL Reading Achievement." *Modern Language Journal,* 71.3: 267–76.

Knepler, M. 1984. "Impromptu Writing to Increase Fluency." *TESOL Newsletter Supplement No. 1: Writing and Composition.* 18: 15–16.

Koda, K. 1987. "Cognitive Strategy Transfer in Second Language Reading. *Research in Reading in English as a Second Language.* Eds. J. Devine, P. C. Carrell, and D. E. Eskey. Washington, DC: TESOL. 125–44.

Krashen, S. 1981. *Second Language Acquisition and Second Language Learning.* Oxford: Pergamon.

Krashen, S., J. Butler, R. Birnbaum, and J. Robertson. 1978. "Two Studies in Language Acquisition and Language Learning." *ITL: Review of Applied Linguistics* 39–40: 73–92.

Lantolf, J. P. 1988. "The Syntactic Complexity of Written Texts in Spanish as a Foreign Language: A Markedness Perspective." *Hispania* 71.4: 933–40.

Laufer, B. 1978. "An Experiment in Teaching Reading Comprehension With Written Answers in the Mother Tongue." *System* 6: 11–20.

Laufer-Dvorkin, B. 1981. " 'Intensive' versus 'Extensive' Reading for Improving University Students' Comprehension in English as a Foreign Language." *Journal of Reading* 25.1: 40–3.

Lay, N. D. S. 1982. "Composing Processes of Adult ESL Learners: A Case Study." *TESOL Quarterly* 16: 406.

Lee, J. F. 1986a. "Background Knowledge and L2 Reading." *Modern Language Journal* 70: 350–54.

———. 1986b. "On the Use of the Recall Task to Measure L2 Reading Comprehension." *Studies in Second Language Acquisition* 8: 83–93.

Lee, J. F., and D. Musumeci. 1988. "On Hierarchies of Reading Skills and Text Types." *Modern Language Journal* 72.2: 173–87.

Lutjeharms, M. 1985. "Testing Reading Comprehension: An Example From German for Academic Purposes." *Reading for Professional Purposes: Methods and Materials in Teaching Languages.* Eds. J. M. Ulijn, and A. K. Pugh. Leuven, Belgium: Acco.

MacLean, M., and A. d'Anglejan. 1986. "Rational Cloze and Retrospection: Insights Into First and Second Language Reading Comprehension." *Canadian Modern Language Review* 42: 814–26.

McColly, W. 1970. "What Does Educational Research Say About the Judging of Writing Ability?" *Journal of Educational Research* 64: 148–56.

McDougall, A., and M. Bruck. 1976. "English Reading Within the French Immersion Program: A Comparison of the Effects of the Introduction of English at Different Grade Levels." *Language Learning* 26: 37–44.

McKay, S. 1984. "Some Limitations in Teaching Composition." *On TESOL '83.* Eds. J. Handscombe, *et al.* Bloomington, Ill.: Pantagraph. 187–94.

McLeod, B., and B. McLaughlin. 1986. "Restructuring or Automaticity? Reading in a Second Language." *Language Learning* 36: 109–23.

Markham, P. 1985. "The Rational Deletion Cloze and Global Comprehension in German." *Language Learning* 35: 423–30.

Mazurkewich, I. 1984. "Dative Questions and Markedness." *Universals of Second Language Acquisition*. Eds. F. R. Eckman, L. H. Bell, and D. Nelson. Rowley, Mass.: Newbury House. 119–31.

Meara, P. 1984. "Word Recognition in Foreign Languages." *Reading for Professional Purposes: Studies and Practices in Native and Foreign Languages*. Eds. A. K. Pugh and J. M. Ulijn. London: Heinemann Educational Books.

Mohammed, M. A. H., and J. M. Swales. 1984. "Factors Affecting the Successful Reading of Technical Instructions." *Reading in a Foreign Language* 2: 206–17.

Mohan, B. A., and W. A. Lo. 1985. "Academic Writing and Chinese Students: Transfer and Developmental Factors." *TESOL Quarterly* 19: 515–34.

Moore, B. 1982. "English Reading Skills of Multilingual Pupils in Singapore." *Reading Teacher* 35: 696–701.

Mott, B. 1981. "A Miscue Analysis of German Speakers Reading in German and English. *Learning to Read in Different Languages*. Ed. S. Hudelson. Washington, D.C.: Center for Applied Linguistics.

Muchisky, D. M. 1983. "Relationships Between Speech and Reading Among Second Language Learners." *Language Learning* 33: 77–102.

Mullen, K. A. 1980. "Evaluating Writing Proficiency in ESL." *Research in Language Testing*. Eds. J. W. Oller, Jr., and K. Perkins. Rowley, Mass.: Newbury House. 160–70.

Mustapha, H., P. Nelson, and J. Thomas. 1985. "Reading for Specific Purposes: The Course for the Faculty of Earth Sciences at King Abdulaziz University." *Reading for Professional Purposes: Methods and Materials in Teaching Languages*. Eds. J. M. Ulijn and A. K. Pugh. Leuven, Belgium: Acco.

Narayanaswamy, K. R. 1982. "ESP for Islamic School-Learners." *System* 10: 159–70.

Nehr, M. 1984. "Audio-Lingual Behavior in Learning to Read Foreign Languages." *Reading for Professional Purposes: Studies and Practices in Native and Foreign Languages*. Eds. A. K. Pugh and J. M. Ulijn. London: Heinemann Educational Books.

Neville, M. H. 1979. "An Englishwoman Reads Spanish: Self-Observation and Speculation." *English Language Teaching Journal* 33: 274–81.

Neville, M. H., and A. K. Pugh. 1975. "An Exploratory Study of the Application of Time-Compressed and Time-Expanded Speech in the Development of the English Reading Proficiency of Foreign Students." *English Language Teaching Journal* 29: 320–29.

Nunan, D. 1985. "Content Familiarity and the Perception of Textual Relationships in Second Language Reading." *RELC Journal* 16: 43–51.

O'Flanagan, M. J. R. 1985. "A Program for Teaching and Learning to Read Professional Texts in a Second/Foreign Language at Siemens AG." *Reading for Professional Purposes: Methods and Materials in Teaching Languages.* Eds. J. M. Ulijn and A. K. Pugh. Leuven, Belgium: Acco.

Olah, E. 1984. "How Special Is Special English?" *Reading for Professional Purposes: Studies and Practices in Native and Foreign Languages.* Eds. A. K. Pugh and J. M. Ulijn. London: Heinemann Educational Books.

Olshtain, E. 1982. "English Nominal Components and the ESL/EFL Reader." *On TESOL '81.* Eds. M. Hines and W. Rutherford. Washington, D.C.: TESOL.

Omaggio, A. C. 1979. "Pictures and Second Language Comprehension: Do They Help?" *Foreign Language Annals* 12: 107–16.

Ostler, S. 1987. "English in Parallels: A Comparison of English and Arabic Prose." *Writing Across Languages: Analysis of L2 Text.* Eds. U. Connor and R. B. Kaplan. Reading, Mass.: Addison-Wesley. 169–85.

Padron, Y. N., and H. C. Waxman. 1988. "The Effect of ESL Students' Perceptions of Their Cognitive Strategies on Reading Achievement." *TESOL Quarterly* 22.1: 146–50.

Parry, K. J. 1987. "Reading in a Second Culture." *Research in Reading in English as a Second Language.* Eds. J. Devine, P. L. Carrell, and D. E. Eskey. Washington, D.C.: TESOL. 59–70.

Pearson, P. D. 1975. "The Effects of Grammatical Complexity on Children's Comprehension, Recall, and Conception of Certain Grammatical Relations." *Reading Research Quarterly* 10: 155–92.

Pederson, K. 1986. "An Experiment in Computer Assisted Second-Language Reading." *Modern Language Journal* 70: 36–41.

Perkins, K. 1980. "Using Objective Methods of Attained Writing Proficiency to Discriminate Among Holistic Evaluations." *TESOL Quarterly* 14: 61–9.

———. 1983a. "Semantic Constructivity in ESL Reading Comprehension." *TESOL Quarterly* 17: 19–27.

———. 1983b. "On the Use of Composition Scoring Techniques, Objective Measures, and Objective Tests to Evaluate ESL Writing Ability." *TESOL Quarterly* 17: 651–71.

———. 1984. "An Analysis of Four Common Item Types Used in Testing EFL Reading Comprehension." *RELC Journal* 15: 29–43.

———. 1987. "The Relationship Between Nonverbal Schematic Concept Formation and Story Comprehension." *Research in Reading in English as a Second Language.* Eds. J. Devine, P. L. Carrell, and D. E. Eskey. Washington, D.C.: TESOL. 151–71.

Perkins, K., and P. J. Angelis. 1985. "Schematic Concept Formation: Concurrent Validity for Attained English as a Second Language Reading Comprehension?" *Language Learning* 35: 269–83.

Perkins, K., and S. R. Brutten. 1988. "A Behavioral Anchoring Analysis of Three ESL Reading Comprehension Tests." *TESOL Quarterly* 22.4: 607–22.

Propst, I. K., Jr., and R. B. Baldauf, Jr. 1979. "Using Matching Cloze Tests for Elementary ESL Students." *Reading Teacher* 32: 683–90.

Pugh, A. K. 1977. "Implications of Problems of Language Testing for the Validity of Speed Reading Courses." *System* 5: 29–39.

Pugh, A. K., and J. M. Ulijn, eds. 1984. *Reading for Professional Purposes: Studies and Practices in Native and Foreign Languages.* London: Heinemann Educational Books.

Purves, A. C., and W. C. Purves. 1986. "Cultures, Text Models, and the Activity of Writing." *Research in the Teaching of English* 20: 174–97.

Raimes, A. 1979. "Problems and Teaching Strategies in ESL Composition." In *Language in Education: Theory and Practice* 14. Arlington, Va.: Center for Applied Linguistics.

———. 1983. "Anguish as a Second Language? Remedies for Composition Teachers." *Composing in a Second Language.* Ed. S. McKay. Rowley, Mass.: Newbury House. 81–96.

———. 1985. "What Unskilled ESL Writers Do As They Write: A Classroom Study of Composing." *TESOL Quarterly* 19: 229–58.

Reeds, J. A., H. Winitz, and P. A. Garcia. 1977. A Test of Reading Following Comprehension Training." *IRAL* 15: 307–19.

Rigg, P. 1978. "The Miscue-ESL Project." *On TESOL '87.* Eds. D. Brown, C. Yorio, and R. Crymes. Washington, D.C.: TESOL.

Robb, T., S. Ross, and I. Shortreed. 1986. "Salience of Feedback on Error and Its Effect on EFL Writing Quality." *TESOL Quarterly* 20: 83–93.

Robbins, B. 1983. "Language Proficiency Level and the Comprehension of Anaphoric Subject Pronouns by Bilingual and Monolingual Children." *On TESOL '84.* Eds. P. Larson, E. L. Judd, and D. S. Messerschmitt. Washington, D.C.: TESOL.

Roller, C. M. 1988. "Transfer of Cognitive Academic Competence and L2 Reading in a Rural Zimbabwean Primary School." *TESOL Quarterly* 22.2: 303–28.

Romatowski, J. 1981. "A Study of Oral Reading in Polish and English: A Psycholinguistic Perspective." *Learning to Read in Different Languages.* Ed. S. Hudelson. Washington, D.C.: Center for Applied Linguistics.

Santos, T. 1988. "Professors' Reactions to the Academic Writing of Non-Native–Speaking Students." *TESOL Quarterly* 22.1: 69–90.

Sarig, G. 1987. "High-Level Reading in the First and in the Foreign Language: Some Comparative Process Data." *Research in Reading in English as a Second Language.* Eds. J. Devine, P. L. Carrell, and D. E. Eskey. Washington, D.C.: TESOL. 105–20.

Saville-Troike, M. 1984a. "What *Really* Matters in Second Language Learning for Academic Achievement?" *TESOL Quarterly* 18: 199–219.

————. 1984b. "Where's the Beef in ESL?" Paper presented at the Ohio Conference of Language and Literacy for the Culturally Different Child, Columbus, Ohio, December 1984.

Scarcella, R. 1984. "How Writers Orient Their Readers in Expository Essays: A Comparative Study of Native and Nonnative English Writers." *TESOL Quarterly* 18.4: 671–88.

Scott, M., and G. R. Tucker. 1974. "Error Analysis and English-Language Strategies of Arab Students." *Language Learning* 24: 69–97.

Shohamy, E. 1984. "Does the Testing Method Make a Difference? The Case of Reading Comprehension." *Language Testing* 1: 147–70.

Sim, D., and M. Bensoussan. 1979. "Control of Contextualized Function and Content Words as It Affects EFL Reading Comprehension Test Scores." *Reading in a Second Language*. Eds. R. Mackay, B. Barkman, and R. R. Jordan. Rowley, Mass.: Newbury House.

Spack, R., and C. Sadow. 1983. "Student-Teacher Working Journals in ESL Freshman Composition." *TESOL Quarterly* 17: 575–93.

Stanley, R. M. 1984. "The Recognition of Macrostructure: A Pilot Study." *Reading in a Foreign Language* 2: 156–68.

Steffensen, M. S. 1988. "Changes in Cohesion in the Recall of Native and Foreign Texts." *Interactive Approaches to Second Language Reading*. Eds. P. L. Carrell, J. Devine, and D. E. Eskey. Cambridge: Cambridge UP. 140–51.

Steffensen, M. S., C. Joag-Dev, and R. C. Anderson. 1979. "A Cross-Cultural Perspective on Reading Comprehension." *Reading Research Quarterly* 15: 10–29.

Stokes, E. 1984. "An ESL Writing Workshop." *TESOL Newsletter Supplement No. 1: Writing and Composition* 18: 4–5.

Strother, J. B. and J. M. Ulijn. 1987. "Does Syntactic Rewriting Affect English for Science and Technology Text Comprehension?" *Research in Reading in English as a Second Language*. Eds. J. Devine, P. L. Carrell, and D. E. Eskey. Washington, D.C.: TESOL. 89–100.

Swain, M. 1985. "Communicative Competence: Some Roles of Comprehensible Input and Comprehensible Output in Its Development." *Input in Second Language Acquisition*. Eds. S. M. Gass and C. G. Madden. Rowley, Mass.: Newbury House.

deSuarez, J. 1985. "Using Translation Communicatively in ESP Courses for Science Studies." *Reading for Professional Purposes: Methods and Materials in Teaching Languages*. Eds. J. M. Ulijn and A. K. Pugh. Leuven, Belgium: Acco.

Taglieber, C. K., L. L. Johnson, and D. B. Yarbrough. 1988. "Effects of Prereading Activities on EFL Reading by Brazilian College Students." *TESOL Quarterly* 22.3: 455–72.

Takala, S., A. C. Purves, and A. Buckmaster. 1982. "On the Interrelationships Between Language, Perception, Thought and Culture, and Their Relevance to the Assessment of Written Composition." *Evaluation in Education: An International Review Series* 5: 317–42.

Tang, B. A. 1974. "A Psycholinguistic Study of the Relationships Between Children's Ethnic-Linguistic Attitudes and the Effectiveness of Methods Used in Second-Language Reading Instruction." *TESOL Quarterly* 8: 233–51.

Tatlonghari, M. 1984. "Miscue Analysis in an ESL Context." *RELC Journal* 15: 75–84.

Taylor, B. P. 1981. "Content and Written Form: A Two-Way Street." *TESOL Quarterly* 15: 5–13.

Tedick, D. J. 1988. "The Effects of Topic Familiarity on the Writing Performance of Non-Native Writers of English at the Graduate Level." Unpublished diss., Ohio State University.

Tierney, R. J., and P. D. Pearson. 1985. "Towards a Composing Model of Reading." *Contexts of Reading*. Eds. C. N. Hedley and A. N. Baratta. Norwood, N.J.: Ablex.

Ulijn, J. M., and A. K. Pugh, eds. 1985. *Reading for Professional Puposes: Methods and Materials in Teaching Languages*. Leuven, Belgium: Acco.

Urquhart, A. H. 1984. "The Effect of Rhetorical Ordering on Readability." *Reading in a Foreign Language*. Eds. J. C. Alderson and A. H. Urquhart. London: Longman.

Urzua, C. 1987. " 'You Stopped Too Soon' : Second Language Children Composing and Revising." *TESOL Quarterly* 21: 279–304.

Vann, R. J. 1979. "Oral and Written Syntactic Relationships in Second Language Learning." *On TESOL '89*. Eds. C. Yorio, K. Perkins, and J. Schachter. Washington, D.C.: TESOL. 322–29.

VanParreren, C. F., and M. C. Schouten-VanParreren. 1981. Contextual Guessing: A Trainable Reader Strategy." *System* 15: 235–41.

Wagner, D. A., J. E. Spratt, and A. Ezzaki. 1989. "Does Learning to Read in a Second Language Always Put the Child at a Disadvantage? Some Counter Evidence from Morocco." *Applied Psycholinguistics* 10: 31–48.

Walker, L. J. 1983. "Word Identification Strategies in Reading in a Foreign Language." *Foreign Language Annals* 16: 293–99.

Wallace, C. 1986. *Learning to Read in a Multicultural Society*. Oxford: Pergamon.

Williams, D. 1981. "Factors Related to Performance in Reading English as a Second Language." *Language Learning* 31: 31–50.

Winfield, F. E., and P. Barnes-Felfeli. 1982. "The Effects of Familiar and Unfamiliar Cultural Context on Foreign Language Composition." *Modern Language Journal* 66: 373–78.

Wipf, J. A. 1979. "Improving Reading Fluency Through Lexical Cuing." *Lesen in der Fremdsprache*. Eds. R. Berger and U. Haider. Munich: Kemmler und Hoch.

Zamel, V. 1976. "Teaching Composition in the ESL Classroom: What We Can Learn from Research in the Teaching of English." *TESOL Quarterly* 10: 67–76.

———. 1982. "Writing: The Process of Discovering Meaning." *TESOL Quarterly* 16: 189–204.

———. 1983. "The Composing Processes of Advanced ESL Students: Six Case Studies." *TESOL Quarterly* 17: 165–87.

———. 1985. "Responding to Student Writing." *TESOL Quarterly* 19: 79–101.

———. 1987. "Recent Research on Writing Pedagogy." *TESOL Quarterly* 21: 697–715.

Zuck, L. V., and J. G. Zuck. 1984. "The Main Idea: Specialist and Non-Specialist Judgments." *Reading for Professional Purposes: Studies and Practices in Native and Foreign Languages.* Eds. A. K. Pugh and J. M. Ulijn. London: Heinemann Educational Books.

Chapter 15

Language Learning Is More than Learning Language: Rethinking Reading and Writing Tasks in Textbooks for Beginning Language Study

Janet K. Swaffar

University of Texas at Austin

In the last decade, learner-centered research has rewritten the conventional wisdom, the traditional canon of foreign language teaching, particularly with regard to literate students of English who are learning European languages. Two major extralinguistic factors have been introduced that impact on our current practices in teaching beginning students of European languages how to read and write. First, recent studies suggest that, regardless of the learners' language level, more successful learning outcomes result when assessment measures of reading and writing acknowledge the learners' metacognitive processes. Second, another group of studies reveal that—again, regardless of the learners' language level— prior knowledge impacts heavily on how well a text is comprehended or presented in a student composition.[1] These insights can be summed up in what at first blush appears to be an anomaly: language learning is more than learning language. And if this assertion bears scrutiny, the apparent anomaly has significant practical implications for classroom practice.

AUTOMATIC AND CONTROLLED PROCESSING

The claim that language learning is more than learning language reflects the profession's acknowledgment that cognitive processes, attention of the learner, monitoring of new information, and its storage in long-term memory, all result from an admixture of multiple neurological and phenomenological events (Shiffrin and Schneider, 1977). The language product depends on the individual learner's processing of information.[2] Recent neurological research suggests that learning *combines* controlled and automatic processes. Schneider and Shiffrin define controlled processes as those that utilize "a temporary sequence of nodes activated under control of, and through attention by, the subject" (156). Automatic processes are those that are an established sequence of nodes "activated without the necessity of active control or attention by the subject" (155). In other words, to become automatic, apprehension processes must first use learner attention, which is controlled—cognitively focused. Drill alone will not suffice. Only a "focal attention" builds configurations that can become automatic. Unfortunately, controlled processing interferes with comprehension (McLaughlin, Rossman, and McLeod, 1983). Language learners, whether L1 or L2, need a good store of automatic processes. Otherwise they have difficulty comprehending or expressing connected ideas.

All learners must conduct memory searches (operations of working memory) to link new information with the already known. Intentional performance of a new skill, such as language learning, puts high demands on various memory functions. Focal attention is diffused. Short-term memory has, by the most generous estimates, an outside limit of only a few seconds. If, in that time, the amount of incoming information proves too unfamiliar or too extensive to be linked to existing memory patterns, learning cannot occur. If the learner must, for example, transfer too much new phonological, orthographic, lexical, morphological, or syntactic information from short-term memory to long-term memory, incoming data will interrupt concentration. As Rivers and Temperley (1987) stress, interruption interferes not only with comprehension but with storage processes as well.

RECONSIDERING THE LEARNING SEQUENCE IN TERMS OF COGNITIVE PROCESSING

Despite publisher and author rhetoric about proficiency-based or communicatively based instruction, presumably a term that encompasses reading and writing as well as speaking and listening proficiencies, most textbooks in beginning language instruction fail to differentiate between the cognitive levels appropriate for oral work and listening comprehension on the one hand, and those appropriate for reading and writing on the other.

How do the needs of listeners and speakers differ from those of readers and writers? First of all, the processing of speaking and listening puts different real-world constraints on the learner. Speaking involves simultaneous use of macro- and micromemory functions which must operate without much time for reflection. Hence they are, cognitively speaking, *immediacy tasks*. The learner's ability to use prior knowledge and metacognitive processes is restricted by time factors. Speakers must forge ahead or lose their platform. Hence, self-correction by a speaker is often made at the cost of that speaker's focal attention on her message. The listener is at a similar disadvantage. Readers and writers, however, can reread, check data, and reconsider. Hence, these options are cognitively linked as *recursive tasks*. Recursions allow attention to focus on language detail, and allow one to chunk or recombine ideas. Consequently, controlled attention can focus on the micro- or bottom-up processing. The traditional matching of receptive (listening and reading) with productive (speaking and writing) is, from the standpoint of cognitive processing, a mismatch.

If similarity in cognitive strategies is considered, arguments can be made for relating writing to reading tasks. The range of purposes in reading (skimming for information, scanning for main ideas, rereading to reconsider content or apprehension) make excellent writing exercises as well. They combine cognitive interest (high focal attention) with an accessible, reviewable language source. Hence writing tasks, if structured so that they commence with cognitive rather than linguistic demands, can reinforce reading comprehension, even in beginning instruction. Asking students to reduce complex ideas to fundamental linguistic units engages them in valuable cognitive as well as linguistic practice (Felix, 1981). The point can be illustrated if we imagine the following sentences being read aloud: "A recent research report indicates that forests throughout the world are being subjected to a variety of ecological changes brought about by pollution problems. Apparently all kinds of trees are vulnerable to this destructive trend." As a listening task, recapitulation would be difficult even for native speakers. Yet, as a combined reading and writing exercise, the processing involves no more than rereading to match redundant propositions. Students can then proceed to express the longer statement in a variety of simpler ways:

Trees are dying all over the world.
Ecological problems kill trees.
Pollution kills all kinds of trees.[3]

Such statements simplify complex surface structures of the original statement, yet use the vocabulary of its topics and comments. An exercise of this type can, in subsequent classroom comparison of statements, acknowledge the comprehension of different students. In class, focal attention can be on communicative message. As an outside assignment, however, the learner's focal attention can be on message *and* accurate usage. As a writing assignment, the language model is available visually and need not be stored in memory.

Reading and writing assignments must concentrate on messages rather than concern for linear translation. The use of familiar messages (texts about the L1 culture of familiar international events) eases the cognitive load because the second or foreign language learner can anticipate textual ideas rather than rely exclusively on language to convey those ideas (Carrell, 1984, 1985; Lee, 1986; Levine and Haus, 1985; Melendez and Pritchard, 1985; Wolff, 1987). If, for example, the former Surgeon General's views on smoking are familiar to a learner, even a fairly sophisticated discussion of these views has predictive value for automatic processing. A student versed in Dr. Koop's opinions who reads and understands the words, *By the year 2000 the former Surgeon General wants Americans to. . . .* , can generally complete the thought, *quit smoking, stop using cigarettes,* or *give up their addiction to nicotine.* Films and video can, when treated as recursive tasks (that is, repeated viewing, recognition and restatement of textual language), serve similar functions.

If the content and context are familiar or established in prereading instruction, students have recourse to their own, cognitively driven rereading or reviewing when attention overload occurs. New linguistic information need not be held in short-term memory until linked to preexisting knowledge. The written word facilitates controlled processing of lexicon and grammar because it enables recursive reading. When focal attention and macroprocessing deal with familiar schemata, they activate well-trained pathways. Recognition and replication of unfamiliar textual language as components of a familiar message reduce the processing load. Such reading and writing tasks capitalize on the students' familiarity with textual schemata on the one hand, yet free memory for attention to details of unfamiliar language on the other.

Practically, then, reading and writing allow students to use higher-order cognitive skills to apprehend language detail. Both activities access adult capabilities and enable a level of learning more appropriate to the adult learner than one based exclusively on speaking and listening activities, tasks that necessarily rely more heavily on automaticity. Conversely, if the limits to input are bound by the limits of immediacy tasks such as student speaking ability, both the texts and the language to be learned are necessarily restricted as well.

Beyond these cognitive considerations are the changing demographics of language learners themselves. Increasingly, foreign languages have an audience of adult learners who are fully literate. Ever-larger numbers are over twenty-five years old (Dannerbeck, 1987). The success of content or multidisciplinary orientations at Rhode Island, Pennsylvania, and Earlham—to mention only a few of the programs emerging across the United States that integrate reading and writing with the learning of subject matter—reflects the success of the adult immersion or shelter programs Swain describes elsewhere in this volume. The fact that language can be learned in conjunction with subject matter makes good sense for the literate adult learner of a European language. Adults in our culture read to learn about new information and ideas; they write to record that information and express a point of view. Consequently, the practice of learning foreign languages by reading for information and writing to record that information dovetails with broader educational practice. Postponing reading and writing tasks until an unspecified level of language mastery probably does our adult learners a practical as well as a cognitive disservice.

COMBINING RECURSIVE TASKS (READING AND WRITING) WITH IMMEDIACY TASKS (LISTENING AND SPEAKING)

Will earlier introduction of reading and writing as reflective processes interfere with acquisition of speaking and listening abilities? Although the answer to this question lies in teacher practice, mounting evidence suggests that recursive tasks can support the tasks demanding more immediate and hence more automatic responses. Translation of texts of correct answers to discrete point questions seem to be no guarantee of comprehension, nor do accurate answers based on mechanical clues (fill-ins, dehydrated sentences) guarantee coherent self-expression.[4] By the same token, practice devoted solely to sentence-level transactions apparently has negligible impact on writing performance. One of the few areas of virtual unanimity in research on composition correction regards correction of surface errors. Although students, particularly those studying a second language, often claim to need and use it (Cohen, forthcoming), corrective feedback on mechanics addresses only one aspect of the writing process. Studies comparing correction styles conclude that "detailed feedback may be not worth the instructors' time and effort" (Robb, Ross, and Shortreed, 1986, 91). Zamel's suggestions (1976) based on English composition research, as well as Dvorak's (1986) summary of foreign language research on writing, cite similar conclusions.

Since Zamel's plea for more intersentential writing, evidence has mounted in favor of assigning compositions as well as sentence-level writing to improve language mechanics in FL work (Robb, Ross, and Shortreed, 1986). Yet studies about teacher corrections of ESL compositions reveal that "the teachers overwhelmingly view themselves as language teachers rather than writing teachers; they attend primarily to surface level features of writing and seem to read and react to a text as a series of separate sentences or even clauses, rather than as a whole unit of discourse. They are in fact so distracted by language-related local problems that they often correct these without realizing that a much larger meaning-related problem has totally escaped their notice" (Zamel, 1986, 86).

Zamel's analysis of criticisms that deal with content-related and organizational problems ("getting away from the topic," "unclear reference," "what are your subtopics?" and so on) revealed that, like the suggestions for improved mechanics, these comments failed to help students in revision. As a result, she concludes that "we need to replace vague commentary and references to abstract rules and principles with text-specific strategies, directions, guidelines, and recommendations" (95). In this vein, Connor's (1987) research summary concludes that the profession needs to develop content-based criteria for textual analysis in order to foster our student's writing processes. Semke (1984) and Kassen (1990) have arrived at similar conclusions about teachers of foreign languages.

TEXTBOOK TREATMENTS OF READING AND WRITING

In the last decade, prompted largely by a move toward functional language use represented in the *ACTFL Guidelines,* L2 textbooks reflect greater emphasis on learner-created language. Most newer books strive to present communicative goals, contextual practice, and linguistic rules. Their illustrations of language structures enhance focal attention through visual emphases. Increasingly, rote drill has been supplanted with contextual practice. Practice with sentence-level grammar and word-level memory checks are found in workbooks. Presumably, this means less classroom time is spent on rote learning.[5]

The four first-year textbooks analyzed below stress themes and situations with real-world speech constraints. Their formats optimize speaking and listening practice in context. Yet these books often ignore two notions emerging from current research about reading and writing: first, that considerations about the language levels appropriate for speaking and listening tasks may be inappropriate for reading and writing (for example, Allen, *et al.,* 1988; Lee & Musumeci, 1988) and second, that composition practice may foster sentential skills more effectively than sentence-level practice (Shih, 1986; Zamel, 1986; Dvorak, 1986).

Despite their acknowledged virtues, these beginning texts appear to be consistently reluctant to implement cognitively challenging reading or related writing tasks. Where such assignments occur, they are often peripheral to the focus of the language lesson. In terms of presumed time allotted, these assignments play an adjunct function when compared to other types of assignments. Even in *Entradas,* Heinle and Heinle's new Spanish textbook, the accompanying workbook presents a breadth of authentic texts, but treats them as sources of discrete information rather than systems of meaning. In other words, the workbook apparatus fails to provide exercises that activate a student's cognitive strategies for encoding authentic texts.

A brief survey of space allotment in four textbooks for beginning language instruction illustrates a hesitancy to rely on the students' capacity to integrate recursive tasks with beginning instruction in language. Three of the books assessed are French texts: *Voilà* from Harper and Row (1988), *C'est à dire* from Heinle and Heinle (1989), and *Invitation,* from Holt, Rinehart and Winston (1989). *Voilà* and *C'est à dire* are first editions. *Invitation* is a fourth edition. In addition, the Spanish text, *Dos mundos,* from Random House (1986) was analyzed using the same criteria.[6] Although *Dos mundos* has more recent French and German variants, arguably the assessment of the series of texts in the natural approach should be made with its flagship volume. All four books have introductions that refer to concepts we associate with recent research insights: communicative message in conjunction with formal accuracy, various reading techniques rather than reading word for word, sentence-level writing exercises in which students express their own ideas rather than manipulate language forms. French was chosen because in French the largest number of major publishing houses have textbooks and workbooks that claim to represent these insights.[7] As suggested earlier, these claims do not extend, in my view, to cognitively based, communicative use of reading and writing.

The coding system had three major categories: language production, language comprehension, and explanations.[8] Segments were coded in this way to establish a weighting for the exercise style and to see whether that emphasis changed in the course of the semester. The discussion here compares the uses of reading and writing overall revealed in purely quantitative measures. *No claim is made that quantity in the textbook represents the weighting given to an exercise in class or as an assignment.* For example, two composition assignments may represent only 2% of the textbook space allotted to their description, yet involve extensive writing practice and classroom effort. The purpose of the charts is to illustrate two relationships: first, the comparison between cognitively challenging reading and written work and the relative emphasis on language mechanics represented by structural presentations and sentential (sentence-level) practice, and second, the relative isolation of reading and suprasentential writing with respect to the other activities in the chapter.

In each case, the coding for the charts attempts to distinguish between the type of assignment and the applications for that assignment. Integrated reading and writing tasks have two potentials. The first use is the traditional one: reading or writing to learn the foreign language. The second use is largely neglected in first-year language texts for college: reading for the information or entertainment value of the text, writing to reveal comprehension of the content of a text or analysis of its messages.

The coding excludes workbooks from consideration for two reasons. First, presumably the textbook is the focus for *classroom* activity. Second, most workbooks currently are used for drills on the mechanics of language, and the extent of their use will vary with the institution, student audience, and instructional emphasis. Unlike *Entradas,* none of the workbooks of the four books discussed here offer either longer authentic texts (that is, over five hundred words) or regular, systematic progression of activities culminating in creative writing or composition. Several workbooks include discourse gambits—scenarios of conversations or interviews to be worked out between students. In the charts coding exercise objectives, discourse gambits were considered suprasentential rather than sentential. However, the caveat with discourse gambits is that, without a textual basis for informed exchange, students practice only expression of their preconceived notions in a foreign language. If language practice encourages uninformed opinion, it fails concomitantly to encourage cognitive synthesis.

The pie chart illustrations include cultural notes as edited readings or authentic texts as appropriate. Parenthetically, it should be noted that these textbook presentations of culture vary widely. Some integrate generic assertions about cultural differences with contextual drill (*Dos mundos*); others present particular social behaviors and ethnographic differences within the culture as background and language reading practice (*Invitation*); still others deal with generic attitudes and values to which students respond (*Voilà, C'est à dire*). Some textbooks prefer to provide comments in English, some in French or Spanish.

Regardless of treatment, each text generalizes about cultural components—values, cognitive styles, and prevalent assumptions. As such, they illustrate problems of promoting cultural awareness that Kramsch and Byrnes address elsewhere in this volume.[9] While all of the texts ask students to express opinions about cultural differences or contrast American practices with French or Spanish counterparts, none uses Byrnes's suggestion that authentic materials about the C1 be the basis for that task. Rarely are students asked to analyze assertions or distinguish views on the basis of what is said or not said, how a statement *from* (rather than *about*) the foreign culture contrasts with alternative attitudes, behaviors, or values expressed in the United States.

TEXT AND EXERCISE TYPES FOR READING

All of the text discussed here state in their introductions that students should practice skimming, scanning, reading for main ideas, and recognition of implicit as well as explicit information. However, regardless of such advice, most reading is restricted to short, glossed texts. Such texts often appear to have been written to illustrate the language and subject matter of the particular chapter. Simplified or not, their very brevity encourages reliance on command of lexical and syntactic detail, micro- rather than macrostrategies. Without exercises that encourage alternative reading styles, FL students, particularly those with limited proficiency, tend to read word for word. Of the four textbooks, only *Invitation* and *Dos mundos* have readings longer than one page. In both cases, however, the texts appear to have been created for that chapter.[10]

To compare treatments of reading, page space devoted to texts written for native speakers were coded separately from total pages featuring dialogues and edited texts (see Appendix for inventory). The coding defines edited texts in terms of four factors:

1. The text is written to teach the linguistic features and vocabulary of the chapter.

2. The print reflects textbook style rather than a reprint from a newspaper or other original source.

3. The excerpt lacks indications about possible simplification or abbreviation.

4. Texts are glossed.

The fourth column merges data from the three chapters in each of the four books examined.[11] The first three columns of pie charts in Figure 1 reflect samples from approximately the same beginning (p. 20*ff.*), midpoint (p. 150*ff.*), and concluding chapters of each book (the second to the last chapter in each case).

— *Figure 1*

A Comparison of Reading Passages.

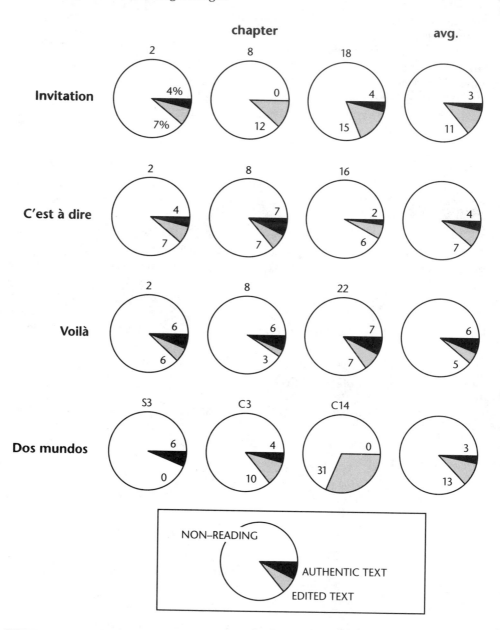

Treatments of reading vary widely. Several books encourage schematizing. *Invitation,* for example, precedes readings with exercises to stimulate encoding strategies and to focus reader attention on specific information in the text, and employs follow-up questions to check comprehension. *Dos mundos* relies on instructions to the teacher about how to preview. The book places longer texts, that is, two pages, in a special segment labeled *additional readings.* The only exercises included in the text are interrogative questions at the end of the passage. Since *Dos mundos* uses encoding comprehension checks for dialogues (sequencing events or identifying speakers), the discrepant practice with regard to the narrative texts is the more striking.

Figure 2 illustrates how instructional use of the foreign language varies from text to text. Of the four, *Dos mundos* and *Invitation* reduce proportionally more of the English used in the course of the first year, especially when compared with *Voilà.* The reduction reflects an increase in French, not only for exercises but also for later explanations of formal usage, in *Invitation.* In *Dos mundos* the increase in Spanish occurs primarily in explanations of contextual drills and discourse exercises.

The disparate use of foreign language in explanations and assignments in first-year books deserves research attention. At present the profession lacks data to confirm or disconfirm these divergent practices for reading, performance on assignments, or overall learning. A major consideration is the influence that the use of English or the foreign language in the textbook will have on the language spoken by teacher and students in the classroom. Since a number of beginning textbooks use Spanish, French, and German exclusively, a comparison of classroom and testing treatments, as well as assessments of attitude and achievement, is overdue.[12]

With both edited texts and authentic texts, assignment style varies widely, but is consistent within each book. *Invitation,* for example, uses only comprehension checks; *Dos mundos* uses only interrogative questions. *C'est à dire* and *Voilà* have both reading strategy exercises and encoding exercises that ask for written or oral work on the basis of reading. In all four books authentic materials often constitute no more than a form of realia for practical applications—maps, ads, charts, headlines, or forms. Authentic realia are used for speaking and writing practice at the micro level at initial learning stages. But as such they fail to offer the same challenges as longer prose passages. Hence, there are actually fewer authentic texts and exercises in later stages in all books. Where authentic prose occurs, selections are very short—200 to 350 words.[13] This practice probably inhibits activation of metacognitive strategies, since short texts are processed differently than texts of over five hundred words (Kintsch and van Dijk, 1987). Sometimes such texts appear in reduced script as marginal notations. In *Voilà* short authentic materials are sometimes used in culture capsules with clarification in English. As was doubtless true for many of the decisions in all the textbooks analyzed here, the relatively small number of authentic texts in *Voilà* resulted from the publisher's insistence, and was a decision vigorously protested by the authors.[14] Figure 3 illustrates the relationship between authentic and edited readings.

— *Figure 2*

A Comparison of FL and English Use.

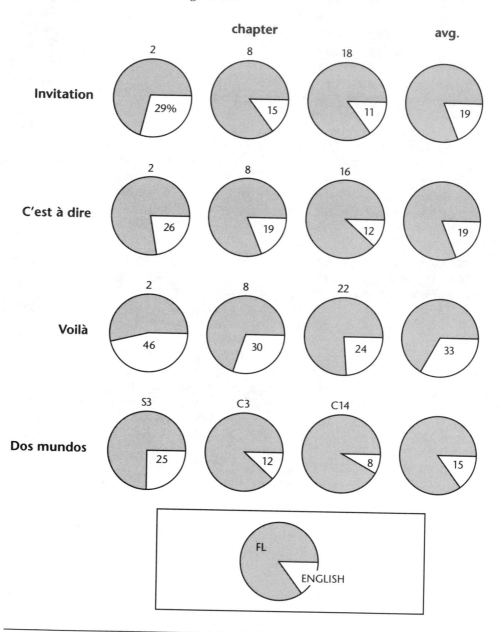

— *Figure 3* ───────────────────────────

A Comparison of Reading Exercises.

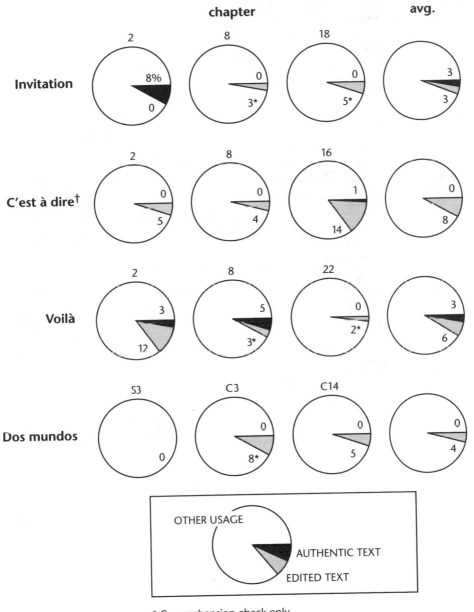

chapter   avg.

Invitation

C'est à dire†

Voilà

Dos mundos

OTHER USAGE

AUTHENTIC TEXT

EDITED TEXT

* Comprehension check only
† Listening comprehension exercises are 1% of total book

How do the relative proportions allotted these tasks impact on our communicative goals? Do such formats allow students to capitalize on the fact that language learning can be more than learning language? In most beginning language textbooks the vocabulary applies to spoken exercises. Reliance on command of vocabulary, however, undercuts the notion that reading not be conducted word for word.

In looking at the differences among language production exercises, the category entitled *functional use* attempts to codify textbook efforts to point out how usage changes meaning. The difference between *functional use* and *grammar* in the coding may be contrasted as follows: the distinction might ask students to identify the already learned infinitives of inflected strong tense verbs in a text (functional use). Or it could ask them to memorize the strong verbs presented in paradigm fashion (rule explanation or paradigm).[15] As a recognition task, a functional-use exercise might identify plural forms of noun subjects through application of knowledge about verb inflection—a review of previous comprehension linked to recognizing the meaning of new information. Alternatively, a formal grammar exercise provides the learner with lists of nouns to be substituted in a sentence drill. As an initial writing task, the functional-use exercise might ask students to identify pronominal references, followed by a cloze passage in which they decide when and which pronominal references are appropriate in extended discourse. The formal grammar has students practice reference at the individual sentence level. The proportions illustrated in Figure 4 reveal relatively few presentations of functional applications for all books except *C'est à dire.* However, even in *C'est à dire,* the larger share of practice is at the sentential rather than suprasentential level. And this practice commences with production rather than recognition and reflection about use and usage in a text.

Space allotted to discussion of linguistic rules and their illustration in the four texts is strikingly similar. In view of the presumption of wide divergence in treatments of formal accuracy in "communicative" and "proficiency" orientations, the fact of the matter is that presentation of linguistic rules in all four books is similar. Most of the time these books tend to deal with linguistic rules and communicative objectives as separate categories. Treatments, however, vary somewhat. Two books in particular link formal features to specific types of pragmatic use. The functional-use exercises in *C'est à dire* present tasks designed to promote student illocution and perlocution, the syntax and modalities of speech acts. In *Voilà* the exercises emphasize a particular contextual situation within each chapter and hence focus more attention on lexical and morphological learning. *Voilà* tends, as a result, somewhat more toward language practice for descriptions or facts (locutions), and *C'est à dire* more toward expression of intents and opinions (illocutions).

As indicated earlier, despite the concern for cultural issues and their linguistic implications (all four have cultural notes), none of the books affords students regular opportunity to explore authentic cultural information in the comparative sense—texts that reflect a cross-section of cultural values or authentic texts that

— *Figure 4*

A Comparison of Grammar Explanation and Illustration of Grammar in Functional Use.

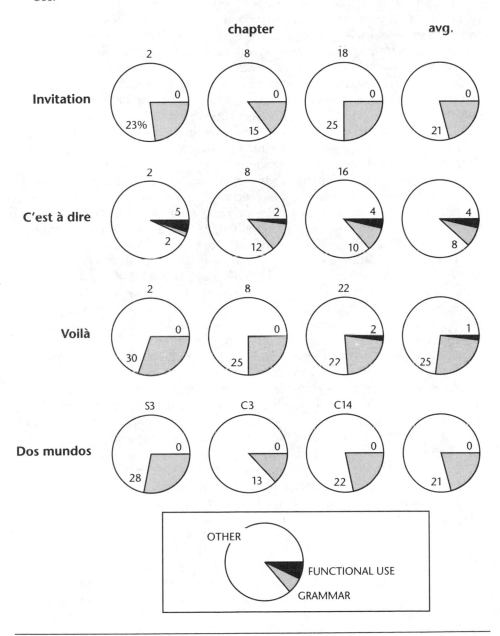

present cultural values different from those in the United States. Only rarely, primarily in discourse gambits, can students develop arguments that express the basis for textual or personal opinions.

The charts fail to distinguish between written and oral work, since choice in execution of the exercises appears to be optional in many instances. Perhaps that observation is in itself revealing, since it suggests implicitly that composition ability evolves from speaking skills. Traditionally teachers have argued that accurate sentences were the first stage toward writing accurate paragraphs. In ESL analyses, however, written performance in a controlled situation (prescribed usage with specified performance variables) and free writing do not always reveal corresponding proficiency increments (Lightbown, 1983; Larsen-Freeman, 1983). To extrapolate, a good sentence in a structured drill does not automatically result in good paragraph writing any more than the ability to read word for word guarantees comprehension of authentic texts.

As do the foregoing charts, Figure 5 attempts to illustrate how beginning textbooks treat material (in this case, writing), not to fault the textbook treatments. At this point in time the profession lacks information about how students most effectively learn to write in a foreign language. We have only the parameters established by the ESL work cited above.

One striking feature about presentation of linguistic rules emerges. The relative allotments and exercise styles of reading, and reading and writing exercises, remain surprisingly similar throughout first-year work. Later work in the semester reveals virtually no trend toward composition. In this way the first-year textbooks imply assumptions about skill development: students near the end of their first year of language study are still expected to read and write largely on the basis of practice in comprehending and expressing individual propositions rather than practice in expanding discourse.

Until further research confirmation is available, the assertion that reading authentic texts in conjunction with guided suprasentential writing is a valuable exercise for the learners of a foreign language can have only experiential confirmation. The current enthusiasm for journal writing is supported by reports from classroom studies about positive student attitudes toward such assignments. Nonetheless, as the style of reading exercises and the distribution of sentence level to suprasentential exercises reveal, the profession seems to be far from including top-down processing in the first year of college instruction in a foreign language.

How would a research project assess the hypothesis that structured composition yields more successful results than structured sentential practice? Recent studies in both ESL and FL look at T-units—the shortest possible sentence units that express ideas.[16] The length of the T-unit is compared with the number of structural errors per T-unit to discriminate between proficiency levels. In light of the paucity of evidence about FL writing that Bernhardt (1983 and this volume) has documented, the profession needs to investigate whether measures of structured and unstructured writing reveal differences in performance among our students, particularly adult students of beginning languages. We need to find out

— *Figure 5*

A Comparison of Sentential and Suprasentential Exercises.

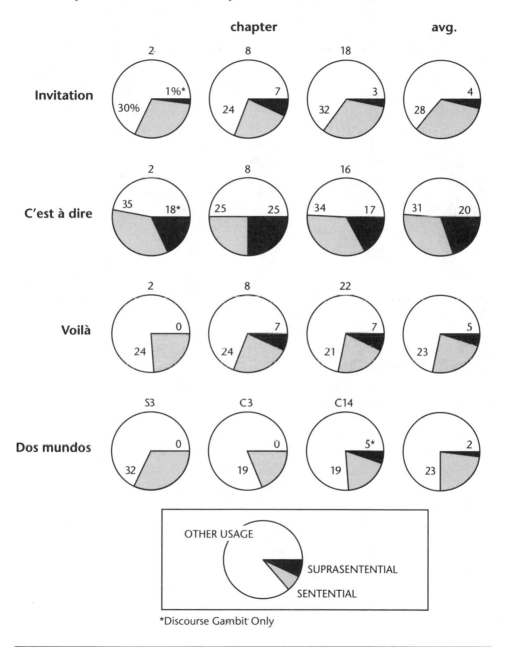

chapter   **avg.**

*Discourse Gambit Only

what types of writing or what sequence of writing assignments promote improvement. We need to know how different performance variables discriminate between proficiency levels in composition or journal writing. We need to establish whether work with the content and organization of compositions correlates with proficiency assessments in other skills.

In view of the learner-centered, communicative orientation, why does reluctance about reading longer authentic texts and engaging in suprasentential writing persist? Why does the profession continue to resist tasks that activate the adult learners' metacognitive capabilities with challenging texts and related writing during early stages of instruction? Perhaps it is because the profession confuses methodological differences with differences in instructional strategies. Whereas methods focus on presentational mode, strategies are concerned with optimal learning sequences and diagnoses of learner problems. Methods tend to be teacher-based, strategy approaches learner-based. Unfortunately, the research program until now has conducted few studies about variables in learner-based instruction.

HOW INADEQUATE RESEARCH HAS MITIGATED AGAINST INTEGRATION OF READING AND WRITING INTO THE CURRICULUM AT THE INTRODUCTORY LEVEL

We in foreign languages have insufficient studies about both reading and writing. The ESL studies on which we largely rely deal with intermediate or advanced, not beginning, learners. Raimes (1985) and Connor (1987) have researched intermediate or advanced level ESL students; Robb *et al.* (1986) have researched advanced students of composition who were studying English in Japanese colleges. Hence, the presumption remains that it may be essential for FL students, especially beginners who, unlike ESL students, lack immersion options or exposure to multiple courses in the FL, to focus exclusively on sentence mechanics and vocabulary mastery. Many assume that only thereafter can a discourse effort be undertaken. Compared with traditional treatments, however, several FL studies indicate that beginners seem to learn more effectively by reading authentic texts and writing their own thoughts about things they have learned.[17] Yet, as the textbooks reveal, the FL profession remains largely convinced that communicative efforts in writing must be restricted to a structural model at the sentence level.

Despite a larger body of research, a not dissimilar situation exists for reading. For although colleagues in ESL have undertaken extensive investigation of L2 reading, neither ESL nor FL research has explored reading and writing as related recursive tasks. Presumably our inadequate research base explains the profession's reluctance to offer adult learners challenging reading and writing tasks.

SUGGESTIONS FOR AUGMENTING
CURRENT INSTRUCTIONAL STRATEGIES

Unquestionably, a great frustration in the initial years of foreign language learning is that students must attend to language and message information simultaneously. Traditionally, the language profession has accepted this "memory load" problem as a necessary price, which every low-proficiency learner must pay. But is this price, a costly one both in teacher and student effort and student attrition or eventual disinterest, truly inevitable? Our learning models, together with the research data on extralinguistic knowledge, suggest, if not solutions, then at least mitigation of the burden.[18]

Three modifications in current practice come to mind. First, instead of an initial instruction in foreign languages that focuses solely on language per se, students need early exposure to familiar content and quantitative reading. Second, and as a consequence of the first suggestion, instead of curricular adherence to a "canonical sequence" that commences with speaking and listening comprehension (*immediacy tasks*), the *recursive tasks,* intellectually challenging content for reading and writing, deserve an initial, more prominent role. Third, instead of emphasizing production and immediate control of the linguistic rules, instruction should forge more links between recognition of formal accuracy and comprehension of meaningful subject matter. Those same links should ask students to reflect about how to express meaning in suprasentential writing. Students would be asked to *reduce a complex text to its fundamental propositions,* to its T-units. Equally important for advanced speaking facility, paring complex language down to fundamental components provides real-world training in how to use circumlocution to communicative advantage, how to be intelligible with limited command of language structures.[19]

I suggest an enhanced canon, which would introduce a three-stage cognitive sequence:

1. reading an authentic text about a familiar topic in order to locate some global concepts students can link to illustrative detail (that is, students display ability to select coherent language appropriate to specified meanings)

2. a second reading, in which students identify particular relationships between grammatical form and expressive function

3. reproduction of concepts in the texts in terms of student conceptualization (students demonstrate they are capable of manipulating the expression of those ideas by carefully attending to the language detail of the text).

Thereafter students would have sufficient familiarity with the language and concepts of the passage to express opinions or analyze what they have read. An integration of this sequence into any one of the textbooks examined in this paper might be illustrated as in Table 1.

In the ongoing debates about accuracy and the causes of a learner's failure to develop beyond sentence-level communication, an important factor has been overlooked. We are failing to offer students opportunities to practice reading and

— **Table 1** ───────────────────

Shifts in the Canon of Foreign Language Instruction

Language Adds: Component	Past Canon	Current Canon Learning Activities	Revised Canon Learner Activities
Vocabulary	lists	semantic or linguistic categories illustrated in context	categorizing in context, authentic texts of varying lengths
Grammar	detailed explanation, multiple examples	minimal explanation + examples	recognition of function, manipulation (T-units)
Practice	rote	contextual drill (opinion)	discourse gambits
Writing	mechanical	generic situations, sentential	suprasentential compositions based on textual data
Reading	edited texts	authentic texts for language learning (illus. of vocabulary, grammar, isolated textual facts)	authentic texts for multiple strategies including analysis of new information, ideas, cultural features

writing as complementary tasks that involve different cognitive processes than those demanded in speech and listening. Increments in speaking facility as illustrated in the *ACTFL Guidelines* need not be interpreted as statements about how linguistic rules drive proficiency—quite the contrary: given the paucity of data at present, an equally strong case can be built for activation of our students' critical thinking as an alternative remedy for error production.[20] The reading and writing stages illustrated in the right-hand column of Table 1 encourage students to monitor and control their cognitive assessment of input as the first step in monitoring and controlling their language output.

A second, equally cogent argument in behalf of a revised canon is that teachers cannot expect students to produce communicatively complex language without practice. Students need opportunities to reflect in terms of that language's propositions or idea units. The ability to engage in discourse beyond descriptive or factual sentence series, to articulate wishes, requests, gratitude, or irritation in a manner that reveals sensitivity to the foreign norms, commences with cognitive practice. FL students need early, consistent opportunities for such practice, because sophisticated language can only develop from sophisticated thought.

ENDNOTES

1. For a review of recent research in L1 and FL reading and writing and presumptions about their relationship, see chapters three through six in Wing (1986).

2. Cognitive scientists have created models that illustrate current knowledge about the sequence and features of learner processing. Their concepts have been adapted by researchers in both second and foreign language learning (Gagné, 1985; Nagle and Sanders, 1986). To be sure, like their antecedents, many of the language learning models differ in their specifications. Some, for example, refer to cognitive and communicative hierarchies (Tollefson, *et al.,* 1983) whereas others prefer terms such as explicit and implicit linguistic knowledge (Bialystock, 1978, 1983). Dulay, Burt, and Krashen's model for internal processors (1982) stresses the inhibitions on communication that can result from undue attention to form—the explicit linguistic knowledge in Bialystock's model.

3. These examples are student writing samples based on the initial statement of a newspaper article from *Die Zeit,* entitled "Ein Dickicht von Hypothesen." The level was a fourth semester German class at the University of Texas. In the original German their comments read: Bäume sterben überall auf der Welt. Ökologische Probleme töten Baume [sic] fast überall. Umweltschmutz tötet alle [sic] Art Bäume. These statements were the result of an assignment asking students to reduce the information in the initial paragraph of the article to its essential topic and comment.

4. Lightbown (1983) in her longitudinal study of morpheme development among sixth-grade speakers of French who received formal ESL instruction, concludes that "one important observation of this study is that there was relatively little improvement over time in the accuracy of learners' use of the six grammatical morphemes in obligatory contexts even though grammatical accuracy was always the focus of their ESL classes" (211).

5. By its very nature, rote learning involves a peripheral focus of attention in the sense of McLaughlin *et al.* (1983) unless driven by individual motivation. A serious oversight in the workbooks is that they lack an answer chart, thereby failing to acknowledge the importance of immediate feedback to reinforce automaticity, and encouraging a reliance on teacher rather than student responsibility for self-correction.

6. The discussion omits less commonly taught languages of non-Western cultures and languages written in other than a Latin alphabet, since research about the relative impact of cognitive sequence and extralinguistic knowledge for learners of these languages is still in its infancy.

7. As of this writing, the workbook portion of Heinle and Heinle's *Entradas* was not available.

8. The assessment procedures I use are the result of several efforts to codify exercises and explanations. My impetus for the entire undertaking arose out

of frustration with the criteria used by publishers who ask teachers to assess textbook manuscripts or departments who set up in-house criteria to adopt textbooks. Questions such as "Are grammatical explanations clear and presented in an amount of detail that is suitable for your students?" or "Will exercises be effective in developing students' mastery of the structural points in question?" beg the real questions on which such judgments rest. In order to make a judgment about clarity, teachers need to identify what makes grammatical explanations clear. An educated opinion about mastery will depend not only on the exercise in question, but on instructional goals. For example, do teachers think that exercises ought to present grammar usage in formal exemplification only or also in the context of functional use? Should cultural information be taught to or should it be interpreted by the learner? Should readings be selected to serve as language lessons or also to serve as lessons in various ways to comprehend meaning? What balance is sought between language and cognitive tasks?

9. As Howard Nostrand (1989) points out, "Without doubt, the most urgent need is to press on toward a nationwide consensus on the meaning of cultural competence. Agreement on a common core will permit research to evaluate and compare alternative approaches, while still allowing for great diversity surrounding the core" (191). My alternative suggestion is that we identify the strategies students need in order to develop awareness of cultural differences and their implications in the sense of Thomas.

10. I wish to thank Bob Swaffar for drawing Figures 2–5 and Table 1 and for his assistance in tabulating textbook data and subjecting them to a series of alternative analyses.

11. Selections of representative books were made after consultation with coordinators in the respective language departments at the University of Texas. Coordinators were consulted about books they considered leading examples of proficiency orientation, communicative approaches, and a middle-of-the-road text that was designed to accommodate traditional expectations as well as current theory. For my final selection, I relied on the introductory remarks of the authors, as well. My thanks to my colleagues Frank Donahue, Dieter Waeltermann (German), Dale Koike, Dolly Young (Spanish), Patricia Kyle, and Richard Kern (French) for their insights regarding text selections in their various departments.

12. I am indebted to Professor Shumway for calling this point to my attention.

13. Short texts elicit a different reading style and are presumed to influence language retention in a manner quite different from a text of more than one thousand words. Shorter texts are generally more difficult to read, since they lack redundant features and clear breaks in structure such as change of topic or focus. Students who read about the Surgeon General's views on smoking will be likely to understand at least some of the text if five opinions are discussed in relative depth in a longer passage than if one opinion is briefly summarized in a single paragraph or two. Kintsch and van Dijk (1987) point

out that the long-term memory functions are also different when the reader must synthesize larger quantities of information.

14. Personal communication, Isabel Kaplan, October 14, 1989.

15. For a succinct discussion of these principles and their applications in current textbooks, see the discussion by Byrnes (1988, 30).

16. Larsen-Freeman's study (1983) was of a "fairly homogeneous population—UCLA students studying ESL" (300). She allows that her techniques may work well only for English as a second language but not for Spanish, French, Chinese, and so forth, as second languages (301). Robb, Ross, and Shortreed (1986) arrived at similar conclusions for EFL students in Japan, however. They recommend systematic sentence-combining practice and the writing of weekly compositions, concluding that "the fact that students in all of the groups in this study wrote more complex structures as the course progressed indicates that improvement was independent of type of feedback" (91). Two caveats are important here: the subjects were in a composition class and participants in six concurrent language courses. We can only speculate about whether these assertions would prove equally valid for beginning students of a foreign language.

17. In one of these relatively rare studies that investigates a modification of the language based cognitive sequence, Vigil (1987) compared use of authentic texts with a control section that used conventional procedures (dialogues, initial speech practice) for beginning instruction in Spanish. When measured against the control group, the experimental group showed significant gains in all skills, although one feature of authentic text use was that the students in the experiment experienced delay periods before engaging in speaking and writing. In a description of curricular innovations with more advanced ESL students, Cortese's (1985) experiential report concluded that "reversing the canonical sequence of skills (listening, speaking, reading, and writing)" proved to be an effective sequence (7).

18. Unfortunately, little research exists concerning the relationship between memory functions in foreign language learning and saliency factors. Most assumptions are based on L1 research (for example, Loftus and Loftus, 1976; Meyer, 1975). Cook's (1977) data suggest that speech processing in short-term memory of adult second language learners is similar to those functions in the native language, but that the retention capacity will reflect language proficiency.

19. Vigil's (1987) results with first-semester students who read authentic texts revealed greater inclination to express opinions and points of view over the control group that used the edited texts and a traditional speaking emphasis during the same period. The control group had better spelling and attendance to grammar detail. Vigil's students, however, did not examine authentic texts as norms for grammaticality. Morgan's comparison of speaking ability between a four-skills control group and a communicative experimental group of German students revealed similar patterns.

20. Magnan's recent analysis of error incidence between proficiency levels corroborates the notion that while cognitive complexity gives rise to higher incidence of errors initially, students rapidly self-correct.

APPENDIX

Descriptors: Coding and Definitions

Language Production Exercise Types

MD   Mechanical Drill = manipulation of form at sentence level

CMD   Contextual Mechanical Drill = sentential manipulations within a discourse frame

CD   Contextual Drill = sentential production driven by text situation or student intent
Also included: opinion and discussion *without* textual model for suprasentential expansion

DD   Discourse Drill = speech act models to elicit suprasentential production (* = writing)

DG   Dialogue Gambit = verbal scenarios created from short models (4+ sentences + speech acts)

CVD   Cognitive Vocabulary Drill = charts or texts guide intent driven selection

FG   Functional Grammar = model of how context or intent change function of surface features

CC   Cultural Comparisons = identification of contrasts and similarities

Explanation Types

IV   Illustrations of Vocabulary = drawings, charts that define words in lieu of English glosses

VL   Vocabulary Lists = alphabetical or categorized by grammar function + English translation

CV   Contextualized Vocabulary = grouped by chart, speech acts, or context in narrative text

CN   Cultural Notes = explanations of contrasts in values, attitudes, or behaviors

CNV   Cultural Notes about Vocabulary = usage linked to cultural phenomena

G   Grammar = explanation or illustrative models outside a speech act context, includes pronunciation, orthographic, lexical information

I   Illustrations = pictures or drawings

Comprehension Exercise Types

D   Dialogues = assumed to be edited texts

ET   Edited Texts = texts with vocabulary glosses, textbook formats, illustrate language use

AT   Authentic Texts = reprinted from natural sources, no glosses (*Note:* * = charts, headlines, forms, ads, maps intended to be read as opposed to adjunct illustrative value)

RSD   Reading Strategies Dialogue = previewing or reading exercises

RST   Reading Strategies for Texts (edited) = previewing or reading exercises

RSAT   Reading Strategies Authentic Texts = previewing or reading exercises

DES   Dialogue Encoding Strategies = recognition and production of various levels of information

ETES   Edited Text Encoding Strategies = (as above)

ATES   Authentic Texts Encoding Strategies (as above + * = charts, maps, forms, ads, headlines)

CCh   Comprehension Check = true/false, multiple choice, confirmation in text or through identifying event or logical sequences

IQ   Interrogative Questions = Discrete point questions about textual facts (who, what, where)

LC   Listening Comprehension = cassettes or in class

LCES   Listening Comprehension Encoding Strategies = recognition and production of information

REFERENCES

Allen, Edward D., Elizabeth B. Bernhardt, Mary Therese Berry, and Marjorie Demel. 1988. "Comprehension and Text Genre: An Analysis of Secondary School Foreign Language Readers." *Modern Language Journal* 72: 163–87.

American Council on the Teaching of Foreign Languages. 1986. *ACTFL Proficiency Guidelines*. Hastings-on-Hudson, N.Y.: ACTFL Materials Center.

Ariew, Robert, and Anne Nerenz. 1989. *C'est à dire*. Boston: Heinle & Heinle.

Barnett, Marva. 1986. "Syntactic and Lexical/Semantic Skill in Foreign Language Reading: Importance and Interaction." *Modern Language Journal* 70: 343–49.

Berman, Ruth A. 1984. "Syntactic Components of the Foreign Language Reading Process." *Reading in a Foreign Language*. Eds. J. Charles Alderson and A. H. Urquhart. Essex: Longman. 139–56.

Bernhardt, Elizabeth. 1983. "Testing Foreign Language Reading Comprehension: The Immediate Recall Protocol." *Die Unterrichtspraxis* 16: 17–33.

Bialystock, Ellen B. 1978. "A Theoretical Model of Second Language Learning." *Language Learning* 28: 69–83.

———. 1983. "Inferencing: Testing the 'Hypothesis Testing' Hypothesis." *Classroom Research in Second Language Acquisition.* Eds. Herbert W. Seliger and Michael H. Long. Rowley, Mass.: Newbury House. 104–23.

Bransford, John, J. Richard Barclay, and Jeffrey Franks. 1972. "Sentence Memory: A Constructive versus Interpretive Approach." *Cognitive Psychology* 3: 193–209.

Byrnes, Heidi. 1988. "Whither Foreign Language Pedagogy: Reflections in Textbooks—Reflections on Textbooks." *Unterrichtspraxis* 21: 29–36.

Carrell, Patricia. 1984. "The Effects of Rhetorical Organization on ESL Readers." *TESOL Quarterly* 18: 441–69.

———. 1985. "Facilitating ESL Reading by Teaching Text Structure." *TESOL Quarterly* 19: 727–52.

Carroll, John. 1967. *The Foreign Language Attainments of Language Majors in the Senior Year: A Survey Conducted in U.S. Colleges and Universities.* Cambridge, Mass.: Graduate School of Education, Harvard University. ED 013 343.

Chastain, Kenneth D. 1970. "A Methodological Study Comparing the Audio-Lingual Habit Theory and the Cognitive Code-Learning Theory—A Continuation." *Modern Language Journal* 54: 257–66.

Chastain, Kenneth D., and Frank J. Woerdehoff. 1968. "A Methodological Study Comparing the Audio-Lingual Habit Theory and the Cognitive Code-Learning Theory." *Modern Language Journal* 52: 268–79.

Chaudron, Craig. 1988. *Second Language Classrooms: Research on Teaching and Learning.* New York: Cambridge UP.

Cohen, Andrew. Forthcoming. "The Processing of Feedback on Student Papers." *Research on Learner Strategies.* Eds. A. L. Wenden and J. Rubin. Oxford: Pergamon Press.

Connor, Ulla. 1987. "Research Frontiers in Writing Analysis." *TESOL Quarterly* 21: 677–96.

Cook, Vivian J. 1977. "Cognitive Processes in Second Language Learning." *International Review of Applied Linguistics* 15: 1–20.

Cortese, Guiseppina. 1985. "From Receptive to Productive in Post-Intermediate EFL Classes: A Pedagogical 'Experiment.'" *TESOL Quarterly* 19: 7–25.

Dannerbeck, Francis J. 1987. "Adult Second-Language Learning: Toward an American Adaptation with a European Perspective." *Foreign Language Annals* 20: 413–19.

Dulay, Heidi, Marina K. Burt, and Stephen Krashen. 1982. *Language Two.* New York: Oxford UP. 46.

Dvorak, Trisha. 1986. "Writing in a Foreign Language." *Listening, Reading, and*

Writing: Analysis and Application. Ed. Barbara H. Wing. Middlebury, Vt.: Northeast Conference on the Teaching of Foreign Languages.

Felix, Sascha W. 1981. "The Effect of Formal Instruction on Second Language Acquisition." *Language Learning* 31: 87–112.

Gagné, Ellen. 1985. *The Cognitive Psychology of School Learning.* Boston: Little, Brown.

Heilenman, Kathy L., Isabelle Kaplan, and Claude Toussant Tournier, eds. 1989. *Voilà! An Introduction to French.* New York: Harper and Row.

Higgs, Theodore V., and Ray Clifford. 1982. "The Push Toward Communication." *Curriculum, Competence, and the Foreign Language Teacher.* Skokie, Ill.: National Textbook Co. 57–79.

Jarvis, Gilbert A., Therese N. Bonin, and Diane W. Birckbichler, eds. 1988. *Invitation.* 3rd ed. New York: Holt, Rinehart and Winston.

Kassen, Margaret Ann. 1990. "Native Speaker and Non-Native Speaker Teacher Response to FL Composition: A Study of Beginning, Intermediate, and Advanced Level French." Diss. U. of Texas.

Kintsch, Walter, and Teun A. van Dijk. 1987. "Towards a Model of Discourse Comprehension and Production." *Psychological Review* 85: 363–94.

Larsen-Freeman, Diane. 1983. "Assessing Global Second Language Proficiency." *Classroom Oriented Research in Second Language Acquisition.* Eds. Herbert W. Seliger and Michael Long. Rowley, Mass.: Newbury House. 287–304.

Lee, James F. 1986. "Background Knowledge and L2 Reading." *Modern Language Journal* 70: 350–54.

———. 1987. "Comprehending the Spanish Subjunctive: An Information Processing Perspective." *Modern Language Journal* 71: 51–7.

Lee, James F., and Diane Musumeci. 1988. "On Hierarchies of Reading Skills and Text Types." *Modern Language Journal* 72: 173–87.

Levine, Martin, and George Haus. 1985. "The Effect of Background Knowledge on the Reading Comprehension of Second Language Learners." *Foreign Language Annals* 18: 391–97.

Lightbown, Patsy M. 1983. "Input, Interaction, and Acquisition in the SL Classroom." *Classroom Oriented Research in Second Language Acquisition.* Eds. Herbert W. Seliger and Michael Long. Rowley, Mass.: Newbury House. 217–43.

Loftus, Geoffrey, R., and Elizabeth Loftus. 1976. *Human Memory: The Processing of Information.* Hillsdale, N.J.: Lawrence Erbaum.

McLaughlin, B., T. Rossman, and B. McLeod. 1983. "Second Language Learning: An Information-Processing Perspective." *Language Learning* 33: 135–58.

Magnan, Sally Sieloff. 1986. "Assessing Speaking Proficiency in the Undergraduate Curriculum: Data from French." *Foreign Language Annals* 19: 429–38.

Melendez, E. Jane, and Robert H. Pritchard. 1985. "Applying Schema Theory to Foreign Language Reading." *Foreign Language Annals* 18: 399–403.

Meyer, Bonnie J. F. 1975. *The Organization of Prose and Its Effects on Memory.* New York: North-Holland.

Morgan, Martha. 1980. "The Achievement of First-Year College German Students at the University of Texas at Austin: A Comparison of a Comprehension-Based Reading Curriculum and a Speaking-Based Four Skills Curriculum." Masters Thesis, Univ. of Texas.

Nagle, Stephen, and Sara Sanders. 1986. "Comprehension Theory and Second Language Pedagogy." *TESOL Quarterly* 20: 9–26.

Nostrand, Howard Lee. 1989. "The Beginning Teacher's Cultural Competence: Goal and Strategy." *Foreign Language Annals* 22: 189–93.

Raimes, Ann. 1985. "What Unskilled ESL Students Do As They Write: A Classroom Study of Composing." *TESOL Quarterly* 19: 229–58.

Rivers, Wilga. 1971. "Linguistic and Psychological Factors in Speech Perception and Their Implications for Teaching Materials." *The Psychology of Second Language Learning.* Eds. Paul Pimsleur and Terence Quinn. Cambridge, Mass.: Cambridge UP. 123–34.

Rivers, Wilga, and Mary S. Temperley. 1987. *A Practical Guide to the Teaching of English as a Second or Foreign Language.* New York: Oxford UP.

Robb, Thomas, Steven Ross, and Ian Shortreed. 1986. "Salience of Feedback on Error and Its Effect on EFL Writing Quality." *TESOL Quarterly* 20: 83–95.

Schneider, Walter, and Richard M. Shiffrin. 1977. "Controlled and Automatic Information Processing: I. Detection, Search, and Attention." *Psychological Review* 84: 1–55.

Seliger, Herbert W., and Michael Long, eds. 1983. *Classroom Research in Second Language Acquisition.* Rowley, Mass.: Newbury House.

Semke, Harriet D. 1984. "Effects of the Red Pen." *Foreign Language Annals* 17: 195–202.

Shiffrin, Richard M., and Walter Schneider. 1977. "Controlled and Automatic Information Processing: II. Detection, Search, and Attention." *Psychological Review* 84: 127–90.

Shih, Mary. 1986. "Content Approaches to Teaching Academic Writing." *TESOL Quarterly* 20: 617–48.

Thomas, Jenny. 1983. "Cross-Cultural Pragmatic Failure." *Applied Linguistics* 4: 92–112.

Thomas, Margarat-Hanraity, and John N. Dister. 1987. "The Positive Effects of Writing Practice on Integration of Foreign Words in Memory." *Journal of Educational Psychology* 79: 219–53.

Tollefson, John W., Bob Jacobs, and Elaine J. Selipsky. 1983. "The Monitor

Model and Neurofunctional Theory: An Integrated View." *Studies in Second Language Acquisition* 6: 1–16.

Vigil, Virginia Dorothea. 1987. "Authentic Text in the College-Level Spanish I Class as the Primary Vehicle of Instruction." Diss. Univ. of Texas.

Wing, Barbara H., ed. 1986. *Listening, Reading, and Writing: Analysis and Application*. Middlebury, Vt.: Northeast Conference on the Teaching of Foreign Languages.

Wolff, Dieter. 1987. "Some Assumptions About Second Language Text Comprehension." *Studies in Second Language Acquisition* 9: 307–26.

Zamel, Vivian. 1976. "Teaching Composition in the ESL Classroom: What We Can Learn from Research on the Teaching of English." *TESOL Quarterly* 10: 67–76.

———. 1986. "Responding to Student Writing." *TESOL Quarterly* 20: 79–102.

Perspectives on Language Teaching Methodology

Psychological Validation of Methodological Approaches and Foreign Language Classroom Practices

Wilga M. Rivers

Harvard University

The swings and cycles of language teaching approaches continue. Everyone talks about them, but few people analyze them. As Gleick has pointed out in a fascinating way, there is patterning within patterning in nature (1987); and new ideas have long been recognized as recombinations of early thinking, the human mind associating and interrelating existing and entering material in a multitude of unexpected ways. So it behooves us to try to identify this patterning within teaching approaches, so that we may pinpoint what each new approach is emphasizing. Differences among approaches are, for the most part, differences in emphases, frequently because of changing demands and expectations that come from outside the foreign language learning/teaching domain. What appear to be radically new theoretical premises are, as often as not, variants of ways of looking at the same basic questions about language learning, sometimes with the fresh paint of a new terminology that camouflages their fundamental similarity.

The fundamental question in second language teaching that we are always considering and reconsidering, researching and hypothesizing about, can be stated succinctly: how do we internalize a language system so that we can enter into meaningful communication with speakers or writers of that language? Is the internalization a priming of something innate, something we already know, "one element in a system of cognitive structure," (Chomsky, 1980, 220) that is, the setting of parameters for the new language based on an inborn abstract competence or universal grammar, in Chomskyan terms? Alternatively, is it an ingestion of new knowledge from without? Is it perhaps a combination of both? Is it a priming of innate abstract capacities, whether linguistic or logical, by contact with new forms of expression essential for well-being, that sets in motion the process of absorption of these new forms into the dynamic networks of the human mind/brain,[1] in which are already incorporated what the learner knows of a first, and sometimes a second and third language? We have much evidence from diaries of the way learners do interrelate new linguistic knowledge with what is known of other languages,[2] and further evidence that strategies of approach to a third, fourth, or fifth language are guided by experience with the systemic way other languages have organized their phonology, syntax, or semantics.[3] From birth, nothing is learned in a vacuum.

All evidence points to an organized system at the core of any language—a system that is basic to communicating messages even at a very simple level. Whether this core is considered in essence lexico-syntactic (as Chomsky maintains)[4] or semantic-pragmatic (as in Halliday's (1985) theory of meaning-potential and "goings-on" in language), there is clearly a formal framework that enables one to use a language systematically to convey meaning to other individuals. Interwoven within this basic framework are the phonological system and the semantic, syntactic, and pragmatic systems (in whichever ways they are considered to be interrelated). Although there are universals at the base of these systems, in each case the usage specific to a particular language and culture must be acquired in the language environment, although previous experience with language has sensitized the learner to the role of each in the communication of meaning. We will refer to this basic framework as *grammar* in its broadest sense, even at the risk of being misinterpreted and misquoted.

In all language-learning approaches, there has been awareness of the existence of this vital core, without which mutual comprehension is impossible. Leontiev (1981) has spoken of the "absolute minimum . . . the foundations of the language without which the learning of any speech activity would be impossible." But all theorists have been aware that language learning must be more than learning the grammar, even in this broad sense. Ploetz, the foremost grammar-translation protagonist of the late nineteenth century, believed that "grammar should be the most important part of a linguistic training and all language courses should begin with this basic training. But," he continued, "it is dangerous to believe that everything is done once the grammar is learned" (1865). Newmark, a more radical methodologist, acknowledges the existence of this basic core, but not the "study" of it. At the opposite pole from Ploetz, he says, "The study of grammar as such is neither necessary nor sufficient for learning to use a language" (1966). Frequently misquoted, he clearly states "the study of grammar as such." He thus distances himself from Ploetz, while emphasizing what Ploetz was referring to when he said, "It is dangerous to believe everything is done" once grammar has been absorbed (though in all probability not *internalized,* as Ploetz was well aware). Newmark advocates using the language and letting the students imitate as best they can. He believes "Language is learned a whole act at a time rather than learned as an assemblage of constituent skills." Consequently, he maintains that "situational rather than grammatical cohesion is what is necessary and sufficient for language learning to take place" (1968). By using the word *cohesion* in this context, Newmark makes clear that there is some core to the many situations in which language is used, and even permits of a "limited kind of structural drill," where "learning is embedded in a meaningful context," in which small variations in situations being acted out call for "partial innovations in the previously learned role" (1966, 83).

Nicole, in 1670, discussed the ideas "of those who will have no truck with grammar," maintaining that this approach, "far from being a help . . . loads (the learners) infinitely more than rules, because it deprives them of an aid." Experience with replacing rules with functions and notions has been found by some to load students with many apparently unrelated items (Omaggio, 1986), which could have been linked in memory in dynamic and recursive ways through the acquisition of a framework.

Methodologists have nailed this problem down as one of approach rather than principle. In 1964, Brooks affirmed that "we first learn the grammar by actual use of communication, thinking of rules only after having learned many examples very well. . . . There is little point in asking or explaining 'why' grammar . . . [is] as [it is], until the grammar in question [is] familiar through actual use." Article 6 of the International Phonetic Association (Passy and Rambeau, 1879) states that "in the early stages grammar should be taught inductively, complementing and generalizing language facts observed during reading. A more systematic study of grammar should be postponed to the advanced stages of the course" (in Stern 1983, 89). The apparent dichotomy of views on the role of grammar clearly lies along the induction-deduction continuum, with direct method as the prototype at one end and grammar-translation at the other, with other methodological approaches falling somewhere in between. Even Krashen, who objects to "teaching grammar as subject matter" in his more recent work, maintaining that "any subject matter that held (the students') attention would do as well," since "their progress is coming from the medium [use of the language] and not the message" (1982), thus coming down on the inductive side, had earlier stated that "the isolation of rules and words of the target language" may be a crucial ingredient of formal instruction" (he calls this + DEDUCTIVE) and that "informal learners may well be using formal instruction, via bilingual dictionaries and grammars or through using native-speaking informants" (Krashen and Seliger, 1975: 181).

Leaders in methodological theory like Brooks, Gattegno, Curran, and Lozanov have all favored the inductive assimilation of grammar and opposed "teaching grammar as subject matter," while recognizing the need for internal control of the basic framework.[5] Terrell's *affective acquisition activities* foster this control, once the students' attention has been focused briefly on aspects of the overall system through *advance organizers* (such as drawing attention to markers of grammatical gender or morphological affixal indicators of person and tense)—a mixture of inductive and deductive techniques, while still strongly on the inductive side.[6] Gattegno (1972) speaks of "the integrative schemata of meaning and structure" that the learner internalizes through the development of "inner criteria." His approach is inductive, but his materials are designed to present structural features, as are Lozanov's. Even Curran, whose Counseling-Learning/Community Language Learning sessions are at the extreme inductive end of the continuum, advocates deductive discussions at a later stage of the material taped during the students' attempts at communication within the group.

We may consider these inductive or deductive emphases as indicative of whether the stress is laid on language knowledge or language control[7]—knowing the system of the language or knowing how to operate within it to express personal meanings. It is notable that in the most deductive approaches, learners express the teacher's or textbook writer's meanings, as in the grammar-translation approach, whereas in the most inductive approaches, they express their own meanings, as in Curran's Community Language Learning. Many blend one with the other. All methodologies that favor the inductive emphasize autonomous language use in a distinctive context, context being essential for the inferencing induction requires, and most encourage student initiative in generating utterances. Curran (1976) emphasizes the predicament of "learners who may, in fact, learn the laws of grammar and be able to analyze a sentence and yet never really arrive at the freedom to speak. But representation," he says, "has come into being when, in a certain sense, the law is cast off by being internalized into a living reality. Representation and being have come together in an integrity of meaning and value. In language learning, the person speaks correctly but without any consciousness of rules." This is the ultimate objective of most contemporary language programs.

It is this notion of representation that is at the heart of the internalization-of-language question, "Basic to language use is a mental representation of how the language works" (Rivers, 1989, 4). What we need to know is how this mental representation is developed, what is represented, and the role of the mental representation in the individual's production of language. For an answer, we must turn to the field in which mental representations and mental models are being studied intensely, the field of cognitive psychology—a field to which linguistics rightfully belongs, according to Chomsky (1988). Intensive study of the human mind/brain, particularly through computer simulation, is throwing much light on this subject. Since the field is still very young and in a certain ferment, we cannot expect to find definitive answers, neatly tied up in packets, but there are theoretical models and research findings that are provocative of thought in this area. To establish their applicability to our field will require further research in language-related areas.

As Chomsky has pointed out, each human being is "an organism whose behavior, we have every reason to believe, is determined by the interaction of numerous internal systems operating under conditions of great variety and complexity" (1980, 218). Knowledge of the language of a particular speech community is "uniformly represented in the mind of each of its members, as one element in a system of cognitive structure" (220). Whether or not they accept the innateness of the Universal Grammar (UG) component at the base of an individual's linguistic competence, cognitive psychologists generally do accept the innateness of certain cognitive structures. Whether the activation of the use of a specific language is a matter of setting the parameters of an inborn competence to the features of the new language or the derivation from social interaction of the ways that language meets interactional needs, as Bruner would maintain (1983), the product is a mental representation of the way the language works, or may be made to work, to convey an infinity of meanings for a multiplicity of social and personal functions.

As language teachers, we should be wary of hitching our wagon too closely to the Chomskyan concept of a purely linguistic mental representation for language. We are interested in our students being able to use language in a messy practical way, not in the idealized way to which Chomskyan linguistics has deliberately limited itself. Its primary object of research is *grammatical competence,* as Chomsky has frequently stated, while accepting the existence of *pragmatic competence* as an important element determining linguistic performance, by "relating intentions and purposes to the linguistic means at hand" (1980, 224). For our part we care greatly about appropriate use of the language in various circumstances by our language learners. Chomsky says that "if non-linguistic factors must be included in grammar beliefs, attitudes, etc. [this would] amount to a to a rejection of the initial idealization of language as an object of study." This, he continues, would lead him to "conclude that language is a chaos that is not worth studying" (1979, 140). Yet it is this very chaos into which our students are plunged from their very first efforts to express themselves in a new language. As language learners rather than students of language as a phenomenon, our students (and we as their teachers) need to "recognize that human beings inhabit a communicational space which is not neatly compartmentalized into language and non-language," as Harris puts it (1981). Our students need to develop mental representations of aspects of the culture and culturally determined forms of interaction before they can effectively operate within the semantic-syntactic framework of their new language.

For our purposes we need a broader view of mental representation. In this regard, Shanon (1987) makes an interesting distinction between what he calls the presentational as process of acquisition of knowledge and the representational as product established in the mind. "The representational facets of mind," he says, "are not primary or basic but rather secondary or derived." He sees "a progression from the unidimensional level, which does not distinguish between medium and message, to the symbolic level . . . —from that which is ill defined, undifferentiated, and multifaceted to that which is well defined, differentiated, and articulated; from activities that are part and parcel of one's being in the world to ones that attest to the increasing autonomy of the individual." He sees "cognition as a dynamic movement between two poles, the presentational and the representational." This seems an applicable description of what takes place in inductive learning, with the student passing through a mist, as it were, of undifferentiated linguistic features, which gradually clarify and take distinct form as learners develop mental representations. These enable them to achieve a state of autonomy where personal meanings can be expressed apart from external stimuli; they can now extract, store, and interrelate information, and are able to perform other indispensable cognitive activities in the language.

This mental representation, according to Shanon (1987), is distinct from other cognitive activity in the mind and allows for "reflection on one's own cognitions." The continual dynamic movement between the presentational in the world of the senses and the representational in the mind enables mental schemas to be adapted and readapted, chameleonlike, as new material is encountered in the environment. "Action in the world, not symbolic reference [then becomes] the basis for cognition." We see evidence of the existence of mental representations in such metacognitive abilities of individuals as explaining why they expressed themselves as they did, recognizing acceptable and unacceptable ways, on the part of themselves and others, of encoding ideas in their dialect or in a new language; and challenging as veridical or not an imitation of their utterances. (Young children already demonstrate the latter capacity when imitation by others does not tally with their own mental representations of their utterances.) As Shanon concludes, "Without representations, neither precise human communication nor conscious reflection could have been achieved." As we shall see in a moment, mental representation also explains linguistic action. Language knowledge in the mental representation is the product that provides the capacity for language control in many varied situations, which is the process of language use.

At this point, we would do well to look carefully at what we can learn from neoconnectionist parallel distributed processing systems (PDP) (Hinton and Anderson, 1989), and J. R. Anderson's (1983) model of cognition, ACT* (Adaptive Control of Thought, final version). Both of these theoretical positions regard memory processes as the component linking knowledge to action, a process that deeply concerns all who teach language for communication, in speech or writing.

Memory in cognitive studies is no longer regarded as a locatable storage space. We have passed through the period when memory was considered to resemble a series of bins or stores through which material passed on its way to long-term storage. The push-down storage of the sixties is way behind us, as is the Broadbent model (1967), where memory capacity is calculated in bits of information. Certain concepts from Broadbent's influential model are, however, still regarded as valid—such concepts as the selective filter that decides what will be extracted from the intial message for processing, the short-term and intermediate stores of material being processed (now more likely to be called working memory), the long-term store of past events, and the processes of rehearsal and recirculation; these are incorporated into more recent models, with new interpretations based on later research and experimentation, particularly through computer simulation. Many of Miller's ideas on chunking and organizing, and recoding for storage (1967), and Neisser's enlightening observations on the subjective nature of perception in its relation to memory (1967) are still found to be extremely useful.

More recent models are notably dynamic and process-oriented. Memory is now viewed as a process whereby knowledge (factual and experience-derived) enters into networks with a multiplicity of interconnected nodes (like the neurons in the nervous system). The nodes are conceptual and the interconnecting networks are relational. Entering information activates nodes, which activate nodes on nodes, so that processing of the information is effected by many processes occurring at the same time, that is, in parallel. Anything that one encounters, and selectively or peripherally perceives, enters the networks and is immediately bounced around, compared, discriminated, matched, linked up in the networks with information related to it in a multiplicity of obvious and unexpected ways, to serve some purpose eventually along with all the other elements operating in parallel. Because of these interrelated networks, items of knowledge and memory traces of events are distributed throughout the system. Rather than our being able to retrieve them from one node or one spot in long-term storage, through a few cues or triggers, memory traces can be accessed anywhere in the system through the multitude of different connections firing simultaneously. "The multiple connections allow much of the knowledge of the entire system to be applied in any instance of recognition or problem-solving" (Gardner, 1985, 319). As Rumelhart and Norman (1989) express it, "Information is better thought of as 'evoked' than 'found' "; it is the relationships that are important. Consequently, memories come to us in many unexpected ways and through a variety of sensory stimuli. This approach tallies with common experience, where we are frequently bombarded with activated memories, perhaps on encountering a particular scent or taste (as with Proust's famous madeleine), or in searching for a word or name. Such networks make the "subconscious acquisition" and "the din in the head," of which Krashen speaks, readily explicable, but cast doubt on the validity of a nonpermeable division between what is "acquired" and what is "learned."[8]

With this approach to memory, accessibility becomes the key word, as basic to retrieval. In language teaching this means constant reactivation of language material within the networks in all kinds of student-maintained interactive activities where students themselves follow the direction in language use that their own minds project. It adds support to Lozanov's insistence on the importance of peripheral intake, with his attention to the surroundings, his wall charts and pictures, and his emphasis on allowing the whole mind to work in its own way with language material presented to it. It supports the present emphasis on learning in context in a variety of different but similar situations (something that textbook writers have been conscious of for some time). Rumelhart and Normal (1989) point out that "information that is related to, but different from, previously stored information tends to evoke the original pattern of activity . . . similarity and the ability to generalize [comprise] a central component. Similar items of information interact with one another in such a way as to reinforce those aspects they have in common and cancel out those aspects on which they differ." And finally, we find support in this model for using every possible medium and modality to reinforce learning.

As Spolsky (1989) points out, parallel distributed processing implies processes made up of "large numbers of microscale elements that occur in large networks, which may be variously connected internally to each other or externally, receiving input from the outside world or sending output. A network," he points out, "learns a new behavior pattern by changing the 'weight' of its various connections on the basis of patterns received from input to it. These patterns of 'weights' rather than the fixed connections determine the new patterns of behavior."[9] Thus, the system learns from the input and corrects its errors as it has more experience with a certain behavior pattern. De Saussure has pointed out the importance of "value" (compare *weights*) in meaning. In language, he says, "the value of each term results solely from the simultaneous presence of the others" (1959, 114), as in a game of chess where the value of each piece derives from the values of all the others at a particular moment, as it enters into the relationships that develop among them. To learn these "weights" or "internal parameters," our language learners need frequent opportunities to observe certain features of language as used by native speakers and, at times, to have these features drawn to their attention when they seem not to observe them, because there is also here a basis of language knowledge that cannot be brushed under the mat. We would do well to reexamine the question of microlanguage learning and macrolanguage use and the intimate way in which they interact (Rivers, 1983, 108–9). These are insights that merit our attention if we are to produce adept language users.

Networks of the type we have been discussing are basic to Anderson's ACT* model, which is fundamentally "learning by doing," and learning from past doing (1983, 20). ACT* incorporates three memory systems—working, declarative, and production—and attempts to relate knowledge to action, with memory in its distinctive form in the model as the basic force in action. Anderson's work is a bold attempt to bring together in a coherent framework much that has been discovered through psychological investigation about the acquisition and use of knowledge. Although it is undoubtedly not the last word in a fast-changing field, it contains interesting proposals that may lead us to ponder more deeply certain basic questions that concern our work.

In the ACT* system, knowledge that reaches us in whatever form (facts, ideas, images, events, sense impressions), either through focused attention and selection or peripherally, is encoded for storage in declarative memory (which takes the form of associative networks); from declarative memory it can be retrieved for use in working memory when the need for action, emanating from production memory, calls for it. Production memory is a thinking process that reflects previous experience with events. When an event is encountered, working memory calls on production memory to match circumstances and facts (drawing on the contents of declarative memory) and to decide on an appropriate form of execution (or production). In working memory, this production (or intention) is fleshed out with requisite language, motor information, or whatever, from declarative memory and initiates performances to meet the needs of the situation. Experience with the situation results in further encoding into working memory, which augments both declarative and production memory for further informed action. Memories will be strengthened as they are drawn out of storage and involved in performances and will be enriched by further experience. How long a memory is kept depends on how frequently it is used, but we must keep in mind that, in associative parallel-processing theory, memories are continually changing and evolving as new events and new facts enter the network. (At this point, one might challenge Spolsky's use of the word *fixed* in the comment just cited.)

Knowing and doing are thus intimately associated. Knowledge is essential to action, and without action knowledge declines and even disintegrates. Through action (which includes, in this model, thinking and other cognitive activities) knowledge grows, evolves, and is strengthened. In our domain, language knowledge (lexico-syntactic and semantic-pragmatic) is essential to performance in the language (which demonstrates control of language), but knowledge of facts about language without language experience is not knowledge of language in the ACT* sense, the two combine in working memory, which drives performance, and each matching for language use increases the usability of language knowledge on future occasions. Just as success breeds success, language use strengthens and increases both declarative memory and production memory. To consider one without the other is impossible within this system.

Along with parallel distributed processing, ACT* theory encourages us to design our courses so that students are continually involved in using whatever they know (not just whatever they are learning at a certain point) and in reflecting on what they are learning as they are using it. Call this monitoring if you will, but reflective matching for appropriateness seems to be an essential part of the execution process. Some language operations may be performed automatically after a certain amount of experience but, as circumstances vary, we as thinking beings need to be able to contemplate our performance even as we are executing a production procedure, so as to continue comparing and matching with information from the ever-active associative networks. In this way we can adapt our performance, in mid-breath if necessary, as we seek for relevance and appropriateness in our verbal and nonverbal responses.

There is an essential difference between the automaticity of habitual performance and skillful performance. Ryle (1949) argued that "a person's performance is described as careful or skillful if in his operations he is ready to detect and correct lapses, to repeat and improve on successes, to profit from the examples of others." Bailin (1987), who quotes Ryle, maintains that original and expressive use of language, which may involve "breaking rules" can occur only when one has a command of the rules and knows what he or she can and cannot accomplish. (Such a command comes from performing rules, not reciting them, of course [Rivers, 1989, 4].) A skilled performance can adapt to changing circumstances, which an habitual one cannot. We exercise control over even routine skills that seem automatic and can adapt them rapidly should an unforeseen circumstance arise (Bailin, 1987, 329). In our classes, we need to develop skilled language users, who are aware of what they are doing even when performing familiar linguistic routines, and who possess the knowledge (in the ACT* sense) to guide their selection of productive options to convey what they really want to convey in pragmatically, culturally, syntactically, and semantically appropriate ways. Then, and only then, knowledge and action become one, and we have done our part.

ENDNOTES

1. At this point I will not enter into a discussion of the identity of or distinction between these two.

2. See, for example, W. M. Rivers, "Learning a Sixth Language: An Adult Learner's Daily Diary," Appendix B of *Teaching Foreign-Language Skills.*

3. For example, see N. Naiman, M. Frohlich, H. H. Stern, and A. Todesco, *The Good Language Learner.*

4. In Government Binding (GB) theory, "the lexicon is not a separate issue, a list of words and meanings; it plays a dynamic and necessary part in the syntax." V. J. Cook, *Chomsky's Universal Grammar: An Introduction,* p. 11.

5. For further information on Gattegno, Curran, and Lozanov, see "Student-centered Trends: A Rationale," in W. M. Rivers, *Communicating Naturally in a Second Language: Theory and Practice in Language Teaching,* pp. 80–84.

6. T. Terrell, Presentation at the ACTFL Annual Meeting, Monterey, Calif., 1988. Lozanov also gives such indications.

7. See Principle 5 of W. M. Rivers, "Ten Principles of Interactive Language Learning and Teaching," p. 4.

8. S. D. Krashen, *The Input Hypothesis: Issues and Implications,* pp. 1, 38. "The din in the head" refers to an experience Krashen cites. He had been an undergraduate student of German and had spent a year abroad in Austria. On a later visit he found all kinds of expressions in German that he was hearing around him dancing about in his head.

9. B. Spolsky, *Conditions for Second Language Learning,* pp. 226–27. For "weights" or "internal parameters," see also Hinton and Anderson, eds. (1989), p. 6.

REFERENCES

Anderson, J. R. 1983. *The Architecture of Cognition.* Cambridge, Mass.: Harvard UP.

Bailin, S. 1987. "Creativity and Skill." *Thinking: The Second International Conference.* Hillsdale, N.J.: LEA. 323–32.

Broadbent, D. E. 1967. *Perception and Communication.* London: Pergamon.

Brooks, N. 1964. *Language and Language Learning: Theory and Practice.* 2nd ed. New York: Harcourt Brace and World. 135.

Bruner, J. 1983. *Child's Talk.* Oxford: Oxford UP.

Chomsky, N. 1979. *Language and Responsibility.* New York: Pantheon. 140.

———. 1980. *Rules and Representations.* New York: Columbia UP.

———. 1988. *Language and the Problems of Knowledge: The Managua Lectures.* Cambridge, Mass.: MIT Press. 6.

Cook, V. J. 1988. *Chomsky's Universal Grammar: An Introduction.* Oxford: Basil Blackmore. 11.

Curran, C. A. 1976. *Counseling-Learning in Foreign Languages.* Apple River, Ill. Apple River Press. 57–8.

Gardner, H. 1985. *The Mind's New Science: A History of the Cognitive Revolution.* New York: Basic Books. 57–8.

Gattegno, C. 1972. *Teaching Foreign Languages in Schools: The Silent Way.* New York: Educational Solutions. 8, 14.

Gleick, J. 1987. *Chaos: Making a New Science.* New York: Viking.

Halliday, M. A. K. 1985. *An Introduction to Functional Grammar.* London: Edward Arnold.

Harris, R. 1981. *The Language Myth.* London: Duckworth. 165.

Hinton, G. E., and J. A. Anderson, eds. 1989. *Parellel Models of Associative Memory.* Updated ed. Hillsdale, N.J.: LEA.

Krashen, S. D. 1982. *Principles and Practice in Second Language Acquisition.* Oxford: Pergamon Press. 20.

———. 1985. *The Input Hypothesis: Issues and Implications.* London: Longman.

Krashen, S. D. and H. W. Seliger. 1975. "The Essential Contributions of Formal Instruction in Adult Second Language Learning." *TESOL Quarterly* 9: 181.

Leontiev, A. A. 1981. *Psychology and the Language-Learning Process.* Oxford: Basil Blackmore. 25.

Lozanov, G. 1978. *Suggestology and Outlines of Suggestopedy.* New York: Gordon and Breach.

Miller, G. A. 1967. *The Psychology of Communication: Seven Essays.* New York: Basic Books.

Naiman, N., M. Frohlich, H. H. Stern, and A. Todesco. 1978. *The Good Language Learner.* Toronto: OISE.

Neisser, U. 1967. *Cognitive Psychology.* New York: Appleton-Century-Crofts.

Newmark, L. 1966. "How Not to Interfere with Language Learning." *IJAL* 32: 77–83.

Newmark, L., and D. Reibel. 1968. "Necessity and Sufficiency in Language Learning." *IRAL* 6: 151.

Nicole. 1670. Quoted in L. G. Kelly. 1969. *25 Centuries of Language Teaching. 500 BC–1969.* Rowley, Mass.: Newbury House. 219–20.

Omaggio, A. C. 1986. *Teaching Language in Context: Proficiency-Oriented Instruction.* Boston: Heinle and Heinle. 214–15.

Perkins, D. N., J. Lochhead, and J. Bishop, eds. 1987. *Thinking: The Second International Conference.* Hillsdale, N.J.: LEA.

Ploetz, K. 1865. *Elementarbuch der Franzoesischensprache.* New York. Quoted in L. G. Kelly. 1969. *25 Centiries of Language Teaching. 500 BC–1969.* Rowley, Mass.: Newbury House. 220.

Rivers, W. M. 1981. *Teaching Foreign-Language Skills.* Chicago: University of Chicago Press.

————. 1983. *Communicating Naturally in a Second Language: Theory and Practice in Language Teaching*. Cambridge: Cambridge UP.

————. 1989. "Ten Principles of Interactive Language Learning and Teaching." Washington, D.C.: National Foreign Language Center at the Johns Hopkins University.

Rumelhart, D. E., and D. A. Norman. 1989. Introduction. *Parallel Models of Associative Memory*. Eds. G. E. Hinton and J. A. Anderson. Updated ed. Hillsdale, N.J.: LEA.

Ryle, G. 1949. *The Concept of Mind*. London: Hutchinson. 28–9.

de Saussure, F. 1959. *Course in General Linguistics*. Eds. C. Bally and A. Secherhaye. New York: Philosophical Library.

Shanon, B. 1987. "On the Place of Representations in Cognition." *Thinking: The Second International Conference*. Eds. D. N. Perkins, J. Lockhead, and J. Bishop. Hillsdale, N.J.: LEA. 45–7.

Spolsky, B. 1989. *Conditions for Second Language Learning*. Oxford: Oxford UP.

Stern, H. H. 1983. *Fundamental Concepts of Language Teaching*. Oxford: Oxford UP.

Titone, R. 1968. *Teaching Languages: An Historical Sketch*. Washington, D.C.: Georgetown UP.

Chapter 17

Research on Teaching Methodology: Its Evolution and Prospects

Gilbert A. Jarvis

The Ohio State University

INTRODUCTION

It is important to acknowledge, first of all, that important research in foreign and second language education deals with much more than teaching and learning behavior, or what many call "methods." All language educators need to understand better, for example, how one learns a new language and how various arrangements of language and text influence learning. Clearly, such issues are not unrelated to what happens in classrooms and other learning settings, and there is a certain measure of artificiality in separating them. Indeed, issues of learning ought to be the most fundamental of all. To achieve focus and manageability, this manuscript will be limited to research issues relating directly to teaching and learning behavior in classrooms or other settings.

Historically, foreign language teaching and learning behavior has frequently been viewed through a lens of teaching methods. The consequences of this view are unfortunate for the profession. Indeed, language teaching might be better understood and better executed if the concept of method were not to exist at all. Its fundamental shortcoming is that it is a macroconceptualization that deflects attention away from microlevel teaching and learning activity—the very activity that determines whether or not instruction is successful (in every sense of successful). Viewing oneself as practicing a method is remarkably constraining. It can preclude any attention to moment-to-moment behavior. It can draw attention to what the methodological prescriptions dictate, rather than to whether learning is occurring effectively. One might contrast, for example, the ways in which physicians inquire, test, diagnose, and treat patients versus the way they would function if they were following the dictates of one of several competing methods of doctoring.

Discussions of change in language education—like all of education—frequently include the terms *fads, frills,* and *pendulum swings.* Indeed, more than a half century ago, Charters (1922) referred to the history of education as "a chronicle of fads." This bleak characterization is especially true in relation to teaching methodology. Yet, most histories of language teaching are framed in terms of methodologies.

An extensive search of the pedagogical literature is not necessary to identify methods with labels as diverse as *direct, compromise, reform, grammar translation, psychological, phonetic, reading, eclectic, army, audiolingual, cognitive code, new key, audiovisual, communicative, suggestopoedia, natural, silent way, community language learning, counseling learning,* and *total physical response.* Each represents a particular configuration of teaching behavior, student behavior, and instructional materials. Each has been codified in written descriptions (sometimes promulgated as prescriptions) and often demonstrated at professional meetings. None, however, is a formulation whose origin is a data base describing the nature of language learning—for such a data base does not yet exist. The primary role of research is to develop that data base.

Carroll (1960) entitled an article "Wanted: A Research Basis for Educational Policy on Foreign Language Teaching." Twenty years later, Stern and Cummins (1981) reiterated the same plea. Ten more years later, as we enter the 1990s, the need for this research base is just as great—particularly in the area of teaching and learning behavior. Such a foundation is the only appropriate base for a teaching method—at least, if one makes the assumption that the purpose of teaching is to cause or facilitate learning—to enable the student to perform the tasks of learning. In other words, "studenting" must be made optimally effective.

One cannot avoid noting a significant irony in our history: the best example of teaching methodology being tied closely to a research and theory base is the audiolingualism popular in the 1960s. Unfortunately, the behavioristic base proved to be invalid. Moreover, initially the methodology was widely promulgated through instructional materials and government-funded institutes. Only *after* this extensive effort did language educators discover, via Rivers's (1964) astute analysis, the psychological bases of the method. Truth and understanding came late—and did not come from those who were promoting the method.

Methods have frequently been transmitted via prescriptions about how to teach. They emanate primarily from trial-and-error experience rather than from research. Thus, they represent craft knowledge that is passed from teacher to teacher in workshops, written descriptions, and faculty lounges. Occasionally, it is craft knowledge emanating from a single source, usually involving a quasi-entrepreneurial effort. The method is sold along with the materials utilized in its application. Stern and Cummins have noted that "it is hardly possible to find in the literature unbiased descriptions . . . let alone dispassionate examinations of the effect of these methods on specified groups of students" (1981, 223). Sometimes the origins are outside of language education expertise, in fields such as linguistics or psychology. Enormous leaps are made from paradigms such as nonsense-syllable research to language classrooms. Such errors are characteristic of primitive stages of disciplines.

Given such origins, our methods conceptualizations are prone to many kinds of error that would be diminished by the safeguards built into research by the scientific method. Sometimes our methods are packaged, promoted, and sold as if they are commercial products. The result has been strong instructor loyalties and emotions in a matter that ought to be predominantly intellectual. Faith has become more important than understanding.

Why have we evolved as we have? Why have we not emphasized research as a basis for teaching behavior if that is a better *modus operandi?* Several reasons are clear. First, we have not had the requisite expertise in educational research. It was only in the late 1960s that doctoral programs in language education were developed in a handful of institutions. Prior to that time, our pedagogical literature was created by language educators who typically were prepared in literary research but who were interested in teaching-learning issues. In the early years of doctoral programs, the curricula frequently did not emphasize sophisticated research skills; they often taught little more than teaching methods. Some programs that are labeled foreign or second language education still do not appear to emphasize research—at least if one can judge by the titles of dissertations being completed in the field (Benseler, 1988). Many of them appear to be nonresearch activity.

Thus, competent researchers are a recent phenomenon and represent a very small minority of those engaged in language teaching. More powerful an influence still, perhaps, is the tradition under which they work. In research universities, the roles they occupy often include responsibility for teaching assistant supervision and administration of basic language programs—activities that have not been given high status by colleagues with whom they work. Their instructional and supervisory loads in these roles have been extraordinarily heavy, thus making inquiry more difficult. Their inquiry is also different from that of their colleagues and has often been poorly understood by them. They have further jeopardized their own status in many major research universities by not making basic distinctions between research and service activities and by devoting excessive efforts to service activity. Conducting workshops for language teachers is simply not research and should not be a basis for promotion and tenure in any department.

During the past decade or two, when human resources that created potential for progress started to become available, little research funding was provided. The meager amounts that were provided were often utilized for short-term, glamorous-appearing goals, such as the development of model programs that others would presumably emulate. There appeared to be little patience for the quest for the long-term isolated insight, which, when combined with other such insights, might improve language teaching early in the twenty-first century. Research on teaching and learning behavior is furthermore remarkably difficult to conduct and is therefore often avoided by many researchers. It involves working with instructors and students who function within complex bureaucracies and whose roles entail another complex of ethical constraints. Among the forty-five dissertations listed in foreign language education for 1987 (Benseler, 1988), only four clearly relate directly to teaching and learning behavior.

One consequence of meager funding levels during these years is a skewed topography of the research in this area. Much of the inquiry appears to be dissertation research. Because of that fact, our research has clearly discernible characteristics. It is inexpensive; few doctoral students have the resources to fund their own research. It is short-term; few doctoral students choose to invest several years in data gathering to accomplish, for example, a longitudinal goal, no matter how important it may be. It is apprenticeship research; for better or worse, it is enthusiastically done by a neophyte doing his or her first inquiry.

Another consequence of the paucity of funding is the very small number of long-term research programs discernible in the literature. Few faculty (or researchers outside of academia) appear to create opportunities for the neophyte to apprentice in a well-developed research program.

AN HISTORICAL PERSPECTIVE

If one makes the assumption that methods research must be empirical—that data relating to instruction must be collected—the first noteworthy efforts that were widely disseminated were broad methods comparisons in the 1960s. Such comparisons utilized a hard-science model of true experiments in which an independent variable was manipulated in order to observe the effects on one or more dependent variables. We researched in a way similar to the horticulturalist who might manipulate the rate of application of potassium on several plots of beans to observe the effect on plant height and weight of the yield.

In our profession, these comparisons typically involved two methods that were compared in two or more classrooms. Chastain and Woerdehoff (1968), for example, compared audiolingual and cognitive code methods. At the end of a year, students who were taught by these methods were compared in terms of several measures of language ability. Audiolingual students received significantly higher scores in repeating sentences; cognitive-code students received significantly higher reading scores. Listening and writing scores favored the cognitive students, but not significantly. This study, which probably represents the best effort within language education to make such methods comparisons, extended through a second year by following the progress of the students through the succeeding year of instruction where they were mixed with students who had not participated in the experiment. Results indicated that the effects of the second-year of instruction overwhelmed any effects from the methods used in the first year. Students learned essentially what they were taught.

Words should not be spent on the results of such methods comparisons. In light of today's knowledge they were generally not productive inquiry; in fact, if precise definitions are employed, they really cannot even he considered research. They are comparative *evaluations* of entities that defy operational definitions. One essential characteristic of research is a need for generalizability of the knowledge—a need for transportability. Such comparisons fail that test.

In the context of a positivist paradigm, a method is not amenable to isolating and maximizing treatment conditions while controlling all other factors so that cause and effect can be established. A teaching method is a configuration of thousands of variables, each of which contributes positively or negatively to the impact of the totality. A method cannot be realized in the same way by even two teachers in adjacent classrooms. In many cases, the method variable cannot be defined, and in virtually all situations, it is not controllable. Thus, the inquiry becomes an evaluation of the effectiveness of an individual teacher, with one class of students, in a unique classroom, at a single moment in time, compared to another such unique classroom. In light of the control demands of scientific inquiry, we have to acknowledge that even the same instructor could not replicate his or her teaching in two succeeding semesters with the same course. Thus, the question being answered in this type of inquiry is really how well Professor Jones or Professor Smith did with the nine-o'clock Spanish 102 section in a particular semester at Oakview College. Such evaluation may well be a worthwhile activity; it simply is not research.

One strategy that has been tried to overcome this problem is to create a large-scale experiment involving a large number of classrooms. If fifty teachers utilize method A and fifty others, method B (or if a large number of teachers each taught both methods), the assumption is that the variations would average out, and we would end up with an average version of method A being compared with an average version of method B. Unfortunately, the variability within methods becomes greater than the variability between methods. When one factors in the variance due to the many powerful variables outside of teaching method, effects are inevitably masked. We must remember, for example, that what students know already that is related to the new material to be learned is a far more powerful influence than what is done in the classroom.

In foreign and second language education, the Pennsylvania Project is an heroic example of this large-scale strategy. In this most extensive methods comparison, Smith (1970) compared audiolingual with what was called a "traditional" method in a large number of Pennsylvania schools. The results indicated that traditional students equalled or exceeded the audiolingual students on all measures of achievement. By and large, in this experiment one sees once again that in language education, as in other fields, *students learn essentially what is taught, what is emphasized,* in their instruction, and they do not learn what is not emphasized. That does not now, of course, appear to be a remarkable conclusion.

In the literature of the early 1970s, a strategy that was designed to overcome the weaknesses of methods comparisons appeared. This strategy involved the manipulation of a single instructional variable or a small configuration of variables. Good examples of this strategy are efforts to manipulate and compare types of practice occurring in the language classroom (for example, Jarvis, 1970; Joiner, 1974).

This strategy is a plausible means to come to understand better the factors within the classroom that influence learning. It achieves much better control than earlier designs. The problem that became apparent in such research, however, is that in seeking to detect the effects of a single variable, the researcher was implicitly making the assumption that it was such a powerful variable that its effects would not be masked by the thousands of other variables that would presumably be held constant across the several levels of the independent variable. The effects were in fact likely to be masked, and only an unusually powerful variable would have a detectable effect. The stone tossed into a river does indeed make ripples, but they may not be detected on the bank on the other side of the stream. This research strategy can therefore be used only with the most influential of variables—and we typically have little a priori basis for identifying them.

By the late 1970s, one can observe in the literature occasional application of a min-max principle in order to address the masking problem. In this approach the context in which the research is taking place is minimized in every possible way, and the distinction between the levels of the independent variable is maximized. To use the same metaphor—the stone tossed into the stream is a large one and it is tossed into the narrowest, calmest part of the stream. The research might, for example, take place within one class hour's time; it might involve only one learning task; and it would probably involve only one group of subjects. The researcher might, as in the case of Schaeffer (1979), maximize control by delivering the experiment via the computer, where all student behavior can also be recorded. This min-max approach remains today a viable application of the experimental paradigm to educational phenomena. By virtue of its goal of decontextualizing phenomena it cannot, of course, address many important questions. Ecological validity remains an issue.

Today, as we enter the 1990s, research dealing with teaching behavior must be described with terms such as eclectic, diverse, or even random. Although limited in quantity, one encounters many different paradigms, or as some (for example, Shulman, 1986) prefer, "research programs." Qualitative approaches are no longer universally viewed as second class and, in the view of some critics (for example, Jarvis, 1981; Lambert, this volume; Erickson, this volume), may have potential to lead to certain kinds of understanding that are not attainable via any other approach. Other approaches, such as case studies, that had once been denigrated, especially by "number crunchers," now occasionally appear in the pages of respected journals.

One conspicuous characteristic of research in classroom behavior is the lack of descriptive research. We have skipped a fundamental step in the evolution of research. Our history is dominated by the several forms of experimental designs that have been delineated. We have asked in many different ways what happens to Y when we manipulate X in particular ways. We have not, however, accomplished the prerequisite steps of describing what happens typically in classrooms with X and Y. Does X have a thousand different renditions in the hands of a thousand different instructors, or does it vary little? We need to know what X is before we can hypothesize how to manipulate it.

Research in any field is not guided by an overseer who can see the total picture and who can direct the process, delineating what is most needed at any given time in the grand scheme of knowledge development. Research is done because of idiosyncratic interests, inclinations, and circumstances. It is prompted by accidental factors such as the proximity of one's office to a colleague with a particular research interest. It is prompted by political factors, such as a decision in Washington to provide funding for research in a particular area.

Within the broad arena of educational research, our historical emphasis on experimental designs places most research in language education into the process-product paradigm. Anderson, Evertson, and Brophy (1979) have described the basic tenets of process-product research:

> . . . to define relationships between what teachers do in the classroom (the processes of teaching) and what happens to their students (the products of learning). . . . Research in this tradition assumes that greater knowledge of such relationships will lead to improved instruction (1979, 193).

Although process-product has been the dominant research mode in classroom behavior research, recently it has lost favor in the larger educational research community. Shulman (1986) suggests that a

> . . . most important reason for the erosion of the process-product program was its unabashedly empirical and nontheoretical tenor. Even as it moved to experimental treatments, the emphasis was pragmatically on what worked, rather than on why it worked. Causes were sought in behaviors, not in theoretically meaningful mechanisms or explanations. The perspective was that of engineering rather than that of science or even of history (1986, 13).

This research, in effect, was designed to identify means-ends relationships. Although that is a limited goal in the grand scheme of inquiry, means-ends relationships can be seen as foundations for testing more specific hypotheses and for theory building. Occasionally, such relationships have enormous value in and of themselves. The classic example is aspirin, whose workings are still not well understood but whose effects are well established.

In the broad educational research community, Fenstermacher (1986) sees a positive trend toward a more pluralistic approach to inquiry.

> Educational research currently makes use of a number of different methods, many of them classifiable as either quantitative or qualitative. Depending on how they are applied in specific contexts, quantitative methods are also known as confirmatory, hypothesis testing, or predictive methods. Qualitative methods are also often known as exploratory, hypothesis generating, descriptive, or interpretive methods. Among the techniques of quantitative methods are the experiment, quasi-experiment, correlational study, and survey research. These methods typically employ both logical design and statistical techniques as controls for the collection, analysis, and interpretation of data. Among qualitative methods are the techniques used in ethnography, ethnomethodology, and . . . ecological research (1986, 41).

Shulman (1986) delineates a similar perspective on current educational research.

> [A] healthy current trend is the emergence of more complex research designs and research programs that include concern for a wide range of determinants influencing teaching practice and its consequences. These "hybrid" designs, which mix experiment with ethnography, multiple regressions with multiple case studies, process-product designs with analyses of student mediation, sur-

veys with personal diaries, are exciting new developments in the study of teaching (1986, 4).

The reign of quantitative methods in both psychology and education for most of this century has now clearly been altered.

> Over the last two decades . . . the pristine splendor of the experiment has accumulated more tarnish than patina. . . . Perhaps the most damaging attack on quantitative methods came from the critics of behaviorism, who saw the experiment, the covering law (hypothetic-deductive) model of explanation, the generalizability criterion, and many of the other trappings of predictive inquiry as part and parcel of the research tradition of behaviorism. . . . As behaviorists sought to make their inquiries "truly scientific," they adopted the procedures and controls that brought them as close as possible to methodological isomorphism with the natural sciences.
>
> The problems with this approach are now rather well-known among social scientists. The methods of the physical sciences are grounded in presuppositions and assumptions that pertain to events, activities, and phenomena generally without will and purpose; things like atoms, molecules, ball bearings, and planets. As psychologists adopted these physical science methods, they also imported the presuppositions and assumptions under-girding them (e.g., causal regularities, law-like generalizations, predictability, and near-perfect confirmation). To make these methods work, behaviorists either had to ignore the telic properties of human behavior, or deny that human beings had the capacity to act with purpose (including the capacity to act stupidly or inconsistently) (Fenstermacher, 1986, 41–42).

PROSPECTS

Essential issues for the future center around who does the research, how they are enabled to do it, and what kinds of research they will do. First, we must acknowledge that the number of individuals who have the requisite expertise remains small. Those who do most of the language teaching have scholarship skills in areas other than inquiry into educational phenomena. Language and literary scholarship is different from educational research, and the preparation of teachers for elementary and secondary schools does not (and really cannot) include research methodology. Contrary to some claims, research—as the term has been used here—is not synonymous with a teacher's problem solving, which is sometimes called action research.

> The purpose of research is to generate knowledge—to come to understand. The purpose of action research is to solve a problem—to "make something work." These are very different aims. A person with the aim of understanding will not behave in the same way as a person with the aim of solving a problem. This is a fundamental difference that is often overlooked or misunderstood—probably because knowledge generated in research is subsequently often used to solve problems, though not in a simplistic, direct manner (Jarvis, 1981).

What then is an appropriate role for the instructor in research? Strong arguments can be made for a genuinely *collaborative* role. This same label was often used in the past to refer to a situation in which the instructor simply granted permission to the researcher to do research "on" the class. That arrangement was hierarchical with the researcher at the top and the instructor at the bottom, and it rarely led to productive research. It has been characterized by the anecdote about the teacher in the high school faculty lounge who, upon seeing the car from the state university pull up in front of the high school, said, "Here they come from State U to do research on us." A new teacher asks, "Where is State U?" The first responds, "Twenty-two miles down the road and twenty-six miles up in the air."

Genuinely collaborative research creates new potential. First, nearly all complex matters are better managed by teamed expertise than by a single individual. Any scholar will be a more successful researcher if multiple perspectives enter into the design of the research. Experienced researchers recognize that it is the planning of research, not the doing, that is the challenge in successful research.

Second, we have come to understand that the way in which instructors conceptualize their roles or make decisions is important in the educational process. Access to instructor thinking provides an additional perspective on the behavior occurring in the classroom.

Third, the kinds of research questions that are asked are likely to be shaped by the interaction between the two (or more) kinds of expertise. One's orientation and day-to-day activity inevitably influence the kind of inquiry in which one engages. Experienced researchers are more likely, for example, to pursue questions that are more easily answered. An instructor is oriented toward what he or she really feels a need to know. The dynamic tension between such different perspectives is itself healthy for a profession like ours.

Last of all, collaborative research, occurring enough times with enough language teachers, will influence the attitudes of practitioners. There is no doubt that we disadvantage ourselves with attitudes that reject research for the "real" first-hand insight that we gain in our own teaching.

The preparation of researchers must improve. One should not encounter dissertation titles that resemble "A Manual for the Teaching of. . . ." Foreign and second language education programs have to demand strong research methodology skills from their students. It was only a decade ago that inclusion of a single statistics course in such programs was viewed primarily as a novelty. Now it is clear that strong sequences of quantitative and qualitative methodology courses as well as research practicum experiences that precede the dissertation are needed. Graduate students should have opportunities to participate in faculty research programs. Thus, there is a need for programs that have a critical resource mass to achieve such activity.

Once such individuals are employed—and more and more of them are being employed in language departments—they must be rigorously but fairly evaluated for promotion and tenure. *Fairly* is a challenging term in this context. The research that they do is very different from that of their departmental peers. It is from a different tradition, and it entails different kinds of expertise in making judgments about it. What should not be different is the standard of excellence. In major universities such individuals should be promoted because they have done competent peer-reviewed research, not because they have conducted teacher workshops, written "how-to" articles, or served as officers in professional organizations.

The type of research that is done must continue to diversify methodologically. Inquiry becomes a matter of asking what we want to find out and then how we can get that information. The *how* requires artful design. There is considerable risk in this direction; the "newer" approaches and hybrid designs do not follow clear principles and procedures. They require a great deal of decision-making and planning without clear models to imitate. They risk, therefore, creating an impression of disorganization where any activity qualifies as research. On the contrary, this research requires greater skill than that which follows established convention.

We need many *descriptive* studies utilizing all research methodologies and hybrid combinations of them. What is happening in language teaching? What is the range of lenses that we can use to understand teaching and learning behavior? Is there great diversity from classroom to classroom or relatively little? How is time used? In what ways do students become active in the classroom? What does the instructor's behavior indicate about his or her conception of language learning? The questions are endless. They must be answered, however, prior to our becoming able to manipulate variables in order to observe their effects on other variables.

The second needed emphasis is research on learning. Only when we better understand language learning will we be able to improve our teaching practice. We benefit in this late twentieth century from the ready availability of technology. Enormous amounts of student data can be collected, organized, and analyzed in unobtrusive ways via readily accessible microcomputers. Control, efficiency, and accessibility to important student variables can now be achieved as never before.

The vehicles for disseminating our knowledge remain insufficient. Some journals have not been able to overcome their schizoid approach to goals: do they provide "how-to" manuscripts for the large number of practitioners among their subscribers, or do they dedicate pages to research that will today be read by a small number of peers? The issue is complicated by uncertainty about how many practitioners really read any content in the journals. Similar comments can be made about the professional conferences in our field.

Second, some of the journals in which our literature appears are tangential to our field. They may be outstanding in terms of their linguistic, literary, or general education manuscripts, but they are less regularly read by the professionals who would do research on language classroom behavior.

New potential for sharing research results may result from technological advances. A network—perhaps a version of electronic mail or a bulletin board, on which research reports could be shared, and with reactions to them available to everyone on the network as a permanent part of the "folio"—could dramatically increase our research dialogue. Research is often a lonely activity, and it should not be.

Perhaps the most important change of all is a needed change in attitudes, for increased faith in the potential of inquiry into classroom behavior. Such a posture will lead to a badly needed increase in the volume of research. We cannot progress if our research is done by graduate students and assistant professors who remain active only until they are tenured. We cannot expect needed levels of research funding if research is viewed as a fringe activity. We must recognize that knowledge development is a slow process. Too many decision makers—and I particularly single out those in funding agencies—are not sufficiently patient. They fund glamorous model programs, for example, and then wonder why they are never replicated elsewhere.

Exhortations for more research are not new. What is new is the opportunity created by the current context. The value of cross-cultural understanding is increasingly recognized; technology is empowering us; and the human resources are gradually becoming available. *Carpe diem* would be a wise motto for language education.

REFERENCES

Anderson, L., C. Evertson, and J. Brophy. 1979. "An Experimental Study of Effective Teaching in First-Grade Reading Groups." *Elementary School Journal* 79: 193–223.

Benseler, David P. 1988. "Doctoral Degrees Granted in Foreign Language in 1987." *Modern Language Journal* 72: 304–17.

Carroll, John B. 1960. "Wanted: A Research Basis for Educational Policy on Foreign Language Teaching." *Harvard Educational Review* 30: 128–40.

Charters, W. W. 1922. "Regulating the Project." *Journal of Educational Research* 5: 245–46.

Chastain, K. A., and F. J. Woerdehoff. 1968. "A Methodological Study Comparing the Audio-Lingual Habit Theory and the Cognitive-Code Learning Theory." *Modern Language Journal* 52: 268–79.

Fenstermacher, Gary D. 1986. "Philosophy of Research on Teaching: Three Aspects." *Handbook of Research on Teaching*. Ed. Merlin C. Wittrock. 3rd ed. New York: Macmillan Publishing Company. 37–49.

Jarvis, Gilbert A. 1970. "A Comparison of Contextualized Practice with Particularized Referents versus Practice with Generic Meaning in the Teaching of Beginning College French." Diss. Purdue University.

———. 1981. "Action Research versus Needed Research for the 1980's." *Proceedings of the National Conference on Professional Priorities*. Ed. Dale L. Lange. Hastings-on-Hudson, N.Y.: ACTFL Materials Center.

Joiner, Elizabeth G. 1974. "Communicative versus Non-Communicative Language Practice in the Teaching of Beginning College French: A Comparison of Two Treatments." Diss. Ohio State University.

Rivers, Wilga M. 1964. *The Psychologist and the Foreign Language Teacher.* Chicago: University of Chicago Press.

Schaeffer, Reiner H. 1979. "A Comparison Between Computer-Supplemented Structural and Semantic Drill Practice with Beginning College German Students: An Experiment." Diss. Ohio State University.

Shulman, Lee A. 1986. "Paradigms and Research Programs in the Study of Teaching: A Contemporary Perspective." *Handbook of Research on Teaching.* Ed. Merlin C. Wittrock. 3rd ed. New York: Macmillan Publishing Company. 3–46.

Smith. Philip D. 1970. *A Comparison of the Cognitive and Audio-Lingual Approaches to Foreign Language Instruction: The Pennsylvania Foreign Language Project.* Philadelphia: Center for Curriculum Development.

Stern, H. H., and Jim Cummins. 1981. "Language Teaching/Learning Research: A Canadian Perspective on Status and Directions." *Action for the 80's: A Political, Professional, and Public Program for Foreign Language Education.* ACTFL Foreign Language Education Series. Ed. June K. Phillips. Skokie, Ill.: National Textbook Company. 195–248.

Research Design in Foreign Language Acquisition Research

The Design and Psycholinguistic Motivation of Research on Foreign Language Learning

Michael H. Long

University of Hawaii at Manoa

Data-based study of foreign language learning and teaching has a relatively brief history, yet three major phases in such research can already be discerned. The phases overlap to some degree, but there is a clear chronology nonetheless, and given the history of language teaching this century, a certain logic to the sequence: product-oriented methods comparisons; process-oriented microstudies; and process-process and process-product experiments.

PHASE 1: PRODUCT-ORIENTED METHODS COMPARISONS

The 1950s and 1960s were a time of some confidence in foreign language teaching. The (U.S.) "army method" had supposedly been used successfully in training certain kinds of language learners during World War II, and neo-behaviorist psychologists and structuralist linguists claimed to have understood human learning and human language, respectively. Consequently, related teaching methods and approaches (such as the ALM and the aural-oral approach) received widespread and initially uncritical acceptance in many parts of the world. Moreover, since particular methods and approaches were believed to work, it is understandable that the constructs themselves went unchallenged and were considered suitable for manipulation in experimental work. Thus, whereas research typically proceeds from description through correlation to experiment, the first phase of second language classroom research, the so-called comparative methods studies, bypassed the first two stages and attempted to address outcomes and causal relationships from the outset.

Again, perhaps reflecting the optimism of the times, most European and North American comparative methods studies of the 1960s and early 1970s were large-scale, long-term, general, and product-oriented. The typical procedure was for researchers to use proficiency tests to evaluate the progress of fairly large numbers of students in intact classes over relatively long periods (often one or two years) while half the teachers supposedly used one method or approach, for example, audiolingual or inductive, and half used another, for example, grammar-translation or deductive. The studies were general in that whole teaching methods or approaches were ostensibly being manipulated simply because certain programs or schools were labeled as using a particular method or approach. They were product-oriented in that the dependent variables were almost exclusively proficiency test scores or gain scores. Little or no consideration was given to the classroom teaching and learning processes that produced the scores. Process-product relationships were largely ignored.

Well-known examples of this kind of research in the United States were the Colorado and Pennsylvania Projects (Scherer and Wertheimer, 1964; Smith, 1970). These and other comparative methods studies generally reported short-lived advantages or no advantage for one method or approach over another. As has often been pointed out, however, since researchers rarely examined what was actually going on in the classrooms concerned, there was no way of knowing whether teachers had adhered uniquely to the method or approach they were supposed to have been using, that is, whether the "treatments" had been delivered, or if so, delivered to the right groups. (For review, see Allwright, 1983; Long, 1980; Mitchell, 1985; Oskarsson, 1972). That this concern was justified is suggested strongly by the findings of more recent studies, which *have* looked inside classrooms or have debriefed teachers after a study was completed and found considerable overlap between methods and approaches and a lack of clarity in teachers' minds as to differences between them, even after those teachers received explicit training in the methods and approaches (see, for example, Swaffar, Arens, and Morgan, 1982; Spada, 1987; Nunan, 1987).

PHASE 2: PROCESS-ORIENTED MICROSTUDIES

The failure of the comparative methods studies to produce meaningful results bred a healthy appreciation of the complexity of foreign language learning among a new generation of researchers. As a result, whereas work in phase 1 had been large-scale, long-term, general, and product-oriented, most second language classroom research in the 1970s and 1980s was small-scale, short-term, particular, and process-oriented. Experiment and quasi-experiment gave way to description—the reverse of the normal cycle—with the majority of studies now ignoring product data and process-product relationships and instead focusing exclusively on the details of language use surrounding pedagogic processes.

Phase 2 studies (which are still continuing and still needed) have tended to be small-scale and short-term for the simple reason that this kind of work is extremely labor-intensive and, like most language teaching classroom research, is usually funded out of researchers' pockets. In fact, with the exception of the diary studies (for review, see Bailey and Ochsner, 1983) and a tiny number of true ethnographic inquiries (for example, Ulichny, 1989; and for review, Watson-Gegeo, 1988; Watson-Gegeo and Ulichny, 1988), almost all the the second generation work has been cross-sectional, with consequently severe limitations on what can be investigated and the kinds of claims that can be made. Findings are frequently based on one lesson each by just three or four teachers and their students, sometimes on just a single lesson.

The amount of work involved in producing even the limited findings of most phase 2 studies is difficult to appreciate unless one has done this kind of research. Discovering what goes on in language teaching means getting inside classrooms, or at the very least getting a tape recorder inside, and this in turn involves often lengthy and delicate negotiations with administrators, parents, teachers, and students, and then hours of observation to collect the data. There follow many more hours spent in transcribing audio or video tapes (usually around ten hours for every hour of classroom recording, even for a rough transcription) and in verifying the transcription, time to develop operational definitions of analytic categories, to train coders in the system of analysis and to conduct one or more inter-rater reliability checks, and then time to code the transcripts—all this just to get the data into a form that can be quantified (for a review of procedures, see Chaudron, Crookes, and Long, 1988). In contrast, where product data are concerned, thousands of proficiency test answer sheets, attitude inventories, and the like can be machine-scored and the results manipulated statistically by a computer in a fraction of the time.

Phase 2 studies are particular in that they typically concentrate on just one aspect of classroom discourse, ignoring much more than the immediate context in which the phenomenon of interest occurs. A study of the language elicited by different types of pedagogic tasks, for example, may code student talk for evidence of various kinds of negotiation work and for syntactic complexity, but say nothing about the grammatical accuracy of the language produced, the relationship of performance on those task types to teacher-supervised lockstep work in the same lessons, or about the kinds of power relationships operating in the class and the wider school and societal context. Examples include studies of turn-taking (Allwright, 1980), feedback on error (Chaudron, 1977), teacher questions (Long and Sato, 1983), ethnic styles in classroom discourse (Sato, 1982), task type and incorporation of corrective feedback (Crookes and Rulon, 1985) and negotiation work in interlanguage talk (Varonis and Gass, 1985). (For review, see Allwright, 1988; Chaudron, 1988; van Lier, 1988).

Research of this kind is sometimes criticized for "atomizing" classroom life and ignoring setting variables. The validity of its findings is questioned for being decontextualized and, as a result, for the research failing to *explain* the processes being studied. However, a careful reading shows that researchers doing this kind of work have generally been extremely circumspect in reporting their results and have rarely claimed to be providing either the only possible analysis of a phenomenon or (because of the labor involved) more than partial descriptions, whose cumulative impact it is hoped will be useful. Such criticisms also miss the point that the primary purpose of these studies is to *describe* classroom processes so that they may later be systematically manipulated in experimental work. It would be premature and unwarranted to make causal claims on the basis of descriptive studies or to offer anything more than hypotheses as to potential explanations of the findings.

Phase 2 studies have not been without some serious shortcomings, nevertheless. Thus, however understandable, *n*-sizes have undoubtedly been too small to support the generalizations made in some studies, and they have usually involved convenience samples. Interobserver agreement data are seldom reported, meaning that the reliability of analyses is questionable, especially in a field that often employs high inference category systems. Where existing observation instruments and analytic categories have been employed (for example, interaction and discourse analysis systems devised by Flanders, Moskowitz, Bellack, Sinclair and Coulthard, Fanselow, and others), there has typically been no attempt to establish either the reliability of their application or their validity for the studies concerned. Findings are often unquantified or not analyzed statistically, meaning that the reader is offered sample utterances or excerpts from transcripts with no idea how representative they were of the corpus involved, much less of language teaching in general. Finally, no attempt is made to relate findings to product data, and even the potential relevance to language learning of some process phenomena that have been studied remains a mystery.

Limited and occasionally flawed though they have been, phase 2 studies have nonetheless produced many useful findings. As Fanselow (1977) has pointed out, the procedures and systems that researchers have developed for recording and analysing classroom process data have provided a common language (or several dialects, at least) through which not only researchers but also trainees and teacher educators can discuss teaching and learning intelligibly. It is frustrating for novice teachers to be told to "involve the students more" or that they need to "vary their questions," for example. Such admonitions are impressionistic, vague, and uninformative. Conversely, if a supervisor can tell the same trainees that they spoke 80% of the time and their students 20%, that 90% of the questions they asked were "known information" or "display" questions (What's my name? Is Tokyo the capital of Japan?), that 75% of those questions occurred as general solicits, and that, as found in studies of ethnic differences in classroom turn-taking, (say) the Japanese students in the class did not offer a response to any of those soliciting moves, whereas Chinese and other, non-Asian, students did, then the supervisor's feedback is likely to be (and to be perceived as being) objective, precise, and nonarbitrary.

Further, if trainees are told that some proven alternatives include use of "referential" questions (Do you agree? In your opinion, which city would be a better capital, and why?) and encoding some of them as directed solicits first, then the feedback is likely to give (and to be perceived as giving) specific, usable information about at least some mechanisms by which the current state of affairs can be changed, should such changes be thought desirable.

The findings of phase 2 studies have also made it possible for methodologists, materials writers, and program designers to discuss a number of foreign language classroom phenomena with some objective understanding of what they involve. Terms like *question, error correction, teacher-fronted, group work,* and *grammar teaching,* for example, now have some empirical content. We know something about the kinds of questions teachers ask, about the kinds of errors they ignore and "correct" and the most frequent forms the "corrections" take, about differences in the quality and quantity of language use in teacher-fronted lockstep work and small-group and pair work, and about how that varies according to certain characteristics of the tasks that teachers and learners are engaged in.

Another common finding of phase 2 studies is that the constructs, *method* and *approach,* ostensibly manipulated in phase 1 studies, have little validity or relevance at the classroom level. Researchers have consistently found few differences between lessons supposedly taught using different methods, teachers supposedly trained to teach different methods, teachers believing they were using different methods, and lessons using materials supposedly embodying different methods, suggesting that at the classroom level, methods do not exist (for review, see Long, 1988a, 1989; Nunan, 1988). This in turn makes them weak candidates for manipulation in process-product studies and argues for deeper analysis to identify more promising variables for phase 3 research.

PHASE 3: PROCESS-PROCESS AND PROCESS-PRODUCT EXPERIMENTS

While the descriptive, process-oriented microstudies of phase 2 are still needed and continue on a variety of topics, reports from a new, third phase in modern foreign language research have already begun to appear in the literature. Phase 3 studies manipulate one or more classroom process variables and endeavor to relate the modifications either to changes in other processes or to variance in learning outcomes. The process-process and process-product studies of phase 3 can be seen as renewed attempts to achieve the goals set by the phase 1 comparative methods studies, but with several important differences.

Foremost among the improvements observable is that the recent studies are better informed about the variables that can be manipulated, since researchers now have descriptions available from phase 2 research about what actually goes on in foreign language classrooms. Second, many researchers doing the phase 3 work have learned the importance of carefully monitoring classroom processes in their studies in order to ascertain whether the variables selected for manipulation are in fact successfully isolated, that is, whether the intended treatments are delivered to the appropriate groups. Third, the new studies eschew "method" as a variable for manipulation.

There are several interesting lines of work under way involving process-process relationships. Two simple examples concern the possible connections between question types and student production, and the effects of two types of input modification on student comprehension. In the first case, preliminary findings suggest that teachers can easily learn to increase the frequency with which they employ referential questions (those to which the speaker does not know the answer) in their lessons, and that those referential questions elicit significantly longer utterances, syntactically more complex utterances, more use of sentential connectives, more utterances per turn, and more communicative language use from learners than do display questions (see, for example, Long, Brock, Crookes, Deicke, Potter, and Zhang, 1984; Brock, 1986; Tollefson, 1988).

Where input comprehensibility is concerned, several researchers have taken findings from descriptive studies of processes in foreigner talk and teacher talk (for review, see Long, 1983; Chaudron, 1988) and applied them to the design of listening and reading comprehension materials. Studies have found that modifying spoken or written discourse by *elaboration* of texts in various ways achieves improvements in student comprehension over that of unmodified (native speaker) baseline texts equal to the improvements achieved by traditional linguistic simplification of the same texts (see, for example, Brown, 1987; Long, 1985; Pica, Doughty, and Young, 1986; and for review, Parker and Chaudron, 1987). This finding is of potential significance for language teaching, since the traditional approach to text simplification obtains the improvement in comprehension by reducing sentence length and removing both unknown lexis and complex syntax from the input, modifications that are counterproductive as far as language development is concerned, because they deny learners exposure to precisely the unknown items they need to learn.

There has been relatively little process-product research to date, but it has begun to appear. A study by Spada (1987) will serve to illustrate the interesting work of that kind. Using a quasi-experimental design, Spada monitored processes in three intact ESL classes over a six-week period using the COLT (Communicative Orientation of Language Teaching) observation system (Allen, Frolich, and Spada, 1984), and then tested for relationships between interclass differences in the degree of focus on language form and student scores on a variety of post-test proficiency measures. Although one class was found to spend between one and one-half and three times as much time on overtly form-focused instruction as the other two, the difference between classes was not statistically significant, and improvement in grammatical accuracy assessed by ANCOVA was also found not to differ across classes.

Although it produced null findings in this instance, the design of Spada's study is indicative in some respects of the kind of work to be hoped for in phase 3, notably in its choice of a previously documented classroom process as the independent variable; in its systematic monitoring of classroom instruction in the study; its use of an observation system specifically developed for use in language teaching classrooms; and in its focus on links between process and product. Moreover, the study built on research findings in second language acquisition, which had identified the issue of focus on form as a likely candidate for promoting certain aspects of language development.

Additional examples of psycholinguistically motivated experimental work are to be found in the growing body of research on the role of instruction in second language learning. These phase 3 studies no longer select items for instruction in the intuitive or arbitrary manner of structural and notional-functional syllabi. Rather, building on second language acquisition research on developmental sequences, investigators target particular grammatical constructions at particular times for particular learners, the decisions in various studies being made with reference to theories of speech processing, learnability, and markedness (see, for example, Pienemann, 1984; Eckman, Bell, and Nelson, 1988; Doughty, 1988). To date, at least, a salient characteristic of these studies is that they work. Unlike so many earlier efforts, instruction is found to make a difference in these studies, presumably because researchers are using theories of second language acquisition, which guide them to the right places to look for its effects.

The study by Spada (1987) is interesting also because it reveals some methodological problems that remain to be addressed in phase 3 work. These include the need for true experiments, not only in order to demonstrate causal relationships, but also because of the control that experimental work offers the investigator. Quasi-experimentation typically means that two or more learner or setting variables are confounded due to lack of random assignment of subjects to treatment groups, with the usual problems in analysis and interpretation this creates. The use of natural intact groups also means, however, that the outcome of a study rests in the hands of the teachers and students in an additional undesirable sense in that, as was the case in Spada's study, the researcher has little chance of ensuring that the treatments of interest are sufficiently differentiated and delivered, especially over time. A possible solution to the lowering of external validity, which is the price of such control, is the combination of parallel lines of quasi- and true experimental research on the same issue, in an effort to determine whether results from work with intact groups and laboratory studies will converge on the same findings. If they do, each kind of work can be used to compensate for the admitted weaknesses of the other, that is, problems of internal validity with quasi-experiments and external validity with true experiments.

A final methodological issue needing attention is the question of theoretical motivation. This has been a weakness in all three phases of research on foreign language acquisition. In phase 1, even if the comparative methods studies had been free of other methodological problems, it would have been difficult to know how to interpret an advantage for one method over another, since the individual methods studied were never chosen as representative of superordinate categories, for example, cognitivist or behaviorist, input rich or input poor, and structurally isolating or nonisolating.

In phase 2 research, the use of convenience samples and inadequate n-sizes has frequently precluded generalization of potentially interesting findings from the individual cases studied to teachers, learners, or materials of particular types. In addition, the motivation for studying some classroom processes at all has often been left to the imagination of the reader rather than explained by the researcher. For example, systems of discourse analysis, such as those of Bellack, Kliebard, Hyman, and Smith (1966) and Sinclair and Coulthard (1975), have frequently been applied to classroom foreign language data by researchers ostensibly interested in improving language learning and teaching. Each system has proven itself a highly useful research tool for other purposes, but neither was developed with language learning classrooms in mind or has any obvious relevance to language learning issues. The categories they employ may yet turn out to be relevant, of course, but these and other systems currently seem to be adopted not for that reason, but rather because they have gained academic respectability in other fields or simply because they exist.

Similarly, in phase 3, some of the process-process work is being conducted at too low a level of abstraction to permit potentially useful generalizations. To illustrate, several studies of relationships between pedagogic tasks and interlanguage use compare performance only on single tasks in two or more categories, yet individual tasks themselves have little or no interest beyond a particular study or program. It is the language development potential of *task types* that is of interest. To investigate that issue efficiently, researchers need to employ at least two tasks in each of two or more categories, to define and operationalize the categories, and to classify the tasks in their study into those superordinate categories before the study begins, using criteria independent of the interlanguage performance data (see Crookes (1986) for a review of task-classification possibilities). Failure to address task classification a priori delegates to third-party reviewers the hazardous job of *post hoc* classification, interpretation and generalization (see, for example, Long, 1989). The lack of a common theoretical framework makes the problem more difficult and increases the chance of error, because the original researchers often have used similar labels with different meanings or, more often, have addressed different dimensions of tasks. As with any theoretically unmotivated research program, some of the current work is less likely to be cumulative, since the choice of which dimensions of tasks to study is unprincipled, for lack of the guidance that a theory provides when conceptualizing and designing research. This is not an efficient use of time or money.

Work on error correction is in a similar state. Otherwise rather well-designed process-product studies (for example, Robb, Ross, and Shortreed, 1986) continue to find no effect for error treatment, yet if a focus on form facilitates language development as research findings indicate it does (for review, see Long, 1988b), it is surely predictable that error treatment should help, too, and for the same reasons. A way of improving on the experimental work on error correction thus far would be to target two sets of errors in a corpus (and to ignore the remainder): one set that a theory of second language acquisition predicts would benefit from treatment and one set that the same theory predicts would not. The current approach is to target all errors indiscriminately, a procedure that several different second language acquisition theories independently predict will be unsuccessful.

Last but not least, it would be especially appropriate for researchers who do motivate their studies theoretically (and an increasing number do) to pay particular attention to the *psycholinguistic* rationale for their work, and more specifically, to theory and research findings in second language acquisition. The ultimate goal of this work, after all, is to facilitate classroom foreign language development.

REFERENCES

Allen, John P. B., Maria Frolich, and Nina Spada. 1984. "The Communicative Orientation of Language Teaching: An Observation Scheme." *On TESOL '83: The Question of Control.* Eds. John Handscombe, Richard A. Orem, and Barry Taylor. Washington, D.C.: TESOL. 231–52.

Allwright, Richard L. 1980. "Turns, Topics and Tasks: Patterns of Participation in Language Learning and Teaching." *Discourse Analysis in Second Language Research.* Ed. Diane Larsen-Freeman. Rowley, Mass.: Newbury House. 165–87.

———. 1983. "Classroom-Centered Research on Language Teaching and Learning: An Overview." *TESOL Quarterly* 17: 191–217.

———. 1988. *Observation in the Language Classroom.* London: Longman.

Bailey, Kathleen M., and Robert Ochsner. 1983. "A Methodological Review of the Diary Studies: Windmill Tilting or Social Science?" *Classroom-Oriented Research in Second Language Acquisition.* Eds. Herbert W. Seliger and Michael H. Long. Rowley, Mass.: Newbury House. 188–98.

Bellack, Arno, Herbert M. Kliebard, Ronald T. Hyman, and Frank L. Smith. 1966. *The Language of the Classroom.* New York: Teachers College Press.

Brock, Cynthia. 1986. "The Effects of Referential Questions on ESL Classroom Discourse." *TESOL Quarterly* 20: 47–59.

Brown, Ronald. 1987. "A Comparison of the Comprehensibility of Modified and Unmodified Reading Materials for ESL." *University of Hawaii Working Papers in ESL* 6: 49–79.

Chaudron, Craig. 1977. "A Descriptive Model of Discourse in the Corrective Treatment of Learners' Errors." *Language Learning* 27: 29–46.

———. 1983. "Foreigner Talk in the Classroom—An Aid to Learning?" *Classroom-Oriented Research in Second Language Acquisition.* Eds. Herbert W. Seliger and Michael H. Long: 127–43.

———. 1988. *Second Language Classrooms: Research on Teaching and Learning.* Cambridge: Cambridge UP.

Chaudron, Craig, Graham Crookes, and Michael H. Long. 1988. *Reliability and Validity in Second Language Classroom Research.* Technical Report No. 8. Honolulu: Center for Second Language Classroom Research, Social Science Research Institute, University of Hawaii at Manoa.

Crookes, Graham. 1986. *Task Classification: A Cross-Disciplinary Review.* Technical Report No. 4. Honolulu: Center for Second Language Classroom Research, Social Science Research Institute, University of Hawaii at Manoa.

Crookes, Graham, and Katherine Rulon. 1985. *Incorporation of Corrective Feedback in Native Speaker/Non-Native Speaker Conversation.* Technical Report

No. 3. Honolulu: Center for Second Language Classroom Research, Social Science Research Institute, University of Hawaii at Manoa.

Doughty, Catherine. 1988. "The Effect of Instruction on the Acquisition of Relativization in ESL." Unpublished Ph.D. Diss. Philadelphia: University of Pennsylvania.

Eckman, Fred R., Lawrence Bell, and Diane Nelson. 1988. "On the Generalization of Relative Clause Instruction in the Acquisition of English as a Second Language." *Applied Linguistics* 9: 1–20.

Fanselow, John F. 1977. "Beyond 'Rashomon'—Conceptualizing and Describing the Teaching Act." *TESOL Quarterly* 11: 17–39.

Long, Michael H. 1980. "Inside the 'Black Box': Methodological Issues in Classroom Research on Language Learning." *Language Learning* 30: 1–42.

———. 1983. "Linguistic and Conversational Adjustments to Non-Native Speakers." *Studies in Second Language Acquisition* 5: 177–93.

———. 1985. "Input and Second Language Acquisition Theory." *Input in Second Language Acquisition.* Eds. Susan M. Gass and Carolyn G. Madden. Rowley, Mass.: Newbury House. 377–93.

———. 1988a. "Focus on Form: A Design Feature in Language Teaching Methodology." Paper presented at the National Foreign Language Center/European Cultural Foundation Conference on Empirical Research on Second Language Learning in Instructional Settings. Bellagio, Italy, Rockefeller Center, June 20–24.

———. 1988b. "Instructed Interlanguage Development." *Issues in Second Language Acquisition: Multiple Perspectives.* Ed. Leslie M. Beebe. New York: Newbury House/Harper and Row. 115–41.

———. 1989. "Task, Group and Task-Group Interactions." Plenary address to the RELC Regional Seminar: Language Teaching Methodology for the Nineties, Singapore, April 10–14.

Long, Michael H. and Charlene J. Sato. 1983. "Classroom Foreigner Talk Discourse: Forms and Functions of Teachers' Questions." *Classroom-Oriented Research in Second Language Acquisition.* Eds. Herbert W. Seliger and Michael H. Long. Rowley, Mass.: Newbury House: 268–85.

Long, Michael H., Cynthia Brock, Graham Crookes, Carla Deicke, Lynn Potter, and Shuquiang Zhang. 1984. *The Effects of Teachers' Questioning Patterns and Wait-Time on Pupil Participation in Public High School Classes in Hawaii for Students of Limited English Proficiency.* Technical Report No. 1. Honolulu: Center for Second Language Classroom Research, Social Science Research Institute, University of Hawaii at Manoa.

Mitchell, Rosalind. 1985. "Process Research in Second Language Classrooms." *Language Teaching* 18: 330–52.

Nunan, David. 1987. "Communicative Language Teaching: Making it Work." *English Language Teaching Journal* 41: 136–45.

————. 1988. *The Learner-Centered Curriculum*. Cambridge: Cambridge UP.

Oskarsson, Mats. 1972. "Comparative Methods Studies in Foreign Language Teaching." *Moderna Sprak* 56: 350–66.

Parker, Katherine, and Craig Chaudron. 1987. "The Effects of Linguistic Simplification and Elaborative Modifications on L2 Comprehension." *University of Hawaii Working Papers in ESL* 6: 107–33.

Pica, Teresa, Catherine Doughty, and Richard Young. 1986. "Making Input Comprehensible: Do Interactional Modifications Help?" *ITL Review of Applied Linguistics* 72: 1–25.

Pienemann, Manfred. 1984. "Psychological Constraints on the Teachability of Languages." *Studies in Second Language Acquisition* 6: 186–214.

Robb, Thom, Stephen Ross, and Ian Shortreed. 1986. "Salience of Feedback on Error and Its Effect on EFL Writing Quality." *TESOL Quarterly* 20: 83–95.

Sato, Charlene J. 1982. "Ethnic Styles in Classroom Discourse." *On TESOL '81*. Eds. Mary Hynes and William Rutherford. Washington, D.C.: TESOL. 11–24.

Scherer, George A. C., and Michael Wertheimer. 1964. *A Psycholinguistic Experiment in Foreign Language Teaching*. New York: McGraw-Hill.

Seliger, Herbert W., and Michael H. Long, eds. 1983. *Classroom-Oriented Research in Second Language Acquisition*. Rowley, Mass.: Newbury House.

Sinclair, John McH., and Malcolm Coulthard. 1975. *Towards an Analysis of Discourse*. Oxford: Oxford UP.

Smith, Phillip D. 1970. *A Comparison of the Cognitive and Audiolingual Approaches to Foreign Language Instruction: The Pennsylvania Foreign Language Project*. Philadelphia: Center for Curriculum Development.

Spada, Nina. 1987. "Relationships Between Instructional Differences and Learning Outcomes: A Process-Product Study of Communicative Language Teaching." *Applied Linguistics* 8: 137–61.

Swaffar, Janet K., Katherine Arens, and Michelle Morgan. 1982. "Teacher Classroom Practices: Redefining Method as Task Hierarchy." *Modern Language Journal* 66: 24–33.

Tollefson, James. 1988. "Measuring Communication in ESL/EFL Classes." *Cross Currents* 15: 37–46.

Ulichny, Polly. 1989. "Exploring a Teacher's Practice: Collaborative Research in an Adult ESL Reading Class." Unpublished Ph.D. Diss. Cambridge, Mass.: Harvard University, Graduate School of Education.

van Lier, Leo. 1988. *The Classroom and the Language Learner*. London: Longman.

Varonis, Evangeline, and Susan Gass. 1985. "Non-Native/Non-Native Conversations: A Model for the Negotiation of Meaning." *Applied Linguistics* 6.1: 71–90.

Watson-Gegeo, Karen A. 1988. "Ethnography in ESL: Defining the Essentials." *TESOL Quarterly* 22: 575–92.

Watson-Gegeo, Karen A., and Polly Ulichny. 1988. "Ethnographic Inquiry into Second Language Acquisition and Instruction." *University of Hawaii Working Papers in ESL* 7: 75–92.

Chapter 19

Pros, Cons, and Limits to Quantitative Approaches in Foreign Language Acquisition Research

Wallace E. Lambert

McGill University

I was asked to focus my remarks on the advantages and disadvantages of quantitative approaches and designs in research on foreign language acquisition, with illustrative examples. In addition, the remarks were to be pertinent not only for scholars in this specialized field but also for everyday members of college language faculties who have to deal with classrooms of real, live students.

Two preliminary apologies are in order. First, several of my examples will be drawn from research on elementary or high school youngsters. Even so, I believe they are appropriate for college-level educators because the processes of teaching and learning are fundamentally common ones running their course at all age levels. The examples are also relevant to college educators because the new twists in early language education are affecting large numbers of pupils who are already bringing their new experiences and competencies along with them to college. For instance, the Canadian language "immersion" experience to which I will refer has changed dramatically the recent waves of foreign language (FL) or second language (SL) learners, who expect a great deal more of high school and college FL education than was formerly the case. As a consequence, the goals, means, and overall purpose of college-level courses have had to be modified to accommodate a new breed of FL or SL students.

Second, I should explain, if not apologize, for making comments at all about quantification because actually I see matters of research design as no more than good common sense, and statistical experts as officiators or rule-keepers who have to be tested periodically for their certainty and to be outfoxed when they are inattentive. But I *should* be qualified to talk on this topic because, in years past, I was a statistical assistant for Leon Thurstone and have been a colleague for years of John Carroll, George Ferguson, and Lee Cronbach, who have tried to keep me honest, statistically speaking. Furthermore, I have been knee-deep in quantitative research on language-related issues for many years. That experience has made me a proponent of tight designs and quantitative checkouts because all other alternatives in language research turn out to be too subjective and personally biased. The only way I can see to be tough or rigorous on ourselves and our ideas in this field is to put those ideas to a serious quantitative, experimental test. This bias of mine, however, has clear limits, and what I want to do here is present what I see as the pros and cons of quantitative approaches.

Complying with this topic assignment meant reading recent reports on statistical procedures for dealing with performance changes over time when large-scale evaluation studies are conducted (for example, the papers of Willett, 1988; Bryk and Raudenbush, 1987; and Rogosa, Brandt, and Zimowski, 1982); reading through several large-scale, ongoing empirical studies on foreign language pedagogy in order to get some idea of what is going on in North America; and then, thinking back on my own involvement in studies of language pedagogy and attempting to explain what has been going on in these cases, too.

The upshot of all this is that I have three macroconcerns that will be the schema for organizing the comments to follow. The concerns are bigness versus manageability in the breadth of empirical studies; the nature of "process" in the product versus process debate in empirical research; and the tailoring of design and statistics to accommodate more moderately sized investigations that will be able to explore deep processes or underlying mechanisms.

BIGNESS IN LANGUAGE-RELATED RESEARCH

The United States is big, and research directors as well as fund suppliers seem to want to make their studies big, as if one can keep up the feeling of national unity only if one brings the whole nation or some large region of it into each empirical test of an educational or social innovation. The common argument is that if a researcher has a really strong new pedagogical treatment in hand or a really important teacher or learner characteristic to examine, its effects should be robust enough to emerge even when tested across the nation. Consequently, it is common to hear administrators in federal posts (for example, in the United States Department of Education) say that they have two or three somewhat related empirical studies under way that are national in scope, each at a cost of some five million dollars. The problem I have with this is that one can convincingly argue that there are many nations all within the United States. For example, one recent estimate is that only 14% of the American population have Anglo-Saxon roots, which makes them not much more important than the 13% who have Germanic origins, the 11% who have African roots, the 11% who have Hispanic roots, and so forth (see Sowell, 1983). In fact, I believe that if one were to scale down distances in North America to a European size, it might well be that there are equivalent *culture* differences in a San Diego-Albuquerque-Chicago-Boston network (to take a random example of sites), as there are in a Zurich-Milan-Paris-Amsterdam-London network.

The point is that when research projects become too large, they are forced to overlook the socially distinctive characteristics of regional sites, school districts, schools, and particularly classrooms. To attempt to attend to these potentially distinctive features usually overtaxes the capacities of the research team, and in most cases such issues are bypassed in the search for across-site trends. Researchers usually realize that there are regional, district, and school variations in their data that are clear and possibly significant, but they normally can't deal with them; and this usually means that they are "averaged out." For example, samples of pupils from various schools are amalgamated in a treatment-comparison investigation, even though obvious school-to-school differences in academic atmosphere exist, that is, differences in the attention or priority given to certain subject matter or to learning in general. My argument here is that language-related studies should be kept as small as possible so that regional, district, school, principal, teacher, and student variations can be dealt with adequately. If one were to combine data collected in London and Amsterdam to test out some particular pedagogical approach, one would likely have to overlook enormously different views about language learning in the two sites. But no more so, I would argue, than would transpire in a Boston-Chicago amalgamation.

Here are two examples of bigness troubles that I have in mind. The first is the Baker and de Kanter (1981) review of all methodologically adequate studies of bilingual education up to the 1980s that were developed for language minority children and conducted *across the United States*. The aim of the Baker and de Kanter report was to assess the impact of bilingual educational offerings on math and English achievement scores. The basic criterion for a successful program was that it showed more learning than would have been the case without the program. Setting aside the clear need for either random-assignment controls for those in or outside a bilingual program, or some quasi-experimental approximation (see, for example, Campbell and Boruch, 1975), Baker and de Kanter concluded on the basis of the studies available that bilingual education didn't have much if any positive effect. Overall, perhaps that is a relatively true evaluation, but *overall* in this case covered a multitude of sins. When the patient and insightful Ann Willig (1985) conducted a meta-analysis of the same studies reviewed by Baker and de Kanter, she was able to uncover enough of the sins to come to a much more convincing conclusion and one that was very favorable toward bilingual education. For instance, Willig found, "In every instance where there did not appear to be crucial inequalities between experimental and comparison groups, children in the bilingual programs averaged higher than the comparison children on criterion instruments" (1985, 312). My point here is that much of the confusion in the overview of Baker and de Kanter was due to the fact that they had to look beyond specific cases that were regional, district, or school specific, and it took a Willig not only to consider them but to show their importance. In her conclusions, she makes direct reference to the bigness factor:

The cost of the national Title VII evaluation could have financed several programs that included sound, integrated research in the design. Not only would such an endeavor have produced additional programs for a number of students, it would also have produced information useful for both evaluation and program planning. In discussing the necessity for smaller scale, randomized experiments of educational programs, Campbell & Erlebacher (1970, 207) write, "We are sure that data from 400 children in such an experiment would be far more informative than 4,000 tested by the best of quasi-experiments, to say nothing of an ex post facto study." The results of this synthesis have confirmed that observation (Willig, 1985, 313).

My second example is a research project directed by my good friend, David Ramirez, and I'm an outside adviser on this one. It is big and expensive, but it is a very good one, in large part because the research team was dedicated, interested, and coordinated (Ramirez et al., 1988). The project was solicited by the Department of Education and was designed for Hispanic American children, especially those with limited English proficiency. Its purpose was to test which of three approaches was most effective: early schooling in an all-English program (a type of sink-or-swim option that circumvents the Spanish home language); a traditional transitional bilingual program (wherein some, but not much, Spanish is used in order to assist the children to reprogram themselves into the all-English stream); or a quasi maintenance-of-home-language bilingual program that provides for language arts in Spanish and instruction for part of the day through Spanish. The first option is called the *immersion strategy* program, the second is the *early exit* alternative, where *exit* means out of the program to all-English classes, and the third is late exit, to indicate more emphasis on helping the children juggle two languages and cultures. (Of course, we Canadians dislike the misuse of the term *immersion* in the first case because actually it is a reversal of the intent of immersion education, as I will explain later.)

The implementation of this project has been instructive in several respects. It was a study requested by the government, through the Department of Education (DOE), and was motivated by a keen interest in the potential of the immersion strategy option. My guess is that the immersion-in-English option was congruent with the Reagan administration's views about language minorities, that is, that it is basically un-American to have American citizens or citizens-to-be speaking home languages in American public schools. Things like that, the argument goes, stigmatize minorities and slow their progress toward Americanization. Better to dive right into English and stay away from maintenance bilingual programs or even traditional ones if possible, because both alternatives only stretch out the assimilation period. Since a few districts around the country were trying out an immersion-in-English option, the DOE indicated in the original contract that they wanted a large-scale investigation of the immersion strategy classes then starting and a comparison of them with comparable early exit programs—the most common form of education available for minorities. The study would be restricted to Hispanic children only. Thus, the study was to be big, and also expensive, because it would follow children for a four year period. A small group of experienced research consultants would meet twice a year first to help design the study and then to monitor it.

At the first design-planning meeting, the consultants argued fast and furiously to change the immersion name to *sink-or-swim, submersion, drowning, brainwashing* or some such alternative. But the DOE kept it as *immersion strategy*. Then we argued for the inclusion of one alternative—the late exit option—to add a bit of sunshine to the project, and on this point the DOE was persuaded our way.

Then much time was spent on another exciting approach to the basic question, and this alternative almost worked out. The idea was to run a real experiment comparing the three alternatives. We realized that few district supervisors in the United States could differentiate one of these alternatives from another. In fact, few school principals or teachers in bilingual/bicultural programs in the United States know about alternative approaches to teaching minority children, other than the alternative with which they have been asked to comply. Thus, we had the opportunity to work with one or two districts and to set up, through random placement of pupils, the three alternatives and test their relative effectiveness. Parents certainly were no better informed about the alternatives, and they would likely have been willing to participate, since, as is, they take whatever program the district has decided to offer. This possibility pleased the researchers because it would have satisfied the basic demands of "good" experiments according to Donald Campbell's and Ann Willig's specifications. Note that it would have been relatively small in scale, providing control over district and region effects, the things that a bigger study can't handle properly. In addition, treatment specifications and teacher selection and training could have been easily undertaken and monitored, and most important of all, pupils from a common district or community could have been placed at random in one treatment or another. Later, contrasting communities could be included. But rather than crying over a missed opportunity, we as consultants could adjust to the generosity of DOE to permit the late exit alternative to be added to the contract.

The main point here, however, is that bigness stalks this project, as it does so many American educational evaluations or surveys. Let me illustrate.

1. In order to get a nationwide view of the relative strengths and weaknesses of the three options, five states are included: California, Texas, Florida, New York, and New Jersey (likely equivalents to Moscow, Athens, Bucarest, Amsterdam, and London, in my mind). This spread, it was argued, would give representation to the major Spanish-speaking groups in the United States. But this approach means that little or no attention can be given to the differences in program effects for the various cultural-historical subgroups classified together here as Hispanic, that is, Mexican and Chicano in particular regions and Cuban and Puerto Rican in other regions.

2. Some states have only one or two of the alternatives in operation in their schools and few districts or school systems available across the country have all three alternatives in place. This means that the researcher can not deter-

mine why a particular state, region or district has inherited one alternative or another, nor what effect the values and attitudes underlying the choice of alternative in vogue might have on that program's relative success or failure.

3. States, regions, districts, and schools within a district vary also with respect to the socioeconomic and educational background of Hispanic families, and these factors affect salaries and social-class backgrounds of public school teachers, and ultimately the achievement scores of pupils.

In sum, then, this large-scale research project, exemplary in many respects and designed to circumvent as many of these potentially confounding variables as possible, has been from its start too big for its britches. It has had to overlook or work around variables that are clearly socially significant: ethnic differences within America's Spanish-speaking population; state and regional variations in socioeconomic status of families, in demographic clusters of language minorities, and in educational programs; and school-specific variations in climates or atmospheres that encourage or discourage learning and teaching. My argument is that less money would be spent to conduct a coordinated set of real or quasi-*experiments* in different regional sites, permitting researchers to concentrate on a manageable subset of sites for separate studies that could be kept small enough to allow researchers to give attention to as many socially relevant factors as possible. Smaller, multiple-site approaches to a national issue of this sort could provide a type of "construct validity" checkout on each of the alternatives. Then university researchers and student assistants who know about each site could be involved, thereby making the project less expensive, and testers could be drawn from the various language minorities in the local communities.

PRODUCT RESEARCH VERSUS PROCESS RESEARCH: A QUESTION OF DEPTH

Michael Long (1984 and this volume) has described some important differences between process-oriented research and product-oriented research, a differentiation similar in many respects to formative versus summative evaluations in research on second language learning (see Scriven, 1967). Product research sets out to answer questions about the effectiveness, reflected in achievement scores, of one program (approach or treatment) compared to another program. Generally, each new educational innovation is ultimately tested for its presumed merits by means of product evaluations, and, theoretically, well-conducted evaluations could test out and thereby inform policy makers on the best course of education possible. One need never know *why* a particular approach is the best alternative if one could be confident that the evaluation had been carefully conducted: the product outcomes would simply determine which alternative is the most effective. But it is difficult for human researchers to be careful enough to satisfy all possible critics, and, especially in big studies, unbeknownst to the evaluator, happenings intervene while the product is being tested.

For example, pupils following an early exit option in the example above might perform poorest at the time of post-testing because all the best students in that program had been exited out (the issue of subject "mortality"). Researchers might still have big enough samples to deal with the slow early exiters, but one would begin to see weaknesses in the evaluation. Or it could be that the supposedly bilingual instruction given to one treatment group was actually reduced to having a bicultural teacher instruct through English, possibly with non-native command of the English language. Consequently, researchers are required to be as process-oriented in their evaluations as possible, that is, to find out what actually transpires in each classroom under each treatment. This includes the details of teacher-pupil interactions, analyses of the content of instruction and its form, as well as the pupil variability in receptivity to the instruction. Clearly, there is a need for some balance here, as Long recognizes:

> Process evaluations offer many benefits for teachers and administrators alike. Of these, the most important is that they can document what is going on in classrooms, as opposed to what is thought to be going on. Using process and product evaluations in combination, one can then determine not only whether a program really works, or works better, but if so, why, and if not, why not (Long, 1984, 422).

The examples Long gives of what can be done in process research are instructive and interesting. Consider the issue of teacher-pupil interactions. Suppose we videotape or audiotape a sample of classes in an educational experiment on language pedagogy; some samples would be taken from an innovative, new approach in one case and from a standard, old approach in the other. The tapes are transcribed, and transcriptions usually take five minutes per minute of tape. To check on transcription accuracy, one might want two transcriptors to work independently and calculate their agreement; but note how costs can accumulate here. Nonetheless, information about the fine-textured differences between programs can be made apparent in this fashion; for example, one set of classes might be found to stress

> 1) structural grading, 2) immediate, forced oral production by students, 3) avoidance and correction of errors—focus on form, 4) both mechanical and meaningful language practice, chiefly through memorization of short dialogues built around basic sentence patterns, and 5) large doses of drillwork (Long, 1984, 416).

There is no question that researchers would be delighted with such data, because then they could pinpoint factors that have an effect on product-oriented achievement measures. There is good common sense here that researchers appreciate. For instance, Merrill Swain (1987) got such transcripts from classes in French immersion programs in Canada and found that teachers hardly ever used the past tense when teaching a history course in French to anglophone students. And product assessments had noted that these students were not too swift in the use of the French past tenses! The major point is that researchers, like Swain in this example, might miss entirely what is going on in the classroom if they neglect process concerns in their research.

Process, however, can be overstressed, and clearly a reasonable balance has to be struck. Here's an example of too much process at the expense of product, an example that bothers me. The researchers were searching for "significant bilingual instructional features"; that is, they attempted to "identify, describe, and analyze significant instructional features in successful bilingual instructional settings" and to explore the consequences of these features on the progress of language minority pupils (Tikunoff, 1980, 1, and 1981; Fisher and Guthrie, 1983). For this purpose they collected detailed information on what went on in the classrooms, including teaching styles, whether active or not, among many other features, assuring the reader that process aspects of research were admirably covered. The trouble is that, for determining which programs were successful, they relied on opinions of local people—administrators, teachers, parents, and former students. No other independent check on success is mentioned and *no* attention is given to a contrast or comparison group that did *not* receive "significant bilingual instruction." In fact, *significant* is presumed to be the instruction that transpires in successful classrooms. Again, there is no introduction of comparison groups who were not successful.

There is much valuable information in this work. But it was expensive and spread through three years, and there is no way to determine and no evidence given to convince me that these instructional features were either significant or successful. The neglect of product information in this case means that the researchers did not go after data from matched groups of limited-English-proficient students who received either one set of instructional features or a comparison set, and who then were found to be either successful or not in terms of achievement growth or improvement. To me, it is a shame to have missed this opportunity as Long suggests, to combine product and process concerns in the research. A valuable suggestion for those wanting to explore the process-product issue in more detail is the work by Craig Chaudron (1988) that demonstrates very nicely the need for researchers to give ample attention to both process and product.

DEEPER FORMS OF PROCESS

There is, however, another way to consider process and product research, a way that I think goes deeper and captures the interests of another type of researcher. The particular way I have in mind was introduced by Lev Vygotsky back in 1934, although his book appeared in English only in 1962. Here's an example:

> It seems to us that [this] phenomenon has not received a sufficiently convincing psychological explanation, and this for two reasons: First, investigations have tended to focus on the contents of the phenomenon and to ignore the mental operations involved, i.e., *to study the product rather than the process;* second,

no adequate attempts have been made to view the phenomenon in the context of other bonds and relationships . . . (Vygotsky, 1962, 71; emphasis added by W. L.).

The phenomenon Vygotsky was referring to was the changes that transpire in the normal development of thought from infancy to young adulthood, a progression from thinking in "complexes" to "pseudo-concepts" or from potential concepts to genuine concepts.

> The processes leading to concept formation develop along two main lines. The first is "complex" formation: The child unites diverse objects in groups under a common "family name"; this process passes through various stages. The second line of development is the formation of "potential concepts," based on singling out certain common attributes. In both, the use of the word is an integral part of the developing processes, and the word maintains its guiding function in the formation of genuine concepts, to which these processes lead (Vygotsky, 1962, 81).

This endeavor permitted Vygotsky to be

> the first modern psychologist to suggest the mechanism by which culture becomes part of each person's nature. The internalization of socially rooted and historically developed activities is the distinguishing feature of human psychology (Cole, 1987, 6, 57)

To study these processes and to find a potential mechanism of the sort referred to here led Vygotsky not only to conduct experiments, using the now-famous Vygotsky blocks, (see Vygotsky, 1962, 52–81), but to experiment with children who fit somewhere on a continuum of developmental age steps. Vygotsky was interested in how children of different ages performed (the product dimension) and how each child in each age group interacted with the experimenter, in terms of the details of what was said by each member of the dyad and what each member meant by what was said (the conventional process concern). More important, he was also interested in the mental operations involved in each attempted solution of the problems presented.

It is this last step in Vygotsky's overall approach that I see as a deeper form of process research, a form that could be a helpful model for research on foreign language learning. Standard process research can make us aware of what is going on in a classroom and it can help us be certain that the planned treatment offered to pupils in that classroom is or is not transpiring (the treatment verification function of process research, referred to earlier). For me, the more fundamental processes in foreign language learning are those that take place in students' minds and in the social systems students find themselves in, rather than in the classroom processes or in the teacher-student interactions. The only way I see to get at these more social-psychological processes is through a combined product-process orientation on the part of the researcher. But to get at the deeper levels, the researcher has to have some relevant theoretical ideas, even if only commonsense hunches, to orient the long-range plan of the research. Let me illustrate what I mean through four examples from the Montreal setting.

ILLUSTRATION 1: TWO SOLITUDES

In Montreal, French and English school systems are and have been separate; the administration is separate, the schools are in different sites, and consequently, students and staff are kept exclusively in their own linguistic worlds. This separateness is nicely represented in an important Canadian novel on the two major ethnolinguistic communities in Quebec, entitled *Two Solitudes* (McClennan, 1945). Ailie Cleghorn and Fred Genesee (1984) were interested in what happens when French- and English-speaking teachers become members of a common teaching staff in English language schools that have French immersion programs under way. Their hunch was that the social interactions of the two groups of teachers would likely reflect the social realities of distant, separate existences.

Data were collected, using observational procedures, over a one-year period. Thus, an observer recorded relevant events in the schools, in classrooms, in principals' offices, and in teachers' rooms, especially at break times and lunch times. It was an unusual event, for both the French teachers and the English schools involved, to have a sizable subgroup of French teachers working in otherwise all-English schools. At first, the English-speaking teachers showed normal amounts of politeness and welcome. In the common teachers' room at lunch period, for example, small tables were arranged so as to accommodate all staff, and suggestions were made that French might be the language of communication (a type of "French table") from time to time, so that the English teachers could get some experience using French, and at the same time, they reasoned, the French teachers would be made to feel at home.

The Cleghorn and Genesee study is noteworthy because it chronicles in the teacher-to-teacher contacts the slow but sure emergence of the deep, long-standing conflictual nature of English-French relations in the general society. For instance, there was a gradual separation and segregation of social contacts, including the use of separate tables, separate burners on the common stove, schedules for French and English usage of the stove. French teachers slowly switched to English (no matter how poorly they commanded it) for intergroup contacts, which for generations had been the expected thing for French-Canadians to do in the presence of anglophones.

To me, this informative study is a good example of a carefully documented, standard, process-oriented study that was designed to go far beyond the structure and content of the interaction between teachers. Instead, the basic process data were used to explore a fundamental social-context process involving society's impact on the school and on cross-group contacts that take place in this novel form of mixed-group setting. The impact of this deeper societal process on anglophone children's progress in French, their reluctance to initiate French conversations outside school, and their expectations that French people speak English with anglophones were all evident in the product results of the immersion classes.

ILLUSTRATION 2:
BILINGUALISM'S EFFECTS
ON CREATIVE-TYPE THINKING

This is an example of a research project that accompanied a standard product-oriented evaluation of the progress of anglophone students enrolled in French immersion programs (see Scott, 1973). The basic idea was to see if becoming bilingual would expand or enhance "mental flexibility," an idea that other research (for example, Peal and Lambert, 1962) had suggested as a possibility because a very pronounced *association* had been found between certain aspects of IQ and bilingualism. An opportunity was seized to explore the causal direction of this association, especially the possibility that becoming bilingual *causes* an increase in cognitive flexibility.

By the early 1970s, the structure of Canadian French immersion programs in schools had been routinized in terms of agenda and procedure. Consequently, it was possible to test a group of anglophone children on a measure of cognitive flexibility (in this case, a measure of "divergent thinking" taken from the work of Getzels and Jackson (1962) at the kindergarten and grade 1 levels, *before* the youngsters were launched on immersion, and again at the grade 5 and 6 level by which time a good degree of functional bilingualism was already evident. Anglophone control groups who followed a conventional all-English program served as an appropriate comparison, since most of the parents of these pupils would also have taken the immersion option, had it been available to them. The controls, however, were selected to be of equivalent IQ's and socioeconomic backgrounds as the treatment (that is, immersion) groups. Thus, we were confident that at the start of elementary school, the treatment and control groups were as alike as one can ever get them and their *early* scores on the divergent thinking tests were essentially identical. The important finding, however, was that the later scores at the end of grades 5 and 6 were significantly different in favor of the immersion group, even when tested via English, which was used much less than 50% of the time in the schooling of the immersion student.

This outcome not only says something important about the causal link between becoming bilingual and cognitive flexibility, but it also casts light on a very important underlying mental process that permits one to infer what likely goes on in the immersion experience, something far below the surface events of teacher-student interaction patterns. Thus, this study is a clear illustration of a Vygotsky-type process that was studied through an apparently product type (pre-post) testing of the performance of the children on a standard, psychometrically sound measure of cognitive activity.

ILLUSTRATION 3: THE EFFECTS OF ATTITUDES AND MOTIVATION ON FOREIGN LANGUAGE STUDY

Robert Gardner and I have had a long-standing interest in the role played by students' attitudes toward the foreign group whose language they are studying, whether they are motivated by instrumental reasons (those with a practical pay-off) or integrative reasons (for example, interest in or inquisitiveness about the foreign people and their culture) (see Gardner and Lambert, 1972). Since our early work, Gardner (1981) has accumulated an impressive array of empirical studies that explore the ways in which attitudes and motivations affect language acquisition proficiency, performance in the classroom, and willingness to take advanced courses in the language. The basic research design is to measure, as of the start of FL training, the foreign language aptitude, the verbal IQ, the socioeconomic background, and the attitude-motivational profile of large numbers of primary and secondary school students and to follow them through one or more years of FL training, with repeated tests of FL achievement. Thus, a basically product-oriented approach is followed.

Numerous, small-scale replications reveal that measures of attitudes toward the other cultural group and motivational interest in mastering the FL are correlated, forming a cluster that stands apart from a second cluster made up of tests of aptitude for learning a FL and verbal intelligence. Furthermore, each cluster is as closely correlated to FL achievement as the other. The fact that the attitude-motivation cluster is as good a predictor of FL achievement as verbal intelligence or language aptitude and that it is statistically independent from the aptitude-intelligence cluster has great social significance, because it indicates that anyone, even the intellectually and linguistically nongifted, can be successful in FL study if they want to and especially if they want to for the "right" attitudinal reasons.

The more recent research of Gardner and his students shows that the attitude-motivation index is also strongly associated with perseverance in the FL study (Gardner and Smythe, 1975; Gardner, 1981); that is, the more integratively oriented the attitudes and motivation of students are, the more they avail themselves of opportunities to practice the second language, and the more often they decide to take advanced courses at the college level. It is also clear that attitudes and motivation affect classroom interactions (Glicksman, 1981; Gardner, 1981). Trained observers of FL classrooms found that the more integratively oriented students (those with favorable attitudes and nonpractical motivations) volunteered more frequently, gave more correct answers publicly, and received more positive feedback from teachers than did those less integratively oriented. There were no subgroup differences, however, in asking the teacher questions, in demonstrating knowledge beyond that solicited, nor in indications of classroom anxiety.

For me, these results indicate that a deeper process, reflected in an attitude-motivation complex, is at work in FL learning. Furthermore, this deeper process seems to have an effect on the content and structure of the teacher-student interaction—the more standard form of classroom process, the type more commonly dealt with by FL researchers.

ILLUSTRATION 4: PROCESSES UNDERLYING THE TRANSFORMATION OF SUBTRACTIVE TO ADDITIVE FORMS OF BILINGUALISM

My final example is both societal and personal in nature. It deals with small communities in northern New England whose residents have French as a heritage language, being third- or fourth-generation immigrants from French Canada, but who function otherwise in an all-English American society. These "Franco-Americans" have kept French up mainly as an informal social language, especially with family members, and mainly for oral communication; there is very little reading or writing in French. As these families function more and more in English, they gradually lose French. Their stage of bilinguality reflects the gradual substitution of English for French, what we refer to as subtractive bilingualism, meaning that even though at a certain time in their lives they are functionally bilingual, French is being eliminated from their lives and replaced by English (Dube and Herbert, 1975; Lambert, Giles, and Picard, 1975; Lambert, Giles, and Albert, 1976).

The implied contrast is with an additive form of bilingualism, where speakers of a dominant, prestigious, and communicationally useful language (such as English in the United States or French in France) can add a second or foreign language to their linguistic repertoires with no fear that the first language and its cultural supports will be upset in any sense. Rather, they experience numerous cognitive, intellectual, and social advantages as they become bilingual. The question that prompted us was this: can researchers successfully effect a change at the school/community level that will transform a subtractive bilingual experience into an additive one?

Working as research collaborators of school administrators in Madawaska, Frenchville, and Fort Kent, small communities in northern Maine, we selected at random a subset of elementary school classrooms, and assigned available bilingual teachers to teach half the day in French and half in English. They were to follow the conventional academic curriculum, supplementing English textbooks with French ones from France or Quebec or with French mimeographed materials covering curriculum content. The families were mainly from working- or lower-middle class socioeconomic standing, and nearly 90% of the children had some audiolingual skill with French at home and in social settings. The random selection of classrooms and pupils provided us with two essentially similar groups of Franco-American youngsters: the treatment group received a four- to five-year experience with 50% of their instruction in French (which meant that they had only 50% of school time spent in English instruction) while the control group followed a conventional all-English program. Both groups had teachers who were from the region and all of these were also Franco-American.

The results revealed progressive improvement in French skills (writing and reading as well as audiolingual) for the treatment group, as expected; the *same,* and in several respects *better,* scores on standardized measures of *English* skills for the immersion group over the controls; and the same or better achievement than the controls in subject matters taught through French (like math and social science), even when tested in *English.*

How can one explain these outcomes? The explanation I find most reasonable is that the fate of language-minority children in public schooling can be substantially improved if they are given a chance to study and learn through their heritage languages. Here we had apparently successfully transformed a subtractive bilingual experience into an additive one, and our guess was that some deeper underlying process was likely a key mediator of these favorable outcomes. More specifically, we had hypothesized that a sense of pride in having a French heredity and a sense of value attached to the French language were likely involved (see Lambert, 1984). This prompted us to administer pre-post tests, for both the treatment and control children, of self views and of evaluations of heritage culture and language. Statistical comparisons revealed a significant difference, favoring the treatment group of pupils, who in contrast to the controls were proud and happy to be *both* American and French, and who were pleasantly surprised and equally proud that French was as useful and precise a language for school learning as was English—a set of ideas the control children had no way to develop.

This example, I suggest, is both small and community-based, and it is by design as carefully control-group, product-oriented as we could make it, and yet it was much more. It provided us with an opportunity to test out potentially important underlying processes that help us understand the different meanings that being bilingual/bicultural can have on both language minority and language majority families in an American setting.

Considering all four illustrations, what are the essential features of this deeper type of process research or this "Vygotsky style" search for underlying processes? I see two important features:

1. All such examples are applications of a hypothetical-deductive research model (cf. Underwood, 1957; Hull, 1952) that makes active use of *hypothetical constructs* or *intervening variables* (see MacCorquodale and Meehl, 1948). These hypothetical constructs are often simply sophisticated guesses on the part of the researcher. Their importance lies in the fact that they can be linked, through experiments, with particular input variables (also known as *independent variables*) that are systematically related to one or several output variables (*dependent variables*).

2. The basic model also implies *multiple* hypothetical deductions and testings of the central construct, and thus, there is an implied requirement that the researcher-theoretician strive for construct validity so as to enhance the believability of the basic construct (see Cronbach and Meehl, 1955; Underwood, 1957, 117*ff*). This old, dependable model gets new names and new twists from time to time, but never any substantive changes. And as is apparent in the examples, the constructs or basic processes can be psychological in nature, group- or community-oriented, and even culture-oriented.

This suggested model does imply, however, that valuable research on foreign or second language learning requires much more than linguistic or pedagogical training and interest; it requires also some extensive experience and interest in one or more of the behavioral sciences, either on the part of the researcher or on the part of research collaborators. The important message, however, is that progress in FL or SL research calls for prime attention to underlying hypothetical constructs or, more simply, to educated guesses that experienced teachers are so competent at generating. Progress also calls for careful and systematic testing using product-type, quantitative research approaches that incorporate as much process data as is economically feasible. The smaller the scale of the design and the more local its scope, the greater the progress is likely to be.

REFERENCES

Baker, K., and A. A. de Kanter. 1981. *Effectiveness of Bilingual Education: A Review of the Literature.* Washington, D.C.: Office of Planning, Budget and Evaluation, U.S. Department of Education.

Bryk, A. S., and S. W. Raudenbush. 1987. "Application of Hierarchical Linear Models to Assessing Change." *Psychological Bulletin* 101: 147–58.

Campbell, D. T., and R. F. Boruch. 1975. "Making the Case for Randomized Assignment to Treatments by Considering Alternatives." *Evaluation and Experiment.* Eds. C. A. Bennett and A. A. Lumsdaine. New York: Academic Press.

Chaudron, C. 1988. *Second Language Classrooms: Research on Teaching and Learning.* New York: Cambridge UP.

Cleghorn, A., and F. Genesee. 1984. "Languages in Contact: An Ethnographic Study of Interaction in an Immersion School." *TESOL Quarterly* 18: 595–625.

Cole, M. 1987. Quoted in L. S. Hearnshaw, *The Shaping of Modern Psychology.* London: Routledge & Kegan Paul. 177.

Cronbach, L., and P. E. Meehl. 1955. "Construct Validity in Psychological Tests." *Psychological Bulletin* 52: 281–302.

Dube, N. C., and G. Herbert. 1975. *The St. John Valley Bilingual Education Project.* Washington, D.C.: U.S. Department of Health, Education and Welfare.

Fisher, C. W., and L. F. Guthrie. 1981. *Executive Summary: The Significant Bilingual Instructional Features Study.* Document SBIF-83-R.14.

Gardner, R. C. 1981. "Second Language Learning." *A Canadian Social Psychology of Ethnic Relations.* Eds. R. C. Gardner and R. Kalin. Toronto: Methuen.

Gardner, R. C., and W. E. Lambert. 1972. *Attitudes and Motivation in Second Language Learning.* Rowley, Mass.: Newbury House.

Gardner, R. C., and P. C. Smythe. 1975. *Second Language Acquisition: A Social Psychological Approach.* London, Ontario: University of Western Ontario, Department of Psychology, Research Bulletin No. 332.

Getzels, J. W., and P. W. Jackson. 1962. *Creativity and Intelligence.* New York: Wiley & Sons.

Glicksman, L. 1981. "Improving the Prediction of Behaviors Associated with Second Language Acquisition." Unpublished doctoral dissertation, University of Western Ontario, London, Ontario, Canada.

Harley, B., *et al.* 1987. *The Development of Bilingual Proficiency: Final Report.* Toronto: Modern Language Center, O.I.S.E.

Hull, C. L. 1952. *A Behavior System.* New Haven: Yale UP.

Lambert, W. E. 1984. "An Overview of Issues in Immersion Education." *Studies on Immersion Education.* Ed. Office of Bilingual Bicultural Education. Sacramento: California State Department of Education.

Lambert, W. E., H. Giles, and A. Albert. 1976. "Language Attitudes in a Rural Community in Northern Maine." Unpublished manuscript, Psychology Department, McGill University, Montreal.

Lambert, W. E., H. Giles, and O. Picard. 1975. "Language Attitudes in a French-American Community." *International Journal of the Sociology of Language* 4: 127–52.

Long, M. 1984. "Process and Product in ESL Program Evaluation." *TESOL Quarterly* 18: 409–25.

McClennan, H. 1945. *Two Solitudes.* New York: Duell, Sloan and Pearce.

MacCorquodale, K., and P. E. Meehl. 1948. "On a Distinction Between Hypothetical Constructs and Intervening Variables." *Psychological Review* 55: 95–107.

Peal, E., and W. E. Lambert. 1962. "The Relation of Bilingualism to Intelligence." *Psychological Monographs* 76: 1–23.

Ramirez, D., S. D. Yuen, and D. S. Ramey. 1988. *Longitudinal Study of Immersion, Early-Exit and Late-Exit Transitional Bilingual Education Programs for Language Minority Children: Study Design Overview.* San Mateo, Calif.: Aguirre International, 411 Borel Avenue, 94402.

Rogosa, D., D. Brandt, and M. Zimowski. 1982. "A Growth Curve Approach to the Measurement of Change." *Psychological Bulletin* 92: 726–48.

Scott, S. 1973. "The Relation of Divergent Thinking to Bilingualism: Cause or Effect?" Unpublished manuscript, Psychology Department, McGill University.

Scriven, M. 1967. "The Methodology of Evaluation." *Perspectives on Curriculum Evaluation.* Ed. R. W. Tyler. Chicago: Rand McNally.

Sowell, T. 1983. *The Economics and Politics of Race.* New York: Morrow and Co.

Swain, M. 1987. Personal communication.

Tikunoff, W. J. 1980. *Overview of the Significant Bilingual Instructional Features Study.* San Francisco: Far West Laboratory, Document SBIF-80-D.1.1.

———. 1981. *Significant Bilingual Instructional Features Study: A Report of the State-of-the-Study.* San Francisco: Far West Laboratory, Document SBIF-81-R.8.

Underwood, B. J. 1957. *Psychological Research*. New York: Appleton-Century-Crofts, Inc.

Vygotsky, L. 1962. *Thought and Language*. Cambridge, Mass.: MIT Press.

Willett, J. B. 1988. "Questions and Answers in the Measurement of Change." *Review of Research in Education*. Vol. 15, in press.

Willig, A. C. 1985. "A Meta-Analysis of Selected Studies on the Effectiveness of Bilingual Education." *Review of Educational Research* 55: 269–317.

Chapter 20

Advantages and Disadvantages of Qualitative Research Design on Foreign Language Research

Frederick Erickson

University of Pennsylvania

INTRODUCTION

In this paper I will review some of the kinds of issues that are appropriate for study by qualitative methods. I will discuss the limitations of those methods for the study of other kinds of issues. Before beginning, however, I want to issue a disclaimer.

Use of the terms *qualitative* and *quantitative* implies a dichotomy that I believe to be misleading. To avoid misunderstanding, I have been using the term *interpretive* in my own recent writing (for example, Erickson 1986) to characterize the family of research approaches that emphasizes description and analysis of routine events, focusing centrally on the meanings of those events to the actors engaged in them. That family of approaches, variously called ethnography, case study, documentation, sociolinguistic microanalysis, and qualitative research, involves study primarily by means of participant observation and interviewing, which is increasingly often accompanied by audio or video recording. Sometimes in interpretive work, phenomena of interest are quantified and occasionally those data are subjected to statistical analysis. It is, in fact, common to make use of quantitative techniques in studies whose overall purpose is qualitative. Hence, I think it is confusing, especially to beginning researchers, to adopt a term that characterizes studies of member-defined qualities of things and events as if such studies were antithetical to considerations of frequency—of asking how often and in what circumstances certain phenomena in the social world typically occur.

If the term qualitative is not entirely satisfactory, it follows that quantitative is not quite appropriate as a contrast term. I find it most useful to contrast interpretive research with surveys and experiments. In survey research (which includes testing as one form of survey instrument) and in experimental research, the data are often reported and analyzed in terms of their frequency distribution. This is why, in ordinary usage, we refer to such research as quantitative.

Yet some experiments do not have frequency data as the center of research interest. And to contrast surveys and experiments with interpretive research points to two significant dimensions on which the two research approaches differ. One dimension involves what can be called the texture of data. In survey research and in large-scale experiments, one collects relatively few bits of information about many research subjects, whereas in interpretive research, one collects many bits of information about relatively few subjects. Another dimension or aspect of comparison involves the role of causal analysis in the study. In survey and experimental research, one usually conceives of *cause* in ways akin to those held in the natural sciences, that is, a physical notion of cause. In interpretive research one is not so much interested in cause per se as one is interested in explanation in terms of meanings and understandings held by those who one has studied (see the discussion in Bredo and Feinberg, 1982). These differences—in the texture of data and in the notions of cause—are more fundamental than the distinction between counting or not counting things. To my mind the crucial distinction between interpretation and surveys or experiments lies not in whether one counts but in what kinds of things one decides to count, which depends on the nature of the research questions one poses.

Accordingly, I will begin here by reviewing some of the kinds of research topics and questions that are most appropriately addressed by interpretive methods. I will conclude by reflecting on the advantages and disadvantages of interpretive methods and of surveys and experiments.

TOPICS APPROPRIATE FOR QUALITATIVE RESEARCH ON FOREIGN LANGUAGE TEACHING

The issues most appropriate for study by interpretive means involve questions regarding foreign language use in reading, writing, listening, and speaking, rather than on questions regarding knowledge of literature or correctness of expression (strictly speaking) in the foreign language. Using language in a given moment draws upon only some parts of the individual's total sociolinguistic repertoire; that is, one does not make use of the entire set of grammatical, lexical, and rhetorical resources for making meaning, which are available in a language system considered as a whole. Rather, language use is specific to particular situations of use, each requiring the speaker/hearer or writer/reader to draw upon a particular subset of necessary linguistic and sociolinguistic knowledge. Business executives who write memos to each other, for example, require different knowledge of a foreign language from that needed by parents talking with a teacher about the school progress of their child or by a person trying to get her car repaired. The differences involve kinds of knowledge as well as amounts of knowledge. Interpretive research can discover what the customary situations and usages are within a given speech community (thus discovering what kinds of knowledge of a foreign language are required to act appropriately in those situations). Interpretive research can also determine what happens in various modes of classroom instruction as a teacher attempts to teach functional knowledge of a foreign language.

FOUNDATIONS IN SOCIOLINGUISTIC THEORY

Two theoretical notions are of special importance in the study of foreign language teaching for functional language use—the nature of social interaction as a learning environment, and the nature of communicative competence. Let us first consider social interaction as it constitutes the situations within which language learning takes place.

In a perspective that situates language learning within social interaction, speaking/writing and hearing/reading are conceived as acts that are fundamentally social in nature.[1] There is always another present, in relation to whom one's own actions take account. Audience members, individually and collectively, are active participants in the speaker's production of oral discourse (just as they have been metaphorically considered as active in relations with authors of written discourse). Research must thus answer such questions as "What are others doing while the speaker(s) is (are) talking?"

Listeners, by showing comprehension through gaze, nodding, or by brief vocalizations (termed *backchannels*) can encourage speakers or inhibit their production of talk. In informal conversation interlocutors may provide one another additional assistance by completing one another's utterances by adding a word or clause to what another has said, completing the syntactic unit or discourse unit that the first speaker was projecting. These utterance completions can be done as prompts or even more smoothly in discourse patterns of co-narration and co-exposition. Interlocutors also can echo one another. Speaking in a conversational environment in which interlocutors provide frequent backchanneling, complete many of one another's utterances, and echo a great deal is a very different situation for learning (rich in "assists" and in modeling by interlocutors) from one in which interlocutors refrain from such conjoint activity with the speaker. The alternative social participation structures according to which conversations can be organized as ecosystems of interaction (see Shultz, Florio, and Erickson, 1982; Erickson, in press) can thus be seen as qualitatively different kinds of learning environments. Conversational arrangements, as they are differentially organized in terms of speaker/audience relations, provide different kinds of opportunities for verbal practice, not only in terms of the *content* that is being uttered (it is in terms of variation in content of talk that second language teachers usually think of variation in speech situations) but also in terms of the social *process* by which the talk is done.

Support of speakers by listeners is one aspect of assistance in language acquisition that Ninio and Bruner (1978) called *scaffolding*. This is related to Vygotsky's theory of learning as radically socially constituted. He sees all knowledge and skill that a learner is eventually able to perform unaided as first being practiced with scaffoldlike assistance from another person in social interaction. From this view comes his dictum: all knowledge exists first on the social plane and only then is acquired on the individual plane (see Wertsch, 1985).

A related notion is that of the *zone of proximal development*. Vygotsky defines this as the distance between what the individual can perform unaided (as in usual tests of knowledge and skill in which the learner is asked to perform alone) and what one can perform through interaction with another person. In sequences of good teaching, the more adept partner provides some assistance but withdraws assistance progressively as the competence of the less adept partner increases with learning. (See the discussion in Cazden, 1988, 99–110.)

To summarize, persons in interaction situations speaking a foreign language in which one party is more fluent than the other may create positive learning environments for the less fluent partner provided that the scaffolding assistance provided by the more fluent partner occurs within the less fluent partner's zone of proximal development. One can study situations of interaction observationally to determine whether scaffolding assistance by the more fluent speaker is being pitched above, below, or within the less fluent speaker's zone of proximal development.

In the preceding discussion, linguistic knowledge has been viewed as continually being used for social purposes. Indeed, the relationships in speaking and listening between interlocutors are so dialectically intertwined that we can say that interlocution consists in co-locution. Thus, in our attempts to understand language acquisition, it is just as important to identify specifically the social aims, the social relations between persons, and the actual behaviors of interaction as they unfold in time, as it is to identify the specific linguistic means or resources (that is the linguistic competence or knowledge) by which the purposes and processes of interaction are realized. It follows that social interaction is the fundamental learning environment for language acquisition. We must ask about the specific ways in which this environment is organized, and how organism-environment interaction happens in specific ways such that certain kinds of language learning take place or fail to take place.

Social interaction, in classrooms and in daily life, presents a language learner with differing kinds of stimulation for foreign language acquisition. An interlocutor (whom we can call *alter*), whether that alter is a reader/writer or is a conversational partner in immediate co-presence with the speaker/hearer of a foreign language (whom we can call *ego*), provides a situation of interaction in which, sometimes alternatively and sometimes simultaneously, the environmental press draws more on ego's knowledge of lexicon, or more on grammar, or on prosody to show, deixis and contrast, or more on the various linguistic and nonverbal means for realizing social strategies in interaction (for example, persuading or being persuaded, showing deference or recognizing it in the actions of others, commanding or seeing that one is being told to obey, or inviting or being invited to join another in playfulness).

The environmental press that requires the successful interactant to use distinct subsets of linguistic and sociolinguistic knowledge can change from moment to moment in face-to-face interaction, and from one discourse unit to another in a written text with which ego is confronted. Talk and writing occur in different situational frames, alternating discourse frames, which invite, as it were, the speaker/hearer's use of alternating subgenres. Thus, variation in context of situation accounts for part of the heteroglossia (that is, the full range of variation in forms and functions of speaking/listening across all situations, and across all class/gender/age divisions within the community) that is inherent in language use. Interaction with others in producing these diverse verbal and written texts constitutes practice in language use. In recent studies of child language acquisition, we have begun to learn more about how differing kinds of texts in the speech environment that surrounds the child present the child with different kinds of opportunities for engagement situations for practice. The child's active participation in those situations—different language learning environments— stimulates the acquisition of various aspects of knowledge and skill in language and in social strategy.

That much is clear from current research in first language acquisition. Some scholars have begun to study how different kinds of environments of speaking operate as situations of practice in second language acquisition as it occurs among immigrants. To my knowledge, this perspective on the nature of language use and on the nature of language learning has not yet been used in research on situations of practice in the foreign language classroom.

The second theoretical notion, communicative competence, has already been alluded to in the preceding discussion. Communicative competence (Hymes, 1974) refers to the content of knowledge and skill required in order to participate with others communicatively in social life in ways that are not only intelligible but appropriate and effective. Such knowledge goes beyond the narrow bounds of linguistic competence in the strict sense of the term as employed by Chomsky— knowledge of the sound system, grammar, and lexicon of a language. The capacity to judge the appropriateness of discourse and to participate in it involves cultural knowledge beyond that of the language itself.

Judgments of appropriateness relate to the social uses of writing, speaking, reading, and hearing. As Hymes noted once, we would interpret as bizarre the communicative actions of an adult speaker who possessed full linguistic competence but who had acquired so little communicative competence that she did not know when to stop or start talking. We might understand the literal meaning of what she was saying but would not understand the metaphoric, social meaning we would assume was being implied in her speech. Since her words would be intelligible but not her deeds in using them with us we would wonder. "Is she trying to defy us or tease us? Is she having a psychotic episode?" We might become frightened or angered by her breach of our assumptions of social order in communication. The judgments we would make in trying to interpret her communicative intent are one aspect of our communicative competence.

Two specific aspects of communicative competence bear mention here. One is the speaker/hearer's capacity to match speech or writing style to the overall situation at hand. The other aspect is the speaker/hearer's capacity to recognize and perform subtle cues during the course of interaction that at once indicate change in the definition of situation of the moment and influence that change's accomplishment. This notion draws on the insight of Bateson (1956) that communicative behavior contains within itself cues that point to the frame or schema of interpretation within which the intent of the communication is to be understood. Gumperz (1982, 1990) has extended that insight in his work on contextualization in speaking, showing how speakers signal implicitly their intentions by verbal, paralinguistic, and nonverbal means.

Style-matching to the overall shape of a situation can be thought of as what one must know in order to be generally appropriate in a social scene. A limitation in that notion is that, taken literally and narrowly, it portrays the speaker/hearer in a one-dimensional way as passive, constantly and stereotypically polite. The notion of contextualization as located in part within the communicative text itself, rather than standing outside it[2] points not only to the subtlety with which situations are continually being reframed in social intercourse, but to the speaker/ hearer as an active agent in negotiating the definition of situation in the moment at hand. Persons are not simply being accommodating and appropriate in interaction, following the cultural rules and cues provided by others. They are also motivated and act in strategic ways, influencing others as well as being influenced by them.

It would seem then that both aspects of communicative competence must be taken together—the speaker/hearer's capacity to match verbal production to situation and the capacity to use that production in changing the definition of situation—as we consider what a speaker must know and be able to do in order to communicate in ways that are not only appropriate but effective (see the discussion in Cazden, 1988, 43–45). The speaker/hearer can be thought of as actively engaged in interpretation of the immediate situations of communication encountered in daily life. We can presume a capacity to recognize social situations as *Gestalten*, whose rough outlines indicate certain overall definitions of situation and of situationally appropriate style. We can presume as well a more finely tuned capacity to read situated interaction as it evolves during the course of its enactment.

These are members' interpretations. Just as when we acquire and hold knowledge of a first language, the cultural knowledge that informs such interpretations is learned and held in memory outside reflective awareness, for the most part. Fluency in a foreign language requires that we learn communicative competence as well as linguistic competence. Yet we acquire communicative competence in our first language by being immersed in situations in which we observe others using language for social purposes and by practicing it ourselves. As infants we do this without the risk of much embarrassment, because adults do not hold us accountable for each of our errors in our beginning attempts to communicate. However, in learning a foreign language in a classroom, the learning environment is far different from that in which we acquired our first language. We are no longer free to make the kinds of mistakes we could make with relative impunity as small children. This presents serious challenges to the foreign language teacher in attempting to teach sociolinguistic knowledge and skill that is largely implicit, and it presents the researcher with challenges and opportunities in any attempt to study foreign language instruction.

QUALITATIVE RESEARCH QUESTIONS: WITHIN THE FOREIGN LANGUAGE CLASSROOM AND BEYOND IT

It should be obvious from the previous discussion that some of the necessary interpretive research needs to go beyond the classroom. As a foundation for curriculum and pedagogy in teaching functional language use, studies of naturally occurring social situations are needed in the foreign country or in networks of first-generation immigrants within a host country. Ideally, through participant observational research, the full range of heteroglossia should be identified within specific speech communities or speech networks. These studies of variation in practical language use, formally called ethnography of communication and sociolinguistic microanalysis or microethnography of communication (see Erickson, 1988, for further discussion) might focus on the forms and uses of written and oral communication in scenes of special interest, because of the time and expense involved in doing a general ethnography of ways of speaking in the community. It should be noted, however, that the more general ethnography that is done so as to provide rich background information on patterns of value and use regarding language in the community, institution, or speech network as a whole, the more illuminating becomes the microethnographic case-study analysis that is done on specific speech situations.

In studying functional language use in business, for example, one might compare situations of collaboration among coworkers in the office, negotiation of sales with employees of another company, and informal recreational interaction among coworkers as it occurs at the office and after work. The studies might also focus on the daily rounds of individuals of special interest, for example, business executives, physicians, parents at home. In either approach one would be identifying specific actions of individuals in situations, and comparing specific aspects of different kinds of situations. One would ask not only what native speakers do, typically and uniquely, in those situations but what their purposes are and how they think and feel about the intentions and styles of others with whom they interact.

What results from such study is information on social interactions as environments for speaking/hearing and writing/reading; information about partial models of the sociolinguistic competence (that is, the linguistic and communicative competence) of individuals who are fluent in the foreign language; and information about those individuals' purposes and tastes in communication, considering them both as typical members of cultural groups and as individuals with distinct personal preferences. Such research might well change the notions of fluency that teachers of a foreign language bring with them to the classroom.

Within the foreign language classroom, one could take a similar approach. This would be to view the classroom as a small-scale speech community that provides contrasting situations for language use. One might concentrate on a range of situations for speaking and writing in the classroom, observing recurrent instances of those situations. Or one might follow individuals of interest through the full range of communicative situations they encounter during a class period. One might look for contrast in students. Do the most fluent and least fluent students encounter similar or different situations during a class period? Do they participate differently in the same situation? In either case, whether they seek out different communication situations using the foreign language or whether, when they meet in the same situations, they tend to locate themselves in different places within the communicative ecology of the interaction that typically occurs, they would be encountering different kinds of opportunities for foreign language practice and learning.

What, more specifically, is it about particular kinds of practice in certain kinds of situations that stimulates acquisition of differing aspects of linguistic and sociolinguistic knowledge and skill? Does a certain kind of participation by a speaker or writer seem to foster acquisition of certain aspects of grammar, or of lexicon, or of forms of politeness, or of authoritative voice, or of direct or indirect persuasion? These are questions that can be answered, at least in part, by close and sensitive participant observation and interviewing, in combination with microanalysis of audiovisual records.[3] (See, for example, Moll and Diaz, 1987.) Some of these questions can also be answered by experiments, but naturalistic observation is desirable first, in order to determine how to design such experiments in the most effective ways.

As in studies of naturally occurring interaction among native speakers, one needs to ask not only about what happens in communication but about what those happenings mean to those engaged in them. How do different students think and feel about their participation in the varying communicative ecologies they encounter in the class? Are there recurring scenes in which it is more or less safe to make mistakes? Is there a relationship between risk and opportunity for certain kinds of learning, within and across situations? Are there differences among students in a given classroom in their willingness to take risks? Do some students acquire certain aspects of communicative competence faster than they acquire grammar and lexicon? What distinguishes those students from the ones who speak more correctly, in a prescriptive sense, but whose sociolinguistic repertoires are relatively less developed? Do the two different kinds of students seek out different kinds of opportunities for practice in language use? How do they feel about the language they are learning and its use? How do they feel about themselves as learners of a foreign language?

The set of questions presented here is intended to be illustrative rather than exhaustive. They address the interpretive sense-making of the persons studied as well as the actions those persons take and the cultural and social structural rules and constraints they appear to be following and confronting as they use language in social interaction. Such questions are best answered by means of interpretive, qualitative research methods.

VALIDITY AND DATA QUALITY IN INTERPRETIVE RESEARCH

Data collection in answering these kinds of questions consists of participant observation, audio- and video-recording of interaction, collection and review of texts written *in situ,* and formal and informal interviewing. Those means of data collection are characteristic of interpretive research and they have been discussed extensively in a burgeoning literature on methods of interpretive research (see, for example, Agar, 1980; Bogdan and Biklen, 1982; and Hammersly and Atkinson, 1983). I have discussed these methods in a review article that focuses on classroom teaching specifically (Erickson, 1986) and in another that focuses on ethnographic description in sociolinguistic research more generally (Erickson, 1988). Accordingly I will not elaborate here on the concrete procedures of interpretive research.

It is appropriate, however, to make a few general observations on data collection and analysis. Interpretive research, in my judgment, is done best when one collects a variety of kinds of evidence about a given topic, presents both specific description and general description in reporting the evidence, and searches deliberately for discrepant cases in the process of analytic induction by which conclusions are reached.

Evidence for a given conclusion one wishes to make can vary in kind as well as in amount. If one has much evidence (for example, many observations of many individuals across time), one is more confident of a conclusion than if one has only a little evidence to warrant an assertion that one wishes to make. But even if one has much evidence of a single type (for example, evidence collected by means of participant observation), one is in an even stronger position to warrant an analytic claim if one also has some evidence of another type (for example, interviews, videotape, in addition to firsthand observation, entries in journals written by students) that corroborates the patterns that are apparent in the first type of evidence. I would rather have fewer bits of information across different types of data sources than a large number of bits of information derived from a single data source. Diversity of evidence enables the researcher to demonstrate what is technically called *convergent validity* (Cook and Campbell, 1979) in marshaling evidence to justify the claims that one wishes to make as an interpretive researcher, about typical patterns in subjects' actions and points of view.

Interpretive research is reported primarily through description. Three types of descriptive reporting are common—specific description, medium-range description, and general description. Specific description is reported by means of rich, concrete narrative vignettes, by means of direct quotes from interviews, and occasionally by transcripts from recordings or from documents written by members at the research site. Specific description gives both a sense of immediacy and finely nuanced detail in reporting what happened in a particular event. It also clarifies the meaning of key analytic constructs (for example, from the previous discussion, *risk, contextualization cues,* the type of practice that stimulates acquisition of authoritative voice in the foreign language).

Medium-range description summarizes happenings across a number of events, for example, "Students who were sloppy about grammar but adept at the use of social strategies in the foreign language tended to seek out opportunities to try out and practice strategies in situations that took them beyond what they knew grammatically. Their mastery of grammar appeared to follow their attempts to communicate even though they did not deliberately engage in practicing the grammatical forms they mastered. It seems that their zest for communication carried them along." Often medium-range description is used to report the broad patterns of customary action the researcher has discovered. This is necessary if the reader is not to be overwhelmed with particular detail as reported in vignettes, direct quotes, and transcripts. Medium-range description enables the reader to get a sense of the forest as well as the trees. Yet there is a danger in medium-range reporting. It is apparent in the preceding example. Statements reporting patterns make claims of frequency without warranting those claims with data. "Students who were ... tended to seek out opportunities to ..." makes claims about occurences that are typical. But typicality is a matter of preponderant frequency. We need to be able to show the reader that, in fact, students of type X very often did behavior Y rather than behavior Z.

This is the point in a report where general description is necessary. The assertions made in summary description at a medium level of descriptive specificity need to be accompanied by reporting at a general level that surveys the frequencies (or at least the overall shape of the patterns) that obtain in the data corpus as a whole. If we know that out of 273 observations of type X students, they did behavior Y 262 times and behavior Z only 11 times, we can be far more confident of the assertion about the typicality of behavior Y than if it went unsupported by data reported by means of general description. General description is reported through some sort of tabulation, sometimes through analytic charts (for example, flow charts, tree diagrams, figures illustrating taxonomic contrast) and often through simple frequency tables. Descriptive statistics are the most summary form of general description, and as the example here indicates, this kind of counting is very desirable in warranting the validity of the conclusions of interpretive research. This is why I said at the outset that I thought the distinction between qualitative and quantitative research was misleading.

A final support for the validity of conclusions comes from the deliberate search for and analysis of discrepant cases. To return to our example, it would be important to identify and scrutinize the eleven instances of behavior Z, even though behavior Y occurred far more frequently. The instances of behavior Z are interesting precisely because they are the rare occurrences. Considering them can tell us more about the overall pattern we have discovered than if we were to ignore them. Perhaps we might find that behavior Z occurs only in situations A and B, while behavior Y occurs only in situations C, D, and E. Something is special about situations A and B. Upon closer investigation it appears that these are situations in which there is greater risk of embarrassment over errors in language form than in situations C, D, and E. The discrepant cases are explained as adaptive action in a situation of risk. This not only clarifies why they are infrequent, it sheds light on a general pattern in which attempts at language use are related to risk factors in the social situation of communication. The teacher might wish, for certain pedagogical purposes, to increase or decrease risk of student embarrassment in certain situations. The analysis of the atypical, infrequent cases as well as the more frequent ones can bring more insight than consideration of the typical cases alone. The approach to analysis that I have been describing is termed *analytic induction*. It is a hallmark of method in interpretive research and has been discussed extensively in the literature, beginning with the classic statement of Lindesmith (1947) and elaborated by Glaser and Strauss (1967).

RELATIVE ADVANTAGES OF INTERPRETIVE, SURVEY, AND EXPERIMENTAL RESEARCH: SOME POSSIBILITIES FOR COMPETITION AND COLLABORATION ACROSS PARADIGMS

I have said that one must consider the advantages and disadvantages of alternative research methods in terms of the kinds of issues and questions one wishes to investigate. Interpretive methods are most useful when one wants to document in subtle detail what is happening among a particular set of participants and what those happenings mean to those participants. These methods are especially useful when the objects of the research are routine and are taken for granted by the participants. People very often are unclear about the details of their performance in routine activities that have been overlearned and that thus fall outside reflective awareness. Consequently, self-report is not a valid means of determining what they do or how they think and feel about it.

This is a major disadvantage of survey methods in the study of routine activities like teaching and learning—teachers and students are usually unable to give a researcher a detailed account of what they did and thought. They are, as are any subjects, too close to their own routines to be able to see them clearly. Questionnaires and even open-ended interviews often ask for self-report data about language use that informants simply cannot provide validly. Informants try to be helpful and produce an account or answer the items on the questionnaire but what they provide is usually a far more rational and streamlined version of what happened than what actually occurred. Open-ended interviews in combination with participant observation and videotaping or audiotaping, however, allow one to check the accuracy of informants' self-reports about their behavior and to inform the analysis of what they were observed to have been doing by information about their perspectives on their actions. If researchers want to understand the subtleties of language use in social situations, considering the social situation as a learning environment, then self-report data alone are inadequate to that task.

Another problem with survey research is that because tests and questionnaires predetermine the information they seek from research subjects and collect relatively little information on each individual subject, compared to participant observation, survey data do not permit the researcher to examine the environmental context in which discrepant cases have arisen. Surveys and tests always reveal *outliers*—those individuals whose responses are atypical. Often the statistical analyses of survey data reveal *error variance*, frequency variation that is not explained by the prespecified set of variables identified in the research design. Outliers and error variance cannot be explained within the data sets collected through surveys. Those data have been context-stripped for the sake of efficiency, since a survey is a cost-effective, capital-intensive procedure (provided that the researcher knew enough or was lucky enough at the outset of the study to ask the right questions in the survey instrument). Participant observation is labor intensive—a liability—but by collecting much information on a few subjects, participant observation provides the contextual information within the data sets collected so that dicrepant cases do not simply remain inscrutable anomalies but can be analyzed to provide opportunities for new learning. Participant observation can also be targeted to follow on surveys, clarifying through direct observation some of the reasons that error variance and other statistical anomalies occurred. Following this topic-focused interpretive research, surveys (and experiments) can be redesigned and readministered.

Let us turn now to consider experiments. The most fundamental disadvantage of experiments is their lack of *ecological validity*. Often in experiments one attempts a simulation of activities that occur naturally. The advantage of the experiment is that some of the complexities of the naturally occurring environment can be simplified, and the action sequences can be simplified, in order to make relationships of analytic interest appear more clearly or more frequently than they would in nature. But this advantage carries with it a liability—the experimental simulation may be artificial as an environment for action and the experimental subjects' purposes are not as genuine as when they are performing similar actions to further their own ends in naturally occurring situations of action.

Another disadvantage is that in experiments, as in surveys, the major dimensions of analytic contrast in examining cause-effect relationships (in experiments these are called *variables* and *parameters*) are decided upon in advance, on theoretical grounds and on practical grounds of the monetary and social costs of collecting certain kinds of information. This works well in the physical sciences. Yet because social life is so complex (and some would argue, inherently various and unstable), often it is impossible to anticipate all the variables and parameters that may bear on the issue being studied. A crucial variable gets left out of the research design and thus no information on it is collected. This has been called (Raoul Naroll, personal communication) the "problem of the lurking variable." It is a perverse, frustrating liability in the use of experiments in social research. Participant observation, by collecting a wide range of information across an extended period during which the researcher engages in cycles of observation and reflection, is much more likely than experimentation to capture a wide range of kinds of variation that obtain in the natural setting (although it should be admitted that interpretive researchers can sometimes be just as perversely blind as experimenters to key features of the situations they observe). Consequently, data collection and analysis by means of participant observation is less liable, at least potentially so, to the problem of the lurking variable than is the classical experiment, in which simplification of the experimental task environment for analytic reasons leaves unexamined some aspects of the natural situation that turn out later to have been crucially entailed in the cause-effect relationships the experimenter was trying to study.

The problems of ecological validity and of lurking variables can be reduced somewhat by designing experimental tasks in ways that resemble as closely as possible those that occur in everyday life. We can return to Vygotsky for insight on this point, for in his pedagogical experiments in the study of language and thinking he attempted to design experimental tasks that were relatively high-fidelity simulations of tasks from ordinary life. He observed closely what the research subjects did in accomplishing the tasks, describing their actions in detail as would an ethnographer (Vygotsky, 1978, 58–75). Michael Cole, a cognitive psychologist with strong interests in the study of language, thought, and learning, is adept in designing actual learning tasks for children that function as high-fidelity experimental simulations, in the spirit of Vygotsky (see Newman, Griffin, and Cole, 1984). Cazden and her students (1979) have also taken this approach in designing peer tutoring situations as experimental tasks in the study of children's language use in classrooms. In these naturalistic approaches to experimentation, the actions of the learner in addressing the experimental task are observed and documented carefully, using methods of interpretive research. Thus, variables that were unanticipated in the initial conception of the experiment can be identified in *post hoc* analysis, and the experimental situation is closer to real life than the typical laboratory-like experiments.

The chief advantage of experimentation is that, of all methods of research, it provides the clearest evidence for statements about cause. Certain treatments or interventions, within the simplified world of the experiment, can be shown to result in certain outcomes of learning and/or performance. Sometimes experimental or quasi-experimental studies can be done with fairly large numbers of subjects, or with small samples of subjects who are randomly selected for the treatment group. This makes it possible to claim that what was found for the subjects in the experiment is true in general for a larger population.

Disadvantages of experiments, besides the problem of ecological validity (which calls into question the validity of generalizing from what subjects did in an experiment to what people do in everyday life) involve problems of ethics, politics, and logistics in successfully carrying out an experiment. Informed-consent guidelines, which are legally binding for much research in the United States, require that in social research those studied must be told the purposes of the study before they participate in it. This can invalidate the experimental results. Yet it may be ethically necessary. There are some political problems with classic experimental designs in which two comparison groups are used, with individuals assigned randomly to each. One comparison group gets the treatment and the other gets a placebo or some alternative kind of treatment. If the experimental treatment is highly desirable socially, for example, a life-sustaining drug or a teaching method that many citizens want for their children, denying some individuals the desired treatment may be politically impossible. Moreover, in school settings true random assignment to comparison groups can be very difficult logistically. What often happens is that ecological validity is sacrificed to ethical and political considerations, because the experiments that actually can be conducted rigorously are the most narrow and trivial in scope and conclusions. These easy experiments may not be controversial or complicated but they are often not very interesting, either. Rather than trying to study teaching and learning in experimental conditions that are inadequate because of ethical, political, and logistical considerations, it is often simpler and more useful to use interpretive methods to observe smaller numbers of subjects in classrooms as interaction occurs there naturally.

A major disadvantage of interpretive methods is that they are so labor-intensive that only small numbers of subjects can be studied in detail at any given point in time. That raises questions of generalization. If we collect many bits of information about teaching and learning in one classroom what does that tell us about teaching and learning in other classrooms, with other teachers and other students? Might we be better off collecting fewer bits of information about more subjects?

Not necessarily, the interpretive researcher would argue. One can say that generalization, as traditionally conceived, is next to impossible to achieve even in studies of foreign language learning, which aim to demonstrate generalization by use of surveys and experiments, because of the problems of validity of self-report data in surveys and testing and the problems of ecological validity, the lurking variable, and ethical and logistical constraints in experimentation.

Another way to think about generalization is to consider it as an empirical problem rather than one of formal matters of experimental design, sampling, and statistical inference. This is to place the determination of generalization in the hands of the reader of a research study rather than in that of the writer (see the discussion in Hamilton, 1980). In the hypothetical example sketched earlier, in which levels and kinds of risk and certain kinds of language learning were seen to be associated, readers of the research report could test the generalizability of that finding by looking in their own classroom to see if something similar were operating there. Another approach would be to take the findings from the single case study and design special surveys or experiments by which the generalizability of the findings could be tested on other sets of students and teachers. Yet another form of cooperation across the research paradigms is for topic-focused interpretive researchers to do follow-up detective work on the anomalies and error variance found in survey data. Ideally, "data-thin" short-term surveys and experiments with large numbers of subjects, and "data-thick" long-term interpretive studies of small numbers of subjects should alternate, preceding and following one another in a sequential program of inquiry.

Little of this collaborative work has been done across the two main kinds of research approaches. Some would argue that such collaboration is impossible because of paradigm conflict—fundamental differences in philosophy of science that underlie the two approaches to social research. Others claim that such collaboration could be fruitful. As of this writing the question remains open.

ENDNOTES

1. For the sake of simplicity in the text that follows, the terms *speaker, speaker/hearer,* and *speaking* will be used to indicate knowledge of writing and reading as well as of speech.

2. The conception does not draw the conventional strong distinction between text and context but sees context as residing in part within the text itself.

3. For discussion of the uses of audiovisual recording together with participant observation, see the special issue of *Sociological Methods and Research* that is entirely devoted to that topic (Grimshaw, 1982).

REFERENCES

Agar, M. 1980. *The Professional Stranger: An Informal Introduction to Ethnography.* New York: Academic Press.

Bateson, G. 1956. "The Message 'This is Play'." *Group Processes.* Ed. B. Schaffner. New York: Josiah Macy Jr. Foundation. 195–242.

Bogdan, R. D., and S. K. Biklen. 1982. *Qualitative Research for Education: An Introduction to Theory and Methods.* Boston: Allyn & Bacon.

Bredo, Eric, and Walter Feinberg. 1982. *Knowledge and Values in Social and Educational Research.* Philadelphia: Temple UP.

Cazden, Courtney B. 1988. *Classroom Discourse: The Language of Teaching and Learning.* Portsmouth, N.H.: Heineman.

Cazden, Courtney, Martha Cox, David Dickinson, Zena Steinberg, and Catherine Stone. 1979. "You All Gonna Hafta Listen: Peer Teaching in a Primary Classroom." *Children's Language and Communication.* Ed. W. A. Collins. Twelfth Annual Minnesota Symposium on Child Development. Hillside, N.J.: Erlbaum.

Cook, T. D., and D. T. Campbell. 1979. *Quasi-Experimentation: Design and Analysis Issues for Field Settings.* Chicago: Rand McNally.

Erickson, Frederick. 1986. "Qualitative Methods in Research on Teaching." *Handbook of Research on Teaching.* 3rd ed. Ed. M. C. Whittrock. New York: Macmillan.

———. 1988. "Ethnographic Description." *An International Handbook of the Science of Language and Society.* Vol. 2. Eds. Ulrich Ammon, Norbert Dittmar, and Klaus J. Matthier. Berlin, N.Y.: Walter deGruyter. 1081–95.

———. 1990. "The Social Construction of Topical Coherence in a Family Dinner Table Conversation." *The Talk of Children and Adolescents.* Ed. Bruce Dorval. Norwood, N.J.: Ablex. 207–38.

———. 1990 (in press). *The Social Construction of Discourse Coherence in a Family Dinner Table Conversation.* Norwood, N.J.: Ablex.

Glaser, G., and A. Strauss. 1967. *The Discovery of Grounded Theory: Strategies for Qualitative Research.* New York: Aldine Publishing Co.

Grimshaw, A. D., ed. 1982. "Uses of Sound and Visual Records in Studies of Social Interaction." *Journal of Sociological Methods and Research* 11.2.

Gumperz, John J. 1982. *Discourse Process.* New York: Cambridge UP.

———. 1990. "Contextualization and Understanding." *Rethinking Context.* Eds. Alessandro Duranti and Charles Goodwin. New York: Cambridge UP.

Hamilton, D. 1980. "Generalization in the Educational Sciences: Problems and Purposes." *The Study of Schooling: Field-Based Methodologies in Education Research.* Eds. T. Popkewitz and R. Tabachnick. New York: Praeger.

Hammersley, Martyn, and Paul Atkinson. 1983. *Ethnography: Principles in Practice.* London: Tavistock.

Hymes, D. 1974. *Foundations in Sociolinguistics: An Ethnographic Approach.* Philadelphia: University of Pennsylvania Press.

Lindesmith, A. R. 1947. *Addiction and Opiates.* Chicago: Aldine.

Moll, Luis, and Stephen Diaz. 1987. "Change of the Goal of Educational Research." *Anthropology and Educational Quarterly* 18.4: 300–11.

Newman, Denis, Peg Griffin, and Michael Cole. 1984. "Social Constraints in Laboratory and Classroom Tasks." *Everyday Cognition: Its Development in Social Context.* Eds. Barbara Rogoff and Jean Lave. Cambridge, Mass.: Harvard UP.

Ninio, A., and Jerome Bruner. 1978. "The Achievement and Antecedents of Labeling." *Journal of Child Language* 5: 1–15.

Shultz, J., S. Florio, and Frederick Erikson. 1982. "Where's the Floor?: Aspects of the Cultural Organization of Social Relationships in Communication at Home and at School." *Ethnography and Education: Children In and Out of School.* Eds. P. Gilmore and A. Glatthorn. Washington, D.C.: Center for Applied Linguistics. 88–123.

Vygotsky, L. S. 1978. *Mind in Society: The Development of Higher Psychological Processes.* Eds. Michael Cole, Vera John-Steiner, Sylvia Scribner, and Ellen Souberman. Cambridge, Mass.: Harvard UP.

Wertsch, James V. 1981. "From Social Interaction to High Psychological Processes: A Clarification and Application of Vygotsky's Theory." *Human Development* 22: 1–22.

———. 1985. *Vygotysky and the Social Formation of Mind.* Cambridge, Mass.: Harvard UP.

Wittrock, M. C., ed. *Handbook of Research on Teaching.* 3rd ed. New York: Macmillan.

Chapter 21

Implications for Classroom-Based Research of Various Research Designs[1]

Jerome L. Packard

University of Pennsylvania

This paper addresses the implications that different research designs have for classroom research. What I would like to do first is define how I will use the term *classroom-based*, and then illustrate how research designs that are often considered at cross purposes—namely, quantitative versus qualitative—are in fact complementary, as we try to determine how students optimally learn a second language in the classroom.

When we consider how various research designs affect classroom second language acquisition research, it is important for us to consider what the term *classroom-based* actually means. It clearly means different things to different researchers. Allwright (1983), for example, considers the term to be very narrowly defined. He defines *classroom-centered* research as

> just that—research *centered* on the classroom, as distinct from, for example, research that concentrates on the *inputs to* the classroom (the syllabus, the teaching materials) or on the *outputs from* the classroom (learner achievement scores) (Allwright, 1983, 191).

I believe that this definition of classroom-based is too narrow and restrictive to provide us with the most useful information on second language acquisition. I would like to define classroom-based more broadly than the definition given by Allwright, and then briefly defend this broader interpretation by showing how classroom research so defined enhances our ability to evaluate those processes that *do* occur strictly within the classroom environment.

If we as language teachers and researchers are interested in what goes on in the language classroom, and are interested in implementing those classroom techniques and procedures that are optimal for learning language, then we must extend our horizons beyond the four walls of the classroom when performing our classroom-based research. By this I mean that while we may want to keep the classroom itself as the primary focus of our investigation, we nonetheless should allow our methods of evaluation to extend outside the classroom. Also, our work in *planning* what will happen in class necessarily extends beyond the classroom, and is also a valid object of our classroom-based research.

Externally obtained test scores can be a good evaluation metric of certain activities that go on in the classroom. For example, if you want to determine how two methods of classroom presentation—for example, an inductive versus a deductive method—affect the mastery of a given grammatical pattern, a good (although admittedly not perfect) way of doing this is to use each presentation method with a different group, and then test both groups on their knowledge of that grammatical pattern, controlling other potential confounding variables as much as possible. The performance of the two groups is then compared to see how the groups differ in their knowledge of the target structure. This would be an example of using an extraclassroom factor (test performance) as a means of evaluating an intraclassroom activity (method of classroom presentation).

Some researchers argue that extraclassroom evaluation of an in-class procedure includes confounding factors such as students' response to test pressure, their level of test preparedness, the effect of time delay between the presentation of the material and when it is tested, and so on. However, it cannot be said that confining the evaluation to in-class observation will necessarily remove these influences. Any method of research that uses the classroom setting as its arena of observation is just as likely to be affected by confounding influences as is external evaluation. For example, if a researcher is performing in-class evaluation based on direct observation of student performance, such performance will necessarily be affected by factors such as response to classroom pressure, level of preparedness, level of attention, the performance of the other students, and the presence of the evaluator. It is difficult if not impossible for the in-class observer to eliminate these influencing factors, or take them into account in any systematic way.

One of the problems with strictly limiting our research domain to classroom-internal data is that we often fail to take into account the relationship between what happens in class and such external influences as teaching materials, curriculum, or even cultural background. If we restrict our research focus to in-class factors, then it is possible to view those factors in isolation. But in reality, we are also interested in knowing how the classroom-internal factors and the classroom-external factors interact. One of the advantages of allowing ourselves a broader interpretation of the notion *classroom-based* is that the classroom-internal factors may be investigated either in isolation or as they systematically interact with classroom-external factors.

To give an example, suppose we are interested in the ratio of student-to-teacher spoken language production in the foreign language classroom. It is possible to determine how this ratio varies in isolation—as, for example, a diagnostic for the amount students are speaking—or it is possible to view the ratio as it is affected by an external factor such as a certain design feature of the syllabus. Knowing merely what the ratio *is* provides us with information such as the ability of a certain teacher to elicit responses. However, knowing how that ratio varies as a result of changes in curriculum design may give us valuable information about how the curriculum should be structured.

It is only after a careful investigation of what transpires in the classroom in isolation, *as well as* how this is affected by external influences such as curriculum design and teaching materials, that it will be possible to design an optimal learning situation for the second language learner.

Now that I have defended the broader interpretation of the term classroom-based, let us use this broader interpretation as a context for considering what implications the two different research designs—namely, qualitative versus quantitative—have for classroom-based research. From here on, instead of using the term *qualitative*, I will use the term *interpretive*, which has been suggested by Erickson (this volume).

Is either one of these two types of research to be considered inherently less desirable than the other? Consider some of the characteristics that are said to be disadvantages of each type of research.

For quantitative research, problems are said to be the following:

1. The experimental environment is unnaturally manipulated or simplified, leading to conclusions that may not be valid in the real world. This is the problem of *ecological validity* (Erickson, this volume).
2. The variables of interest are decided upon in advance, causing the experimenter to focus on those variables and miss other potentially crucial variables. This is the *straitjacket* or *lurking variable* problem (Gaies, 1983; Long, 1986; Erickson, this volume).
3. There are ethical, political, or logistical problems involved in the artificial manipulation of the environment (Erickson, this volume).
4. Truly random assignment to an experimental group is difficult to achieve (Long, Erickson, this volume).
5. It is difficult to ensure that subjects are actually exposed to the experimental treatment (Lambert, Long, this volume).
6. Individual and contextual differences, which are potentially enlightening, are ignored (Erickson, this volume).

Turning now to interpretive research, the following problems are often cited:

1. It is inherently more amenable to subjective interpretation, resulting in a lack of scientific objectivity (Long, 1980).
2. It is labor-intensive, and therefore small-scale and short-term (Long, Erickson, this volume).
3. It results in conclusions that may not generalize over the larger population, due to the small size of the subject population, or because individual and contextual variation is not factored out (Long, this volume).

4. It does not provide clear enough evidence for statements about cause and effect (Lambert, Long, this volume).

5. The problem of *observer paradox*, that is, subjects in the presence of an observer or evaluator often behave in a different, perhaps nonnatural, fashion.

6. Claims of frequency are often made without the support of actual frequency data (Erickson, Long, this volume).

It is clear that each type of research design is perceived as having its own particular set of problems. I would like to argue that, in fact, neither research method is inherently preferable, and that the perceived weaknesses in each type of research design may be explained away or dealt with in one of four ways. First, the perceived weakness may be a problem with *both* types of research; second, the problem may be easily *addressable*; third, the problem may be a matter of *resource* availability; and fourth, the problem may be inherent to the nature of the *questions* being asked.

Note that the first letters of each explanation form an acronym—BARQ—which would be pronounced *bark*. In this regard, I would suggest that critics who feel that one type of research is inherently preferable to the other are barking up the wrong tree.

Let me first point out those problems that appear to be inherent in both types of research design.

Consider statements of causality. Interpretive research is often said not to provide clear evidence for statements about cause and effect. This problem, however, exists in quantitative research as well. This is because a researcher cannot necessarily assume causation simply because a statistical relationship has been demonstrated.

I once performed a statistical test to see whether a standardized test of English verbal ability would predict my students' ability to learn the grammar of the target language. Imagine my surprise when I found a negative correlation between the standardized verbal test score and the target language grammar score! In other words, I found that the better my students scored on the standardized verbal test, the worse they performed in learning the grammar of the target language. It turned out that in this case, the real reason for the statistical relationship—the so-called lurking variable—was that many of the students had had prior experience with the target language (and were therefore able to learn the grammar more quickly, resulting in higher grammar scores), and these same students tended to have lower scores on the standardized verbal test.

The moral of the story is that rather than being seen as a weakness only of interpretive research, the assumption of causation should be considered a potential weakness of quantitative research as well, since quantitative studies sometimes assume a cause-and-effect relationship when no such assumption is warranted.

To provide another example of disadvantages of both types of research, consider the question of objectivity. It is often said that quantitative research is better because it is objective, whereas it is said that interpretive research, on the other hand, is more subjective in nature, and therefore not to be preferred.

We may not, however, assume that quantitative experimental studies are devoid of observer or investigator bias. Studies that use a quantitative research design often contain a real but imperceptible bias in the choice of hypotheses that are to be tested (Gaies, 1983; Long, 1980), which Long calls a *hypothesis-generating bias*. In addition, in quantitative studies the data collector or data scorer may sometimes impose a systematic or nonrandom bias on the data being collected or scored. Although it is the responsibility of the primary investigator to reduce these sources of nonrandom error to a minimum, nonetheless we must not fool ourselves into believing that quantitative studies never contain elements of subjectivity.

Providing another example of how the same weakness may befall both quantitative and interpretive research, consider the straitjacket or lurking variable problem. This problem is often spoken of as though it is a problem only for quantitative research. In reality, as noted by Erickson (this volume), it is a problem for interpretive research as well. An interpretive researcher may be just as likely to couch his observations in terms of a preexisting category or bias, and by doing so neglect other plausible explanations for a given phenomenon.

Finally, the ethical, political, and logistic problems involved in the artificial manipulation of the environment, which are assumed to be disadvantages of quantitative research, are also a problem for interpretive research. This is because, as noted by Long (this volume), the use of outside observers and recording equipment in the classroom often involves lengthy and delicate discussions with various educators and administrators.

Now that I have demonstrated how some weaknesses of each type of research are in fact common to both types, let us see how the rest of these problems are easily addressable, or are simply a function of the resources available and questions asked.

First, the quantitative. Consider the problem of ecological validity. I would say that this is an *addressable* problem, and would follow Erickson's (this volume) suggestion that, where the experiment is performed in a manipulated non-classroom setting, the experimental situation should be made as natural or close to real-life as possible. A better solution to the problem would be to use the actual classroom setting and not unnaturally manipulate the environment at all. Examples of this would be to expose the regular and control groups to different curricula, or, as in the study (Allen, Frolich, and Spada, 1984) cited by Long (this volume), to have the teacher of the experimental and control groups emphasize different aspects of instructional technique.

Regarding the problem of truly random assignment to experimental group being difficult to achieve, I would say that this is also an *addressable* problem. In situations where it is thought that assignment to experimental group is nonrandom with respect to a crucial variable, a pretreatment measure of that variable may be taken, and used as a covariate in the statistical analysis. In this way, the possibility of nonrandom assignment of subjects to experimental group is controlled for.[2]

Concerning the difficulty of ensuring that subjects are actually exposed to the experimental treatment (Long, 1980; Long, Lambert, this volume), I feel that this problem falls into the *addressable* category, and may be addressed by following the advice of Lambert and of Long to more fully use process observational techniques and instructor feedback to ensure that experimental treatments are in fact applied. Since the control of the primary investigator over what treatments are applied decreases as the size of the study increases, I would follow the advice of Lambert (this volume) to keep the size of our studies to manageable levels.

Addressing the problem that in quantitative work individual and contextual differences are largely ignored, it is clear that this is due to the nature of the *question* being asked. The primary function of quantitative experimental research is to abstract away from individual and contextual differences, in order to find a result that is generalizable over different individuals and contexts. Since the loss of individual and contextual variation is the actual goal of this type of investigation, we may regard this weakness as being inherent to the question we are asking.

Let us now turn to interpretive research, and see how the purported disadvantages of this type of research are easily addressable, or simply a function of the resources available and questions asked.

Regarding the disadvantage that this type of research is labor-intensive, and therefore limited in scope, I would say that this is a problem of available *resources*. We can perform only the types of research that we have the resources to perform, which means that we must work with what we have. Note that this problem of limited resources also potentially applies to quantitative research, when, for example, a large enough subject population is unavailable, or when access to computers or statistical facilities is restricted.

Concerning the problem of *observer paradox* (that is, that subjects' behavior is often affected by the presence of an observer), I would place this in the category of *addressable* problems. This problem may be minimized by the use of unobtrusive observation techniques, such as the use of a one-way observation glass or the use of relatively unobtrusive audio-visual recording equipment.

For the problem that claims of frequency are sometimes made in interpretive research without the support of data on actual frequency of occurrence, I would also place this problem into the *addressable* category. Here I would follow the advice of Erickson (this volume), who recommends that descriptive frequency statistics be used to support claims of frequency whenever possible.

Finally, a disadvantage of interpretive research is said to be that obtained conclusions may not be generalizable over the larger population, either because of the small size of the sample population, or because individual and contextual variation enters into the interpretive analysis. This problem is the mirror-image counterpart of one of the problems of quantitative research, namely, that individual and contextual variation is ignored. Therefore, this problem also fits into the *question* category. There are times when a researcher wants to get an idea of the possible *range* of behaviors or look specifically at the effects of context (see Erickson, this volume), rather than determine the most normal or frequently observed case. When these types of research questions are being asked, it is to be expected that information regarding the larger segment of the population may be lost in order to include contextual information or information from the population extremes.

I would like to add to this list of advantages and disadvantages another discussion often heard about the perceived *functions* of quantitative versus interpretive research. It is sometimes said that interpretive research serves only to illuminate issues or generate hypotheses that are later to be tested using quantitative research. It seems that for those who subscribe to this view, interpretive research is relegated to being of service to quantitative research, as though the sole *raison d'être* of interpretive research is merely to provide grist for the quantitative mill.

I believe that this view is a bit one-sided, for once the quantitative researchers have crunched their numbers and come up with what appears to be a significant result, it still falls to interpretive researchers to observe whether and to what extent the suggested technique will succeed with individual learners, and in what variety of classroom environments. According to this point of view, it is the quantitative that is serving the interpretive, rather than vice versa. Therefore, instead of the interpretive being only of service to the quantitative or the quantitative being only of service to the interpretive, I would suggest that in fact the two approaches serve each other. Furthermore, both approaches in tandem serve the interests of second language acquisition by providing a more complete and valid analysis. Sometimes in a philosophical discussion, it is difficult to decide which is the chicken and which is the egg. Happily, in our situation, in which the relationship is mutually beneficial, it is not necessary to make such an arbitrary decision.

The main point I would like to make echoes a point that has been made elsewhere in this section. That is, the choice an investigator makes between research designs will depend not on the inherent superiority of one type of research over the other, but rather on the nature of the questions being asked, and the resources the researcher has available.

In the end, it does not really matter what type of research is performed, as long as it *is* performed, and it is done well. The research must be performed with rigor, with concepts and procedures precisely defined. The design must minimize problems and sources of error, and the work itself must be rigorously and meticulously carried out. In this way, we and our colleagues will know precisely by what means we obtain our results.

Furthermore, we must encourage the performing of classroom second language acquisition research at all levels, wherever there is genuine interest in how foreign languages are taught. Initial research efforts may be restricted by limited resources and may ask only the simplest of questions. But however modest such research efforts are, they constitute a contribution to the field, since our field in the long run will be enriched by such interest in the language-learning process. "A journey of a thousand miles begins with a single step," and so rather than discourage a budding researcher who may be in the process of developing the requisite expertise, this interest should be rewarded and guided. The more interest there is in asking principled, answerable questions about how second languages are learned in the classroom, the more classroom-based research will be performed.

And the more such research is performed, the better off our field will be in the long run.

In conclusion, both interpretive and quantitative research have unique and important roles to play in classroom second language acquisition research. Our choice of method is determined by the resources we have available and the questions we seek to ask. In order to minimize the possibility of drawing invalid conclusions, quantitative and interpretive researchers must proceed cooperatively, rigorously, and with eyes wide open.

ENDNOTES

1. I would like to thank Suzanne Flynn and Carol Packard for helpful discussion.

2. Covariates are measures taken of preexisting characteristics of subjects, which may affect their performance scores. These measures are introduced into an analysis of variance (more properly, analysis of covariance) in order to ensure that observed differences between the experimental and control groups on performance scores are not due to differences in those preexisting characteristics. For a more complete discussion, see Winer (1971), Chapter 10.

REFERENCES

Allen, J. P. B., M. Frolich, and N. Spada. 1984. "The Communicative Orientation of Language Teaching: An Observation Scheme." *On TESOL '83: The Question of Control.* Eds. J. Handscombe, R. A. Orem, and B. Taylor. Washington, D.C.: TESOL. 231–52.

Allwright, Dick. 1983. "Classroom-Centered Research on Language Teaching and Learning: A Brief Historical Overview." *TESOL Quarterly* 17.2: 191–204.

Gaies, Stephen. 1983. "The Investigation of Language Classroom Processes." *TESOL Quarterly* 17.2: 205–17.

Long, Donna R. 1986. "A Case for Case Studies." *Foreign Language Annals* 19.3: 225–29.

Long, Michael. 1980. " 'Inside the Black Box': Methodological Issues in Classroom Research on Language Learning." *Language Learning* 30: 1–42.

Winer, B. 1971. *Statistical Principles in Experiment Design.* New York: McGraw-Hill.

Current Foreign Language Learning Projects and Their Implications for Foreign Language Acquisition Research

Chapter 22

The Virtual Classroom Is Born: What Now?

John Barson

Stanford University

The question asked above is not rhetorical, because in addition to the promise of a breakthrough for foreign languages in an electronic classroom, there is also a growing puzzlement stemming from the complexities of this new way of approaching language teaching and learning. Thus, a 1980s phenomenon has gradually appeared at the intersection of a rapidly expanding technology and evolving language-acquisition theory, which the new technology has the potential both to implement and to test.

My particular perspective on what can emerge from the new electronic classroom environment arises from experiences as a practitioner-turned-researcher. It is difficult to resist trying out new designs, especially in a field where we are still looking for that optimal set of teacher-learner strategies that will make language learning more effective, more efficient, more global, more enduring, and, not the least important, more stimulating for the language learner.

It has been even more challenging to be able to conduct this teaching-research within the seemingly irrepressible expansion of computer technology in our decade. We have come a long way since I first started research on CALL nearly twenty years ago, using bouncing-ball Teletype terminals, the clanking sound of which all but drowned out the digitized audio piped into the students' ears through flimsy headsets (Barson, 1981). The advent of computers in the schools and on the college and university campuses is already having a major impact on education, or to be more precise, the mode in which instruction will proceed. One scholar says that "through the emergence of new tools, we come to a changing awareness of human nature and human action, which in turn leads to a new technological development" (Winograd and Flores, 1987, 163). The model described here has evolved over a period of four to five years and is the result of a search for a formula that could incorporate computers in a dual capacity, tapping into their instrumental as well as their agentive potential. This distinction between computers as tools (instruments to be used in some purposeful human activity) and computers as servers of more or less smart programs (containing specific knowledge or practice material to which students may expose themselves) can serve as a convenient means of characterizing divergent but not necessarily warring ways of exploiting the new technology.

Our first efforts led to practice-type software of the agentive type, *Blankity-Blank*, recently renamed *Zippity-Zap* (Barson, 1986), essentially a blanking device capable of providing a fairly wide variety of exercises (both discrete point and contextual) at all levels of instruction. By the time the software was developed, tested, debugged, and in use in various campus locations, the computer network and word processing (primarily in Macintosh environment) had progressed to the point where a number of activities in the instrumental vein could be undertaken.

Consequently, the focus was placed on means of achieving a readily practicable (or *practice-able* or even practical) environment through the *instrumental* use of computers, as opposed to their more widespread *agentive* application (that is, in fixed programs presenting either information or practice). This distinction, as understood by Terry Winograd, particularly in his study *Understanding Computers and Cognition* (Winograd and Flores, 1987), and by his student and our co-researcher, Françoise Herrmann, is central to the current bifurcation in the development of CALL. For now, suffice it to say that the instrumental classroom use of the computer, which will be illustrated in the teaching experiments described below, involves utilizing the computer both for writing and communication (messaging) in the accomplishment of clearly defined tasks. These experiments in the instrumental vein came to coincide with the theories and hypotheses of Winograd and Herrmann.

Immediate enthusiasm for computers as a powerful word-processing tool prompted an exploration of the possible integration of these machines into a language teaching approach that would make full use of their potential as tools that mediate human action. ". . . [T]he word processor . . . can be used to manipulate text structures that have meaning to those who create and read them. The impact comes not because the programs are 'smart' but because they let people operate effectively in a systematic domain that is relevant to human work" (Winograd and Flores, 1987, 175).

It became essential to explore the effect of positioning the computer with its many functions (word processing, networking, graphic capabilities, program server) as a principal instrument in a new teaching paradigm, which would focus on the accomplishment of tasks rather than on the execution of a given curriculum viewed as content. Students would be linked by the network in various working groups and avail themselves of all computer functionality in achieving their ends.

Proceeding within this framework, various teaching experiments were based on the following tenets:

1. The classroom environment should not be teacher-centered, that is, not teacher-driven for some specific curricular purpose. The interactional dynamic that we envisioned derives its impetus from tasks at hand, which

various groups or individuals have undertaken to accomplish in collaboration. These tasks, as they are carried out, in turn generate new tasks. The commitment to action (Winograd and Flores, 1987, 58) is an essential component of such a paradigm, and classroom discussions deal primarily with these actions and tasks. "The computer is like a tool, in that it is brought up for use by people engaged in some domain of action. The use of the tool shapes the potential for what those actions are and how they are conducted." (170). A similar perspective on the role of contingency in human enterprise is expressed by Lucy Suchman (Suchman, 1987, 28–29, 50–53, 68–69).

Such curricular constraints as might exist within a given course—an introductory grammar syllabus and supportive readings, for example—would float on a well-articulated series of computer-mediated assignments or activities undertaken by students either in collaboration or individually. The direction taken by these communicative tasks shapes the way in which grammar is called upon to inform the writing act.

2. In the execution of tasks, e-mail would be featured as a prominent medium of exchange in addition to classroom "conversation for action," again following Winograd and Flores's theories (1987, 64, 161). This would entail significantly downplaying the formal teaching of structure and literally eliminating all drill practice from the classroom. E-mail can serve as a pretext for piping to students information-rich, comprehensible context at various appropriate levels of discourse, language structure, and usage, thus providing a new and ample avenue for potentially very productive teacher talk. As teachers increasingly experiment with the type of discourse that being in such situations generates, more effective means of functioning in this particular mode may be discovered.[1]

3. Limit point-specific language teaching to providing remediation at the points of disrepair in e-mail messages and in students' drafts of papers to be submitted. This entails refraining from error correction in live conversational exchanges where it almost inevitably interferes with communication. E-mail offers abundant opportunity to correct expression, which tends to be predominantly oral in nature, although different from face-to-face conversation.

There are strong objections to interrupting oral exchanges in class for the purpose of correction, the argument being that shifting the attention from message to form is counterproductive, not necessarily effective, and certainly deleterious to the communication of meaning. With e-mail, the oral message and its meaning are given permanence, allowing one the opportunity to deal with structural aspects without "treading on the footsteps of meaning," as is so frequently the case if one interrupts real-time conversation. And the correction is being applied in the setting of a functional exchange, thus affording the teacher the opportunity to address additional considerations such as appropriateness of style, coherence, sociolinguistic implications. It no longer is necessary to ask students to perform unrelated grammatical exercises and then assume the burden of application to a functional real-world situation where the relationship may not be all that evident. In dealing with actual e-mail exchanges triggered by a real communicative need, a model is set, which can readily be applied to other similar situations or modified according to circumstance. Useful transference is more likely to occur using this approach.

As the various experiments progressed, assessing the broader implications of teaching in this new mode came to include these considerations:

1. Exploring the benefits of longer-term collaborative writing projects where the principal reader (or readers) would not specifically be the teacher. Writing becomes important to students when they know they have a real audience, an argument to sustain, or a story to tell.

2. Expanding the various configurations and capabilities of the electronic classroom as it increasingly became the principle domain of collaborative activity.

3. Examining the usefulness and efficacy of word processing and networking. In interuniversity collaboratives, messaging becomes an essential means of communication. On the local campus, with libraries and residences offering computer clusters for student use, the same potential exists for using technology in a redesigned teaching framework based on tasks.

4. Addressing the many issues raised by the need for testing and, if possible, empirical analysis, of the presumed progress made when students are immersed in a computer-mediated approach to language learning. Obviously, these innovative teaching-learning strategies, unfolding in nonconventional settings, would have to be assessed. Intuitions regarding potentially more effective and efficient language teaching and learning would have to be linked to ongoing research in the field of language acquisition, discourse analysis, writing as process (Donald Murray, 1980; Applebee, 1984, 176, 180) and subjected to the rigors of appropriately designed tests.

THE ROLE OF WRITING

Writing would of course play a key role in this exploration of the instrumental use of computers, since e-mail discourse is a written form of oral communication, albeit one that does not take place in real time. Word processors provide a convenient, powerful means of zeroing in on the writing act as it accomplishes itself over time during the course of revision, expansion, and refinements stemming from very genuinely felt communicative dictates. The electronic classroom, after all, basically implies an advanced medium for facilitating messaging not otherwise readily "activatable" in an ordinary classroom. (Oral, spoken production, on the contrary, is ostensibly available for being put into action by any group of learners and teachers engaged in interactive exchanges.) Interactive writing, on the other hand, can only be fully exploited in an electronic environment. Here, however, writing—as opposed to *written language*—will be taken to signify, first, a dynamic, off-the-cuff, elliptical discourse or a special kind of spoken discourse, or discourse that could almost have been spoken. This is precisely because the speed of computer communication does indeed produce an approximate transcription of what the spoken word might have been. This on-line messaging notion, then, by no means precludes taking on the acquisition of the more evolved, elaborated forms of written discourse that are taken for granted in another register of exchange (style, stylistics, rhetoric, and so forth.) In this regard, Alice Horning has advanced the hypothesis that learning to write is in fact equivalent to acquiring a second language: ". . . basic writers develop writing skills and achieve proficiency in the same way that other adults develop second language skills, principally because, for basic writers, academic, formal, written English is a new and distinct linguistic system" (1987, 2).

As soon as it was possible to meet on a regular basis in a well-equipped electronic classroom, students were encouraged to take a multiple-draft approach to all the written work they handed in. Peer and instructor input along with multiple drafts are recognized as key components of cogent models of teaching writing and literacy (Gaudiani, 1979, 1981). Although my approach was hardly innovative in that regard, implementing it using computers remained an area very much open to research. It was important to furnish on-line corrections (using the footnote mechanism of a fairly easy-to-handle word processor) in an effort to help students deal with important issues in writing: capturing the attention of the reader, organization and development of ideas, consciousness of tone or of differing language levels (formal discourse, familiar speech, and so on.) Clearly, the writing they are doing is an organic process that goes beyond insertion of ready-made phrases, whether they are provided by the teacher or by some convenient on-line resource. The computer definitely facilitates a type of experimentation leading to self-discovery and the sharing of meaning. As Tish Dvorak comments, "the presentation of foreign languages and practice of foreign language skills are increasingly informed by the understanding that language develops fundamentally out of a need and a desire to discover and share meaning. If one accepts this premise, then the primary purpose of writing instruction must be seen as helping students to learn a more effective and coherent way of developing and expressing ideas" (1986, 156).

Consequently, the initial evaluation of papers focused on the interest level of the communication, rather than on its form, since the texts would eventually be emended. Students seemed to benefit from the close attention they were invited to place on their written work. It was understood that they would print out their assignments and submit them at the end of quarter.

The word-processing approach replaced the red-ink-on-error system, which tends so often to leave the student paper sadly mutilated and depressingly messy. The focus is shifted from "you did this wrong" to "you can do this better" with some help from the teacher, from friends, or on your own, or from the crisscrossing sectors of the electronic classroom community, made possible by the instrumentality of the computer. If instructors prefer, or can come to prefer, writing with a keyboard rather than with a pen, then they will discover how much more ample a commentary can be provided. Error correction can be accompanied by additional remarks with examples, thus turning the correction process into a mini-tutorial based on the specific areas of greatest need for the student, highlighting, in a diagnostic perspective, areas where greater student application is called for. There are Macintosh applications, (for example, *Prose*) that offer built-in correction systems and handy features for making on-line corrections. But this is an area where teacher preference should prevail over a preestablished system of highlighting errors. Teachers will perforce have their own systems, and devising one's own on-line correction strategies is in itself making instrumental use of the computer. Teachers' efforts along these lines should not preclude students engaging in similar analysis of certain types of errors they make or tend to repeat (for example misuse of *pour* and *depuis* in French). The teacher diagnostic, rather than a complete picture, merely starts students on the road to a better understanding of their own inaccuracies.

If one is in an IBM environment, *Système-D Writing Assistant for French* (Noblitt *et al.*, 1987 and this volume) provides a highly stimulating environment in which to write, since one has access to an on-line French-English dictionary along with abundant grammar and vocabulary notes. Students can easily browse through these resources as they are writing a paper. At this point teachers could intervene with suggestions and comments.

As willing instructors become increasingly adept at furnishing on-line commentary, they can become, through their own thoughtful and imaginative use of the computer, part of the computer resource from which the students can benefit. The teacher—the human being—provides through the machine what the machine, for all its sophistication and multiple data bases, cannot. Since teacher comments are systematically incorporated into the students' computer-writing world, and thus become part of the permanent data base, they can ultimately function as a diagnostic tool. Teachers will have to decide whether to turn to commercially available annotation programs or to use individually devised applications. These decisions in turn rest on which computers and word-processing packages are in use in a given university.

To the question of how much time can be saved by resorting to the marvels of technology, one might respond by saying "none, so far" during this period of grappling, but there is no doubt about the help such feedback can provide to students. In time, applications will be created to provide this human assistance efficiently as well. What is important about this level of computer use is, specifically, that we not count on the machine to furnish what humans can supply with greater richness, complexity, and appropriateness to individual student needs.

INSTRUMENTAL COMPUTER USE AND INTERACTIVE, TASK-ORIENTED TEACHING

Our first exploration of the instrumental use of computers in a task-oriented classroom took place in the context of a classroom testing site for research on precisely this subject (Herrmann, 1990). The investigator's interests were focused on instrumental versus agentive use of computers, while the essentially improvisational style of the teacher was moving in the direction of increased experimentation with the spontaneous generating of class material from the substance of the interaction between students and between students and teachers. The research design aimed to study how the computer could be placed centrally and instrumentally in a classroom paradigm that had as its principal goal the writing of a newspaper. The teacher was interested in hooking curricular constraints to any and all situations that might arise in the accomplishment of a "real" task. For a number of years, the strategy of turning the classroom exchanges into stories had been in practice. These stories, recyclable in class as reading texts, were also expandable and variable from class to class depending on student contributions. Rather than impose a textbook or teacher construct on the students from which to demonstrate something about the language, a conversation is engaged with the group, which helps it to evolve along lines that will in turn become a vehicle for new structures, new vocabulary. To use Krashen's terms, if not all his theories, the students are involved in generating precisely that $i + 1$ input from which they can derive benefit as acquirers of language (Krashen, 1980). Although one might expect computer-oriented teachers to prefer a situation in which they can anticipate in orderly fashion the diverse components and progression that will make up the day's lesson (after all, is not CALL preponderantly oriented along these lines?), a moment's reflection quickly dispels the apparent contradiction between improvisation-oriented teachers and systematic computer use for language learning and teaching. When the computer is used instrumentally, it serves principally to mediate human communication (conversation), thereby becoming a perfect medium for both preplanned creative activities and spontaneous ones that spring from the classroom exchanges on any given day. It is, on the other hand, precisely the *agentive* use of computers that fits the more prevalent notion of what CALL has been until just recently.

The fact that the experimental group was an end first-year college class added considerably to the challenge. In spite of many obstacles that attended the first experiments—complex work environment using Xerox Dandelions and, user-*unfriendly* mainframe word processors, which at times confounded the computer initiates, a newspaper entitled *Assiette de Crevettes* (or *Shrimp Platter*) finally appeared. A repeat of this experiment in the fall of 1986 produced *L'Etoile française (The French Star)*.

The experience gained in the two local experiments informed the next, far more ambitious task-oriented project—an east-coast–west-coast teaching experiment in collaboration with another instructor who had also long been active in CALL at another institution three thousand miles away.[2] Together, we attempted to join two French classes, one at Harvard, one at Stanford, in a newspaper writing project along lines that had already become familiar from first on-site experiments at Stanford. The requisite environment for an interuniversity, collaborative, task-oriented teaching experiment was created. E-mail would be used for communication between students as they set about co-authoring articles of interest to them. Students would involve themselves as planners, reporters, editors, whatever was called for, to bring the task to fruition. Specifically, after ample discussion, they would commit to carrying out individual and collaborative tasks, completing the project within the deadlines furnished by the collectivity. The formating and printing of the newspaper would also be student-run, and the entire enterprise was to be accomplished in approximately six to seven weeks, using the target language both for writing articles and for e-mail.[3] Macintosh computers with *WriteNow* software for word processing would serve to generate articles, which then could be mailed from one university to the other via the network. In principle, all of the written activity would be preceded by ample discussion at each university and in the mail. As in the past, editorial teams would be formed so that students would, as much as possible, assume responsibilities for managing their project. Teachers were to assume the role of facilitator—being available to students for guidance, some direction, help with language difficulties—but avoiding any direct decision-making intrusion into the process. Pre- and post-testing would take place in the hopes of quantifying the presumed progress to be made by students in the experimental group (our working hypothesis) as compared with control groups set up in both institutions.

As might be expected, numerous problems beset the collaborative experiment: mainframe breakdowns, network malfunctions, inadequate machine facilities, complex protocols for mailing messages and documents in French. Perhaps that is the price one pays for being a pioneer in an environment where breakdown is considered by the hackers and the technicians as the rule of the game. In addition, extensive orientation was needed to assure that all students could use the computers and the network effectively. But the joint efforts were finally published on both campuses as *Le Pont Français* (*The French Bridge*) to mark the link between the two universities.

In conducting this experiment, we gained considerable insight into the manner in which these collaborative, computer-mediated activities unfold. Early periods of vacillation and uncertainty are followed by a moment of crystallization leading to fairly focused activity, research, and writing of preliminary drafts. Then, as the successive drafts are prepared or new articles attempted, there can often be a lag in collective energy. Students are not accustomed to long-term projects in a so-called language course, in a relatively short ten-week quarter. Even their longer, ten- to fifteen-page papers for history, English, or political science courses are often produced in fits of industry, days or even hours prior to their due date. Clearly, the newspaper writing task requires a strong degree of perseverance and, when that fails, ebullient support from the teacher, to bring the project to conclusion.

The presence of a major class project within a given curriculum also means that one must rely to a great extent on student motivation to do other work (such as reading or grammar assimilation) with little and sometimes no class time for going over assignments. For students whose instinctive learning strategies require a high degree of course structure, this is not the optimal learning environment, as they tend to put off everything that is not specifically going to be covered in class. But in this area of providing an out-of-class support for these aspects of the course, computers have a role to play. Software such as *MacLang* (Frommer, 1988) and *Zippity-Zap* (Barson, 1986), to name only two, provide ample discrete-point practice on a wide range of grammar and vocabulary. The positive features of this teaching-learning paradigm are fascinating to observe, and students may well clock in very significant long-term gains (facility, ease of comprehension, diminution of self-consciousness with regard to using a foreign language), gains that at present are not being picked up by our current achievement-oriented tests. Among these benefits are:

1. *Heightened insight into the nature of the writing act.* As students write and revise their individual articles, much attention is placed on the writing act and the relationship between writer and reader. The traditional situation where students are essentially addressing the teacher-evaluator, often a desiccated two-stroke loop, has been changed to include a new audience: the readers of the newspaper at large. Circulating the newspaper and obtaining feedback are essential features of such an activity.

   Writing a good article means, first and foremost, grabbing a reader's attention and then holding on to it by virtue of the strength of the content and the effectiveness of the style. A number of students had ample occasion to grow in this respect. In some cases, addressing the issue of how to pitch an article was fortuitously linked to grammar study as well. A case in point to illustrate:

   A student had opted to write an article describing all the different activities in Plaza, a campus hub of student activities, outdoor speakers, artisans, vendors, lunch wagons. The first version of the article was descriptive and fairly matter-of-fact in tone. "At eight o'clock this, at nine o'clock that. . . " The opening sentence, however, had promise: "White Plaza, five a.m. and all is still."[4] or something to that effect. The student carried out a suggestion that it might be possible, following the opening statement in the present, to write the entire article in the future (so that the humdrum of daily activities could be presented as imminent and in contrast to the morning calm), and perhaps return to the peacefulness of sunset at the conclusion of the article. Since the study of the future tense had just begun in this class, the student had a golden opportunity to use the future with stylistic gains in mind rather than verb endings. These would eventually be addressed at the fine-tuning, proofreading stage. This is important. Certain obvious grammar and spelling errors are often best left uncorrected in the first round of proofreading, since this shifts the emphasis to a counterproductive level of address. In addition, with these corrections tucked neatly away in footnotes, where they don't mar the appearance of the paper, they are available when needed.

2. *Involvement in and out of class in meaningful, authentic activity covering a wide range of comprehension and performance levels.* For example, the assuming of editorial duties by students, within the newspaper writing project, has a significant value for those students who elect to be leaders. The observer is struck by the editors moving into their roles, assuming leadership, giving orders, advice, all of this in French, either during class or in numerous mail messages sent to the entire class or to individuals. The style of these communications is often amusing, a remarkable blend of enthusiasm and frac-

tured French. But a great deal of the French used in these electronic missives is an interlanguage in its own right and is one that until recently has been difficult to set down.

Students working with the teacher or teaching assistant outside of class on preparing their newspaper (as was the case with those who opted to assist with formating and printing) would often spend hours in French dealing with problems, exchanging opinions, making decisions. The conferences with students revising their articles unfold in the same positive atmosphere. The involvement with the task at hand, be it field trips to museums to be reported on, visits to French restaurants to be critiqued, interviews of French-speaking campus figures, takes place through the language.

Even the tutorials and orientations were, in fact, conducted all in French, which with its high incidence of imperatives linked to hands-on activity, represents an intensive language acquisition variant on TPR (Asher *et al.*, 1974). The authenticity of the language use and of the context is striking, one in which the focus is clearly on message and functionality rather than on the language itself as an object of study.

This eliminates—or at least strongly neutralizes—the conventional emphasis that students themselves place on "learning" the language (in the Krashen sense, with the monitor keenly awake), rather than acquiring it as a by-product of meaningful personal involvement in a communicative activity. Hence, a significant lowering of the affective filter can be achieved, thanks to the nonthreatening environment of the collaborative class.

3. *Collaboration with peers.* We have only scratched the surface of what language learners can learn from each other. As Wallace Stegner has commented, "The best teaching that goes on in a college class is done by members of the class, upon one another." The teacher's job, Stegner goes on to say, "is to manage the environment, which may be as hard a job as for God to manage the climate" (Stegner, 1980, 11).

The Harvard-Stanford project, by setting up the instrumental computer link between two universities, between two groups of students united in a common goal, has at least demonstrated the feasibility of long-distance collaboration and the collaborative process, highlighting some of the very real difficulties that attend the undertaking, and shedding light on the nature of the interactive, task-oriented classroom.

In a current repeat-collaboration with Harvard, students will produce a magazine containing their collected stories, debates, surveys of opinions, and film reviews, to mention only a few topics. In addition, all the e-mail exchanges are being archived for future use as a data base for researchers.

E-MAIL

E-mail is making possible the systematic study of conversation, although one must take into account that it is a discourse in its own right, different from real talk in that it does not take place in real time in a face-to-face (or phone-to-phone) setting.

The success of e-mail tends to vary with the student. Some seem to thrive on it and write on a daily basis. Others will try it out at gunpoint (that is, because their grade may depend on it). Among the many uses of e-mail in an academic environment, one could mention the following:

1. Determining course progression on a weekly and sometimes even day-to-day basis.
2. Reminding students of upcoming events.
3. Reminding students of something that one has forgotten to mention in class.
4. Supplying information: grammatical, lexical, or other.
5. Staying in touch with students who are unable to attend class for one reason or another. Send them assignments or copies of any texts distributed in class.
6. Soliciting information from students (for example, What sort of mid-quarter exam would you like? Send mail. We are having some outside visitors in class next week. What activities seem appropriate to you? Send mail. I have to buy a new car. What do you think I should do? Send mail. An article in the paper the other day mentioned that a French student was stealing art treasures from the Louvre. Has anyone ever thought of paying for tuition by looting the campus museum? Send mail. I don't know much about rap music. Please enlighten me! Are you having trouble with any of the technology used in the course? Send mail and I'll try to help).

The e-mail network makes possible increased contact and allows the teacher to give each student customized attention at the appropriate language level for that student. Clearly, the potential is enormous. The establishment of a corpus of e-mail exchanges should shed considerable light not only on the discourse features of e-mail as opposed to real-time conversation, but e-mail as a vehicle for the evolution of interlanguage and information on the order of acquisition of language features, an area that has proven elusive to date.

COMPUTERS AND THE PRODUCTION OF VIDEO SKITS

Writing newspapers in collaboration is not the only use one can make of the electronic environment described above. Projects, such as writing a short video play and producing and filming it, are eminently worthwhile and greatly facilitated by the existence of a network of computers. After an initial brainstorming session or sessions to determine possible plots and characters, students can commit to developing various scenes either individually or in groups. Rough drafts can circulate immediately, using either hard copy or e-mail. This sort of enterprise often entails false starts and development of material that may not be needed at a later date. But no matter. It's all valuable writing experience that students pursue with gusto, since they are intent on making the action of the play work out to their satisfaction. The ease with which subplots can be developed, tried out, revised, and expanded actually makes an entertaining activity out of what other-wise would be drudgery or so slow a process that the play might never get written.

Many benefits accrue from such a collaborative enterprise, not the least of which is facing head-on what is involved in writing good spoken dialogue. Students are quick to perceive that although people talk in plays, it is a special kind of talk that answers to different rules from those governing conversational exchanges. Writing the skit therefore sheds light on at least two major types of discourse. When the time comes to costume, stage, and film the skit, the field-specific vocabulary and interactional language use that is required comes into play. This is an extremely varied and motivating project. A student who once performed in one of these theatrical productions commented, some two years after taking the class, that the highlight of the course was the sense of community that united the students in a common goal of putting together their own play. It was reassuring to hear that this project, conducted entirely in the target language, had left a lasting impression. In the area of play or video production, the technology will also have a major role to play: computers for communication, video cameras, editing machines. It is an elaborate, time-consuming affair to teach this way, but the rewards are many, both in terms of language learning and of pure entertainment with its concomitant result of continually reinforced interest. One often feels like a tightrope walker performing a juggling act over the the Grand Canyon. Perhaps that image can serve to characterize the ever-present challenge of language teaching in the new mode.

THE VIRTUAL CLASSROOM

Just recently, the whole concept of electronic communication was given another push forward when a local Macintosh French file server was set up at Stanford. Using an application called *Minishare,* students could log on to the server with individual usernames and passwords to ensure confidentiality of their work. The file server presently can be accessed from the undergraduate library cluster, from the electronic classroom, and from all the residences on campus.

The need for such a setup had arisen in the context of the Harvard-Stanford experiment, since students often wished to have access to their classroom file server when they were outside of class. In a somewhat makeshift arrangement, two Macintoshes in a central student computer cluster had been linked to the classroom file server, giving students full access to their applications and files once they had logged in properly. *Minishare* was simply an extension and amplification of this system to include any networked Macintosh on campus that loaded the requisite software. By connecting the teacher's office to the network, a new, completely electronic classroom comes into being. The Minishare-French Server environment, in addition to word-processing applications and *MacIP* to be shared by all, contains individual student folders to which the instructor alone has access. Students can now prepare documents in their own private workspaces and turn their work in by dragging an icon to the appropriate turn-in folder. Written assignments can be collected electronically, read and commented on-line, and returned to the appropriate student folders via this network, again simply by moving icons on the computer screen.

Topical material (for example, poems, articles, short stories) can be distributed to students electronically with minimal delay by placing files in special folders open to all students using the shared workspace. Most teachers enjoy supplementing available textbooks with texts of their own choice. The Local Area Network, described here, makes accomplishing this both easy and efficient.

In addition to its usefulness as an information exchange outside of class, the server can also be used in conjunction with overhead projection of the instructor's computer screen, as a means of structuring in-class discussion of student work. With students' permission, work can be displayed and commented on in a positive manner, to the mutual benefit of all. Students can thus give and receive feedback on documents, with teachers serving as mediators of the discussion from their terminal. The spirit of this type of group correction must always avoid stressing what is wrong by focusing on what can be made better with a little extra effort and knowledge.

At some point in the future, provided one were dealing with compatible mainframes, an icon-dragging system of communication between universities could be put into place that would offer certain advantages over our current Internet messaging system or FTP (File Transfer Protocol). Experiments are currently in progress at Harvard and at Stanford with local interfaces that simplify the sending of mail and shipping of document files.

As the walls of the traditional classroom gradually disappear like the Cheshire cat, leaving only an inscrutable grin of things to come, gently fading and making way for a new manifestation, quite real in its functional potential (albeit with the barest definable silhouette in physical space), it seems as if another giant step forward has been taken into the "age of information," as it is now commonplace to refer to our rapidly growing world of computers, data bases, messaging, word processing, graphics, simulations, and so on. We seem to be moving in the direction of information exchange so dramatically described by Nelson (1987) in his spirited book *Literary Machines,* in which he explains in detail the workings of hypertext—Project Xanadu.

REDEFINITION OF STUDENT-TEACHER ROLES IN THE ELECTRONIC CLASSROOM

Teachers who have already worked in an electronic classroom know, as impressive as a room of MacIIs or IBMs may look, that we are not really talking about science-fiction settings, futuristic chambers with strobe lights, buzzers, sirens, electrocognitive ions leaping from sensitized nodes to instill linguistic competence directly into a subject's brain. By the year three thousand, who knows . . . but for the present such visions are more typical of the fantasies depicted in a Woody Allen or Frankenstein movie!

A room equipped with networked IBM, Macintosh, NeXT, or Xerox Sun computers is a workplace, where students, in addition to the many classroom relationships we already know, develop a new one with their individual machine. So intense is this rapport between student and computer that when one finds oneself in an electronic classroom that is humming with activity—groups of students sending messages, individuals writing papers, others printing out papers, others sneaking in a game of *Bricks* or *Tetris,* one sometimes wonders just what teacher comportments are appropriate in this "strange new world." It is easy to feel cast adrift, at times almost not needed. Still, this intense yet informal ambiance is engaging and reassuring, since a great deal of work is being accomplished. It also offers ample opportunity to practice a new and unfamiliar role. The teacher eventually learns a new role, seeking out the most effective way to manage the multiple activities, supporting them without being intrusive, or refocusing student attention on the instructor without undue pressure.

Teachers will no longer rule supreme in the classroom. In fact, they may be in class less and on-line more. They will no longer lecture on language, supervise drill and practice, check up on reading assignments, but make themselves available as living models of various types of functioning and the level of discourse that attends them. They will weave in and out of the web of exchanges, reinforcing, commenting, answering queries, asking for information, giving instructions, participating in discussions or analyses of various types, leaving language tracks in all of these interactions, tracks that can serve as models to observant students. The style of these participations will vary considerably from teacher to teacher, as does the style adopted by various students in their dealings with each other.

The teacher will also have a new role to play as initiator and manager of purposeful e-mail exchanges. Purposeful, because students insist on authenticity and goals in this medium, while they might tolerate fairly high degrees of artificiality in more traditionally structured language practice. If a certain threshold of authentic need for communication—the message's *raison d'être*—is not attained or built into the setup, students will opt for some other avenue of exchange sidestepping the potential gains that could come from playing the game.

What is difficult to structure is a well-integrated series of small (fairly short-term) interactional writing tasks involving either teacher and student or various combinations of students in such a way as to make language use in the accomplishment of some immediate end an instrument of discovery about language function and form in the broader area of mental process, the shaping of reality, the sharing of human experience. In Winograd's words, "Much of our theory is a theory of language, and our understanding of the computer centers on the rôle it will play in mediating and facilitating linguistic action as the essential human activity. In asking what computers can do, we are drawn into asking what people do with them, and in the end into addressing the fundamental question of what it means to be human" (Winograd and Flores, 1987, 7).

If student purpose does not tap into a richer source of personal motivation than that of satisfying a teacher's dictates, no matter how well-meaning or even well-framed, that student's performance is likely to fall short of offering the special insights that come from self-motivated discovery. Gide's pronouncement

"Nathanaël, jette mon livre," ("Nathanaël, throw away my book") could be changed to "Student, toss out my assignments . . ." with an additional proviso that the student feel free to discuss the course of action taken with a supportive teacher, who will listen attentively and may even offer a suggestion or two.

CLOZE PRACTICE AND
LANGUAGE-PROCESSING RESEARCH

Zippity-Zap, IBM software initially developed for cloze practice and testing at Stanford, grew to become a general-purpose authoring tool for blanking texts in a variety of ways. In its present state of development, it contains the readings and exercises drawn from a first-year French language textbook[5] and exercises from a second-year French review grammar,[6] both in use at Stanford. In addition, the program contains supplementary beginning- and intermediate-level texts, mainly short stories in French. Other texts could easily be substituted, as has recently been done for a series of Russian texts, which are currently being tested.

Students, by selecting different deletion rates for a given text, can provide themselves with a varied means of checking their awareness of context and knowledge of vocabulary and spelling. Research on cloze as an evaluation procedure is not new. Research on cloze as a learning device is still sparse, but work so far indicates considerable promise.

It is possible to rely substantially on agentive programs such as this one to assist students in addressing the formal aspects of language (for example, verb tenses, declensions, agreement). Machines linked to servers can be available in library computer-clusters, language labs, and ideally, in the residences. Reliance on this out-of-class reinforcement makes possible allocating more in-class time to the accomplishment of tasks in a communicative setting. If one has access to an IBM classroom, software such as *Zippity-Zap* or *MacLang* can also be used for in-class practice or testing. The testing version of *Zippity-Zap,* in addition to scoring the student performances, generates a file containing all the answers the students entered for every blank attempted. In an ongoing research project, ancillary programs are being developed at Stanford, using Q'NIAL,[7] a program that will read the student answer files and display or print them in spreadsheet form, so that multiple attempts at solving blanks can be easily identified and studied. Once completed, this data base may offer some new insight into the processes involved in language production. Preliminary observation of chains of incorrect student answers during controlled tests reveals very interesting learner strategies as students grope for correct answers.

Further investigation of the performance of native speakers working with a number of texts is called for as well, along with systematic attention to those blanks in a cloze text displaying a great deal of activity (multiple attempts at solving the blank). There may be qualitative differences in guessing strategies employed by native or fluent language users as compared with language learners. Identifying viable hypotheses for predicting correctness could well be an important mental faculty to develop in learners during the acquisition process. In this realm there appear to be more questions than answers.

CONCLUSION

Returning to the question posed at the outset: what now, given the technological advances with which we are seeking a new teaching and learning paradigm? Given the present-day configuration of the experimental electronic classroom, more is inevitably in store as we close in on the twenty-first century.

Interactive video is still in its infancy, but we already have the tools to segment movies (or any material for that matter) pressed on video disks. MIT's interactive video project, "A la rencontre de Philippe" (Murray *et al.*, 1988) is a ground-breaking effort to give students a taste of authentic language use in an authentic setting, equipping them at the same time, through various computer tools, with the means to comprehend what they are viewing and hearing.

Computers with ample voice resources are still hampered by the large amount of memory needed to digitize sound, but these constraints fade away when one develops software on the NeXT box. With the NeXT computer just making its debut and Sun machines still relatively expensive, it is hard to predict just how quickly the ultimate workstation will take root at the university level. We seem to be moving in the direction of networked workstations, which have easy, fast access to multiple resources: dictionaries, thesauri, interactive video programs, compilations of all sorts. It is precisely in this environment that the agentive and instrumental use of computers can come together to form a more integrated, dynamic, and far-reaching conception of CALL than has been advanced to date. Learners in all disciplines, not just in languages, will avail themselves of these powerful resources as appropriate, interacting with teachers and peers according to their inherent qualities and abilities to inform the process, discovering new boundaries for human enterprise now that computers are here to stay and to be used for the quest.

Does the model elaborated above work more effectively than others? It is too early to tell. Preliminary empirical evidence from the experiments conducted to date does not support any resounding successes nor does it document any glaring failures. The very tests used are in question, since it is not clear that they are designed to measure what is being accomplished by using a computer-instrumental, interactive, task-oriented approach. Longer-term experiments are called for, increased collaboration between linguists, psycholinguists, sociolinguists, and the teachers who, in collaboration with the theorists, are in a position to put notions into effect, to modify current designs, to prepare the way for whatever developments the technology suggests or makes possible. In the meantime, increased emphasis should be placed on protocol analysis: unobtrusive audiotaping and videotaping of electronic classes in progress, documentation of anecdotal responses from both teacher and students.

For every teaching method one might try (and methods are legion) there always seem to be 15% of a given class who find it unsuitable and 15% who respond with unbridled enthusiasm. Why can't we win them all? Given the constraints imposed by university curricula, student outlook, goals and ambitions, not to mention our own teaching bias, this will probably never be the case. Yet in spite of the difficulties that are faced on a daily basis, this new medium is so intriguing in its ramifications and potential that one can only hope that colleagues, in increasing collaboration across the country, will continue experiments in this electronic teaching and learning environment, where developments in each succeeding week tend to make the previous one look like ancient history.

ENDNOTES

1. There is already some published research on e-mail discourse (Denise Murray, 1987, 1988a, 1988b) although this is not specific to foreign language learning.

2. Judith Frommer, Department of Romance Languages, Harvard University.

3. Underwood had already suggested the use of e-mail (66–67), but cross-country, coast-to-coast, class-to-class, computer correspondence is a far more extended use of e-mail than his brief treatment covers.

4. This sentence and the one quoted above are translated from the student's original version in French.

5. Gérard Jian and Ralph M. Hester, *Découverte et Création,* Houghton Mifflin, 4th ed., 1985.

6. John Barson, *La Grammaire à l'Oeuvre,* 4th ed., New York: CBS College Publishing (Holt, Rinehart, and Winston), 1987.

7. *Queen's University Nested Interactive Array Language,* Kingston, Ontario: Nial Systems, 1985.

REFERENCES

Anderson, D., B. Tschumy, C. Stinson, and A. Jeffrey. 1988. *Write Now for Macintosh.* ver. 2.00. T-Maker Company.

Applebee, Arthur. 1981. "Improving the Teaching of Writing, NCTE Reasearch Report." *Writing in the Secondary Schools: English and the Content Area.* NCTE.

———. 1984. *Contexts for Learning to Write.* Norwood, N.J.: Ablex Publishing Corporation.

Asher, James, J. Kusudo, and R. de la Torre. 1974. "Learning a Second Language Through Commands: The Second Field Test." *Modern Language Journal* 58: 24–32.

Barson, John. 1981. "University-Level CAI in French." *University-Level Computer*

Assisted Instruction at Stanford, 1968–80. Ed. Patrick Suppes. Stanford: Stanford University, Institute for Mathematical Studies in the Social Sciences.

————. 1986. *Zippity-Zap.* Software for cloze practice. Stanford: Stanford University.

————. 1987. *La Grammaire à l'Oeuvre.* 4th ed., New York: Holt Rinehart and Winston–CBS College Publishing.

Bartholomae, D. 1980. "The Study of Error." *College Composition and Communication* 31: 253–69.

Dulay, H., M. Burt, and S. Krashen. 1984. *Language Two.* New York: Oxford UP.

Dvorak, Trisha. 1986. "Writing in the Foreign Language." *Listening, Reading, and Writing: Analysis and Application.* Northeast Conference on the Teaching of Foreign Languages.

Flower, L. 1979. "Writer-Based Prose: A Cognitive Basis for Problems in Writing." *College English* 41: 19–37.

————. 1985. *Problem-Solving Strategies for Writing.* 2nd ed. New York: Harcourt Brace Jovanovich.

Frommer, Judith. 1988. *MacLang.* ver. 3.3. Software for authoring exercises for language practice. Kinko Copies.

Gaudiani, Claire. 1979. "French Composition Teaching: A Student-Generated Text Editing Approach." *French Review* 53.2: 232–38.

————. 1981. "Teaching Writing in the Foreign Language Curriculum in Education: Theory and Practice." 43, Center for Applied Linguistics, Washington, D.C., ERIC Clearinghouse on Languages and Linguistics, Washington, D.C.

Herrmann, Françoise. 1990. "Instrumental and Agentive Use of Computers: Their Role in Learning French as a Foreign Language." Doctoral dissertation, Stanford University.

Horning, Alice. 1987. *Teaching Writing as a Second Language.* Carbondale: Southern Illinois Press.

Jian, Gérard, and Ralph M. Hester. 1985. *Découverte et Création.* 4th ed. Boston: Houghton Mifflin.

Johnson-Laird, Philip. 1988. *The Computer and the Mind.* Cambridge, Mass.: Harvard UP.

Klein, Wolfgang. 1986. *Second Language Acquisition.* New York: Cambridge UP.

Krashen, Stephen. 1980. "The Theoretical and Practical Relevance of Simple Codes in Second Language Acquisition." *Research in Second Language Acquisition.* Selected papers of the Los Angeles Second Language Reserach Forum. Rowley, Mass: Newbury House. 11–12.

————. 1981. *Second Language Acquisition and Learning.* Oxford: Pergamon Press.

————. 1982. *Principles and Practice in Second Language Acquisition.* Oxford: Pergamon Press.

Kroll, B. M., and J. C. Schafer. 1978. "Error Analysis and the Teaching of Composition." *College Composition and Communication* 29: 243–48.

Minsky, Marvin. 1986. *The Society of Mind*. New York: Simon and Schuster.

Murray, Denise. 1985. "Computer Conversation: Adapting the Composing Process to Conversation." Paper presented at the International Conference on Computers and the Humanities. Brigham Young University.

———. 1987. "Computer-Mediated Communication as a Tool for Language Learning." *TESOL Newsletter* June 1987: 13–14.

———. 1988a. "Computer-Mediated Communication: Implication for ESP." *English for Special Purposes* 7.1: 3–18.

———. 1988b. "The Context of Oral and Written Language: A Framework for Mode and Medium Switching." *Language in Society* 17.3: 351–73.

Murray, Donald M. 1980. "Writing as Process: How Writing Finds Its Own Meaning." *Eight Approaches to Teaching Composition*. Eds. T. R. Donovan, and B. W. McClelland. Urbana, Ill.: National Council of Teachers of English.

Murray, Janet, Douglas Morgenstern, and Gilberte Furstenberg. 1988. "The Athena Language Learning Project: Design Issues for the Next Generation of Computer-Based Language-Learning Tools." *Modern Technology in Foreign Language Education: Applications and Projects*. ACTFL/NTC.

Nelson, Theodor. 1987. *Literary Machines*. South Bend: Theodor Nelson.

Noblitt, James, William Sola, and William Pet. 1987. *Système D, Writing Assistant for French*. Software. Boston, Mass.: Heinle and Heinle.

Perl, S. and A. Egendorf. 1979. "The Process of Creative Discovery: Theory, Research and Pedagogical Implications." *Linguistics, Stylistics and the Teaching of Composition*. Ed. D. McQuade. Akron: L and S Books.

Q'NIAL. 1985. *Queen's University Nested Interactive Array Language*. Kingston, Ontario: Nial Systems.

Selinker, L. 1972. "Interlanguage." *International Review of Applied Linguistics* 10.3: 209–31.

Shaughnessy, M. 1977. *Errors and Expectations*. New York: Oxford UP.

Stegner, Wallace. 1980. *On the Teaching of Creative Writing*. Hanover, N.H.: UP of New England.

Suchman, Lucy A. 1987. *Plans and Situated Actions: The Problem of Human Machine Communication*. Cambridge, U.K., and New York: Cambridge UP.

Underwood, John. 1984. *Linguistics Computers and the Language Teacher*. Rowley, Mass.: Newbury House.

Valdes, G., T. Dvorak, and T. Pagan Hannum. 1984. *Composicion: Proceso y Sintesis*. New York: Random House.

Winograd, Terry, and Fernando Flores. 1987. *Understanding Computers and Cognition*. Reading, Mass.: Addison-Wesley.

Chapter 23

The Use of Interactive Video in the Learning of Japanese

Eleanor Harz Jorden

The National Foreign Language Center
The Johns Hopkins University

Probably the greatest challenge of a curriculum in a "truly foreign"[1] language like Japanese is the adequate treatment of the relationship between the language and what might be called the *acquired culture* of the society—the mindset, the patterns of behavior, generally outside the consciousness of natives of the society. Acquired culture, like acquired spoken language, is gained without awareness, and it becomes so much a part of natural, automatic, daily behavior that it is often assumed by natives to be universal human behavior. Some of its features, however, may be recognized by members of the society, often as in-group characteristics not to be discussed with the outside world. Such features constitute hidden or suppressed culture, which may constitute an important segment of a society's acquired culture.

Acquired culture complements *learned culture,* the parallel to learned language, which is deliberately studied (or not, according to choice). In the case of a spoken language, it is the foreigner who learns, consciously and deliberately; but natives and foreigners alike learn to read and write a language as a systematic course of study. Learned culture is also learned by all—both natives and foreigners—if chosen as an object of study. It encompasses aesthetic culture (literature, art, music, and the like), informational culture (facts about the culture), and skill culture (how to perform various activities according to the accepted methods of the society—how to cook, saw wood, wrap a package, and so on).

When the acquired culture of a foreign society differs radically from one's own, it requires extensive treatment within a course that deals with the language of that society, if the learner is to use the language appropriately and communicate effectively. A culturally meaningful transfer from language *A* to language *B* must never be automatically equated with direct translation, no matter how accurate the translation may be linguistically. Nevertheless, this problem is woefully ignored in most language programs, even when the cultural differences involved are of the magnitude of those that obtain between Japan and the United States. Target native instructors are particularly apt to overlook—or, in some instances, conceal—the need for such instruction. And included among the areas most subject to omission are those where surface behaviors may coincide in spite of significant differences in cultural motivation.

It was once suggested, only partly in jest, that before universality or general validity across languages was claimed for any new sociolinguistic theory, it should be checked out in Japanese. A more serious proposition is that the closely related languages and cultures of Western Europe, viewed as a subset of a parent group that includes truly foreign languages and cultures, define a more realistic approach to foreign language analysis and pedagogy. One need only cite the problems and delays in formulating the ACTFL language-proficiency guidelines that resulted from the initial attempt to use the so-called generic guidelines, which had been based specifically on Western European languages, as the basis for the extension to languages like Japanese and Chinese.

The interplay of language and acquired culture can have an effect on pedagogy far more pervasive than is often realized, for instructors are themselves bound by their own native acquired culture, which exerts a strong influence on their attitudes and their teaching. Consider an example from Japanese. Over the years the Japanese have had a preoccupation with uniqueness. One might say that they are indeed unique in that they believe that they alone—they uniquely—are unique. The emphasis on "we Japanese" as opposed to all the rest of the world has important implications for language instruction. A conviction that the language is uniquely difficult and pride in that belief have led many Japanese to alter it deliberately for foreign consumption. It is unusual to find published teaching materials that do not contain countless examples that would *never* be used by native speakers. They may contain distortions and inaccuracies, including stylistic contradictions, that are just as difficult for a learner to master as authentic Japanese would be. The ultimate example of this tendency was the creation last year, after many years of work at the Japanese National Language Research Institute, of a special dialect of Japanese—*kanyaku-nihongo*—to be taught to foreigners. Its promoters see this as a means by which foreigners can cope with their "uniquely difficult" language more easily and Japanese can become more available as an international instrument. However, most foreigners regard it as simply another way to keep them in the out-group—unable to understand the real language or to communicate with any Japanese except those who have mastered this special artificial dialect.

To the Western mind, the justification for the dialect presents a puzzling contradiction. If, as it is claimed by its principal advocate, "teaching Japanese to non-native speakers is in effect teaching them how the Japanese order their world"; and "those who study Japanese are bound to develop at least some understanding of the Japanese mind,"[2] it would seem to be extremely important to leave the language intact, in the interest of providing culturally revealing material. On the other hand, language that has been deliberately altered to make it easier for foreign students to learn will hardly serve as a reliable basis for the revelation of

Japanese acquired culture. It is in fact the actual creation of this dialect and the statements that have been made about it, rather than the special dialect itself, that do indeed provide a window on the nature of Japanese acquired culture.

In the 1960s, I published a two-volume textbook, *Beginning Japanese,* which for that era, represented a new approach for Japanese language learning materials. But with the passage of time, the need for a replacement became increasingly evident. In addition to incorporating revisions in my own analysis of the linguistic structure of the language, I was most anxious to add the cultural component that was missing from the earlier text: I wanted to present authentic language material culturally contextualized, with detailed analysis on both levels—the kind of orientation essential for *learners* of the language.

Of all the new technologies being adapted for foreign language study, video held the most promise for introducing the learner to a spoken language with a cultural orientation. The video I envisioned was *not* of the genre that provides supplementary visual material with a sound track in the target language of an only vaguely defined level of linguistic competence. It was *not* to introduce learners to the temples, art works, food, and scenic beauty of Japan, nor was it to teach students how to make sushi or fold paper cranes; it was *not* to create a fictional story revolving, for example, about the life of an imaginary family in Japan; nor was it to present "skits," the main thrust of which was their plots, with emphasis on humor or the unexpected, for example. Such videos, usually intended to be viewed once or twice at most, focus on the introduction of learned culture of all varieties—aesthetic, informational, and skill—or material that will amuse, with samples of the target language that presuppose previous learning or acquisition. My purpose was different: the introduction of language within a framework of acquired culture that would enable foreigners to interact effectively with cultural natives. These videos were to be scripted as culturally contextualized language *learning* materials, presupposing absolutely no previous knowledge of the language. In this, they would, as far as I knew, represent a new approach.

The materials have now been completed according to plan, with the collaboration of Mari Noda—a native speaker of Japanese, who is also a professional linguist, with background in theoretical linguistics, and an experienced and unusually well-trained, talented teacher of Japanese as a foreign language. Her ability to write materials that satisfied all the constraints that had been established is indeed a rare talent.

The video scripts constitute the core of the curriculum, from which the drills, exercises, and supplements are derived. These are the basic conversations for memorization—but in contrast with the past, learners are provided not only an aural model, but also an authentic picture of where the given conversations might occur and how native speakers would sound *and look* when participating in them. Much more than voice is involved: proxemics, eye contact, gestures, timing, dress—all play a part in the process of communication and all send out important messages. What is more, these communicative features are culture-specific. To ignore them when teaching a language is to forget the primary purpose of language. The linguistic code is only part of the challenge of learning a foreign language: the delivery system must be analyzed and drilled with equal emphasis, and video is an ideal medium for this component of foreign language learning.

The completed video series consists of about 250 scripted scenes on three interactive laser discs (also available on video cassettes), beginning from level-zero competence and proceeding through an intermediate spoken level, systematically introducing the important structural patterns and basic vocabulary of the language. The situations represented in each scene were selected for their relevance for foreign learners. The video series is accompanied by a three-volume textbook, containing extremely detailed, integrated structural and cultural notes, plus response drills (about sixty-five hundred exchanges), application exercises, eavesdropping practice, utilization outlines, and structural checkups, with accompanying audiotapes and video drill tapes.

The laser discs offer distinct advantages over the corresponding videocassettes: immediate access to individual core conversations; a slow-motion capability for paralinguistic study in depth; clearer sound and more realistic color; and durability (laser discs do not wear out).

These materials have as their goal competence in the spoken language only. For the learning of reading and writing, requiring totally different skills and different pedagogical approaches, this kind of video is obviously not a useful medium. However, mastering the written language presents an equally urgent requirement for understanding acquired culture, in order to develop the ability to read between the lines and to understand the written delivery system in Japanese society. All this is learned more efficiently—as we know from the superior reading skill demonstrated by native speakers—when the learner already has some familiarity with the spoken language and its delivery system. An accompanying reading text is now in preparation—each lesson of which presupposes control of the spoken language at least through the level of the corresponding lesson in the spoken text. It is constructed with the specific goal of teaching learners to read the Japanese written language, not decode it through word-for-word direct translation into English. It emphasizes the differences between the spoken and written language, and drills and supplementary materials aim specifically at developing a true facility in reading and writing.

In composing the core conversations that constitute the video scripts, a number of constraints were rigorously observed as essential to the production of maximally useful learning materials:

1. All material is authentic, naturally occurring, spoken Japanese—not "distorted Japanese for foreigner talk," and not written-style Japanese masquerading as spoken, substituted because it is easier for instructors to teach. Students must be able to study whatever is presented with confidence that it is an authentic addition to their target language repertoire. It is not language that must be unlearned later.

2. All core conversations represent situations in which a foreigner could be—or must be—one of the participants. Since they serve as the learners' basic material for memorization—as models for speaking practice, not supplements for comprehension practice—there was no reason for creating dialogues between a Japanese mother and child, or two airport porters, for example; hundreds of such conversations are included in supplementary exercises, recorded on audiotape, for oral comprehension.

3. The core conversations are "clean": structural patterns and vocabulary are analyzed and explained in the lesson in which they first appear. Except in occurrences within greetings and ritual expressions, no structural pattern is temporarily ignored "to be explained in a later lesson." In some instances, explanations are provided over a span of several lessons, with increasing depth, but at least a basic analysis is provided at the time of the initial introduction, covering that initial type of usage.

4. The amount of new vocabulary and structure in each lesson is limited, and the necessity for repeated use in various contexts in both the original lesson and succeeding lessons is recognized.

5. Structural patterns are introduced according to two basic ordering principles: the simple precedes the complex; the frequently occurring precedes the rare.

   However, for putting these principles into practice, an overall structural analysis of the language was a prerequisite. Pedagogically effective ordering could not be determined unless there was a clear notion from the outset of what structural patterns were to be introduced in the entire corpus, and how these patterns related to each other. Well-designed teaching materials demonstrate to the learner that a language is a system and that its pieces interlock. In contrast, a randomized approach in which structural ordering depends only on what patterns happen to occur in various situational contexts can be expected to produce weak grammatical control. They encourage the belief that learning a foreign language involves little more than the mastery of a topically arranged phrase book.

   A pervasive characteristic of a truly foreign language is the lack of precise overlap between its vocabulary and structural patterns and those of the closest equivalents in the native language of the learner. The overall systematic analysis that was the prerequisite for the production of these Japanese materials is presented to the learner in the form of explanatory notes related to the content of each core conversation. These notes are based on the internal system of Japanese structure: they do *not* attempt to substitute translation into an approximate English equivalent for meaningful analysis. Grammatical terms are defined *for Japanese,* not on the basis of the word class to which an English equivalent happens to belong. What is more, the structural notes are sufficiently detailed to satisfy students whose native language offers little help in making accurate predictions. English-speaking learners who assume a generalized relevance of the salient linguistic features of their native language—the distinction between singular and plural, or among past, present, and future, for example—are headed for a shock when they begin their study of Japanese.

   Language learners must be led into the structural system step by step: with each new pattern there should be explanations of how the new integrates with what has previously been introduced. Only in this way can the language unfold as a unified system.

6. The corpus, then, is structurally driven but contextually grounded. Without context—and this applies to drill material as well as basic core material—

language loses its communicative function. However, if the order of introduction is *determined* by context, many of the preceding constraints, all of which I consider essential to the effective learning of Japanese, must be abandoned.

To suggest, for example, that the introductory conversation in a Japanese language curriculum should be a dialogue between a foreigner, newly arrived in Japan, and a Japanese official at the customs counter of the airport—a favorite for some text writers—would mean that either extremely complex structures and vocabulary would be presented to learners for their initial contact with the language, or the dialogue would be a never-to-be-encountered sequence of "funny Japanese for foreigners." The cultural objections are equally serious. In the real world, no Japanese customs official ever initiates a conversation with an American traveler in Japanese; he switches to Japanese only if the foreigner uses the language and speaks it with facility. In contrast, if the scripting is based on linguistically valid ordering, culturally realistic and useful contexts that are appropriate to the language can be selected after the linguistic input is determined.

7. Contexts were selected on the basis of foreigners' needs. They include not only situations related to surviving in the culture in terms of physical requirements (with appropriate accompanying cultural analyses) but also those requiring skill in culture-specific social interaction—inviting, requesting, accepting, refusing, criticizing, complaining, disagreeing, self-effacement, and the use of go-betweens.

The above constraints argued against attempting to use selections from Japanese movies or television programs as a replacement for scripted dialogues. Such material is never prepared with foreign learners in mind as a systematic introduction of structural patterns and maximally useful vocabulary. What is more, before any isolated segment can be interpreted correctly, particularly by foreign learners, detailed and often complicated background information is required: who are these speakers? what is their relationship? what is the ongoing plot/context? what is happening in this segment? what has occurred previously? This is clearly a less efficient approach for the beginning or intermediate learner. Selections from the Japanese media include a structural and lexical sampling that has no pedagogical motivation and rarely involves situations in which foreigners play a role. They can be excellent for comprehension practice—when carefully selected and introduced at an appropriate point in the curriculum—but they are rarely efficient models for the beginning and intermediate student learning to *speak*.

The creation of the core conversations for the initial lessons presented the greatest challenge, given all the above constraints. The solution was to make them extremely short—that is, single exchanges of the kind that occur naturally and constantly in everyday interaction, in situations in which the setting—the shared information—provides background information that disposes of the need for explicit, grammatically complex utterances. Thus, in Lesson 1, the equivalent of *Did you understand? . . . Yes, I did.* constitutes a normal exchange in a situation in which someone has just demonstrated (on the videotape) a computer procedure.

Later on, students learn how to ask the more complicated question, *Did you understand the procedure that was demonstrated on the computer?*, required when the setting does not define the topic.

The next step in succeeding lessons involves expanding single exchanges into longer conversations—a process far more complicated than simply combining them, and one for which English provides a very poor model. However, no core conversation in the entire corpus is longer than six or seven exchanges, with most averaging three or four. This length has proved to be most suitable for extended utilization of the conversations and for their memorization.

Although the core conversations follow no developing story line, nor do they unfold according to a predetermined plot, they do involve a fixed group of characters whose interpersonal relationships are crucial as determinants of the language style they use in speaking with each other. Perhaps the most striking overall characteristic of the Japanese language is the fact that it has no neutral style; every utterance—and every written sequence—reflects a stylistic choice, made on the basis of addressee/audience, referent, topic of conversation, setting, and so forth. There is no single neutral equivalent in Japanese for a neutral English question such as, *Is Mr. Smith here?* Sensitizing learners to this phenomenon and instructing them as to the salient features that determine appropriate choices require constant, careful, detailed treatment in an instructional corpus.

In the core conversations, the relationship between each pair of participants is reflected in their speech styles with meticulous consistency. This provides learners with a wide range of recurring stylistic models as reflections of interpersonal relationships and settings: boss-employee, co-workers in business, professor-student, fellow students, husband-wife, guest-host/hostess, customer-clerk, and more. Thus, as learners progress through the lessons and familiarize themselves with various politeness and formality levels, they also become aware of the centrality of this feature of the language and familiar with the factors of a setting that are salient in the choice of each style.

Following the writing, revision, and checking of the core conversations with a number of native speakers, arrangements were made for the actual production of the video—by a professional Japanese film company with experience in the production of documentary films. The conversations were filmed in realistic settings in Tokyo, with professional and semiprofessional Japanese actors and actresses. The players were not informed until the last day of filming as to the planned utilization of the material, thereby preventing the kind of distortion in speaking style that would undoubtedly have resulted had they known their audience would be composed mainly of foreigners studying the Japanese language.

Some scripts included vocabulary and structural patterns for which alternate forms were acceptable; in such cases, the players were instructed to choose the alternative they preferred. Perhaps the most significant check on the naturalness of the material was the fact that the players were handed their scripts for the first time only minutes before they were to be filmed: it would have taken longer to memorize "funny Japanese" for delivery at normal speaking speed, and retakes would undoubtedly have been the norm rather than the exception.

The professionalism and extraordinary cooperation of the film crew made for an unusually smooth, efficient, rapid production of the video masters. However, one difficult problem did arise for which there was no completely satisfactory solution—one that would never arise in the production of comparable materials in a Western European language. Simply stated, it hinges on the fact that Japanese and Westerners do not look alike. Who, then should fill the roles of the Westerners in the scripts—Japanese or Westerners? In making audiotapes, the desirability of using native speakers goes without saying. But when the visual component is added, the difference in appearance poses a problem. A conscious decision had to be made as to whether the model in the video was to be culturally and linguistically a perfect model of the target (that is, a native Japanese), or an authentic Westerner, who would create problems if regarded as a model for imitation.

Within the framework of Japanese society, no single solution can be totally satisfactory because of the widely divergent Japanese reactions to Westerners who attempt to adopt their paralinguistic code. Clearly, the stronger one's linguistic competence, the more accurately and more appropriately one can speak the language. However, when we move to paralinguistics, Japanese attitudes range from awe and respect for the Westerner who moves and gestures like a Japanese, to a strong antipathy for a foreigner who seems to be deliberately violating native territoriality. Wise foreigners are those who adjust their paralinguistic behavior on the basis of their assessment as to what is more appropriate in each given situation.

Assuming that the Westerner needs no instruction to cover situations in which a Western style of paralinguistic behavior seems more appropriate, what was needed on the videodiscs was a model for the other end of the continuum: how does a native Japanese look in this conversational setting? This argued for native Japanese—not Westerners—as the cultural as well as the linguistic role models on the video. Note that even if a Westerner with native Japanese language competence were available to fill a particular role, the choice of this individual with his or her idiosyncratic interpretation of appropriate Japanese paralinguistic behavior would suggest that *this* was the model to be imitated by all foreign students. Undoubtedly countless Japanese would feel compelled to criticize, as they observed behavior that struck them as foreign, awkward, and inappropriate. The less controversial decision was to use native Japanese exclusively, thus presenting the language of a native speaker of the standard language and the delivery system of a cultural native. The appearance of these Japanese who assume the roles of non-Japanese is explained by identifying them as offspring of international marriages: they look Japanese because their mothers are Japanese, but they are to be identified as Westerners, with names like Miller, Carter, and Brown. Happily, this solution does not seem to be causing any serious difficulties.

The impact on learners of using these materials as an integral part of a study program is significant. They become visually oriented, always concerned with contextualizing language samples in terms of a setting. Even learners who have never been to Japan are able to visualize accurately; through the video, they have actually observed authentic Japanese settings as the conversations are acted out. While our goal was to provide learners with instructional material whose ambience was "just like Japan," Japan has turned out to be "just like the video" when they arrive in the country for a first visit subsequent to their study of the language.

ENDNOTES

1. "Truly foreign" is the designation used for languages non-cognate with English. It contrasts with "less commonly taught," which is really an administrative term, covering everything from Thai (also "truly foreign") to Dutch (not "truly foreign").

2. Kikuo Nomoto, "Simplified Japanese for Language Education," *Japan Echo,* 16, Special Issue, 1989, p. 55.

REFERENCES

Hall, Edward T. 1976. *Beyond Culture.* New York: Anchor Press/Doubleday.

———. 1983. *The Dance of Life.* New York: Anchor Press/Doubleday.

Hall, Edward T., and Mildred Reed Hall. 1987. *Hidden Differences: Doing Business with the Japanese.* New York: Anchor Press/Doubleday.

Horodeck, Richard A. 1987. "The Role of Sound in Reading and Writing Kanji." PhD Dissertation, Cornell University.

Jorden, Eleanor H. 1962–3. *Beginning Japanese, Part 1 and Part 2.* New Haven and London: Yale University Press.

———. 1985. "Japanese Language Education and Science: A New Wave?" *Japan Quarterly* 32.2: 145–51.

———. 1986. "On Teaching Nihongo." *Japan Quarterly* 33.2: 139–47.

———. 1987. "The Target Native and the Base Native: Making the Team." *Journal of the Association of Teachers of Japanese* 21.1: 7–14.

Jorden, Eleanor H., and Hamako Chaplin. 1976. *Reading Japanese.* New Haven and London: Yale University Press.

Jorden, Eleanor H., and A. Ronald Walton. 1987. "Truly Foreign Languages: Instructional Challenges." *Annals of the American Academy of Political and Social Science.* 490: 110–24.

Jorden, Eleanor H., with Mari Noda. 1987–8. *Japanese: The Spoken Language, Part 1 and Part 2.* New Haven and London: Yale University Press.

———. Forthcoming. *Japanese: The Spoken Language, Part 3.* New Haven and London: Yale University Press.

Nomoto, Kikuo. 1989. "Simplified Japanese for Language Education." *Japan Echo* 16, Special issue. 55–57.

Foreign Language Classrooms: Making Them Research-Ready and Research-Able

Teresa Pica

University of Pennsylvania

INTRODUCTION

The language learning projects of John Barson and Eleanor Jorden hold considerable interest for language specialists, whether they be teachers, curriculum planners, or researchers. The opportunities these projects provide for interaction with computers, video, and authentic texts surely have great appeal to the instructors and students fortunate to be a part of them. Their innovative approaches to language teaching and their fascinating blend of technology, culture, and content are to be applauded.

Many of their key contributions are worthy of research in their own right, not only as they pertain to second language (L2) instruction. Information is needed about the impact of the electronic classroom, interactive video, and authentic materials on student motivation and achievement and on how teachers are coping with technology and innovation, for example, whether they are acquiring new teaching techniques or adhering to their old ones. Educational psychologists and classroom ethnographers can shed much light on these questions. What will be of interest to language learning researchers, however, is very basic, so much so that a response to these projects becomes, in effect, a response to all foreign language teachers, from the highly innovative to the more traditional. Much of what is to be covered in the following response, therefore, will relate to common points of activity among teachers and students across a range of foreign language classrooms, and will attempt to discuss them from a researcher's perspective.

LANGUAGE TEACHERS AND RESEARCHERS: COMMON CONCERNS AND DIVERSE PURPOSES

Whether we are teaching language learners or carrying out research on language learning, we share a number of concerns regarding the work that we do. We are concerned with the developmental sequences of language learning, the sources of learner errors, the extent to which the acquisition process can be shaped by input and intervention. Often, however, these common concerns are overlooked because of the very different objectives toward which our work is directed. Both researchers and teachers gather samples of learners' language. Researchers view these samples as data to be analyzed; teachers regard them as a basis for evaluating their students and their teaching. As researchers, we are oriented toward building a data base on learner language, tracing its features to innate structures and input sources and constructing theories about the learning process. As teachers, we also examine our students' language, but do so to chart their progress and, accordingly, to plan classroom activities or reorganize course content. This type of research reflects very practical concerns and is seldom directed toward compiling data bases or building theories about the learning process.

We have volumes of data analysis of learners' linguistic productions and misproductions and on features of the social and linguistic environments available to them, mostly in second language learning contexts. We also have collections of papers on how to teach—how to design the instructional syllabus, create effective classroom materials, and implement practical and productive teaching procedures. However, much of this material is based on experience and common sense more often than it is on formal data.[1] What we have in effect is a situation in which researchers' concerns are shared primarily within the research community, and applied not to classroom decisions but to the interpretation of previous investigations and the design of follow-up studies. Teachers' concerns about learners and their learning are informed by firsthand experience and are seldom disseminated for wide-ranging consumption.

This is not to suggest that language teachers have little interest in or awareness of research on language learning or that language researchers have little concern for teaching practice or for the insights about language learning that teachers can share with them. Increasingly, many teachers are applying to their teaching at least what they *believe* is language acquisition research—even though (as will be elaborated below) what they all too often do apply are actually *theories* on language acquisition or language teaching. Many of these theories make so much sense or are presented so convincingly in the literature on second language acquisition that it is inevitable for teachers to assume that sufficient evidence exists to support them.

At the same time, most researchers are deeply committed to finding appropriate solutions to classroom challenges. Many, in fact, were language teachers at one time. It was their questions and concerns about classrooms that drew them away from teaching and into research in the first place. In spite of their teaching backgrounds and classroom concerns, however, a good number of researchers have expressed reluctance to take their findings about language learning and apply them directly to the classroom (see, for example, Hatch, 1978; Long, 1985b.) And, as will be explained below, this reluctance on the part of researchers has been highly warranted, and actually should be expressed with greater frequency than it is. Teachers have often responded to such reluctance by taking what research they felt was relevant and adapting it to their repertoire of classroom techniques or by displaying impatience with what they viewed as detachment and elitism in the research community, separating themselves from it and working within their own ideas and experiences of language learning.

CONSTRAINTS ON RESEARCH APPLICATION

Researcher's reluctance to apply their findings is well-founded, as the generalizability of language acquisition research to the classroom has been greatly limited by its focus and context. Much language acquisition research, especially that which has been used to generate and support theoretical claims about the learning process and interlanguage outcomes, has been restricted to *adult* learners of a *second* language, who have access to target language communities outside the classroom. The little work that has been done comparing second and foreign language learners has shown similarities in process and outcome (See Felix, 1981; Pica, 1983); however, this research is highly restricted in terms of numbers of subjects studied, number of structures sampled, and types of learners. We cannot say for sure, therefore, that what we have found out about the interlanguage of second language learners is the same as that of foreign language learners. We can only continue to seek more data on this important question.

Another reason for researchers' reluctance to apply their findings to the classroom is that what is known about input to and interaction with learners has come primarily from interview and conversational data, gathered outside the classroom context. It is only recently that *classroom* input and interaction have come under study. Researchers such as Long and Sato (1983), Doughty and Pica (1986), and Pica and Doughty (1985a, 1985b) have found the L2 input and interaction available to learners during classroom activities to be quite different in structure when compared with input and interaction gathered in research contexts. Thus, there may not be much of a basis for application of overall findings on input and interaction to what goes on in classrooms, especially if the classroom is to be the learner's only source of input, as is the case in the foreign language study.

The need is great, therefore, for information on the interlanguage of foreign language learners and on the input and interaction that characterize their language learning experience. But meeting this need may not be so easy—not so easy for foreign language classrooms in general, and not easy at all for the Barson and Jorden classrooms in particular. Obstacles to conducting research on foreign language acquisition arise from the complex nature of the classroom environment and from the insufficiency of its current state of description. These will be discussed in the following section.

CONSTRAINTS ON FOREIGN LANGUAGE ACQUISITION RESEARCH

Classroom Researchability

All classrooms—whether they provide second or foreign language instruction—are complicated social communities. Individual learners come to them with their own constellation of native language and culture, proficiency level, learning style, and motivation and attitudes toward language learning. Individual teachers have their own distinctive styles and use many different materials and teaching techniques in the course of a single classroom session, and use countless others in a given week or semester. To maintain standards of internal consistency, researchers have attempted to investigate second language learning outcomes and processes through systematic study. They have isolated one learner variable or contextual feature at a time, (for example, native language transfer, proficiency level, interlocutor age or gender), and charted its impact on interlanguage, input, and interaction. Unfortunately, there is no guarantee that interlanguage, input, and interaction will be affected in the same way by one of these features in isolation as it will when all of these features come together in the classroom. In fact, this is unlikely to be the case. This is another reason why many researchers warn that their results should not be applied directly to classroom decisions It's not that they feel apathy toward teachers and their instructional concerns. It is just so difficult to do research that leads to results that are valid and reliable from a scientific point of view and that at the same time have direct application to the classroom.

One of the hopes of second language acquisition researchers was that research on foreign language learners would allow for greater opportunity to study input-interlanguage relationships, since these learners were not subject to L2 experiences outside the classroom, over which the researcher had no control. What we can see, however, from the descriptions of Barson and Jorden is that foreign language environments can be very rich and diversified input sources. Their projects provide authentic L2 interaction, a breadth of teaching techniques and high-interest activities. Such classroom contexts make it difficult for researchers to zero in on any one input source, control for all others, and at the same time, maintain the classroom environment that motivated their research to begin with. So it may be nearly impossible to do input-interlanguage studies in the classrooms designed by Barson and Jorden.

What we need to think about are experimental foreign language classrooms in which particular techniques of instruction or correction and their short-term and long-range effects on interlanguage would be isolated and described. Experimental classrooms, designed from a researcher's perspective, would shed light on input-output relationships in language acquisition. Their research, however, would be language acquisition research primarily and classroom research only secondarily. Studies would not seek to describe authentic classrooms, with their myriad possibilities for language use, but they would meet an important need in current language acquisition research and provide a speedy acceptance for foreign language acquisition study as a distinctive enterprise in its own right.

Research Readiness

Another reason why it is at present difficult to do research on foreign language interlanguage, input, and interaction is that most of what gets described and reported about the foreign language classroom, curriculum, and learner is not what might be called *research-ready*. Theories about language learning are often presented to foreign language educators, and indeed second language teachers too, as though these theories were grounded in research findings about the learning process. In consequence, teachers often refer to the availability in their classrooms of comprehensible input, without providing a systematic, linguistic description of the features that make this input comprehensible. References are made to the presence or absence of an affective filter as though this were an operationalized construct, when it is at best an image, seen in a variety of ways by those who talk about it. Learner involvement, peer collaboration, and a pressure-free atmosphere are not described in characteristics that could be compared systematically. Students' progress and point scores are reported, but their interlanguage features are not presented. Students' learning is distinguished from their acquisition as though there were an observable difference between the two. Not only does such presentation of classrooms and learners impede systematic study, but it keeps foreign language educators from the kinds of exchanges that could be mutually beneficial throughout the teaching and research community.

THE CHALLENGE OF FOREIGN LANGUAGE ACQUISITION RESEARCH

The projects of Barson and Jorden share, along with other foreign language instructional endeavors, two of the major challenges facing foreign language acquisition research. First, if there is to be a field called foreign language acquisition research, either autonomous or part of the wider field of language learning research, it cannot afford to think of itself exclusively as classroom- or curriculum-centered. Second, foreign language acquisition researchers need to find ways to present the foreign language learner and the learner's environment in terms that are researchable.

The first challenge is not intrinsic to foreign language learning, but rather is faced by all language acquisition researchers. Certainly, descriptions of the classroom environment available to learners are needed. However, they require presentations that will reveal how the classroom offers language learning experiences. And we need to see much more data—samples of what teachers ask and say to students, what students say in response, and how students speak with each other across a range of classroom activities.

Second language researchers—some, but not all—have handled this first challenge effectively. For example, they have sampled and compared language learners under experimental as well as classroom conditions (see, for example, Long and Sato, 1983). Or they have observed classrooms to identify potential input sources and interactional experiences, then used their observations as a basis for more focused research. For example, in studies on the relevance to second language acquisition of two frequently observed classroom participation patterns—group work and teacher-fronted interaction—on several types of communication tasks, controls were placed on class and group size, learner proficiency level, and task familiarity in the classrooms under study (see Doughty and Pica, 1986; Pica and Doughty, 1985a, 1985b). The classrooms could then be compared in terms of the kinds of modified input and interactional conditions claimed to be necessary for successful language acquisition. In other words, the scope of the research was limited to specific aspects of the classroom, and research questions and hypotheses were confined to acquisition-related variables.

Foreign language researchers could follow the approach taken in these and other second language classroom studies, or as suggested above, could set up experimental classrooms to provide even tighter controls over acquisition variables. This would allow for the kinds of input-output research that are impossible to carry out in second language contexts, no matter how carefully monitored.

The second challenge can be confronted by calling on foreign language teachers, indeed all language teachers, to take terminology from language acquisition research and use it in observing and describing their classrooms in ways that then can be investigated systematically. Although researchers have been wise to delay application of their findings to classroom decisions, this attitude has in effect kept teachers from an understanding and appreciation of these findings, and from recognizing how the findings could inform descriptions of their classrooms and students. As a result, teachers have often accepted theoretical claims as though they were research results and equated theories about effective teaching with theories on language learning.

In spite of the apparent, perceived detachment of the research community from the classroom, there are a number of important findings about interlanguage, input, and interaction that could help teachers begin to describe their students and classrooms in terms that are "researchable." What have researchers found out about input, interaction, and interlanguage that could inform the classrooms of Barson and Jorden? And how might Barson and Jorden employ these findings both to inform their teaching and make their classrooms research-ready? The following are some themes found in their projects to which research could respond and on which researchers could focus their efforts.

AVAILABILITY OF
COMPREHENSIBLE INPUT

A large part of the instructional programs of Barson and, to some extent, Jorden, rest on theoretical claims and popular beliefs about acquisition and the acquisition process, which research has supported, refuted, or modified. One such popular theory is Krashen's monitor theory and its controversial input hypothesis. (See Krashen, 1985, for full elaboration). Barson in particular places a great deal of emphasis on the availability of comprehensible input to his students. So it is important to begin with recent findings on comprehensible input, which can inform not only classroom instruction, but inform also the description of classroom input and interaction and research on them.

Until recently, the term, *comprehensible input* was not within the repertoire of second or foreign language teachers. However, with the publication of *The Natural Approach* (Krashen and Terrell, 1983), this term became synonymous with what was considered the goal of effective language instruction. *The Natural Approach* has had especially widespread appeal because, among other things, it reflects both second and foreign language teaching concerns emanating from the backgrounds of its authors. Krashen makes a distinction between L2 *input* to learners and their actual linguistic *intake*: He argues that new or difficult input must be comprehended as intake in order to assist the acquisition process. Therefore, the first thing for foreign language teachers to appreciate is that it is not *comprehensible input* that aids acquisition, but input that is initially unclear or unfamiliar to the learner, that is, *incomprehensible input*, which is *made* comprehensible, that fuels the acquisition process. This is what they must seek to uncover in research on their classrooms.

Krashen also makes claims about $i + 1$. The best input for acquisition must be meaningful and slightly beyond $(+1)$ the learner's current level of language development (i), but made comprehensible through contextual supports. According to Krashen, learners acquire $+ 1$ when they notice a difference between i and $i + 1$; hypothesize that $i + 1$ is a target feature; and finally, confirm their hypothesis when hearing $i + 1$ again in input. At present, $i + 1$ is not an operationalized construct. It cannot be identified, nor can it be isolated for systematic study. Input and interlanguage are simply too rich, complex, and hierarchical to be characterized with such simple terminology. This is another point for foreign language specialists to recognize. They can only assume that they are offering $i + 1$ to their students. They cannot make claims about its actual availability.

Not all researchers who have studied learners in classrooms agree with Krashen's ideas about the sufficiency of comprehension to successful language acquisition. Nor, given its state of inadequate operationalization, can any researchers comfortably test Krashen's hypothesis about the $i + 1$ construct. However, the overall consensus among researchers is that the learner's linguistic environment is a major contributor to the acquisition process. Therefore, they have focused their research on how input within the learner's environment can be made comprehensible, and they have organized their research to respond to this question.

Long (1985a) has argued that input is made comprehensible through modified and negotiated *interaction* in which learners seek clarification, confirmation, and repetition of L2 utterances that they do not understand. Through these interactional modifications, linguistic adjustments, such as repetitions and rephrasings, are provided to aid the comprehensibility of unclear input. Research by Chaudron (1983), Long (1985a), and others, for example, (Blau, 1980) has shown that if such adjustments are made a priori to text or lecturette input, they aid the learner's comprehension. Additional research by Pica, Young, and Doughty (1987) has strengthened Long's claims regarding negotiated interaction and its effect on input comprehension. They found that learners who heard linguistically unmodified input (directions to a task), with opportunities to negotiate interaction, (for example, by seeking clarification of direction input with the direction giver), understood it better than learners who heard a linguistically simplified version of the direction input, but were offered no opportunity for such clarification requests.

Why was there better comprehension of the unmodified direction input? Research results have shown that negotiation between the learners and their interlocutors led directly to modifications in input complexity and redundancy. Direction input was thus made comprehensible without the need for a priori modification by the researcher. A further possibility posed, but not tested by the researchers, was that negotiated interaction simply increased the amount of time available to the learners for processing the directions. In other words, it was not the linguistic modifications that were crucial to understanding. Rather, the stretch of time the direction-giver took in modifying the directions gave learners an opportunity to process the original direction input so that they could understand it.

How do these research findings inform the description of input and interaction in the foreign language classroom and help make it research-ready and researchable? They suggest that teaching a second or foreign language should be an interactive process between teachers and students and among the students themselves. Students need to comprehend the new language, but can best do this when allowed to ask about what it is that they do not understand rather than relying on their teacher or textbook to anticipate areas of comprehension difficulty and to simplify a priori. What these results also suggest is that simply giving students enough wait time to ask questions about or to internalize input that they do not initially understand may have very positive results on their comprehension, without the need for much talk on the teacher's part at all. When foreign language teachers talk about the availability of comprehensible input in their classrooms, it is these input and interactional features—repetitions and rephrasings, learner requests for clarification and confirmation of input, teacher provision of wait time—that they need to elaborate and study. Saying that comprehensible input is available to foreign language learners is an assertion that needs to be researched, but it cannot be researched unless it is analyzed into features that can be described and studied.

How can research on foreign language acquisition in particular add to the input hypothesis? Further research is needed on the longer-term effects of comprehension on learner proficiency. If we are to provide a basis for the theoretical importance of negotiated interaction to language comprehension, and ultimately to language acquisition, we must be able to demonstrate the effects of interactional contributions to comprehension over time. To do this requires careful monitoring of both all input that the learners receive and their opportunities to hear input adjusted to their comprehension level. This type of monitoring is virtually impossible to carry out in second language environments in which comprehension research has been conducted. Learners in second language settings are engaged with numerous interlocutors and are exposed to various input sources, which are virtually impossible for researchers to monitor. As noted above, foreign language classrooms are complex learning environments, difficult to study systematically. However, an experimental foreign language classroom, with only a few sources of input, with all sources monitored by the teacher, and stored, perhaps, by computer, may provide a favorable site for further research on input comprehension and comprehensibility. Thus, additional and more informed data regarding the importance and sufficiency of comprehensible input to successful language learning await research from the experimental foreign language classroom.

STUDENT INTERACTION AND GROUP WORK

Of the two projects, Barson's places a great deal of emphasis on student-to-student interaction and group work. Given the increased emphasis on interaction in language classrooms, it seems surprising that so little research has been conducted on its relationship to successful language learning. A rationale for arranging students into groups is provided by only a handful of relevant studies. Among these, Varonis and Gass (1985) have shown that when non-native speakers, that is, learners, converse with other learners, as opposed to native-speaking interlocutors such as their teachers, they experience a greater degree of involvement in their interaction, are more persistent in their attempts to get their ideas across, and work harder to modify their interlanguage toward greater comprehensibility.

Still, not all research on group work is completely supportive of this classroom practice. Doughty and Pica (1986) and Pica and Doughty (1985a, 1985b) found that it was the learning tasks or activities in which groups engaged, rather than the group participation pattern itself that were critical in bringing about the kinds of interaction considered suitable for learning. The most effective tasks were those that required a two-way exchange of information, thereby requiring all group members to participate. Tasks that focused on problem-solving or discussion tended to favor participation among more assertive students, often to the point of monologue. Such behavior left other group members with few opportunities to attempt L2 production or to signal difficulty with L2 comprehension.

What these results suggest is that teachers' reports on the benefits of group work as a classroom practice need to be tempered by their examination of the tasks that groups are asked to carry out. Foreign language classroom studies—from those based on informal classroom observation to those that encompass more systematic research—must be designed with this in mind.

Chesterfield, Chesterfield, Hayes-Latimer, and Chavez (1983) addressed the influence of teachers and peers on language acquisition. Looking at bilingual preschool programs, they found that in classrooms where the majority of students were English-speaking, greater proficiency in English L2 was related to peer interaction more than to teacher interaction. In classrooms where the majority of students were Spanish-speaking, greater proficiency in English L2 was related more to teacher interaction than to peer interaction. This finding seems particularly appropriate to foreign language classrooms where learners tend to be homogeneous in the native language, or at least share a common language other than the one they are studying. Working in groups can lead them to turn to their common language and avoid using the second, unless their teacher carefully monitors their language choice.

Findings from research thus suggest that group work by no means guarantees success in language learning, but needs to be tempered in light of social and linguistic conditions in the classroom and the tasks given to learners in their groups. The influence of these social, linguistic, and pedagogical variables, many of which are as yet unstudied, may be why some teachers have continued to have reservations about employing group work in their classrooms. Further research is needed in order to help teachers make more informed decisions about the benefits of this practice to their students' learning. Until then, it is impossible to talk about the effectiveness of group work without acknowledging the possible contributions or unfavorable influences of these other factors.

THE ROLE OF GRAMMAR INSTRUCTION IN THE LEARNING PROCESS

The presentations by Barson and Jorden on these innovative foreign language classrooms seemed to de-emphasize grammar instruction. Yet, in their syllabi, objectives, and lesson content, a concern for grammar knowledge comes through. Recent literature on language teaching methods and textbooks for learners have tended to upgrade the importance of activities for meaningful use of the new language and downgrade the contributions made by exercises that emphasize practice of grammar rules. Learners are considered able to infer the grammar rules of a new language by means of large quantities of meaningful and comprehensible input and abundant opportunities for L2 social interaction.

Unfortunately, for many learners, especially those for whom the classroom is the only context for language learning, meaningful and comprehensible input and opportunities for social interaction may not be possible. Even if such input is provided, the overall amount of input and interaction targeted to individual learners will be reduced in relation to the total number of learners in the classroom. This situation suggests that learners may need a more efficient means to access the grammar rules of the language they are trying to learn than through listening or reading experiences alone.

Since Barson and Jorden have indicated that they do incorporate explicit grammar instruction in the classroom, and other foreign language teachers have strengthened their resolve to teach grammar to their students (unfortunately to the point where they overlook all other instructional inputs), questions remain as to selection and sequencing of grammar rules so that they can be acquired effectively. Fortunately, a handful of studies focused on this topic reveals guiding principles for selection and sequencing decisions based on factors of learnability, linguistic complexity, and learner-readiness.

For Pienemann (1984), for example, there are psychological constraints on language learning that affect the teachability (and hence, learnability) of languages. He has shown that word order sequences in German are acquired in order of increasing complexity, but only when the learner is ready, that is, at an appropriate developmental stage. In studying learners' acquisition of German, he found, for example, that there were four stages of word order through which the learners proceeded sequentially, without skipping a stage:

1. subject-verb-object—*He must study the book tomorrow.*

2. preposing of constituents—*Tomorrow he must study the book.*

3. particle movement from utterance-internal to final position—*Tomorrow he must the book study.*

4. inversion of elements, both utterance-internal—*Tomorrow must he the book study?*

The role of instruction, as Pienemann found through a longitudinal study, was to accelerate the learner's movement across the stages. Thus, the learner at stage 3 quickly moved to stage 4 if taught its rules. However, instruction at the level of stage 4 did not accelerate the L2 development of the learner at stage 2. The stage 3 learner who was not taught stage 4 rules directly also moved to stage 4, based on L2 exposure, but much more slowly than the stage 3 learner given instruction.

The work of Doughty (1988) and Gass (1982) has also shown a positive effect for grammar instruction when the grammatical item was related to other items along the hierarchy of difficulty such as that shown below for relative clauses.

most difficult

object of preposition:	*The students with whom I studied passed the test.*
indirect object:	*The students to whom you gave the book are my friends.*
object relative:	*The students whom you saw are my friends.*
subject relative:	*The students who did their homework passed the test.*

least difficult

What both researchers found was that the range of relative clause constructions in English could be learned faster if instruction began with the most difficult type of relative clause (object of preposition) rather than the easiest (subject). Thus, teaching the learners the more difficult relative clause structure for object of preposition helped them to acquire easier structures such as indirect and direct object and subject relatives. On the other hand, teaching them subject relatives helped them learn these structures but had no impact on other, more difficult structures in the hierarchy.

Another positive aspect of explicit grammar instruction was found for items which are "easy to learn" (that is, have a straightforward form-function relationship), but are difficult to hear in input. Pica (1983), in comparing learners of English as a foreign language with learners of English as a second language who had never had formal instruction, found that instruction appeared to influence production of some structures, but had little effect on others: for plural -s, instructed learners were more accurate than uninstructed learners, who showed greater use of quantifiers with base forms, for example, *three book*. For progressive -ing, instructed learners overgeneralized -ing, as in *I liking the movie, every day I going home for lunch, I want to seeing you*. Uninstructed learners omitted -ing or produced targetlike structures. For article *a*, both instructed and noninstructed learners tended to follow the sequence: *a little, a lot, a few* to *read a book, saw a movie*, to *with a friend, on a chair*.

The effectiveness of grammar instruction appears to depend largely on selection and sequencing of grammar rules and careful assessment of learner readiness. Some items are better off not taught, whereas the learning of others is enhanced, indeed accelerated, through instruction. Research on grammar instruction has thus begun to explain why learners often "do not learn what teachers teach" (to quote Allwright, 1988) and yet master other forms and features quite effectively. So far, a little bit has been uncovered about German and English grammar rules, and some basic principles have been advanced regarding rule selection and sequencing for grammar instruction. There remains an enormous amount of research to be done, however, within individual languages and across different grammatical rules, features, and structures. This has to be *interlanguage* research, with learners' language output described in terms of linguistic units not commonly found in teachers' grammar handbooks. The wide spectrum of foreign languages taught in the United States offers the possibility for a wealth of data on the interlanguages and interlanguage sequences of many different L1s. This is another area in which foreign language acquisition research can make a distinctive contribution.

CORRECTION OF STUDENT ERRORS

One of the most widely held assumptions about the language learning process is that errors indicate learner hypotheses about the target language and that overt correction cannot alter learners' natural path of acquisition (see, for example, reviews of this position in Richards, 1978; Ellis, 1984). Numerous inventories of learner errors have been compiled into the now widely familiar categories of overgeneralization (*She has two childrens, He teached English, Did he teached English*); overuse (*She has one books, She liking school*); omissions (*She is doctor, She has three book, He teach English*); and analogies (*We walk with the girls, We follow with the girls*). It is believed that in producing these errors, learners are testing hypotheses about rules and patterns in the language they are learning. Many instructional settings, such as those reported by Barson and Jorden, have responded to this perspective on errors by individualizing correction, minimizing it, or relegating it to areas of meaning. While not denying the effectiveness of this orientation from a learner-motivational point of view, it is important to reexamine the practice of learner-correction in light of recent theory and research on second language learning.

Recent theories of Bley-Vroman (1986), Schachter (1984), and White (1987) have argued against the belief that learners' incorrect hypotheses should go uncorrected. They claim that explicit and/or implicit correction (also referred to as *negative input* by Schachter, 1984) is essential to a theory that includes hypothesis-testing as part of the second language acquisition process. This is because lack of correction may imply to a learner that a nontargetlike utterance was accurate. Unless otherwise corrected, learners who have two ways of forming structures in their L1 may be misled to believe that these same two options exist in the L2, even though the L2 allows for one option only.

Thus, the learner whose first language allowed the same expression for greetings and partings might believe that *hello* could be used similarly for both functions in English. However, such a flawed hypothesis would inevitably lead to a communication breakdown between the learner and an interlocutor in the course of everyday social interaction, and therefore, it would be corrected quite readily. More serious, however, would be the learner's mistaken hypotheses about L2 structural features. These could become internalized as rules within the learner's interlanguage grammar, since they lead to productions that, although grammatically imprecise, are communicatively functional. For example, if the L1 allowed dative formation within either prepositional phrase (PP) (*gave a book to the girl*) or indirect object (IO) (*gave the girl the book*), but L2 allowed PP only, the learner might assume that L2 allowed both PP and IO but that IO was seldom used. This false hypothesis would lead to ungrammatical IO productions, which although awkward-sounding, could be, nonetheless, sufficiently comprehensible to interlocutors to pass uncorrected during social discourse.

How do these theoretical claims and examples help teachers make informed decisions about correction in the classroom and follow-up research on its effectiveness? This is a difficult question to answer, since, so far, research on the actual practice of classroom correction has shown it to be a highly diversified entity. Correction can be focused sometimes on meaning and other times on structure. It can be provided differentially and unsystematically to and across students, yielding confusing and at times contradictory results. Fanselow (1977) found that in Spanish foreign language classrooms, teachers corrected students more frequently for errors in meaning that errors in grammar. Student answers that teachers treated as errors tended to be those that did not correspond to what the teacher expected to hear from the student. Outside the classroom, Brock, Crookes, Day, and Long (1986) found that correction had no significant effect on destabilizing learners' interlanguage during half-hour research sessions. However, when learners were corrected by their interlocutors during communication games, they quickly adjusted their interlanguage accordingly.

In a diary study of Schmidt's Portuguese L2 learning in Brazil, Schmidt and Frota (1986) found that explicit correction had a differential and inconsistent effect on Schmidt's targetlike use of Portuguese L2. Instead, in order to benefit from corrections, Schmidt claims that he had to know he was being corrected. Hearing a corrected version immediately following what he had just said helped him "notice the gap" between his interlanguage and the target Portuguese. Informal (off-record) correction in the form of interlocutor confirmation checks and clarification requests had no discernible effect on internalization of L2 rules and features.

What has been advanced about the role of correction in the learning process appears to be not only confusing in itself, but also to contradict Krashen's claim that comprehensible input is all that is needed for successful second language acquisition. Much of the confusion and contradiction is based on the fact that so little is known about the nature of correction—or comprehension for that matter—and its effect on the learning process. As has been noted all along in this paper, a carefully controlled approach to such research is difficult to carry out in the L2 settings that have dominated language learning research. Although there is a great deal of difficulty in any research that attempts to trace the impact of correction on the learning process, experimental foreign language classrooms, again, could provide a favorable context for finding answers to this crucial area of language learning.

CULTURAL KNOWLEDGE AND LANGUAGE LEARNING

Cultural knowledge and experience is at the heart of Jorden's project, but is apparent in Barson's as well. Before moving into acquisition-related areas, it is important to acknowledge the ongoing efforts of sociolinguists who have been working to identify the linguistic and interactional features of the cultural variables these project leaders describe (see, for example, Beebe and Takahashi, 1987; Blum-Kulka and Olshtain, 1984; Cohen and Olshtain, 1981; Eisenstein and Bodman, 1986; Holmes and Brown, 1987; Wolfson, 1981, 1983, 1986; and Wolfson and Manes, 1980). What these researchers have emphasized is that we are far from a systematic description of social routines as they are used in individual cultures. A great deal of further research is needed before we will be able to identify accurately their timing and encoding, that is, when and how to use them, and translate these findings into terms that make sense to our students.

It is important for teachers to bear in mind the warnings of researchers as they attempt to expose students to social interaction on video and address their questions about the cultural assumptions behind such interaction. Yet it is equally important for researchers to acknowledge that it is the cultural aspects of language study that are often of greatest interest to foreign language students, and that students and their teachers might not want to wait for researchers to catch up with them in meeting this need. Hopefully, attempts to resolve such conflicts between research goals and classroom needs will generate greater collaboration between foreign language teachers and language acquisition researchers toward the education of language learners.

As for culture and questions about language acquisition, the question of whether and how language learning is conditioned by cultural integration with its users is one that troubles foreign language teachers as they work with students in classrooms, far removed from the culture of the language they are learning. In some respects, second language environments pose problems for cultural integration as well. Just because a learner lives in a country where the language under study is spoken widely in the community does not guarantee opportunities for integration with its users. And even when there are opportunities for integration, the learner may not be willing to access them.

In support of the need for cultural integration in language learning, Schumann (1978) reports on the psychosocial profile of Alberto, whose English L2 development remained virtually unchanged over 10 months of Schumann's research and who revealed *little* adaptation to his U.S. urban community or integration with its speakers. Schmidt (1983) on the other hand, presents the psychosocial profile of Wes, whose English L2 development remained virtually unchanged over several years of Schmidt's research, despite *extensive* adaptation to his U.S. urban community and integration with its speakers. Meisel, Clahsen, and Pienemann (1981) have attempted to sort out these apparent contradictions in the role of cultural integration in the learning process. Their research showed that acquisition of German L2 word order, as discussed above, followed an invariant path based on complexity of linguistic features and cognitive processing, whereas acquisition of inflections and functors varied across learners, in correlation with factors of acculturation.

In a recent study, DeKeyser (this volume) compared learners of Spanish as a foreign language whose contact with the language came from the classroom with students who also participated in a semester-abroad program, with opportunities for cultural as well as linguistic contact. What he found were considerable individual differences in the Spanish learned by the latter group. In an ongoing research project, Freed (1989, 1990) is examining the effects of out-of-class cultural contact for students involved in a study-abroad program. These studies will shed light on relationships among cultural contact, learning processes, and language outcomes. Attempting to separate the contributions of cultural integration from other factors is difficult to do in a second language context, where learners are exposed to a variety of cultural experiences at the same time they are engaged in formal classroom study. Research on study abroad programs, with their sequencing of classroom and target culture contexts, will provide much insight into the role of cultural integration in successful language learning.

FOSSILIZATION OF
LANGUAGE LEARNING

One area not addressed in these innovative instructional programs is the possibility for fossilization or incomplete learning among students. Many claims have been made as to why adult learners do not come to master the rules and features of another language. Second language researchers, such as Schumann (1978), have argued that this occurs when learners have limited opportunities for integration with members of a target culture outside the classroom. Such limitations are intrinsic to foreign language learning. Higgs and Clifford (1982) have argued that an early bias toward communicative activities in the language classroom results in learners who stabilize at functional but formally inaccurate proficiency levels. Yet it is important to bear in mind that such activities are often what attract students who would otherwise avoid foreign language study.

Some researchers have proposed learner-internal explanations for fossilization. Schmidt and Frota (1986), for example, report that fossilized learners who are communicatively functional in L2 do not appear to "notice the gap" between their interlanguage and the standard L2 target. Thus, interlocutor confirmation checks and clarification requests may lead the fossilized learner to revise content, but such moves have no effect on their ability to focus on form or their knowledge of grammatical features.

All of these explanations, whether drawn from the learning environment or learners, themselves, point to the need for informed development of instructional materials and procedures for fossilized learners and for ongoing research on the impact of such instruction. If, as claimed by Schmidt and Frota, fossilized learners do not benefit from interlocutor confirmation checks and clarification requests in revising nontargetlike features, there may be a need for more form-focused materials in the classroom. Certainly Higgs and Clifford would agree with such an orientation. So would Yorio (1985), whose observation of different instructional approaches with fossilized learners led to claims that instruction should proceed from the fossilized learner's strength areas in spoken communication to more challenging reading and writing tasks and from contextualized materials and communicative techniques to decontextualized, grammar-oriented instruction. Responding to the needs of fossilized learners and of the teachers who work with them will depend on finding appropriate materials and procedures and monitoring their impact through careful study. This need opens up a wealth of opportunities for collaborative research between foreign language teachers and language acquisition researchers.

OVERVIEW

The projects of both Barson and Jorden are refreshingly innovative in their use of technology, culture, and content in the classroom. Much more description and analysis are needed of input, interaction, and interlanguage in these classrooms, as well as samples of teacher-to-student and student-to-student discourse and learner productions. Variables relevant to these constructs must be operational-ized and described in acquisition features, and findings on them should inform the design of experimental classroom studies and more focused research. As the foreign language classroom is made research-ready and research-able, foreign language acquisition research will find an important and distinctive place within the broader context of research on language learning. Opportunities will emerge for dialogue and collaboration within and across foreign and second language research and teaching communities. Such a collaboration of teachers and re-searchers will in the end help language learners to be ready and able to learn in a classroom environment and to be as enthusiastic about and as successful in their learning as teachers and researchers can become through their collaboration.

ENDNOTE

1. But see chapters by Pienemann and Lightbown in the edited collection of Hyltenstam and Pienemann (1984) for some noteworthy exceptions.

REFERENCES

Allright, Richard. 1988. *Interaction Analysis*. London: Longman.

Beebe, Leslie, and T. Takahashi. 1987. "Do You Have a Bag? Status and Patterned Variation in Second Language Acquisition." Paper presented at XIth University of Michigan Conference on Applied Linguistics: Variation in Second Language Acquisition. Ann Arbor, Michigan, October, 1987.

Blau, Elaine. 1980. "The Effect of Syntax on Readability for ESL Students in Puerto Rico." *TESOL Quarterly* 16.4: 517–28.

Bley-Vroman, Robert. 1986. "Hypothesis Testing in Second Language Acquisition Theory." *Language Learning* 36.3: 353–76.

Blum-Kulka, Shoshana, and Elite Olshtain. 1984. "Requests and Apologies: A Cross Cultural Study of Speech Act and Realization Pattern." *Applied Linguistics* 5.3: 196–213.

Brock, Cynthia, Graham Crookes, Richard Day, and Michael Long. 1986. "The Differential Effects of Corrective Feedback in Native Speaker-Nonnative Speaker Conversation." *Talking to Learn*. Ed. Richard Day. Rowley, Mass.: Newbury House. 229–36.

Chaudron, Craig. 1983. "Simplification of Input: Topic Reinstatements and Their Effect on L2 Learners' Recognition and Recall." *TESOL Quarterly* 17.3: 437–58.

———. 1988. *Second Language Classrooms*. Cambridge: Cambridge UP.

Chesterfield, Ray, Kathleen Burrows Chesterfield, Katherine Hayes-Latimer, and

Regino Chavez. 1983. "The Influence of Teachers and Peers on Second Language Acquisition in Bilingual Preschool Programs." *TESOL Quarterly* 17.3: 401–19.

Cohen, Andrew, and Elite Olshtain. 1981. "Developing a Measure of Sociolinguistic Competence: The Case of Apology." *Language Learning* 31.1: 113–34.

Doughty, Catherine. 1988. "The Effects of Instruction on the Acquisition of Relative Clauses in English as a Second Language." Ph.D. Dissertation, University of Pennsylvania.

Doughty, Catherine, and Teresa Pica. 1986. "Information Gap Tasks: An Aid to Second Language Acquisition?" *TESOL Quarterly* 20.2: 305–25.

Eisenstein, Miriam, and Jean Bodman. 1986. " 'I Very Appreciate': Expressions of Gratitude by Native and Non-Native Speakers of American English." *Applied Linguistics* 7.2: 167–85.

Ellis, Rod. 1984. *Understanding Second Language Acquisition*. Oxford: Oxford UP.

Fanselow, John. 1977. "The Treatment of Error in Oral Work." *Foreign Language Annals* 10: 583–93.

Felix, Sascha. 1981. "The Effect of Formal Instruction on Second Language Acquisition." *Language Learning* 31.1: 87–112.

Freed, Barbara. 1989. "Informal Language Contact and Its Effect on Foreign Language Achievement and Proficiency." Paper presented at RP-ALLA 1989 Conference. Ohio State University, November 1989.

————. 1990. "Language Learning in a Study Abroad Context: The Effects of Interactive and Non-Interactive Out of Class Contact on Grammatical Achievement and Oral Proficiency." To appear in the proceedings of the Georgetown University Roundtable on Languages and Linguistics 1990, *Linguistics, Language Teaching, and Language Acquisition: The Interdependence of Theory, Practice, and Research.* Ed. Janis Alatis. Washington, D.C.: Georgetown University Press.

Gass, Susan. 1982. "From Theory to Practice." *On TESOL 81.* Eds. Mary Hines and William Rutherford. Washington, D.C.: TESOL. 129–39.

Hatch, Evelyn. 1978. "Apply with Caution." *Studies in Second Language Acquisition* 2.2: 123–42.

Higgs, Theodore, and Ray Clifford. 1982. "The Push Toward Communication." *Curriculum, Competence and the Foreign Language Teacher.* Ed. Theodore Higgs. Skokie, Ill.: National Textbook Co.

Holmes, Janet, and Dorothy Brown. 1987. "Teachers and Students Learning About Compliments." *TESOL Quarterly* 21.2: 523–46.

Krashen, Stephen. 1985. *The Input Hypothesis.* London: Longman.

Krashen, Stephen, and Tracy Terrell. 1983. *The Natural Approach.* Oxford: Pergamon.

Section X

Conclusion

Chapter 25

Comments on a Conference

Charles A. Ferguson

Stanford University

The Conference on Foreign Language Acquisition Research and the Classroom, on which this book is based, brought together for the first time on a large national scale in the United States a group of researchers in second language acquisition (SLA) and foreign language (FL) teachers and administrators to communicate with each other on common interests. In many ways the conference was an outstanding success: the two groups did communicate, and an important first step was taken to break the established pattern of isolation between them. Although both groups are deeply interested in understanding how people actually acquire competence in a language not their own, SLA researchers in the United States have as a rule no regular link with foreign language programs and departments in their universities. Both sides can benefit from dialogue and sustained interaction. At this conference the foreign language teachers in particular had a unique opportunity to become familiar with the issues that drive SLA researchers, to judge the relevance of SLA research for problems of foreign language education, and to consider how to take advantage of the overlap in professional concerns.

The papers presented at the conference and included in this volume were mostly prepared by SLA researchers, and they illustrate well the range of research questions and research methods used in that field. Although several of the papers report directly on innovative instructional programs, most of them report research findings that require theoretical and practical mediation to link them with classroom activities. The dialogue begun at the conference will help the FL teachers to understand what constitutes an interesting and feasible research question, and will help SLA researchers to shift some of their research to issues closer to the perceived needs of FL teachers.

It is not possible in a short space to provide a true synthesis of the papers and discussions, but two things I can do: offer some personal reactions to the papers and sketch some hopes for the future, which grow out of the conference.

First of all, I was pleased to note that a number of speakers took a very general overview of the main goals of the conference, taking into account concerns of both researchers and teachers and putting them into historical and disciplinary perspective. I especially enjoyed in this respect the introduction by Barbara Freed and the papers by Rivers, Huebner, and Pica. Someone who heard or read only these contributions, whether teacher or researcher, might miss a great deal of the rich specificity of the papers but would get a good feel of the area of overlapping interests represented at the conference and the need for more communication of the kind that took place there.

Of the recurrent themes of the conference papers and discussions, some were to be expected and others were more surprising, and I will note several of each. Also, in spite of the impressive range of topics treated, I found that some of my own pet subjects were dealt with marginally or not at all, and I will take the liberty of mentioning several of these as well.

Among the themes that might have been expected were the perennial issues of the role of explicit grammatical explanation in the learning and teaching of language, the language and culture problem, and the argument over quantitative versus qualitative methods of research.

Grammar versus communication is an old, old debate among language educators, and in modern times it has appeared also in research efforts and the construction of theories. Various theories of acquisition take diametrically opposed positions on the importance of metalinguistic information about phonology and syntax. Some theorists hold that exposure to the language itself is what matters in the natural processes of acquisition and that grammatical explanation is unnecessary or even disruptive; others find that appropriate description, correction, and "negative evidence" play a crucial role not only in classroom FL learning but even in untutored, natural acquisition. This issue was not the direct topic of any of the papers, but it lurked just below the surface of a number of papers and came up often in informal discussions. No consensus of views was evident. What seemed significant to me was the general recognition that specific aspects of this issue are researchable and should be investigated, but that no research is likely to offer a principled general answer to how the optimum meshing of linguistic structure and communicative function can be achieved in managing the input in FL instruction.

The place of culture in language learning and language teaching is a problem—or better, a set of problems—for anyone seriously interested in understanding how human beings acquire linguistic competence. How tightly are language and culture interwoven? How much of another culture is needed in order to use the language of that culture? Can cultural considerations be utilized to improve language instruction itself? Such questions are basically unanswerable without reaching agreement on the definition of a host of slippery concepts and without better understanding of the processes of acquisition. Yet this conference was particularly stimulating, not only by virtue of the fine papers by Kramsch and Byrnes on the language and culture issue but also by papers offering two radically different perspectives on culture in the classroom. They both recognize the pervasiveness of cultural differences in foreign language learning but take opposite views of the way to deal with them. One is the freewheeling Barson approach, which sets up a type of creative interaction in the learning situation that has the learners acquire cultural competence hands-on, without too much explicit analysis. The other is the heavily programmed Jorden approach, which is based on detailed analysis of cultural differences and careful sequencing in the presentation of appropriate behaviors. Barson says, "Let's learn by communicating"; Jorden says, "Let's learn by structural control of input"—the two are reminiscent in a way of the communication versus grammar approaches to language without culture. Both perspectives are stimulating for the classroom teacher, and both are stimulating for the researcher, who can see specific questions to investigate and potential contributions to SLA theory.

Quantitative or qualitative methods of research? The speakers who raised this question at the conference did just what they should do, and we all profited from their remarks. Every one of them assured us that there was no real opposition between the two types and both should be appreciated and used, and then they each made clear from their own presentation that their own research would be principally one or the other. The lesson is the right one. The choice of research method should be determined by the nature of the problem to be investigated or hypothesis to be tested, by the resources available, and by the imagination and expertise of the researcher. One point was made rather indirectly by the speakers: many useful research techniques can be learned by study and practice, and researchers as well as teachers-turned-researchers should be encouraged to add to their repertoires of research techniques. People who are used to tightly controlled experiments with sophisticated statistical analyses should be encouraged to explore the value of more qualitative approaches, such as case studies and informal characterizations, and people who are used to intuitive judgments based on personal experience should be encouraged to explore more structured and quantifiable research designs.

Besides these themes and some others like them that one might have predicted in advance, a number of more unexpected themes appeared that I found appealing. Let me comment on four of them.

The first is dear to my heart because it represents a research interest of my own. It is discourse analysis of the kind that seeks to characterize and understand the variation in human language that goes under the names of register and genre. Every human language shows variation in linguistic structure depending on the occasions of its use. We do not talk or write with exactly the same phonology, syntax, and vocabulary when we address different people about different topics, in different settings, and with different communicative aims. This register variation is a fundamental characteristic of human language, and it has not received the attention it deserves in linguistics or in the study of second language learning and teaching. The same holds true for the sister concept of genre. Every speech community develops characteristic message-forms, types of discourse conventionalized for particular classes of messages. Such forms of discourse, or genres, have characteristic internal structure and features of form and content that set them apart from one another. The identities and the structure and use of genres change over time and differ from one speech community to another. Analysis of genres should not be left to literary scholars alone, since genres are a part of everyday language as well as literary discourse. It was good to see references to both register variation and genre analysis in conference papers, even when these two terms were not used.

The second unexpected, but very welcome, theme was that of literacy, reading and writing as part of language learning. Partly because of the linguists' rightful insistence on the primacy of speaking and listening in the nature and functioning of human language, and partly because of dissatisfaction with the oral proficiency of FL students, the bulk of SLA research and FL pedagogical innovation has been devoted to speech, and very little to writing. Since FL instruction in the United States normally involves literate students and quite properly has reading and writing as important components, it is clear that serious research on this aspect of second language acquisition is called for.

The third surprising theme is the discussion of European SLA research. American SLA researchers tend to pay little attention to the work of their European colleagues in general, but recent large-scale international research projects in Europe offer an enormous amount of data from several different source and target languages, and the studies have been conducted in ways sometimes refreshingly different from established types of research in this country. Most of the recent European research has been focused on language learning outside the classroom, on the part of foreign guest workers. This kind of research offers a wealth of stimulating ideas for both researchers and language teachers, even though its setting is different from the usual American SLA research and it does not speak directly to university classrooms.

Some twenty-five years ago I urged linguists to study the structure and use of learner languages as they develop over time, using as an example the growing and complexifying structure of the French language competence of American students of French (Ferguson 1963, 120). I have been disappointed that in spite of all the interest in interlanguage phenomena, very few linguists have tried diachronic tracking of whole "mini-grammars" of such learner languages. Although my original suggestion was for FL classroom learner languages, the Europeans have applied the same research strategy in various ways to the development of untutored learner languages, and the payoff promises to be great. Also, the FL education scene in European countries differs from the American in that more languages are taught and learned to a higher degree of competence in schools and universities there than here. The work of European researchers is of great value to Americans, and it was a pleasure to have it reported so extensively and so well at the conference.

The fourth theme that I did not expect reveals my own failure to keep up with technological change. I should have expected it. I am referring to the emphasis on the use of computers in both research and teaching. I am always suspicious of the American love for gadgetry to solve language problems, and I remember the days when the language lab was going to revolutionize American foreign language learning. Instead, it became an instant status symbol that took long years to find its useful place in the FL teacher's array of pedagogical aids. But the computer is different. Students are prepared to work and play with computers—often more than their teachers are—and there are endless ways in which computers can contribute directly to the learning environment; the field of computer-assisted instruction so far has only scratched the surface. At the conference we were treated to some eloquent, exciting reports of computer use, and I hope that the enthusiasm of their authors will be contagious. Teachers will not make the mistake of seeing the computer as a panacea, and researchers will not shrink from the technical problems; both can exercise their creativity and inform one another of their successes and failures. It is good that the computer was well represented at this unifying conference.

An overall impression that I received from these recurrent themes and the tenor of the discussions was that the participants acknowledged fully the complexity of human language and the complexity of the classroom. People were not leaping to simplistic solutions and were ready to agree that differing—even opposed—perspectives might have something to offer. This view of human language is what I referred to as *reverence for language* in a talk on applied linguistics I gave in 1966 (Ferguson, 1966), and I am pleased to see it spreading. The view of classroom behavior as influenced by many factors and involving dynamic interaction was not as clear in my mind at that time, partly because there had been relatively little detailed study of classroom activity and almost none of foreign language classrooms. But by now we realize that often the factors that we take to be important are "blown away" by factors we had not thought of, and it is a wholesome change to see the growing sophistication in classroom research.

In spite of the excellence of the papers and the appropriateness of the conference themes, four topics that could have contributed fruitfully to the discussions were missing. I cannot really complain about their absence, since the program was very full and we could hardly have absorbed any more information, but my mentioning of them here may bring them to the attention of researchers and teachers and may help to get them on the agenda of future conferences.

The first is phonology. Students learning another language must after all learn to pronounce it, the processes of acquiring a second language phonology are a challenge to researchers, and learners' difficulties with the sounds of the language are the concern of language teachers. A few years ago the research literature on L2 phonology was sparse, mostly anecdotal or programmatic, but in recent years an impressive series of publications have appeared (for example, James and Leather, 1987), and it has become a lively field of research, with all the appurtenances of international conferences, doctoral dissertations, new theoretical models, and programs of empirical research. With all due respect to the importance of syntax, discourse, and culture, phonology has a place, and researchers and teachers have a great deal to say to each other.

The second topic is focus on uncommonly taught languages. The SLA research and FL teaching professions in the United States naturally concentrate their efforts on English, French, Spanish, and German, since these are the most commonly taught modern languages. The conference had one full-scale paper on Japanese and occasional mention of other languages in papers and discussions, but it seems to me that increased attention in the immediate future should be given to Russian, Portuguese, Chinese, Arabic, and a number of other important languages. On the researchers' side, this need is obvious: cross-language generalizations and/or the fleshing out of universal grammar are possible only with research on different pairs of languages of varying structure and use. On the teachers' side, I feel that it is important that FL teachers come to regard themselves as a professional community of common interests, regardless of which language they teach to speakers of which language. In addition, of course, familiarity with what takes place in different FL classrooms inevitably gives ideas about one's own, and in some instances may even make one see how simple some of one's own problems are.

The third is bilingualism. Although bilingualism and bilingual education were mentioned, the issues of bilingual competence and performance were not addressed directly. Since FL teachers are or should be bilingual to a high degree, and since the aim of much second language acquisition is to achieve bilingual control, and since language acquisition of various kinds takes place in bilingual communities, it is not possible to separate completely the fields of bilingualism and second language acquisition. What is the effect of the L2 on the L1? How does early bilingualism resemble and differ from later second language acquisition? These are just two of the researchable questions relevant to the FL teaching enterprise that need to be repeatedly reexamined for insights on the problems of one's own professional goals.

The fourth topic is schools and streets. Almost the whole conference was devoted to learning and teaching at the university level, and I must admit that I found this both appropriate and congenial. We must remind ourselves, however, that the university is a very special site of language learning and that ultimately we want to understand principles and practices that occur in formal education below the university level and learning that takes place outside of formal educational systems.

This has been enough or more than enough counting of themes and personal reaction to topics of discussion. I would like now to turn to more general discussion of the outcomes I hope for and expect from the conference.

As you may have noticed, I have used terms such as learning and acquisition, second language and foreign language, theory and model, and so on, more loosely than some people would like. My purpose in doing so is not to deny the usefulness of careful definition of technical terms but rather to reduce the ways of partitioning the field of shared professional interests that the organizers of the conference must have felt to be the basis for communication among the participants.

Language learning takes place under such varied conditions, for such varied purposes, and with such varied results, that it is tempting to identify a large number of relatively independent subfields and lose sight of a unified conceptual framework. May I suggest that what we are all interested in, from our various perspectives, is the acquisition of nonmother tongues. Some of us may focus on the fascinating question of how adult learning of a second, third, or nth language takes place all over the world without formal education. Others of us may be interested in teaching a nonfirst language, that is, creating an environment of space, time, material objects, and human behavior such that language learning takes place—whether in kindergarten, graduate school, weekend church school, or some other level of the system. Some of us may be interested also in L1 acquisition and the relation between L1 and L2 acquisition. I like to draw the line between those who are primarily interested in child language development (L1 and child bilingualism) and those who are interested in everything else. Child language development is a well-established field with its own intellectual and institutional reasons for existence, and events like this conference lead toward the emergence of a field concerned with learning or teaching a language other than the one acquired in child language development. Instead of drawing hard boundaries among a number of subfields, I would hope that we all see ourselves as part of this large single field, with full recognition of the handful of critical variables likely to have major effects on the shape of learning and teaching.

In the light of our present knowledge, I would name five such variables, which we should all specify when we are designing programs of research or teaching or are telling one another about them. These are age of learner; particular L1 and L2; degree of "tutoredness" in the acquisition situation; patterns of language use in the relevant communities; and language attitudes of learner, (teacher), and relevant communities.

Linguistic scholars have traditionally paid most attention to the L1-L2 variable, since their professional focus is linguistic structure, and structural differences may have a strong effect on the nature and extent of transfer from L1 to L2. Language teachers have traditionally paid most attention to the nature of the "tutoredness," since their professional focus is the pedagogical approach or teaching method employed, and their teaching behavior may have a strong effect on the class achievement. All five variables are important, however, and under particular conditions they can be very differently weighted as causal factors.

During a recent trip to Sweden, I was impressed by the fact that in the various seminars I attended, the faculty and students decided before each session whether to use Swedish or English. Although individual differences were noticeable, all the faculty and students seemed very much at home in either language and participated actively in the discussion. This language competence contrasts sharply with the usual monolingualism of American university seminars, and we could ask what factors account for the difference. No doubt age plays some role, since most Swedes start studying English in the third grade. No doubt some effect also comes from the close structural similarity between Swedish and English. More important than either of those factors is probably the extensive use of English outside the classroom (for example, in radio, books, films, conversation with foreigners, popular music). But probably the most important factor is the widespread set of attitudes toward the acquisition and use of English. Language teachers (who themselves know and use English) expect their students to learn and use English, the students expect to learn and use English, the community (including parents and peers) expects them to learn and use English. It is not surprising that these expectations are fulfilled. Careful longitudinal studies of individual Swedes acquiring English would differ in many respects from comparable studies of Americans acquiring French.

It is my hope that every time we undertake a study of language acquisition or engage in a project of language teaching we will see ourselves as trying to understand better some aspect of this whole field of second language acquisition and place ourselves within it in terms of major variables. Then when we attempt to generalize our findings to other situations and when we report our activities to others in the field, we will sense our professional unity but also share understandings of just where we are in that field.

Barbara Freed in her opening remarks told us that five years ago this conference would not have been organized and suggested that five years later such a conference would hopefully be taken for granted. We are grateful to her and the others involved in the organizing and conducting of the conference. We have a long way to go before our professional communication is as unified and effective as we want it to be, and a long way to go before we will see the basic changes we want in the learning and teaching of foreign languages in the United States and in the study of the processes of language acquisition. But we can be sure that the conference has made a difference and five years ahead that difference will be taken for granted.

REFERENCES

Ferguson, G. A. 1963. "Linguistic Theory and Language Learning." *Georgetown University Monograph Series on Language and Linguistics* 16: 115–22.

———. 1966. "Applied Linguistics." *Language Teaching: Broader Contexts.* Ed. R. G. Mead, Jr. Menasha, Wis.: Northeast Conference on the Teaching of Foreign Languages.

James, A., and J. Leather, eds. 1987. *Sound Patterns in Second Language Acquisition.* Dordrecht: Foris.